Quest

Second Edition

3

Reading and Writing

Pamela Hartmann
Laurie Blass

McGraw-Hill

Quest 3 Reading and Writing, 2nd Edition

Published by McGraw-Hill ESL/ELT, a business unit of The McGraw-Hill Companies, Inc. 1221 Avenue of the Americas, New York, NY 10020.

ISBN 13: 978-0-07-325303-9
ISBN 10: 0-07-325303-0
4 5 6 7 8 9 VNH/VNH 12 11 10 09 08

ISBN 13: 978-0-07-110428-9 (INTERNATIONAL STUDENT BOOK)
ISBN 10: 0-07-110428-3
1 2 3 4 5 6 7 8 9 VNH/VNH 12 11 10 09 08 07 06

Editorial director: Erik Gundersen
Series editor: Linda O'Roke
Development editor: Robyn L. Brinks
Production manager: Juanita Thompson
Production coordinator: MaryRose Malley
Cover designer: David Averbach, Anthology
Interior designer: Martini Graphic Services, Inc.
Artists: Jonathan Massie, Ron Mahoney
Photo researchers: PoYee Oster, David Averbach

INTERNATIONAL EDITION ISBN 0-07-110428-3

McGraw-Hill
www.esl-elt.mcgraw-hill.com
The McGraw·Hill Companies

ACKNOWLEDGEMENTS

The publisher and authors would like to thank the following education professionals whose comments, reviews, and assistance were instrumental in the development of the Quest series.

- **Roberta Alexander,** San Diego Community College District
- **David Dahnke,** North Harris College (Houston, TX)
- **Mary Díaz,** Broward Community College (Davie, FL)
- **Judith García,** Miami-Dade College
- **Elizabeth Giles,** The School District of Hillsborough County, Florida
- **Patricia Heiser,** University of Washington, Seattle
- **Yoshiko Matsubayashi,** Kokusai Junior College, Tokyo
- **Ahmed Motala,** University of Sharjah, United Arab Emirates
- **Dee Parker and Andy Harris,** AUA, Bangkok
- **Alison Rice,** Hunter College, City University of New York
- **Alice Savage,** North Harris College (Houston, TX)
- **Katharine Sherak,** San Francisco State University
- **Leslie Eloise Somers,** Miami-Dade County Public Schools
- **Karen Stanley,** Central Piedmont Community College (Charlotte, NC)
- **Diane Urairat,** Mahidol Language Services, Bangkok
- **Pamela Vittorio,** The New School (New York, NY)
- **Anne Marie Walters,** California State University, Long Beach
- **Lynne Wilkins,** Mills College (Oakland, CA)
- **Sean Wray, Elizabeth Watson, and Mariko Yokota,** Waseda International University, Tokyo

Many, many thanks go to Marguerite Ann Snow, who provided the initial inspiration for the entire series. Heartfelt thanks also to Erik Gundersen and Linda O'Roke, Robyn Brinks, and Jenny Bixby for their help in the development of the second edition. We'd also like to thank Dylan Bryan-Dolman, Susannah MacKay, Kristin Sherman, and Kristin Thalheimer, whose opinions were invaluable. Finally, thank you to Keith Folse for his "word journal quadrant" idea and to Eli Hinkel for his inspiration for the sections on "hedging."

TABLE OF CONTENTS

To the Teacher v

Scope and Sequence viii

Welcome xiv

Unit 1 Anthropology 1
- Chapter 1: Cultural Anthropology 3
- Chapter 2: Physical Anthropology 45
- Vocabulary Workshop 82

Unit 2 Economics 85
- Chapter 3: Developing Nations 87
- Chapter 4: The Global Economy 121
- Vocabulary Workshop 156

Unit 3 Literature 159
- Chapter 5: The Nature of Poetry 161
- Chapter 6: Heroes in Literature 193
- Vocabulary Workshop 230

Unit 4 Ecology 233
- Chapter 7: Endangered Species 235
- Chapter 8: Human Ecology 271
- Vocabulary Workshop 303

Appendix 1: Summary of Conjunctions 306

Appendix 2: Research Paper in MLA Format 309

Appendix 3: Academic Word List 313

Vocabulary Index 317

Skills Index 321

Credits 325

TO THE TEACHER

Quest: The Series

Quest Second Edition prepares students for academic success. The series features two complementary strands—*Reading and Writing* and *Listening and Speaking*—each with four levels. The integrated Quest program provides robust scaffolding to support and accelerate each student's journey from exploring general interest topics to mastering academic content.

Quest parallels and accelerates the process native-speaking students go through when they prepare for success in a variety of academic subjects. By previewing typical college course material, *Quest* helps students get "up to speed" in terms of both academic content and language skills.

In addition, *Quest* prepares students for the daunting amount and type of reading, writing, listening, and speaking required for college success. The four *Reading and Writing* books combine high-interest material from newspapers and magazines with readings from academic textbooks. Reading passages increase in length and difficulty across the four levels. The *Listening and Speaking* books in the *Quest* series contain listening strategies and practice activities based on authentic audio and video recordings from "person on the street" interviews, radio programs, and college lectures. Similar to the *Reading and Writing* books, the four *Listening and Speaking* books increase in difficulty with each level.

Quest Second Edition Features

- New *Intro* level providing on-ramp to Books 1-3
- Redesigned, larger format with captivating photos
- Expanded focus on critical thinking and test-taking strategies
- Addition of research paper to *Reading and Writing* strand
- New unit-ending *Vocabulary Workshops* and end-of-book academic word lists
- Expanded video program (VHS and DVD) with new lecture and updated social language footage
- EZ Test® CD-ROM-based test generator for all *Reading and Writing* titles
- Teacher's Editions with activity-by-activity procedural notes, expansion activities, and tests
- Test-taking strategy boxes that highlight skills needed for success on the new TOEFL® iBT test

Quest Reading and Writing

Quest Reading and Writing includes three or four distinct units, each focusing on a different area of college study—sociology, biology, business, history, psychology, art history, anthropology, literature, or economics. Each unit contains two thematically-related chapters.

Chapter Structure

Each chapter of *Quest 3 Reading and Writing* contains five parts that blend reading and writing skills within the context of a particular academic area of study. Readings and activities build upon one another and increase in difficulty as students work through the five sections of each chapter.

Part 1: Introduction

- Before Reading – discussion activities on photos introduce the chapter topic
- Reading – a high-interest reading captures students' attention
- After Reading – activities check students' understanding and allow for further discussion

Part 2: General Interest Reading

- Before Reading – prediction and vocabulary activities prepare students for reading
- Reading – a high-interest reading at a slightly higher level than the reading in Part 1 allows students to explore the chapter topic in more depth
- After Reading – comprehension, discussion, and vocabulary activities check understanding

Part 3: Academic Reading

- Before Reading – prediction and vocabulary activities prepare students for reading
- Reading – a textbook selection prepares students for academic reading
- After Reading – strategies (such as skimming for main ideas, using a dictionary, and synthesizing) and activities give students the opportunity to use academic skills

Part 4: The Mechanics of Writing

- Chapter-specific writing, grammar, lexical, and punctuation boxes equip students to express their ideas.
- Content-driven grammar boxes are followed by contextualized practice activities that prepare students for independent writing assignments.

Part 5: Academic Writing

- A step-by-step model leads students through the writing process which may include brainstorming, narrowing the topic, writing topic sentences, planning the writing, and developing ideas into a paragraph.
- Writing assignments focus on a variety of rhetorical styles: chronological, description, analysis, persuasive, and process.
- Writing assignments ask students to use the writing mechanics taught.

Teacher's Editions

The *Quest Teacher's Editions* provide instructors with activity-by-activity teaching suggestions, cultural and background notes, Internet links to more information on the unit themes, expansion black-line master activities, chapter tests, and a complete answer key.

The *Quest Teacher's Editions* also provide test-taking boxes that highlight skills found in *Quest* that are needed for success on the new TOEFL® iBT test.

Video Program

For the *Quest Listening and Speaking* books, a newly expanded video program on DVD or VHS incorporates authentic classroom lectures with social language vignettes.

Lectures

The lecture portion of each video features college and university professors delivering high-interest mini-lectures on topics as diverse as animal communication, personal finance, and Greek art. The mini-lectures run from two minutes at the *Intro* level to six minutes by Book 3. As students listen to the lectures they complete structured outlines to model accurate note taking. Well-organized post-listening activities teach students how to use and refer to their notes in order to answer questions about the lecture and to review for a test.

Social Language

The social language portion of the videos gives students the chance to hear authentic conversations on topics relevant to the chapter topic and academic life. A series of scenes shot on or around an urban college campus features nine engaging students participating in a host of curricular and extracurricular activities. The social language portion of the video is designed to help English language students join study groups, interact with professors, and make friends.

Audio Program

Each reading selection on the audio CD or audiocassette program allows students to hear new vocabulary words, listen for intonation cues, and increase their reading speed. Each reading is recorded at an appropriate rate while remaining authentic.

Test Generator

For the *Quest Reading and Writing* books, an EZ Test® CD-ROM test generator allows teachers to create customized tests in a matter of minutes. EZ Test® is a flexible and easy-to-use desktop test generator. It allows teachers to create tests from unit-specific test banks or to write their own questions.

SCOPE AND SEQUENCE

<table>
<tr><th>Chapter</th><th>Reading Strategies</th><th>Writing and Writing Strategies</th></tr>
<tr><td colspan="3">UNIT 1 ANTHROPOLOGY</td></tr>
<tr><td>Chapter 1
Cultural Anthropology
• Introduction: Feng Shui in California
• General Interest: Symbolic Systems and Meanings
• Academic: The Anthropological View of Religion</td><td>• Understanding Italics
• Using a Graphic Organizer to Show Cause and Effect
• Guessing the Meaning from Context
• Outlining Main Ideas, Important Details, and Examples
• Marking a Book
• Understanding Collocations
• Understanding the Organization of a Research Paper</td><td>• Focus: Defining a Term
• Strategy: Writing a Paragraph of Definition
• Strategy: Using Material from a Source</td></tr>
<tr><td>Chapter 2
Physical Anthropology
• Introduction: Orangutans
• General Interest: Humans and Other Primates
• Academic: Modern Stone Age Humans</td><td>• Understanding Pronoun References
• Previewing: Using Headings
• Previewing: Using Pictures and Captions
• Having Questions in Mind
• Understanding Quotation Marks</td><td>• Focus: Paragraph of Comparison
• Strategy: Getting Started by Brainstorming
• Strategy: Paraphrasing
• Strategy: Writing a Paragraph of Comparison</td></tr>
</table>

The Mechanics of Writing	Critical Thinking Strategies	Test-Taking Strategies
UNIT 1 ANTHROPOLOGY		
• Adjective Clauses • Coordinating Conjunctions • Adjective Clauses with Prepositions • Adverbial Conjunctions • Avoiding Sentence Fragments	• Making Inferences • Keeping a Word Journal • Making Connections • Outlining • Summarizing	• Taking an Essay Exam • Underlining
• Review: Adverbial Conjunctions to Show Similarities and Differences • Complex Sentences: Subordinating Conjunctions • Subordinating Conjunctions to Show Differences	• Making Comparisons • Comparing	• Taking a Closed-Book Essay Exam • Defining

Chapter	Reading Strategies	Writing and Writing Strategies
UNIT 2 ECONOMICS		
Chapter 3 **Developing Nations** • Introduction: *What Can One Person Do about Poverty?* • General Interest: *A Bank for the Down and Out* • Academic: *Developing Countries*	• Finding the Meaning of Words with Multiple Definitions • Dealing with Too Much Material: Divide and Conquer • Using Tables to Find Information	• Focus: Paragraph of Argument • Strategy: Writing a Paragraph of Argument: Cause/Effect • Strategy: Organizing a Cause/Effect Paragraph: Idea Mapping
Chapter 4 **The Global Economy** • Introduction: *The Global Marketplace* • General Interest: *Skills for the Global Marketplace* • Academic: *International Trade*	• Providing Definitions and Examples to Check Understanding • Summarizing Your Reading	• Focus: Paragraph about Free Trade • Strategy: Writing a Paragraph of Argument: Inductive Reasoning • Strategy: Providing Evidence
UNIT 3 LITERATURE		
Chapter 5 **The Nature of Poetry** • Introduction: *Poetry Lessons* • General Interest: *Appreciating Poetry* • Academic: *Three More Poems*	• Choosing the Correct Dictionary Definition: Using Parts of Speech • Analyzing Poems • Stating the Theme of a Poem: the Topic and Main Idea	• Focus: Analysis of a Poem • Strategy: Planning a Paragraph of Analysis: Idea Mapping • Strategy: Writing a Paragraph of Analysis

The Mechanics of Writing	Critical Thinking Strategies	Test-Taking Strategies
UNIT 2 ECONOMICS		
• Using Source Material • Finding Supporting Information • Introducing Citations • Knowing When to Quote and When to Paraphrase • Choosing the Right Reporting Verb • Weaving in Quotations	• Synthesizing • Summarizing	• Summarizing • Circling the Best Choice
• Transitions Followed by Phrases • Present Unreal Conditional • Conditionals with *Without* • Transition Expressions of Cause and Effect: Review of Coordinating, Adverbial, and Subordinating Conjunctions	• Evaluating Sources • Making Connections	• Taking a Side • Circling the Best Choice • Finding Errors
UNIT 3 LITERATURE		
• Expressing Possibility and Probability • Using Phrases for Symbols • Using Similes with *as . . . as* • Avoiding and Repairing Problems with Sentence Structure	• Discovering the Meaning of a Poem • Making Inferences	• Hedging • Avoiding Overstatement

Chapter	Reading Strategies	Writing and Writing Strategies
Chapter 6 **Heroes in Literature** • Introduction: *Old Country Advice to the American Traveler* • General Interest: *The Hero's Journey* • Academic: *Ta-Na-E-Ka*	• Understanding Italics for Foreign Words • Finding the Theme of a Story • Recognizing Euphemisms	• Focus: A Persuasive Essay • Strategy: Understanding the Organization of an Essay • Strategy: Writing a Thesis Statement • Strategy: Writing Topic Sentences in an Essay
UNIT 4 ECOLOGY		
Chapter 7 **Endangered Species** • Introduction: *A Dutch Scientist Teaches Indians to Hunt* • General Interest: *The Human Factor* • Academic: *The Edge of Extinction*	• Knowing Which New Words to Focus On • Understanding the Passive Voice • Formal Outlining	• Focus: Reference Lists in APA Format • Strategy: Writing a Research Paper • Strategy: Evaluating Online Sources • Strategy: Doing Library Research • Strategy: Writing a Reference List
Chapter 8 **Human Ecology** • Introduction: *Simple Solutions* • General Interest: *Are Pesticides Safe?* • Academic: *The Effects of E-Waste*	• Organizing Ideas	• Focus: A Research Paper • Strategy: Planning an Essay by Using a Formal Outline • Strategy: Writing Introductions • Strategy: Writing Conclusions

The Mechanics of Writing	Critical Thinking Strategies	Test-Taking Strategies
• Parallelism • Making a Strong Argument: *Should, Ought to,* and *Must* • Using Synonyms • Review: Paraphrasing	• Interpreting • Making Connections • Summarizing	• Writing Supporting Material in an Essay • Circling the Best Choice
UNIT 4 ECOLOGY		
• Understanding Punctuation: Ellipses and Brackets • Review: Using Source Material	• Understanding Irony • Outlining	• Finding Errors
• Reducing Adjective Clauses to Participial Phrases • Using Participial Phrases at the End of a Sentence • Using Participial Phrases at the Beginning of a Sentence • Using Internal Citations • Varying Citation Forms • Citing Sources that Cite Sources • Including Long Quotes	• Seeing Both Sides of an Argument	• Practicing Fill-in-the-Blank Questions • Finding Errors

Welcome

Quest Second Edition prepares students for academic success. The series features two complementary strands—*Reading and Writing* and *Listening and Speaking*—each with four levels. The integrated Quest program provides robust scaffolding to support and accelerate each student's journey from exploring general interest topics to mastering academic content.

New second edition features

- New *Intro* level providing on-ramp to Books 1-3
- Redesigned, larger format with captivating photos
- Expanded focus on critical thinking skills
- Addition of research paper to *Reading and Writing* strand
- New unit-ending *Vocabulary Workshops* and end-of-book Academic Word List (AWL)
- Expanded video program (VHS/DVD) with new lecture and updated social language footage
- EZ Test® CD-ROM test generator for all *Reading and Writing* titles
- Test-Taking strategy boxes that highlight skills needed for success on the new TOEFL® iBT
- Teacher's Editions with activity-by-activity procedural notes, expansion activities, and tests

Captivating photos and graphics capture students' attention while introducing each academic topic.

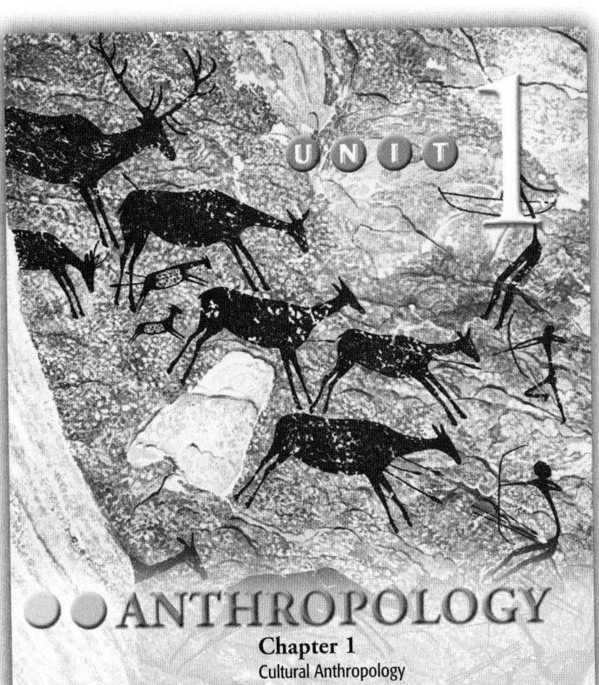

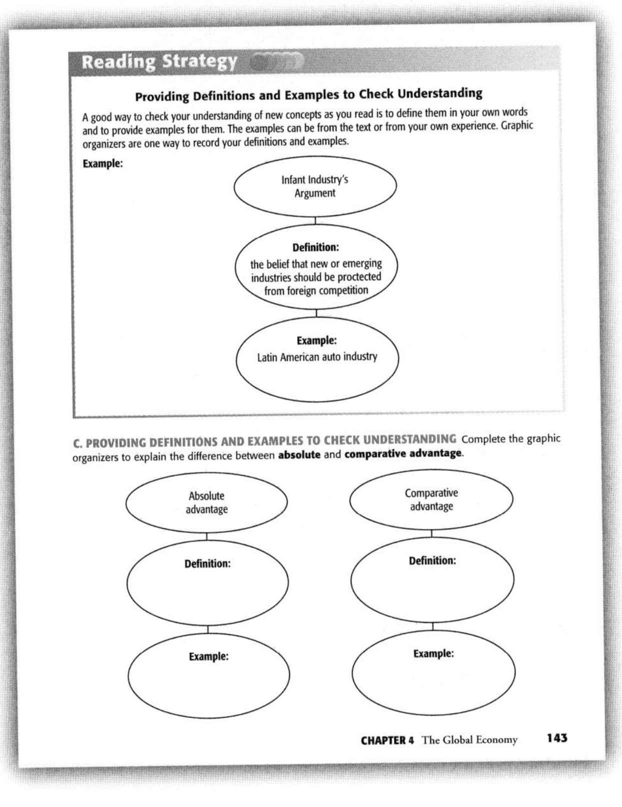
Reading Strategy

Providing Definitions and Examples to Check Understanding

A good way to check your understanding of new concepts as you read is to define them in your own words and to provide examples for them. The examples can be from the text or from your own experience. Graphic organizers are one way to record your definitions and examples.

Example:

Infant Industry's Argument

Definition: the belief that new or emerging industries should be proctected from foreign competition

Example: Latin American auto industry

C. PROVIDING DEFINITIONS AND EXAMPLES TO CHECK UNDERSTANDING Complete the graphic organizers to explain the difference between **absolute** and **comparative advantage**.

Absolute advantage — **Definition:** — **Example:**

Comparative advantage — **Definition:** — **Example:**

CHAPTER 4 The Global Economy **143**

Strategy-based approach develops reading, writing, critical thinking, and test-taking skills needed for academic success.

Three high-interest reading selections in each chapter introduce students to the course content most frequently required by universities.

READING

In the following reading, don't worry about words that are new to you. Instead, try to understand the main ideas. As you read, think about the answer to this question:

- What should companies do when they want to sell products in different countries?

Lost in Translation

When companies want to sell their products globally, they must take into consideration the languages and the cultures in which they want to do business. For example, when translating product names and slogans, companies need to understand the nuances (slight differences in meaning) of other languages; otherwise, they risk offending potential consumers, or worse, creating a bad image for themselves. Take a look at what happens when companies *don't* do this before advertising a product in another country or culture:

- The Scandinavian vacuum manufacturer Electrolux tried to sell its goods in America but didn't help itself with this slogan: "Nothing sucks like an Electrolux."
- When the Pope visited Miami, Florida, an American T-shirt maker printed shirts in both English and Spanish. But instead of "I saw the Pope," the Spanish shirts said: "I saw the potato."
- Parker Pen tried an ad campaign in Mexico that was meant to say, "It won't leak in your pocket and embarrass you." But instead—because the company mistakenly used the word "embarazar" for "embarrass"—the ads said, "It won't leak in your pocket and make you pregnant."
- In Italy, a campaign for Schweppes Tonic Water, a British soft drink, translated the name as "Schweppes Toilet Water."
- A Japanese company wanted to import the sports drink called "Pocari Sweat" to the United States, but quickly realized that it had to remove the second word from the name.
- A French company sold one of its products, a perfume called "Opium," in the United States. Some American consumers (customers) were offended by the product name.

Source: Adapted from "You Say Potato" from *The San Francisco Chronicle* and Global Software (Taylor)

124 **UNIT 2** Economics

International Trade

SECTION 1—ABSOLUTE AND COMPARATIVE ADVANTAGE

The key to trade—whether among people, states, or countries—is specialization.

Some people specialize in cutting hair. Others specialize in fixing computers. These people exchange their services for money, which they then use to buy the specialized goods and services they need from others.

Different regions of a country specialize in certain economic activities in much the same way. New York, for example, is the center of the U.S. financial industry, and Detroit specializes in automobiles. The Midwest and High Plains areas are known for wheat farming. Texas is recognized for oil and cattle, while Florida and California are famous for citrus fruit. All of these states trade with one another so that people in one area can consume the goods and services that workers in other areas offer.

Coca-Cola ad in Moscow, Russia

If you want to find out what a country specializes in, look at its **exports**—the goods and services that it produces and then sells to other nations.

The U.S. and International Trade

International trade is important to all nations. Most of the products exchanged are goods, although services, such as insurance and banking, are being bought and sold in increasing numbers.

In the United States for example, **imports**—goods and services that one country buys from other countries—amounted to about $1,590 billion in 2003. This number corresponds to nearly $5,460 for every person in the country, and it has grown steadily over the years. Figure 4.1 shows the merchandise trade patterns for the United States and the rest of the world. As large as these numbers are, they would be even bigger if we counted the values of services in addition to the **merchandise**, or goods, shown in the figure. The sheer volume of trade between nations of such different geographic, political, and religious characteristics is proof that trade is beneficial.

In fact, nations trade for the same reasons that individuals do—they trade because they believe that the products they receive are worth more than the products they give up.

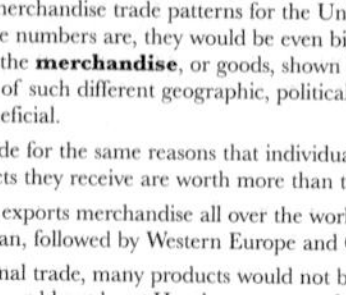

The United States exports merchandise all over the world. The biggest trade imbalance for the U.S. is with Japan, followed by Western Europe and Canada.

Without international trade, many products would not be available on the world market. Bananas, for example, would not leave Honduras, nor would coffee beans leave Colombia or Brazil. Some people think of international trade as a way to obtain exotic products, but trade

136 **UNIT 2** Economics

Gradual curve in each chapter from general interest to academic content supports students as they engage in increasingly more difficult material.

Discussion, pair-work, and group-work activities scaffold the learning process as students move from general interest to academic content.

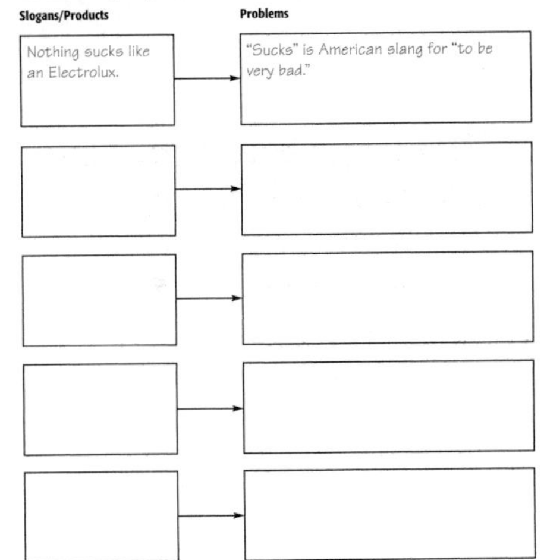

C. UNDERSTANDING DETAILS In small groups, discuss the problem with each example of a mistranslated slogan or product name in the reading. Use the graphic organizer to record your ideas.

Slogans/Products	Problems
Nothing sucks like an Electrolux.	"Sucks" is American slang for "to be very bad."

D. DISCUSSION In small groups, discuss these questions.

1. How could the companies in the reading have avoided problems that they had with ad slogans and product names?
2. Has an ad slogan ever made you want to buy a product? If yes, which one and why? Has a slogan ever made you *not* want to buy a product? If yes, which one and why?
3. How do you make buying decisions?
4. Do you think about where a product is manufactured before you buy it? Does the **country of origin** (the country from which it came) make any difference to you?

126 UNIT 2 Economics

UNIT 2 VOCABULARY WORKSHOP

Review vocabulary items that you learned in Chapters 3 and 4.

A. MATCHING Match the definitions to the words. Write the letters on the lines.

Words	Definitions
______ 1. burden	a. a time in which many people die of hunger
______ 2. capital	b. number of live births per 1,000 people
______ 3. crude birthrate	c. not repay borrowed money
______ 4. default	d. a tax on imports
______ 5. destitute	e. remove completely
______ 6. diversifies	f. money to begin a business
______ 7. eradication	g. complete removal
______ 8. extinguish	h. people who favor few or no trade restrictions
______ 9. famine	i. very, very poor
______ 10. free traders	j. varies; includes a variety
______ 11. revenue	k. something heavy that must be carried
______ 12. tariff	l. income

B. PHRASES USING PREPOSITIONS Write the correct prepositions. When you finish, you can check your answers by looking back at page xx for 1–5 and page xx for 6–10 on the lines.

1. an obstacle __________ economic development
2. a shortage __________ natural and energy resources
3. stand __________ the way __________ economic development
4. compatible __________ the concept __________ economic growth
5. __________ the brink __________ default

156 UNIT 2 Economics

Unit-Ending *Vocabulary Workshops* reinforce key unit vocabulary that appears on the Academic Word List (AWL).

COMPREHENSIVE ANCILLARY PROGRAM

Expanded video program for the *Listening and Speaking* titles now includes mini-lectures to build comprehension and note-taking skills, and updated social language scenes to develop conversation skills.

Audio program selections are indicated with this icon 🎧 and include recordings of all lectures, conversations, pronunciation and intonation activities, and reading selections.

Teacher's Edition provides activity-by-activity teaching suggestions, expansion activities, tests, and special TOEFL® iBT preparation notes.

EZ Test® CD-ROM test generator for the *Reading and Writing* titles allows teachers to create customized tests in a matter of minutes.

UNIT 1

ANTHROPOLOGY

Chapter 1
Cultural Anthropology

Chapter 2
Physical Anthropology

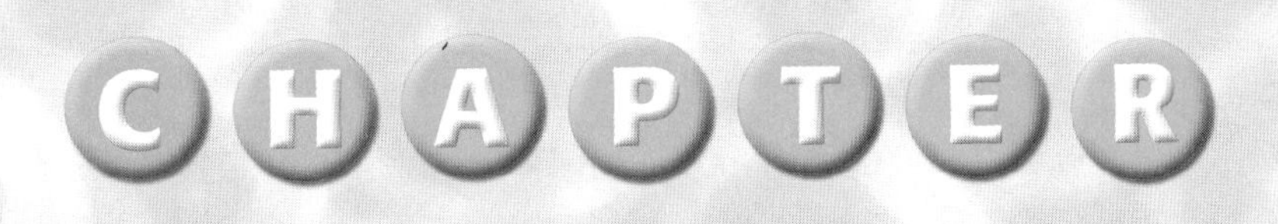

CHAPTER 1

Cultural Anthropology

Discuss these questions:
- What culture do you think the man is from?
- What is his position in society?
- Why is religion important to many people?

PART 1 INTRODUCTION *Feng Shui* in California

BEFORE READING

A neat office space with natural lighting

An elevator panel in an office building

An office filled with **clutter** and with **artificial lighting**

THINKING AHEAD In small groups, look at the pictures and discuss these questions.

1. If you had to work in one of the offices in these photos, which one would put you in a better **mood**—emotional state? What colors put you in a good mood?
2. What is the source of light in each office? In other words, where does it come from?
3. Which floor numbers are missing from the elevator panel? Why?

4. What are some numbers that people think are lucky? Why do they think this? What are some *un*lucky numbers? Why are they considered unlucky?

5. How does a belief in lucky (or unlucky) numbers affect everyday life? Give examples.

6. In modern culture, especially among young people, there are frequent **fads** that come and go. These are things or practices that are *very* popular but for a very short time. Certain hairstyles, video games, diets, music, and sports can be fads. Can you think of any popular fads today?

READING

Read about *feng shui*. As you read, think about this question:

• What new **proposal**—recommendation or suggestion—is one member of the California government making?

San Francisco Legislator Pushes *Feng Shui* Building Codes

A California lawmaker has proposed that the Golden State "adopt building standards that promote *feng shui* principles" in order to increase the "positive energy" available to the state's millions of residents. The proposal was put forth in January of 2004 by Leland Yee, of the California State Assembly, who urged the state architect and cities across the state to adopt design standards consistent with the Chinese principles of *feng shui.* 5

Yee's office explains, "The structure of a building can affect a person's mood, which can influence a person's behavior, which, in turn, can determine the success of a person's personal and professional relationships. The aim of *feng shui* architecture is to study how the environment in which people live may affect their lives and influence their quality of life."

10 *Feng shui,* which translates as "wind and water," is a collection of ancient Chinese traditions intended to improve a person' life through the carefully planned design of buildings and the objects within them. *Feng shui* combines several concepts of Asian mysticism, most essentially the flow of *chi,* or energy. Supposedly, *chi* can be manipulated, redirected, and even blocked by one's environment. According to *feng shui* tradition, positive 15 *chi* is influenced by such things as natural lighting and materials, electronic equipment, and good airflow. Artificial lighting and materials, an "unlucky" or "unbalanced" building shape, clutter, and even items that remind people of bad experiences can all produce negative *chi.*

Feng shui contains many common-sense techniques such as eliminating clutter to reduce stress and painting rooms in certain colors to encourage a good mood. But it is also full of 20 old superstitions, such as avoiding unlucky numbers, keeping toilet lids down to prevent *chi* from going down the drain, and placing mirrors at strategic points to deflect negative energy.

Though the principles originated in China four to five thousand years ago, a simplified version of *feng shui* has become a worldwide fad in recent years, especially among people looking to increase their success. Corporations are also making use of the *feng shui* craze: Merrill 25 Lynch, Citibank, and Donald Trump have all used *feng shui* principles for their properties. But this may have less to do with a desire for good *chi* than with doing smart business: some CEOs may view this as a strategy to win over Asian clients, for whom bad *feng shui* can be a deal-breaker.

Spokespeople for the California Building Standards Commission (CBSC) and the California Building Industry Association have criticized the resolution. "My . . . feeling . . . is
30 that in these times with the budget cuts, . . . we're looking at the highest priority issues," said Stan Nishimura, executive director of the CBSC. "I don't think this is our highest priority."

Source: "San Francisco Legislator Pushes *Feng Shui* Building Codes" (Gaeddert)

AFTER READING

A. COMPREHENSION CHECK Look back at the reading. When you find the answers to these questions, underline them.

1. What does Assemblyman Leland Yee want the state of California to do? Why?
2. What is *feng shui*? What does it do?
3. What is *chi*? What are examples of things that influence good *chi*? What are examples of things that produce negative *chi*?
4. When did the principles of *feng shui* originate? What has happened all over the world in recent years?

Critical Thinking Strategy

Making Inferences

You frequently need to make **inferences** when you read. You need to find small clues that lead you to **infer**—understand—things that the author doesn't explicitly **state** or say.

Example: You read: But it is also full of old superstitions, . . .
You infer: The author doesn't think every aspect of *feng shui* is useful.

B. MAKING INFERENCES The author of the article appears to agree with some of the **principles** of *feng shui*. He seems to disagree with other beliefs. Look in the fourth paragraph (lines 18–21). Discuss these questions with a partner:

- Which techniques does the author like?
- Why does he like them?
- Which ones doesn't he like?
- Which words led you to make these inferences?

Reading Strategy

Understanding Italics

Writers use *italics* (slanted letters) for several reasons, including:

- emphasis or stress of an important word
- the title of a book, newspaper, or magazine
- a foreign word or phrase in an English sentence
- to mean "the word . . ." or "the expression . . ."

Look back at the reading on pages 5–6. Find words in italics. What is the reason for them?

C. VOCABULARY CHECK Look back at the reading on pages 5–6 to find the words and phrases that match these definitions. Don't use a dictionary. Numbers in parentheses refer to line numbers in the reading. Write the correct words on the lines.

1. encouraged; tried to persuade (Lines 1–5) urged
2. not natural (Lines 15–20) artificial
3. many things thrown around in a messy, disorganized way (Lines 15–20) clutter
4. cause something to change its direction (Lines 20–25) deflect
5. a synonym for the word *fad* (Lines 20–25) craze
6. chief executive officers (of big companies) (Lines 25–30) CEOs X
7. reductions in a spending plan (Lines 25–30) [budget] cuts

Reading Strategy

Using a Graphic Organizer to Show Cause and Effect

When you put information into a **graphic organizer**, you can use the organizer to clearly **depict** (show) information. Graphic organizers help you see the relationships or connections among different ideas.

When you organize information from readings in graphic organizers, you can then use them to review and study for exams. There are different types of graphic organizers, and you will work with many of them in this book.

One type of graphic organizer depicts a **chain** of causes and effects. In other words, one situation (a cause) leads to another situation (the effect), which, **in turn**, becomes the cause of another effect. The graphic organizer on page 8 is a cause-and-effect chain.

D. USING A GRAPHIC ORGANIZER Fill in this cause-and-effect chain with information from the second paragraph of the reading on page 5.

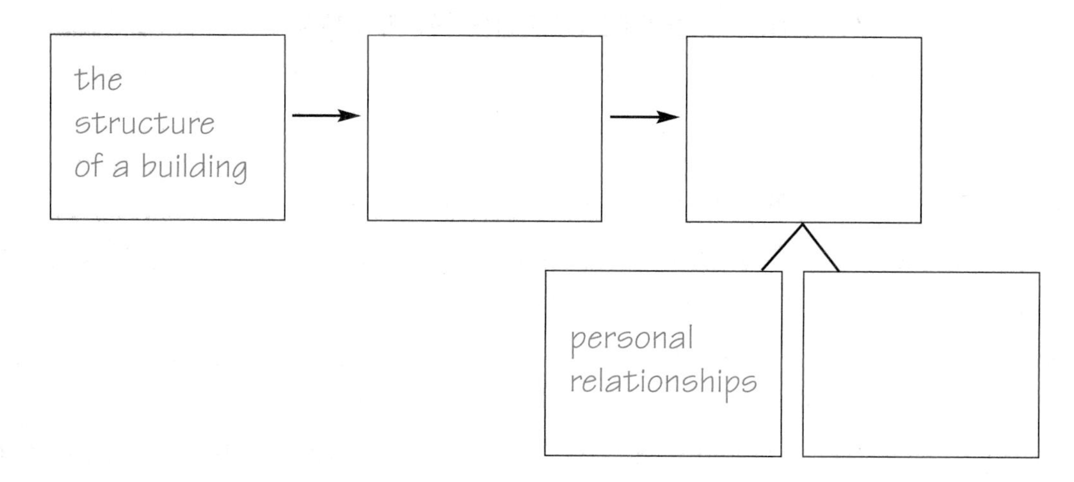

E. TAKING A SURVEY Read the questions in the chart and think about your answers. Then interview three classmates. Ask them the questions in the chart and write their answers.

Questions	Classmate 1	Classmate 2	Classmate 3
Is your mood affected by the space that you are in? If so, how?			
What are some lucky or unlucky signs (animals, food, colors, days, etc.)?			
What are some lucky or unlucky actions—things that people *do*?			

PART 2 GENERAL INTEREST READING
Symbolic Systems and Meanings

BEFORE READING

A. THINKING AHEAD In small groups, discuss these questions.

1. What is a popular sport? Are there any idioms or expressions that come from this sport? (For example, an American may say that someone is "playing hardball.")
2. What different foods are served for different events—for example, a family meal, a business dinner, or a party?
3. What can animals be a **symbol** of? (For example, a dove—a white bird—is a symbol of peace in many countries).
4. Picture a *traditional* house. How are the rooms arranged? In which room do people spend most of their time? How is this house different from modern houses?
5. What are some symbols associated with a position of authority (such as a king or queen)?

A typical Western house

Reading Strategy

Guessing The Meaning from Context

Students often have a lot of reading to do every day. You will not have time to look up every word in a dictionary. It's important to be able to guess the meaning of new words from the context–the words and sentences around the word–whenever possible. This is easy if the context is clear. Here are some clues that will help you avoid using a dictionary.

1. **Definition after *be* or *means*:**
   Feng shui is *a collection of ancient Chinese traditions intended to improve a person's life through the planned design of buildings.*
2. **Definition or synonym after a comma (,) or dash (–) or in parentheses ( ):**
   Metaphor, *a kind of symbol*, is an important analytical concept.
3. **Examples after *such as, for instance, for example,* and *e.g.* or before *and other*:**
   There are also old **superstitions** such as *avoiding unlucky numbers.*
   Brahmins and other **high-ranked people in the Indian caste system** cannot eat with low-ranked people.
4. **Opposites:**
   Political symbols may seem **trivial**, but they are actually very important, and people take them seriously.
5. **The reader's own experience or logic:**
   One player **pitches** the ball, and the other catches it. (The reader needs to know something about baseball.)
6. **Information in another part of the sentence or another sentence:**
   Political cartoonists use symbolic images to **portray** government leaders when they draw them.
7. **The expressions *in other words, that is,* and *i.e.*:**
   Food can be used to distinguish different categories of **rank**; in other words, *people of certain levels of social status* are prohibited from eating certain foods.

Frequently, it's possible to guess *something* about a new word, but you can't guess the exact meaning. In this case, you still probably don't need a dictionary.

Example: People ate stews from a communal pot.

Here you can guess that *stews* are a kind of cooked food, but you don't know exactly what kind. Is it important to know this? Probably not. Often, you will learn more about a word as you keep reading.

Sometimes it's not possible to guess the meaning at all because the context is too limited. In this case, you need to decide how important the word is; if it isn't essential, don't worry about it. Just keep reading. If the word is essential–if you can't understand a paragraph without it–you'll need to use a monolingual dictionary.

B. GUESSING THE MEANING FROM CONTEXT Read the sentences below. The words and phrases in orange are from the next reading. What can you guess about them? Write definitions for the words—*even if you aren't sure about the exact meaning.* Don't use a dictionary.

1. In American society, **the nuclear family** is the unit that regularly eats together.

   nuclear family = ______________________________

2. Physical games demand from the players intelligence, **stamina**, and courage.

   stamina = ______________________________

3. **Acquaintances** can come to cocktail parties, but only relatives may come to Sunday meals in British culture.

   acquaintances = ______________________________

4. Cultural rules determine every aspect of food **consumption**. The people who eat together are a social unit.

   consumption = ______________________________

5. Only **tidbits** and snacks—finger foods—are served at a cocktail party.

   tidbits = ______________________________

6. A nation may be represented by an **array** of symbols: a flag, an animal, certain colors, and so on.

   array = ______________________________

Now compare your answers with a partner's answers.

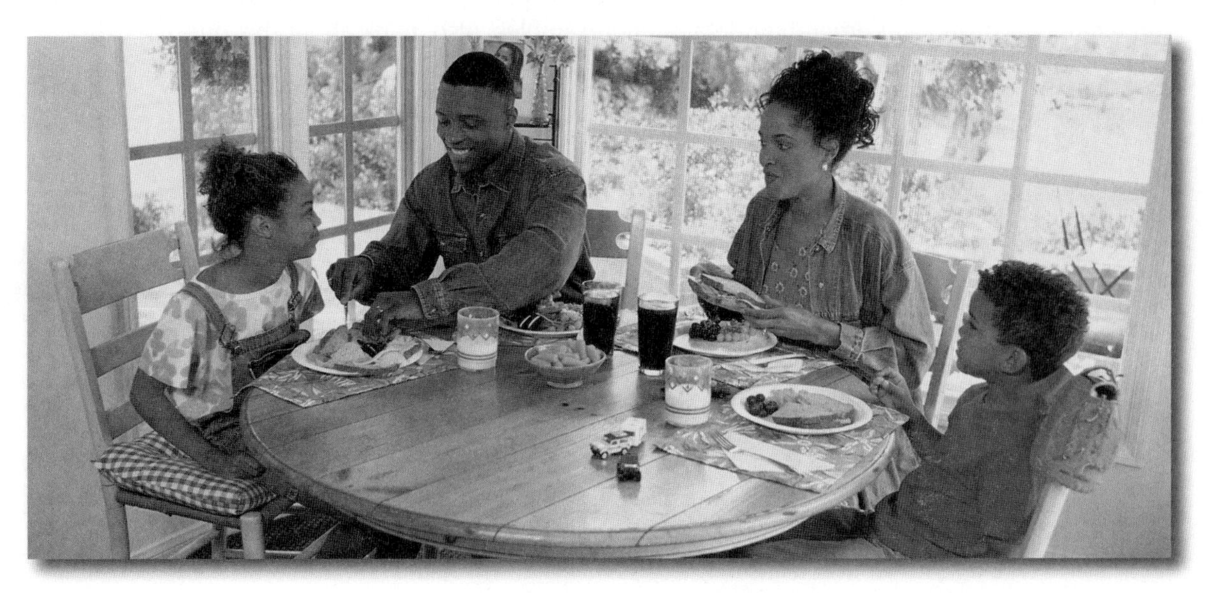

An American family eating breakfast

Reading Strategy

Outlining Main Ideas, Important Details, and Examples

In a reading passage or chapter in a college textbook, there are ideas of different levels of importance. The **one main idea** (an "umbrella" that covers the whole reading) can usually be found in the introductory paragraph. However, there are almost always a number of other **main ideas** about the subtopics. Frequently–but not always–you can find a main idea in the first sentence of a section of the reading. (Look right after the heading.) After the topic sentence of each paragraph (usually the first), there is usually an **important detail** that supports the main idea of that section. Also, there are often **examples**, which are very specific details. They support the important details.

Example: Main idea of the whole reading

- Main idea of Section 1
    - Important detail
        - Example
    - Important detail
- Main idea of Section 2
    - Important detail
        - Example
        - Example

Outlining the main ideas, important ideas, and examples in a reading is one way to make sure you understand its organization.

READING

Read about symbolic systems and meanings. Read the passage without using a dictionary. As you read, underline the main ideas, important details, and examples. Also, think about this question:

- How do symbols represent various areas of everyday life?

Symbolic Systems and Meanings

A symbol, in general, is a sign or object that represents something else. All symbols operate as if they were two-sided coins. On one side are the physical characteristics, and on the other side are the meanings, or what the symbols stand for.

5 Metaphor, a kind of symbol, is an important analytical concept used by anthropologists in the study of symbolic systems. A metaphor is an idea that people use to stand for another set of ideas. Games 10 are often used as a metaphor for life. Games involve struggle and competition.

Idioms in Politics that Come from Sports	
• to play hardball	• to run neck and neck
• to be off and running	• to be on the ropes
• to be down to the wire	• to go to bat for

Sometimes you win and sometimes you lose, but games must be played according to a set of rules. Games demand from the players intelligence, stamina, and courage. Politicians often accuse their rivals of "playing hardball." In this case, baseball is being used to stand for something else—politics—because both include competition, struggle, and some element of danger, though they may differ in many other respects.

Another type of symbol is a metonym. Like a metaphor, a metonym is based on a substitution of one thing for another, but in this case the symbol standing for something else is one of the several things that constitute the something else. Thus, the monarch can be referred to as the head of state, and the crown or throne can stand as a symbol for the monarchy. The capital of any type of government can be referred to as the seat of the government. In each case, a part has been taken and used to stand as a symbol for a more complex whole.

The Symbolism of Food

Cultural rules determine every aspect of food consumption. Who eats together defines social units. For example, in some societies, the nuclear family is the unit that regularly eats together. The anthropologist Mary Douglas (1972) has pointed out that, for the English, the kind of meal and the kind of food that is served relate to the kinds of social links between people who are eating together. She distinguishes between regular meals, Sunday meals when relatives may come, and cocktail parties for acquaintances. The food served symbolizes the occasion and reflects who is present. For example, only tidbits and snacks—finger foods—are served at a cocktail party. It would be inappropriate to serve a steak or hamburgers. The distinctions among cocktails, regular meals, and special dinners mark the social boundaries between those guests who are invited for drinks, those who are invited to dinner, and those who come to a family meal. In this example, the type of food symbolizes the category of guest and with whom it is eaten.

In some New Guinea societies, the nuclear family is not the unit that eats together, as is the case in American society. The men take their meals in a men's house, separately from their wives and children. Women prepare and eat their food in their own houses and take the husband's portion to the men's house. The women eat with their children in their own houses. This pattern is also widespread among Near Eastern societies, where men usually eat with other men and women with other women, and husbands and wives do not eat together.

Eating is a metaphor that is sometimes used to signify marriage. In many New Guinea societies, like that of the Lesu on the island of New Ireland in the Pacific and that of the Trobriand Islanders, marriage is symbolized by the couple's eating together for the first time. Eating symbolizes their new status as a married couple. In U.S. society, it is just the reverse. A couple may go out to dinner on a first date.

A totem pole from the Pacific coast in North America; the creatures represent totemic ancestors.

Other cultural rules have to do with taboos against eating certain things. In some societies, members of a clan, a type of kin (family) group, are not allowed to eat the animal or bird that is their totemic ancestor. Since they believe themselves to be descended from that ancestor, it would be like eating that ancestor or eating themselves.

There is also an association between food prohibitions and rank, which is found in its most extreme form in the caste system of India. A caste system consists of ranked groups, each with a different economic specialization. In India, there is an association between caste and the idea of pollution. Members of highly ranked groups can be polluted by coming into contact with the bodily secretions, particularly saliva, of individuals of lower-ranked castes. Because of the fear of pollution, Brahmans and other high-ranked individuals will not share food with, not eat from the same plate as, not even accept food from an individual from a low-ranking caste.

The Symbolic and Social Meanings of Space

Arrangements of space also make important symbolic statements about social groupings and social relationships. Among the Nuchanulth of the Pacific coast of Canada, each of the large plank houses in the winter villages in which they lived in the 19th century represented a social group. The floor plan of the house was divided into spaces that were ranked (see Figure 1). The place of honor, the left corner of the rear of the house, was occupied by the owner, who was the highest-ranking person in the house, and his family. The next most important man and his family occupied the right rear corner of the house, and so on. Commoners and their families lived in the remaining spaces along the sides of the house. Each location had its own hearth [cooking place]. The house floor plan was like a seating plan according to seniority.

In a village in northeastern Thailand, space in a house is divided to symbolize not rank, but rules about marriage (see Figure 2). The sleeping room is the most sacred part of the house. First cousins, with whom marriage is not permitted, may enter that room but may not sleep there. More distant relatives, whom one may marry, are not allowed to enter the sleeping room and must remain in the guest room.

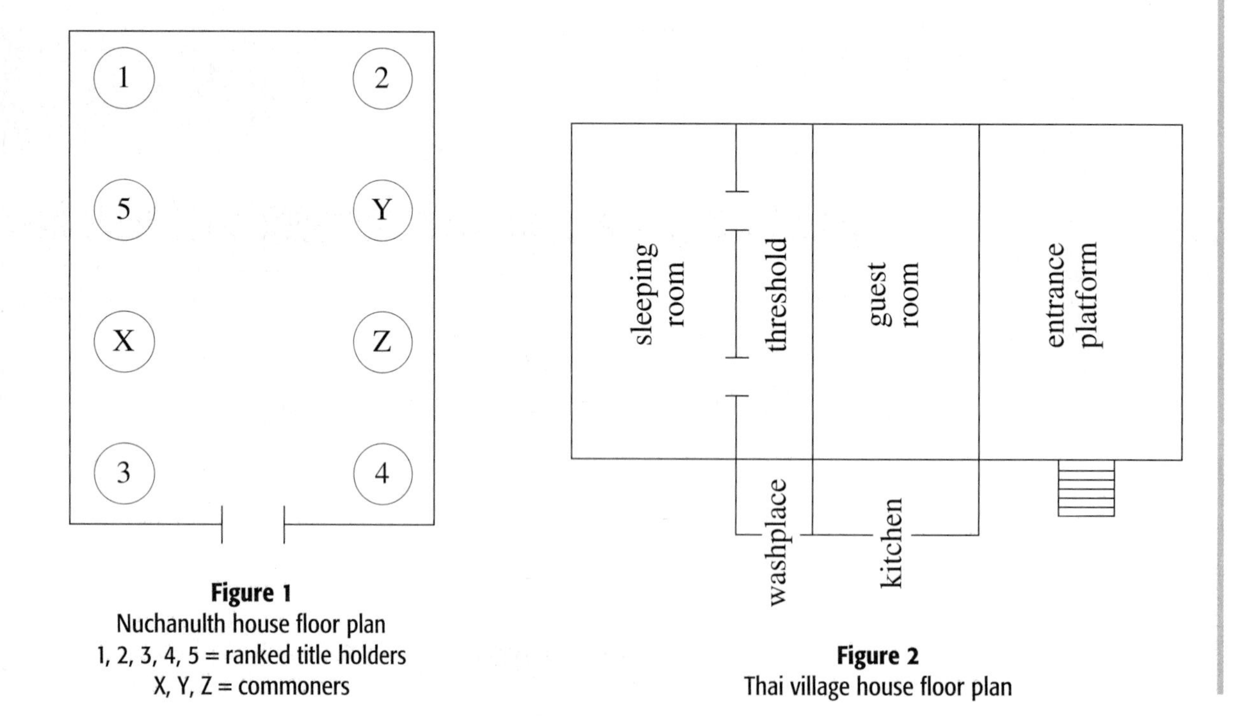

Figure 1
Nuchanulth house floor plan
1, 2, 3, 4, 5 = ranked title holders
X, Y, Z = commoners

Figure 2
Thai village house floor plan

85 The way in which people use social space can also reflect social relationships and ethnic identity. Early immigrants to America from Europe brought with them a communal style of living, which they retained until late in the 18th century. Historical records document group-oriented existence, in which one room was used for eating, entertaining guests, and sleeping (Dietz, 1977; quoted in Pader, 1993, p. 18). People ate stews from a communal pot, shared drinking cups, and used a common pit toilet. 90 With the development of ideas about individualism, people soon began to shift to the use of individual cups and plates; the eating of meals that included meat, starch, and vegetables served on separate plates; and the use of individual chamber pots. They began to build their houses with separate rooms to entertain guests (living rooms), separate bedrooms for sleeping, separate work areas (kitchen, laundry room), and 95 separate bathrooms.

Symbols, Politics, and Authority

An entire nation may be represented by an array of symbols. For example, the combat between symbolic animals—the eagle and the bear—was used by political cartoonists to 100 portray the conflict between the United States and the former Soviet Union.

Individuals in positions of authority are associated with particular objects that become symbols of the office they hold. Sometimes 105 the object is something the officeholder wears, such as a crown, or imperial regalia, which the officeholder alone may put on. Sometimes the officeholder carries a staff, wand, umbrella, or fly whisk. The curved staff 110 of the pharaoh of Egypt was the symbol of office, and so it is seen in the pictures of King Tutankhamen. In our definition of *metonym*, we pointed out how the crown or the throne could stand for the monarchy. A parallel is found in the 115 term referring to the leader of an academic department at a college or university. He or she is referred to as either *the chair* or *the head.* These symbols of authority are metonyms.

King Tutankhamen with symbols of office: a flail and the curved staff

Queen Elizabeth of England shown wearing a crown to symbolize her office

120 If authority is represented by a series of symbols, opposition to that authority is symbolically represented by an inversion of those symbols. In the 1960s in the United

States, all men in authority had short hair. Young men created a symbol of opposition when they allowed their hair to grow long. If authorities have short hair, then long hair is a symbol of opposition to that authority. However, today, wearing one's hair long is acceptable. Long hair is no longer a symbol of opposition to society, but dyeing one's hair fuchsia, blue, or orange is. If the established hierarchy wears *long* hair, then *short* hair becomes a symbol of opposition. During the 17th century, the Cavaliers of King Charles I of England wore their hair long, while those who opposed them, the Puritans led by Oliver Cromwell, wore short hair and were called Roundheads (as depicted in a cartoon of the period). These examples relate to the general principle that those who oppose the established authority will select as their symbol something that is the reverse of the symbol of those in authority. Political symbols may seem trivial, but in reality, people will die rather than deny them or give them up. People's identity as members of a group is powerfully bound up with such symbols.

Which men are Cavaliers? Which are Puritans? Notice their hair—and that of their dogs.

Which men are the authorities? Which are in opposition to them?

Source: *The Tapestry of Culture: An Introduction to Cultural Anthropology* (Rosman & Rubel)

AFTER READING

A. COMPREHENSION CHECK In small groups, compare the lines that you underlined. Discuss these questions.

1. Did you choose most of the same sentences?
2. Which lines contain the main idea of the whole reading?
3. What are the main ideas of the different sections? How many did you underline?
4. Which sentences give important details?
5. What are examples given in the reading?
6. After comparing your underlined information with that of other students, do you want to change your mind about what you underlined?

Reading Strategy

Marking a Book

College and university students usually need to do an enormous amount of reading. Often, there isn't enough time to read a chapter two or three times, so it's important to understand as much as possible the first time. One useful technique is marking a book. There are several ways to do this. One way is to buy several highlighters in yellow, orange, green, and so on. As you read, highlight the more **general, main ideas** with one color. Highlight **important details** with another color. Use a third color for **examples.** For **important vocabulary** (but not every new word), use a fourth color. In the margin, add question marks or notes to yourself.

Note: Be sure not to mark too much! This would be as useless as marking nothing.

B. MARKING A BOOK In the future, you will mark each passage *as you read it* the first time. (Often, in college, you will have time to read a passage only once.) However, for Part 2 in this chapter, you have already underlined the reading. Look back at the reading on pages 12–16 and highlight what you have underlined. Choose three colors—one for each level of importance—and another color for important vocabulary. Use these same colors every time you highlight a reading.

C. VOCABULARY CHECK Look back at the reading to find words and phrases that match these definitions. Numbers in parentheses refer to line numbers in the reading.

1. a type of symbol (Lines 15–20) metronym, [metaphor]
2. a king or queen (Lines 20–25) monarch
3. a type of kin (family) group (Lines 55–60) clan x
4. an animal that people believe their clan is descended from (Lines 55–60) totem
5. a system of ranked groups, especially in India (Lines 60–65) caste system x
6. a cooking place (Lines 75–80) hearth x
7. established hierarchy (Lines 125–130) (heirarchy) authority
8. changing the color of something (Lines 125–130) dyeing
9. connected with; associated with (Lines 130–135) [bound] up with

D. IN YOUR OWN WORDS: SUMMARIZING Choose one of the sections of the reading. Fill in the first blank with the topic of the section. Use a noun or a noun phrase. Fill in the second blank with the main idea. Complete the sentence with an independent clause.

1. The section is about ____

____

2. The author says that ____

____

E. ORGANIZING INFORMATION Use the information you highlighted in the reading to fill in the following chart.

Types of Symbolism	Main Ideas	Important Details	Examples
Food	Cultural rules determine every aspect of food preparation	1. Who eats together defines social units	a. nuclear family b. England: reg. meals (fam.), Sun. meals (rels.), cocktail parties (acquaintances)
		2. Eating—metaphor for marriage	Trobriand Islands: eating together 1st time = marriage
		3. Other cultural rule: taboo against eating certain things	totemic animals
		4. Association between food prohibitions and rank	caste system in India
Space			
Politics and Authority			

F. DISCUSSION In small groups, discuss these questions.

1. In your culture, does the food served at a meal symbolize the occasion and reflect who is present? If so, give an example.
2. What groups of people usually eat together?
3. Are there any animals, paintings, carvings, or territories that are symbolic of a group (such as a family or clan) in your country? If so, give an example.
4. How are houses or apartments organized where you live? In other words, is one room a location for multiple activities, or does each room have a separate use?
5. What are some symbols of your culture?
6. Nowadays, what are some objects or clothes that leaders wear to symbolize their office?

Critical Thinking Strategy

Keeping a Word Journal

Keeping a **word journal** is a good way to study, review, and remember new words. You can do this in a section of your three-ring binder or in a thin spiral notebook. You record words that are important for you to remember. All of the students in a class will be working with the same readings, but each student might find different words from these readings to put in his or her journal. Spend 10–20 minutes each day adding to and reviewing your journal. Include this information:

- the word or phrase
- the part of speech
- a synonym or definition (either your guess or from a dictionary)
- a sentence *from the reading* with the word in it (**especially important**), but with a blank in place of the word.

You can put this information in a four-section grid.

Example:

retain	verb
= keep	Early immigrants to America from Europe ________ed a communal style of living until late in the 18th century.

G. WORD JOURNAL Look back at the readings in Parts 1 and 2. Which new words are important for *you* to remember? Write them in your Word Journal.

PART 3 ACADEMIC READING
The Anthropological View of Religion

BEFORE READING

Many cultures have traditional beliefs about lucky or magical objects.

A. THINKING AHEAD In small groups, discuss these questions.

1. When you think of the word *religion*, what images come to mind?
2. When you think of the word *magic*, what images come to mind?
3. Do you know people who have a lucky **charm** or **amulet**—in other words, something that they wear on a necklace or keep in their pocket to bring them good luck or protect them from bad luck?
4. List as many religions as you can.
   - Who or what are the **supernatural beings** (gods, spirits) in these religions?
   - Who are the human leaders in these religions?
   - Are there any rituals or ceremonies in which people go into a **trance** (a dream-like condition of intense concentration)?
   - What are some symbols in these religions?
5. Do you know of a ritual or ceremony that a young person goes through to make the transition from childhood to adulthood?

B. VOCABULARY PREPARATION Read the sentences below. The words in orange are from the next reading. Try to guess their meanings from the context.

- Circle the part of speech—noun (n), verb (v), or adjective (adj).
- Then write your guess.
- If you are very unsure of your guess, check a dictionary to see if your guess was close. To save time, do the third step with a small group. Divide the group of words; each person can look up several words and then share the answers.

	Parts of Speech		
1. The supernatural is the extraordinary **realm** outside the real world. It is the place of dreams and gods and ghosts.	n	v	adj

Guess: ______________________________

Dictionary Definition: ______________________________

2. Because gods, goddesses, ghosts, and souls are not of the **material** world, we can't touch them.	n	v	adj

Guess: ______________________________

Dictionary Definition: ______________________________

3. In some religions, the gods and goddesses are in the form of animals, but in others, they are **anthropomorphic**.	n	v	adj

Guess: ______________________________

Dictionary Definition: ______________________________

4. The government, the military, and some religions have a strict **hierarchy**, an organized system with lower and higher ranks.	n	v	adj

Guess: ______________________________

Dictionary Definition: ______________________________

5. This idea is similar to the **notion** of luck.	n	v	adj

Guess: ______________________________

Dictionary Definition: ______________________________

6. Fishing in the ocean is **hazardous** at this time of year because there are often sudden, violent storms at sea.	n	v	adj

Guess: ______________________________

Dictionary Definition: ______________________________

7. I need to take another computer class. There's a real **gap** between what I know and what I need to know.	n	v	adj

Guess: ______________________________

Dictionary Definition: ______________________________

Reading Strategy

Understanding Collocations

Your written and spoken English will improve if you learn **collocations** with both new words and words that you already know. A collocation is a phrase. It is a group of words commonly found together. Some collocations are noun phrases, verb phrases, prepositional phrases, or participial phrases.

Examples: In the past, many explorers from Europe went on a quest for the "fountain of youth."

- noun phrase: **fountain of youth**
- verb phrase: **went on a quest**
- prepositional phrases: **in the past, from Europe**

Try these suggestions.

- When you learn a new word, also learn its collocation, if there is one. In time, you will find that many words have more than one collocation.
- As you read, *begin to notice collocations* of both new words and words that you already know. If you think that a group of words is a collocation, mark it in pencil. Ask your teacher or check a collocation dictionary to find out if it *is* one.
- As you read, if you're sure that a group of words is a collocation, highlight it.
- Begin to collect collocations in your Word Journal or a separate notebook section. Review them regularly.

C. UNDERSTANDING COLLOCATIONS Read through the paragraphs below. Notice the collocations in orange. (There are more collocations than those in orange, but you can't mark everything!) Which four are noun phrases? Which three are prepositional phrases? Which five are verb phrases?

Religion—in an array of forms—is a central feature of culture, and this has led anthropologists to focus on it. The questions they seem to ask are, what *is* religion and why is it important? In general, religion is "a system of beliefs usually involving the worship of supernatural forces or beings. Religious beliefs provide shape and meaning to one's perception of the universe" (O'Neill, 2002, ¶ 2). It is concerned with the supernatural world—"the extraordinary realm" outside (but believed to touch on) "the observable world," a realm that "is mysterious and inexplicable" and filled with . . . supernatural beings—gods and goddesses, ghosts, and souls . . . not of the material world" (Kottak, 2004, p. 581).

In 1966, the anthropologist F.C. Wallace identified four types of religion: shamanic, communal, Olympian, and monotheistic (Kottak, 2004, p. 591). Wallace characterized shamanism as the "simplest" religion. It is found mostly among foragers—people who hunt and gather food.

D. HUNTING FOR COLLOCATIONS Go back to Activity B on page 21. Highlight some of the collocations that you find in these sentences. What kind of collocation is each?

READING

Read the research paper without using a dictionary. As you read, highlight main ideas with one color, important details with another, and examples with a third. Highlight important vocabulary with a fourth color. Notice collocations as you read, but don't highlight them yet. Also, think about the answer to this question:

- What are three characteristics of all types of religions? (The sentence that answers this gives the main idea of the entire paper.)

The Anthropological View of Religion

Religion—in an array of forms—is a central feature of culture, and this has led anthropologists to focus on it. The questions they seem to ask are, what *is* religion and why is it important? In general, religion is "a system of beliefs usually involving the worship of supernatural forces or beings. Religious beliefs provide shape and meaning to one's perception of the universe" (O'Neill, 2002, ¶ 2). Religion is concerned with the supernatural world—"the extraordinary realm" outside (but believed to touch on) "the observable world," a realm that "is mysterious and inexplicable" and filled with . . . supernatural beings, gods and goddesses, ghosts, and souls . . . not of the material world" (Kottak, 2004, p. 581).

In 1966, the anthropologist F.C. Wallace identified four types of religion: shamanic, communal, Olympian, and monotheistic (Kottak, 2004, p. 591). Wallace characterized shamanism as the "simplest" religion. It is found mostly among foragers—people who hunt and gather food. The shaman is a part-time practitioner who is a combination of a priest, doctor, psychologist, and pharmacist. Communal religions have community rituals and part-time religious leaders. The believers are polytheistic—in other words, believe in many gods who mainly control nature—and are more often food producers (farmers) than foragers. Olympian religions—named after Mount Olympus, home of the ancient Greek gods—are also polytheistic. Such religions have "powerful anthropomorphic gods with specialized functions, for example, gods of love, war, the sea, and death" (Kottak, 2004, p. 593). Olympian religions exist in societies with a complex state organization and have a full-time priesthood that is organized in a hierarchy—a system of higher and lower ranks. "Wallace's fourth type—monotheism—also has priesthoods and notions of divine power, but it views the supernatural differently. In monotheism, all supernatural phenomena are . . . under the control of a single" all-powerful "supreme being" or god (p. 593). Such religions occur in states and empires and survive in modern organized religions. These religions seem to be very different from one another. However, all four types of religion make use of three characteristics—magic, symbolism, and ritual—to fulfill people's psychological and social needs.

Magic, a part of religion, "refers to supernatural techniques designed to accomplish specific aims" (Kottak, 2004, p. 583). Religion and science are similar in that both are "ways of understanding and influencing the natural world" (Rosman & Rubel, 2004); however, they differ in that "they are based on different theories of knowledge." In using magic, people believe that they can influence the natural world to act in a certain way if the magic words and rituals are performed correctly. Science, in contrast, is based on "knowledge obtained through the five senses" (p. 266) and does not include the supernatural. People often turn to magic when they "face uncertainty and danger" in aspects of their lives "over which they lack control" (Kottak, 2004 p. 584).

In this way, the use of magic fulfills a psychological need by reducing anxiety. There are examples everywhere. In many cultures, people carry a lucky charm or amulet. They may recite certain spells—magic words—to bring rain or stop a storm or make their crops grow well. In the Trobriand Islands, sailors turn to magic to keep their ship safe because sailing is hazardous, and they have no control of the weather. "American baseball players use magic rituals and formulas in areas of the game" that have the most uncertainty—"hitting and pitching." If nothing else, such magic rituals serve to reduce anxiety and increase confidence, which in turn improves performance (Rosman & Rubel, 2004, p. 291).

Symbols, according to Kottak, are "signs that have no necessary or natural connection to the things they signify" (2004, p. 346). Although specific symbols differ from one religion to another, any "religion may be viewed as a vast symbolic system" (Lessa & Vogt, 1965). Symbolism is important because "the human mind comprehends ideas better when they are expressed in visual and auditory symbols" (p. 203). Abstract ideas such as fear, hope, values, and goals are easier to feel and understand when there are gods, objects, and rituals to connect them with. In the ancient Roman religion, an Olympian religion, Venus was both a goddess *and* a symbol of love. In the modern Christian church, a monotheistic religion, bread and wine are symbolic of the body and blood of Christ. In cultures worldwide, a wedding ring symbolizes marriage. Places, too, can have symbolic value. For this reason, in modern Turkey, there may be a mosque built on land where there used to be a Christian church, and before that a temple to an ancient Greek god.

Generally speaking, human beings approach the supernatural by carrying out ritual acts (Rosman & Rubel, 2004, p. 270). According to Kottak (2004, p. 584), "rituals are formal—stylized, repetitive, and stereotyped [acts]. People perform them in special (sacred) places and at set times. . . . Repeated year after year, generation after generation," the function of rituals is to "translate messages, values, and sentiments into observable actions."

An example is the healing ritual in shamanic societies (such as Siberia), which fulfills psychological and social needs in addition to curing a person of a physical illness. In a long and dramatic public ritual that is not frequently practiced in modern times, the shaman enters a trance (Rosman & Rubel, 2004, p. 276). In Siberia, this is accomplished through the constant beating of a drum. In the Amazon, the shaman consumes a hallucinogenic drink. In this trance, he is believed to contact spirits, who tell him the cause of the illness and how to cure it. Part of most healing rituals requires removing some foreign object—a stone or arrowhead or bird feathers—from the patient's body. The shaman appears to suck it out with his mouth. This involves symbolism. Symbolically, the removal of this object means that the person is now free of the illness; it has "left" his body. Because people believe that illness is a punishment for breaking cultural taboos, the ritual is a powerful reminder not to break the rules. This serves to hold the society together.

Important rituals found in cultures worldwide are rites of passage, which "are associated with the transition from one place or stage of life to another . . . Passage rites involve changes in social status, such as from boyhood to manhood and from nonmember to [member]. More generally, a rite of passage may mark any change in place, condition, social position, or age" (Kottak, 2004, pp. 584–585). Baptisms, bar mitzvahs, weddings, and funerals are all rites of passage. Some rites of passage involve physical discomfort or even pain. Among some Native Americans, especially the Plains Indians, there used to be a famous rite called a "vision quest."

In this ritual, a teenage boy spent four days and nights, without food or water, alone in the wilderness. Sometimes drug consumption was part of the ritual. The boy went on a quest for "a vision, which would become his personal guardian spirit. He would then return to his
85 community as an adult" with a new, adult name (Kottak, 2004, p. 585).

Religion exists for many reasons. Among them, it eases psychological anxiety and binds together the members of a community. It makes use of magic, symbolism, and ritual to fill a gap in people's knowledge and to offer an explanation of things that are not understood. It gives meaning to life. Perhaps, too, it gives people perspective, for it reminds them of their
90 need for something greater than themselves.

conclusion

References

Kottak, C.P. (2004). *Anthropology: The Exploration of Human Diversity* (10th ed.). New York: McGraw-Hill.

Lessa, W.A., & Vogt, E.Z. (1965). *Reader in Comparative Religion: An Anthropological Approach* (2nd ed.). New York: Harper & Row.

O'Neil, D. (2002, August 19). *Overview of Religion.* Retrieved September 17, 2004 from http://anthro.palomar.ed/religion/flashcards_1.htm

Rosman, A., & Rubel, P.G. (2004). *The Tapestry of Culture: An Introduction to Cultural Anthropology* (8th ed.). New York: McGraw-Hill.

AFTER READING

A. MAIN IDEA Which sentence do you think includes the main idea of the research paper? Does it answer the questions below? If so, you have found the main idea. If not, try again.

- What needs do religions fulfill?
- What three characteristics do all religions have in common?

Reading Strategy

Understanding the Organization of a Research Paper

You will have to write research papers (also called "term papers" or "papers") throughout your academic life. You will learn to write one later in this book. Papers vary in length from just a few pages to more than 30 pages. They also vary in style, depending on the course for which they are written. For example, courses in anthropology and psychology require a style called APA (American Psychological Association). Courses in literature and languages require the style of the MLA (Modern Language Association).* However, both styles share certain characteristics.

- You will do research and choose books, articles, and/or online sources as the basis of the paper. These sources are listed at the end, on the reference list.
- Research papers have an introduction–one paragraph for a very short paper, several paragraphs for a longer paper.
- The **thesis statement** is a clear sentence at or near the end of the introduction. It has the topic and main idea of the paper. It also introduces the subtopics of the paper.
- The majority of the paper (the body) explores these topics.
- Information from sources are in the bibliography (or reference list), *and credit is given to the source* every time exact words or ideas are used.
- There is a conclusion that re-states the main idea but in different words.

*An example of MLA style is in Appendix 2 on page 309.

B. UNDERSTANDING THE ORGANIZATION OF A RESEARCH PAPER Look closely at the research paper on pages 23–25. In small groups, discuss these questions.

1. How much of the paper is the introduction? Where does the introduction end?
2. What is the thesis statement? How many subtopics does the thesis statement promise to explore?
3. Where does the body of the paper begin? Which three topics does the student write about? What order are these in?
4. Which paragraph is the conclusion? Which part of this re-states the thesis statement?
5. Find places in the paper where the student gives credit to sources. What three pieces of information are included about each source?
6. Sometimes the student uses a source's *ideas* and sometimes the source's *exact words*. How can you tell the difference?
7. Look at the references. How many sources are there? Which sources are books? Which source is a website?

C. COMPREHENSION CHECK Use your highlighted information from pages 23–25 to fill in the chart. One row has been completed as an example.

Characteristics of Religion	Definitions	Functions	Examples
Symbols	signs that have no necessary or natural connection to the things they signify	help people to comprehend abstract ideas such as fear, hope, values, and goals	Venus (in ancient Roman relig.) = love
Magic			
Rituals			

D. COLLOCATIONS WITH PREPOSITIONS Look back at the reading on pages 23–25 to find prepositions that complete the phrases in orange. (Numbers in parentheses refer to line numbers in the reading.) As you find these phrases in the reading, highlight them in the color that you use for important vocabulary.

1. Religion exists in an array ____________ forms. (Lines 1–5)
2. Anthropologists focus ____________ it. (Lines 1–5)
3. A shaman is a combination ____________ a priest, doctor, and psychologist. (Lines 10–15)
4. Olympian religions are named ____________ Mount Olympus. (Lines 15–20)
5. Monotheism has priesthoods and notions ____________ divine power. (Lines 20–25)
6. Science and religion differ in that they are based ____________ different theories of knowledge. (Lines 30–35)
7. People turn ____________ magic when they face uncertainty. (Lines 35–40)
8. Specific symbols differ ____________ one religion ____________ another. (Lines 45–50)
9. Rites of passage are associated ____________ transitions. (Lines 75–80)

E. VOCABULARY CHECK Look back at the reading on pages 23–25 to find words and phrases that match these definitions. Numbers in parentheses refer to line numbers in the reading.

1. people who hunt and gather food (Lines 10–15) ______________________
2. believing in many gods (Lines 15–20) ______________________
3. home of the ancient Greek gods (Lines 15–20) ______________________
4. organization into a system of higher and lower ranks (Lines 20–25) ______________________
5. a religion in which there is one all-powerful supreme being or god (Lines 20–25) ______________________
6. magic words (Lines 40–45) ______________________
7. a stone, arrowhead, bird feathers, or something else that doesn't belong in the human body (Lines 65–70) ______________________

F. APPLICATION In small groups, discuss these questions.

1. Besides the obvious example of the ancient Greek religion, what are some religions (past or present, from anywhere in the world) that fit the description of "Olympian" religions?
2. Before reading, you probably had one idea of what *magic* means. However, as you see, anthropologists have a different idea about what it means. What is the difference?
3. In Part 1 of this chapter, you read about *feng shui*. In Part 3, you read about the anthropological view of magic. What elements of *feng shui* would an anthropologist probably consider as magic?
4. Have you seen a shaman perform a healing ritual, either in real life or in a film? If so, describe what happened.
5. In addition to the examples in the reading, can you think of other rites of passage?
6. You saw the word *hierarchy* once in Part 2 and once in Part 3. Compare the two different meanings of this word.

G. MAKING CONNECTIONS Read an excerpt from a book by a Native American (Indian)* healer, or medicine man, of the Lakhota Sioux tribe. In it, he describes a rite of passage, his own vision quest (which he calls a "vision-seeking").

*Nowadays most people use the term *Native American* instead of *Indian* or *American Indian*.

Alone on a Hilltop

Here I was, crouched in my vision pit, left alone by myself for the first time in my life. I was sixteen then, still had my boy's name and, let me tell you, I was scared. I was shivering and not only from the cold. The nearest human being was many miles away, and four days and nights is a long, long time. Of course, when it was all over, I would no longer be a boy, but a man. I would have had my vision. I would be given a man's name.

Sioux men are not afraid to endure hunger, thirst, and loneliness, and I was only 96 hours away from being a man. The thought was comforting. Comforting, too, was the warmth of the star blanket which old man Chest had wrapped around me to cover my nakedness. My grandmother had made it especially for this, my first *hanblechia*, my first vision-seeking. It was a beautifully designed quilt, white with a large morning star made of many pieces of brightly colored cloth. The star was so big it covered most of the blanket. If Wakan Tanka, the Great Spirit, would give me the vision and the power, I would become a medicine man and perform many ceremonies wrapped in that quilt.

The medicine man had also left a peace pipe with me, together with a bag of *kinnickinnick*—our kind of tobacco made of red willow bark. This pipe was even more of a friend to me than my star blanket. To us, the pipe is like an open Bible. . . . For us Indians, there is just the pipe, the earth we sit on, and the open sky. The spirit is everywhere. Sometimes it shows itself through an animal, a bird, or some trees and hills. Sometimes it speaks from the Badlands, a stone, or even the water. That smoke from the peace pipe, it goes straight up to the spirit world. But this is a two-way thing. Power flows down to us through that smoke, through the pipe stem. You feel that power as you hold your pipe; it moves from the pipe right into your body.

As I ran my fingers along its bowl of smooth red pipestone, red like the blood of my people, I no longer felt scared. That pipe had belonged to my father and to his father before him. It would someday pass to my son and through him, to my grandchildren. As long as we had the pipe, there would be a Sioux nation.

Besides the pipe, the medicine man had also given me a gourd. In it were 40 small squares of flesh which my grandmother had cut from her arm with a razor blade. I had seen her do it. Blood had been streaming down from her shoulder to her elbow as she carefully put down each piece of skin on a handkerchief, anxious not to lose a single one . . . Someone dear to me had undergone pain, given me something of herself, part of her body, to help me pray and make me strong-hearted. . . .

I grasped the rattle with the forty pieces of my grandmother's flesh. It also had many little stones in it, tiny fossils picked up from an ant heap. Ants collect them. Nobody knows why. These little stones are supposed to have a power in them. I shook the rattle and it made a soothing sound, like rain falling on rock. It was talking to me, but it did not calm my fears. I took the sacred pipe in my other hand and began to sing and pray: "Tunkashila, grandfather spirit, help me."

Source: *Lame Deer, Seeker of Visions* (Lame Deer and Erdoes)

H. DISCUSSION In small groups, discuss these questions.

1. What was the purpose of this rite of passage?
2. What are some elements of a rite of passage such as a baptism, bar mitzvah, wedding, or funeral?
3. What are the items that Lame Deer had with him in the vision pit?
4. What do you think is the symbolic importance of each item? In other words, what might each item have represented to his culture or to him personally?

I. WORD JOURNAL Study the vocabulary sections before and after the reading (pages 21 and 28). Also review the words that you highlighted in the reading on pages 23–25. Which new words are important for *you* to remember? Write them in your Word Journal.

J. RESPONSE WRITING In a separate notebook or journal, write about *one* of the topics below for 15 minutes. Don't worry about grammar and don't stop writing to use a dictionary. You won't give this writing to your teacher. Your journal is a place in which you simply write as many ideas as possible without worrying about being "correct."

- your opinion about *feng shui*
- your beliefs about good or bad luck
- something you learned about symbolism
- something you learned about the anthropological view of religion
- an important ritual that you have experienced

PART 4 THE MECHANICS OF WRITING

In Part 4, you will learn to use adjective clauses, adjective clauses with prepositions, coordinating conjunctions, and adverbial conjunctions and to avoid sentence fragments. You will use this knowledge in Part 5 to write a paragraph of definition.

Adjective Clauses

Many definitions include an adjective clause (also called a relative clause). An adjective clause comes immediately after the noun that it modifies and begins with a relative pronoun: *that, which, who, whom, whose, when,* or *where.* In a definition, there is no comma before the adjective clause because this clause gives essential information.

Examples: *Feng shui* is a **practice** that deals with architectural and interior design.

A shaman is a **person** who fills the role of healer and psychologist in many societies.

With the relative pronoun *where*, do not use a preposition.

INCORRECT: A home is a place where people live **in**.

CORRECT: A home is a place where people live.

Note: *Who* refers to a subject. *Whom* refers to an object.

A. ADJECTIVE CLAUSES Combine these pairs of sentences. Make the second sentence in each pair into an adjective clause and add it to the first sentence. Use the relative pronoun in orange.

1. The bear is a symbol. The symbol is associated with Russia. **(that)**
   The bear is a symbol that is associated with Russia.

2. The Puritans were a group of people. This group of people fought against the Cavaliers in 17th-century England. **(who)**

3. The temple was the place. People worshipped in the temple. **(where)**

4. The Melanesians were people. The Melanesians' belief in *mana* affected everything in life. **(whose)**

5. A crown is a symbolic object. Only royalty may wear a crown. **(that)**

6. Oliver Cromwell is the man. We associate the man with opposition to King Charles I of England. **(whom)**

Adjective Clauses with Prepositions

An adjective clause that includes a preposition may be formal or informal. The formal structure is usually found in academic writing. In the formal structure, the clause begins with the preposition and then one of these relative pronouns: *which, whom,* or *whose*. In the informal structure, the preposition comes at the end of the clause. The relative pronoun can be left out in the informal structure.

Examples: A sweat lodge is a tent **in which Sioux Indians take a ritual sweat bath.** (Formal)

A sweat lodge is a tent **that Sioux Indians take a ritual sweat bath in.** (Informal)

A sweat lodge is a tent **Sioux Indians take a ritual sweat bath in.** (Informal)

B. ADJECTIVE CLAUSES WITH PREPOSITIONS Combine these pairs of sentences. Make the second sentence in each pair into a formal adjective clause and add it to the first. The important preposition is in orange.

1. A funeral is a ritual. Europeans wear black **at** a funeral.

   A funeral is a ritual at which Europeans wear black.

2. Informants are people. Anthropologists discuss cultural material **with** informants.

3. A rite of passage is a ritual. People make a transition from one stage of life to another **during** a rite of passage.

4. The Obi is a leader. People have great respect **for** this leader.

5. A cocktail party is an activity. Acquaintances make business contacts **at** a cocktail party.

6. Shamanism is a religious belief. I know nothing **about** this religious belief.

Coordinating Conjunctions

You can join two independent clauses (complete sentences) with a comma and one of the seven coordinating conjunctions.

and	but	or	so (= that's why)
yet* (= but)	for* (= because)	nor**	

Example: The lawmaker believed in the importance of *feng shui*, so he wanted the state to adopt *feng shui* design standards.

If there isn't an independent clause after the coordinating conjunction, don't use a comma.

Example: It is believed that the structure of a building can influence a person's behavior and determine success in relationships.

In a series of three or more nouns, adjectives, verbs, or phrases, use commas to separate each item; this structure occurs with *and* or *or*.

Example: Positive *chi* is influenced by such things as natural lighting, electronic equipment, or good airflow.

* *Yet* and *for* are very formal.
** The rules for *nor* are quite different and are not covered in this chapter. To combine two negatives, you can also use *or.*

C. COORDINATING CONJUNCTIONS Combine these pairs of sentences. Use *and, but, yet, so, for,* or *or*.

1. Anthropologists discuss cultural material with informants. Anthropologists examine actions in a cultural context.

   Anthropologists discuss cultural material with informants and examine actions in a cultural context.

2. Baseball is sometimes used as a metaphor for politics. Both baseball and politics are highly competitive.

   ______

3. In most societies, the family is the unit that regularly eats together. In some societies, men and women eat separately.

   ______

4. Women in New Guinea live in their own houses. Women in New Guinea prepare food there. Women in New Guinea take their husbands' food to the men's house.

   ______

5. In India, members of a high-ranked caste are fearful of ritual pollution. Members of a high-ranked caste will not eat with people from a low-ranked caste.

____

____

6. Brahmans will not share food with low-ranked individuals. Brahmans will not accept food from low-ranked individuals.

____

____

7. Political symbols may seem unimportant. People take them very seriously.

____

____

The Mexican, United States, and Canadian flags

Adverbial Conjunctions

Adverbial conjunctions, like coordinating conjunctions, join two independent clauses. They pull a paragraph together and help the ideas to flow smoothly and logically.

Here are some of the many adverbial conjunctions, grouped by meaning.

in addition
moreover
also
furthermore
= and

however
nevertheless*
even so*
in contrast
= but

therefore
consequently
as a result
for this reason
= so (that's why)

for example
for instance
e.g. (= for example)

in other words
that is (= in other words)
i.e. (= that is)

first
next
finally

afterwards
then

mostly
for the most part
to some extent (= partly)
to a large extent (= mostly)

in short
in conclusion

There is often a period or semicolon before the adverbial conjunction. There is a comma after it (except for *then*).

Examples: In the 1960s, many young American men wore their hair long as a symbol of opposition to authority. **However,** these days long hair is not a form of protest at all.

A social group such as a clan may be represented by different symbols; **for example,** a totemic animal may represent the clan.

Many adverbial conjunctions (especially *moreover, however, therefore,* and *for example*) may appear "inside" the second clause, between commas, or at the end of the second clause, after a comma.

Examples: In the 1960s, many young American men wore their hair long as a symbol of opposition to authority. These days, **however,** long hair is not a form of social protest at all.

Different symbols may represent a social group such as a clan; the clan might be represented by a totemic animal, **for example.**

*Use *nevertheless* and *even so* in surprising situations.

D. ADVERBIAL CONJUNCTIONS Combine the following pairs of sentences. Choose an appropriate adverbial conjunction and correct punctuation.

1. Animals have always represented nations. The eagle and the bear were symbols of the conflict between the United States and the former USSR.

____

____

2. In American society, the color red means danger. Stop signs and traffic signals are red.

____

____

3. In Western cultures, black is the color of mourning. In much of Asia, white is worn at times of death and mourning.

____

____

4. People who practice *feng shui* use many common-sense techniques such as eliminating clutter to reduce stress. They paint rooms in certain colors to encourage a good mood.

____

____

5. Fishing is seasonally hazardous because of violent storms at sea. It is dangerous in some seasons due to bad weather over the ocean.

____

____

Avoiding Sentence Fragments

A common mistake in written English is a sentence fragment. A sentence fragment is an incomplete sentence. It is missing something such as a subject, verb, or main clause.

Examples: A shaman is a person. **Who mediates between the natural and supernatural.** **INCORRECT**

(Here, the second "sentence" is not really a sentence. It is a fragment because it is missing a main clause.)

A shaman is a person **who mediates between the natural and supernatural**. **CORRECT**

In Kwakiutl Indian culture, each clan is represented by an animal. **For example, an eagle.** **INCORRECT**

(Here, the second "sentence" is a fragment because it is missing a verb and object or subject and verb.)

In Kwakiutl Indian culture, each clan is represented by an animal. **For example, an eagle may symbolize the clan.** **CORRECT**

E. AVOIDING SENTENCE FRAGMENTS Read the sentences below. If the sentences are correct, write *OK* on the lines. If the sentences are fragments, write *F* on the lines. Then correct the fragments.

F 1. The unit that regularly eats together is a social unit, for example, the nuclear family.

_______ 2. A metaphor is an idea that stands for another set of ideas.

_______ 3. Games are often used as a metaphor for life. For example, baseball may represent politics.

_______ 4. Baseball may represent politics. And horse racing.

_______ 5. Each caste is a ranked group. Which has an economic specialization.

_______ 6. Length of hair often symbolizes opposition to authority; for example, long hair in the 1960s.

_______ 7. An entire nation may be represented by an array of symbols.

_______ 8. A metonym is a type of symbol. For example, the "head" of a department in a university.

_______ 9. A totem pole with beings representing totemic ancestors.

_______ 10. A shaman has an ability to enter a trance, which he does in different ways. For example, by drinking a hallucinogenic drink, as in the Jivaro tribe, or by beating a drum, as among the Chukchee.

F. ERROR ANALYSIS/EDITING Find and correct the error in each sentence. The error is with either an adjective clause, coordinating conjunction, or adverbial conjunction.

1. A temple is a building where people worship ~~in~~.
2. A funeral is a ritual which Europeans wear black at a funeral.
3. Political symbols may seem unimportant but people take them very seriously.
4. Sports involve competition and struggle, therefore, they are often used as metaphors for politics.
5. In anthropology, magic is not a performance, that we might see on a stage.
6. Magic functions to make people less anxious, for example, in the Trobriand Islands, cricket players recite magic spells when the ball is pitched to help it reach its intended target.
7. In India, members of high-ranked castes are fearful of ritual pollution, for they will not eat with people of low-ranked castes.

PART 5 ACADEMIC WRITING

Test-Taking Strategy

Taking an Essay Exam

On an essay exam, you will need to answer one or more questions in complete paragraphs. The professor wants to find out if you have done the reading for the class and have taken notes from the lectures, understand this material, and can apply it to a new situation.

There are three types of essay exams: closed-book exams (most common), open-book exams, and take-home exams.

- For a **closed-book exam**, do not try to memorize big "chunks" of material such as sentences or paragraphs. Instead, study your highlighted passages and charts and make sure that you *understand* them.
- For an **open-book** or **take-home exam**, know where to find information quickly. Write using *your own words*. However, if you occasionally copy a sentence or part of a sentence, make sure that you put quotation marks around it and give the author's last name.

Here are some points to keep in mind on an essay exam:

- Pay attention to the *verb* in an essay question because this usually indicates what kind of paragraph(s) the professor wants. Often, an essay "question" is not a question at all. Instead, it is an imperative–directions on what to do.
- Remember that *the professor is testing you on what you have learned from the class–not on what you already know.* Do not include information that is outside the class material. (Exception: Sometimes the essay question says, "Include examples from your own experience." In this case, you need to **apply** your own experience to material that you learned in class.)
- Be as specific and detailed as possible.
- Be prepared to **synthesize** information from different materials in the class–e.g., from two separate readings or from the textbook and the lectures.

One common type of question on an essay exam asks you to define a word or term. You will do this in this chapter.

WRITING ASSIGNMENT

Write one paragraph of definition about a word frequently found in anthropology. Do this as either a take-home exam or an open-book exam. (Your teacher will choose.) Use information from the reading in Part 2 (pages 12–16) and from the excerpt by Lame Deer in Part 3 (page 29). You will *use your own words* in your paragraph but may use one quotation from one of these two sources. Follow these steps.

STEP A. CHOOSING A TOPIC Choose the word *metaphor* or *symbol* to define in one paragraph.

STEP B. GATHERING INFORMATION Review the reading in Part 2. Find information about the word that you chose. On the lines below, write a definition of the word, important details in the reading, and examples. Put quotation marks around anything that you copy exactly. Include examples from the reading in Part 2.

From Line

Definition: ______________________________ ________

____

Important Details:

______________________________ ________

______________________________ ________

______________________________ ________

______________________________ ________

______________________________ ________

Examples:

______________________________ ________

______________________________ ________

______________________________ ________

______________________________ ________

______________________________ ________

STEP C. SYNTHESIZING INFORMATION Now look back at the excerpt from Lame Deer's book on page 29. Find additional examples.

Examples:

______________________________ ________

______________________________ ________

______________________________ ________

______________________________ ________

Writing a Paragraph of Definition

Frequently you need to define words or phrases on an essay exam. In a paragraph of definition, you give the meaning of a word or phrase in several ways.

Types of Definitions	**Examples**	**Notes**
synonym	• *Taboo* means forbidden. • The word *taboo* means forbidden.	Use italics (or underlining) to mean *"the word."*
definition	• A rite of passage is a ritual in which a person makes a transition from one stage of life to another. • Magic is a group of "supernatural techniques designed to accomplish specific aims" (Kottak).	This definition is in either *your own words* or—on a take-home exam or open-book exam—*quoted* from class material.
function	• Taboos serve to maintain order in society and prevent anarchy. • Taboos maintain order and prevent anarchy.	Use the verb *serve* or *function*, or simply tell what the subject does.
classification	• Anthropology is a social science that deals with human culture. • A shaman is a medical/religious practitioner who mediates between people and supernatural beings.	Use an adjective clause in this type of definition.
negation	• *Freedom* does not mean that you don't have to do your homework.	Negation is an effective type of definition when you are explaining a word that is commonly misunderstood or understood differently.
example	• One example of a taboo is the prohibition against physical contact between a high chief and commoners in Melanesian society. • Another common taboo forbids the eating of certain kinds of meat, as in Judaism and Islam.	You will almost always include at least one example in a paragraph of definition. Your examples usually come at the end of the paragraph because they are the most specific part of the paragraph. You might have several short examples or one longer example that includes details.

Usually, a paragraph of definition combines several different types of definition. It's a good idea to synthesize information from more than one source that you had in class—from the textbook and supplemental reading, for example. (This proves to the professor that you truly understood the material.) Order your definitions from general to specific. If you include a negation, this should probably be at the beginning.

Example:

Most people think of magic as a form of entertainment. However, in anthropology, *magic* does not refer to a performance on a stage or the pulling of rabbits out of hats. Instead, according to Kottak, it "refers to supernatural techniques designed to accomplish specific aims." It is a part of various religions. People use it when they are afraid and uncertain and when they don't feel that they have control of a situation. It functions to make them less anxious. In the Trobriand Islands, for example, cricket players recite magic spells when the ball is pitched to help it reach its intended target. There are also elements of magic in the practice of *feng shui*. For example, people who believe in *feng shui* don't want their *chi* (energy) to go down the toilet, so they make sure to keep the lid down.

Analysis: What types of definition are there in the example paragraph above? What is copied from a source? Who is the source?

STEP D. ORGANIZING YOUR MATERIAL Choose which information from Steps B and C to include in your paragraph. (You probably won't use all of it.) Have at least three types of definition. Decide what order to put them in.

Writing Strategy

Using Material from a Source

Most essay exams are taken in class, and you will not be able to use your books or notes during the exam. You don't usually have to worry about copying material from the textbook because it's not possible.

However, on a take-home exam or an open-book exam, you *will* have access to your books, so you might be tempted to copy material from one of them. Here are some guidelines.

1. Use your own words for the exam. The best way to do this is to follow these steps:

   Study the information that you highlighted in the readings.

   Study any charts or graphic organizers that you created.

   Understand the material well but *don't memorize complete sentences.* Instead, memorize important phrases, vocabulary and spelling, names, and dates.

   Don't look at the book as you write. You might look back occasionally to check information, but for the most part, *don't copy.*

2. On an exam for which you *do* have access to your books, you may sometimes find information that you want to copy. If so, follow these guidelines:

   Put **quotation marks** around anything that you copy.

   Do not change words that you include inside quotation marks.

   Cite your source. In other words, give credit to the person who wrote it. It's sufficient to give the last name (family name) of the author.

   The simplest ways to cite your source are either to say "According to . . ." or to put the author's last name in parentheses at the end of the quote. You will learn other ways to cite your source later in this book.

   Do not quote a large amount.

Examples: According to Kottak, the word *magic* "refers to supernatural techniques designed to accomplish specific aims."

Feng shui functions "to improve a person's life through the carefully planned design of buildings and the objects within them" (Gaeddert).

Analysis: What punctuation do you notice in the two examples above? Which are the student's words? Which words are from a source? Who is the source in each example? Where is the period in each sentence?

STEP E. WRITING THE PARAGRAPH Write complete sentences in paragraph form. If you can, choose one piece of information to quote. Be sure to include at least one example. You might make some mistakes, but don't worry about them now.

STEP F. EDITING Read your paragraph and answer these questions.

1. Is the paragraph form correct (indentation, margins)?
2. Are there several types of definition?
3. Is there at least one good example?
4. If anything is copied, is the source cited correctly? Is the punctuation correct?
5. Is there correct use of transition words?
6. If there are adjective clauses, are they used correctly?
7. Is sentence structure correct (no fragments)?

STEP G. REWRITING Write your paragraph again. This time try to write with no mistakes.

CHAPTER 2

Physical Anthropology

Discuss these questions:

- What is happening in the picture above?
- How are humans and apes alike? How are they different?
- Do you believe that humans and apes are related? Why or why not?

PART 1 INTRODUCTION Orangutans

BEFORE READING

A chimpanzee

A gorilla

An orangutan

A colobus monkey

THINKING AHEAD In small groups, look at the pictures and discuss these questions.

1. What are primates? What animals do we include in this classification? Are humans primates?
2. What do you know about orangutans? Where do they live? How do they live? Are they **endangered**? (In other words, is their population decreasing due to pollution and/or human activities?)

READING

In the following reading, don't worry about words that are new to you. Instead, try to understand the main ideas. As you read, think about the answer to this question:

- What is one way that orangutans are different from other primates?

2/24

Orangutans

The orangutan—also called Mawas—is literally a "man of the woods." A great ape with long reddish hair, the orangutan spends most of its time moving about in trees and less on the ground. Orangutans live in the hot, wet forests of Sumatra and Kalimantan, in Borneo. Kalimantan orangutans are reddish-brown in color, while 5 their Sumatran cousins are a paler, ginger color. Kalimantan orangutans also have coarser hair.

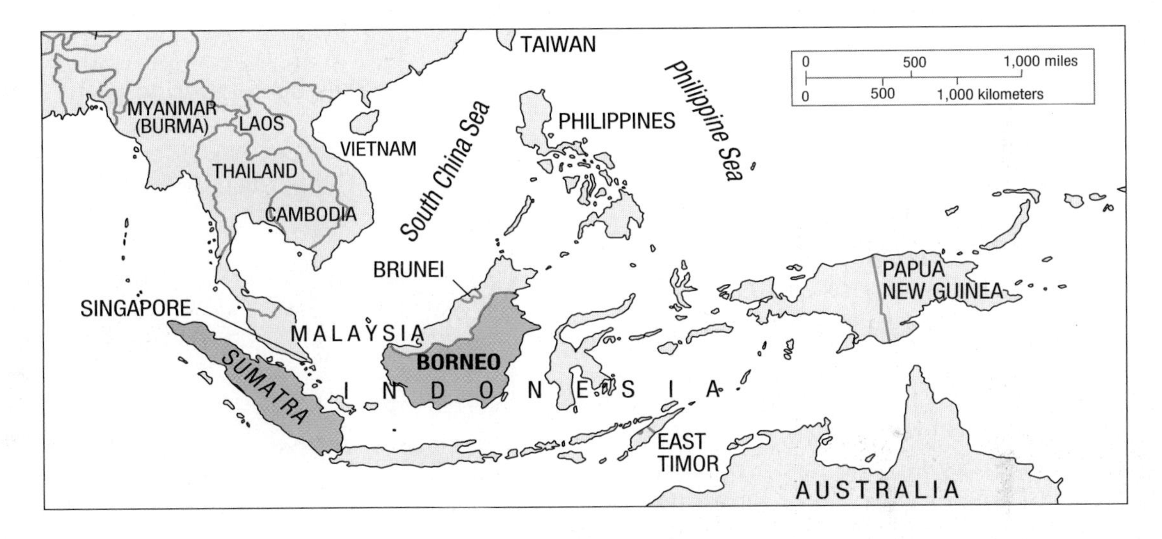

Borneo and the surrounding area

The mature male has fleshy cheek pads and a heavy, hanging throat pouch, and his voice can be heard up to several kilometers away. His height reaches 125 cm (49 in) standing tall, and he weighs up to 110 kg (242 1/2 lbs). The female weighs about half 10 as much.

Orangutans (both Sumatran and Kalimantan) have a varied diet of fruit, bark, leaves, and insects such as ants, termites, and bees. They find food primarily by moving about in the canopy (the tree-tops), but males sometimes descend to the ground to travel longer distances in search of food. Females, however, virtually never 15 leave the trees. Orangutans' lives are nomadic—they travel from place to place depending on food availability. They have a solitary lifestyle and don't live in groups like other primates.

The current number of orangutans left in the wild is estimated at between 15,000 and 24,000. They are an endangered species and are the only big ape found in Asia.

Nonja, an Artistic Orangutan

Like other primates, orangutans have complex brains and are highly intelligent. One orangutan in particular, living at the Schönbrunn Zoo in Vienna, Austria, has shown special talent as a painter.

Her name is Nonja, and she's a female orangutan belonging to the subspecies *pongo pygmaeus pygmaeus*, native to the island of Borneo. She was born in the Vienna zoo on April 21, 1976. Though she grew up with her mother, she had to be fed by caretakers. As a result, Nonja is very outgoing with humans.

Nonja draws with her caretaker early in the morning at least once a week. Like other apes, she has a preference for particular colors (brown and violet) and certain patterns. The motive behind her "artistic" activity seems to be to have fun as well as visual control. For example, if she detects little stains on the paper, she paints over them. Sometimes she will give her undivided attention to a particular spot for several minutes.

Nonja's specialty is a splatter pattern, which she makes by splattering paint onto the paper by flicking her wrist. Pictures painted by apes such as Nonja are a lot like the art of two- or three-year-old children. Their artwork is never representational because apes are not able to draw forms and figures.

Nonja

Nonja's period of concentration has increased over the years from eight minutes at the beginning of her artistic career to between 20 and 60 minutes today. So far, she has produced about 250 pictures, some of which have been shown at exhibitions. More than 200 TV, radio, and newspaper journalists from all over the world have reported on her paintings. The prices for original artwork by Nonja run between 3,500 and 28,000 Austrian schillings (approx. $323.00 to $2,584.00). Two of Nonja's most beautiful pictures have been auctioned off at a charity gala at the Regent Beverly Wilshire Hotel in Los Angeles to raise money to protect orangutans in the wild.

Source: "OrangUtan" (Tourismindonesia.com and Tiergarten Schönbrunn)

AFTER READING

A. COMPREHENSION CHECK Look back at the reading. When you find the answers to these questions, highlight them.

1. What is one way that orangutans are different from other primates?
2. Where in the world do orangutans live?
3. In their natural habitats, where do orangutans spend most of their time?
4. What do orangutans eat?
5. Are orangutans endangered? How do you think researchers have come to this conclusion?
6. Describe Nonja's painting style.

2/24

Critical Thinking Strategy

Making Comparisons

When you read, make comparisons. In other words, think about the similarities and/or differences in things such as individuals, groups, or ideas. This will help you better organize and analyze the information in the reading.

B. MAKING COMPARISONS Look back at the reading on pages 47–48 and compare two types of orangutans. Fill in the chart below.

	Sumatran Orangutans	Kalimantan Orangutans
Similarities		
Differences		

2/24

Reading Strategy

Understanding Quotation Marks

In Chapter 1, you used quotation marks to indicate words that are not your own. Quotation marks have additional uses:

- to give the meaning of a word or phrase
- to show that a word is used differently from what the writer believes it means

Look back at the reading on pages 47–48. Find words in quotation marks. What is the reason for them?

C. VOCABULARY CHECK Look back at the reading on pages 47–48 to find the words and phrases that match these definitions. Don't use a dictionary. Numbers in parentheses refer to the line numbers in the reading.

1. "man of the woods" (Lines 1–5) Orangutan

2. thick, full (skin) (Lines 5–10) fleshy

3. come down (Lines 10–15) descend

4. alone (Lines 15–20) solitary

5. coming from (Lines 25–30) native to

6. not shy (Lines 25–30) outgoing

7. sold (Lines 50–54) auctioned off

2/24

D. DISCUSSION In small groups, discuss these questions.

1. Should art galleries sell an orangutan's art work? Why or why not? Who should get the money?
2. Do you think Nonja is well cared for at the Schönbrunn Zoo? Why or why not?
3. In your opinion, are humans doing enough to take care of nonhuman primates? What kind of legal protection should nonhuman primates have?

PART 2 GENERAL INTEREST READING
Humans and Other Primates

BEFORE READING

A. THINKING AHEAD In small groups, discuss these questions.

1. What similarities are there between humans and other primates?
2. What differences are there between humans and other primates?

B. GUESSING THE MEANING FROM CONTEXT Read the sentences below. The words in orange are from the next reading. Write definitions of the words. Then write the type of context clue that helped you understand the meaning from context.

Context clues:

- definitions or synonyms
- examples
- expressions such as *in other words* or *that is*
- opposites
- information in another sentence part
- logic or your own life experience

1. Scholars used to believe that learned behavior (versus **instinctive** behavior) separated humans from other animals.

   instinctive = not learned / natural

   Clue type = opposites

2. One researcher discovered that **macaques** (a kind of monkey) raised alone didn't form dominance hierarchies when brought together as young adults.

   macaques = kind of monkeys

   Clue type = definition in ( )

3. Anthropologists once believed that only humans manufactured tools with **foresight**, that is, with a specific purpose in mind.

   foresight = specific purpose

   Clue type = definition linked with "that is"

4. Chimpanzees use **twigs**, from which they remove leaves and peel off bark to expose the sticky surface beneath.

   twigs = branches

   Clue type = logic / experience

5. Many Gombe chimps never learn to catch termites well. In fact, human observers have not been able **to master** it, either.

to master = be good at / learn well

Clue type = info. in another sentence

6. Humans have adapted to **an omnivorous diet**—a diet of both plants and animals—over millions of years.

an omnivorous diet = __________

Clue type = __________

7. In one study, macaques were allowed just twenty minutes of daily play with **peers**—macaques of the same age.

peers = __________

Clue type = __________

8. In a troop of **terrestrial monkeys**, monkeys that live on the ground, the strongest and most aggressive members dominate.

terrestrial monkeys = __________

Clue type = __________

Reading Strategy

Previewing: Using Headings

Previewing a reading helps you focus your reading. You can preview the main ideas of a reading by looking quickly at the headings. Headings are usually in bold print.

C. PREVIEWING: USING HEADINGS Preview the reading on pages 53–57. Look at the headings and subheadings. Then answer these questions.

1. Can you tell by previewing which sections will illustrate differences and which will illustrate similarities?
2. Can you tell by previewing which sections will be about primates *in the wild* and which will be about primates *in captivity?*
3. In which five areas will humans and other primates be compared?

__________ __________

__________ __________

____

READING

Read the passage without using a dictionary. As you read, highlight main ideas, important details, and important vocabulary with three different colors. Use a fourth color for new vocabulary. Think about these questions:

- When researchers compare humans and other primates, do they talk about *kinds* of difference, or *degrees* of difference?
- What does *degrees of difference* mean?
- What examples in the reading illustrate this?

Note: There are many new words in the reading. Some of them are glossed; that is, they are defined in footnotes at the bottom of each page.

Comparing Humans with Other Primates

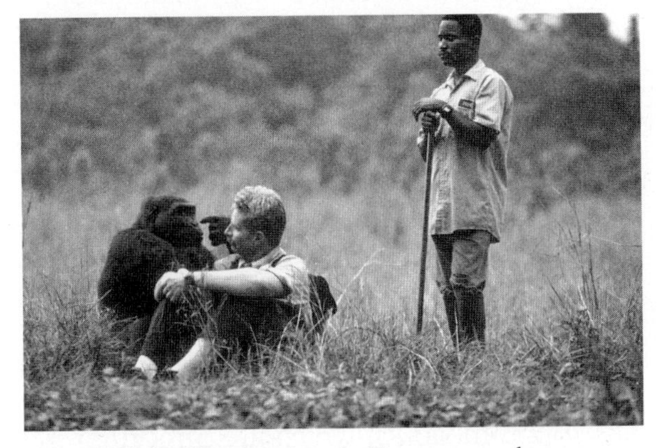

Human-Primate Similarities

There is a large gap between primate society and fully developed human culture. However, studies of primates have revealed many similarities. Scholars used to believe that learned (versus instinctive) behavior separates humans from other animals. We know now that monkeys and apes also rely on learning. Many of the differences between humans and other primates are differences in degree rather than in kind. For example, monkeys learn from experiences, but humans learn much more. Another example is that chimpanzees and orangutans make tools for specific tasks, but human reliance on tools is much greater.

Learning

Common to monkeys, apes, and humans is the fact that behavior and social life are not rigidly[1] programmed by the genes. All these animals learn throughout their lives. A series of famous experiments conducted at the University of Wisconsin under the direction of the psychologist Harry Harlow (1966) demonstrated that many aspects of monkey behavior once thought to be instinctive are not. Rather, they depend on social interaction.

Harlow discovered that macaques (a kind of monkey) raised in isolation didn't form dominance (power) relationships when brought together as young adults. Nor could they engage in a basic biological act—sexual intercourse. However, macaques that had been allowed just twenty minutes of daily play with peers—macaques of the same age—eventually established dominance in relationships. Furthermore, although they had never witnessed copulation, they were able to have sexual intercourse. These two aspects of behavior turn out to be hereditary tendencies that appear only when certain social conditions exist.

[1]**rigidly:** strictly; in an unchanging manner

Monkeys and apes can learn from experience. In several cases, an entire monkey troop has learned from the experiences of some of its members. In one group of Japanese macaques, a three-year-old female monkey started washing dirt off sweet potatoes before she ate them. First her mother, then her peers, and finally the entire troop began washing sweet potatoes, too. The direction of learning was reversed when members of another macaque troop learned to eat wheat. After the dominant males had tried the new food, within four hours the practice had spread throughout the troop. Changes in learned behavior seem to spread more quickly from the top down than from the bottom up.

For monkeys as for people, the ability to learn, to profit from experience, gives a tremendous adaptive advantage, permitting them to avoid fatal mistakes. Faced with environmental change, primates don't have to wait for a genetic or physiological response. Learned behavior and social patterns can be modified instead.

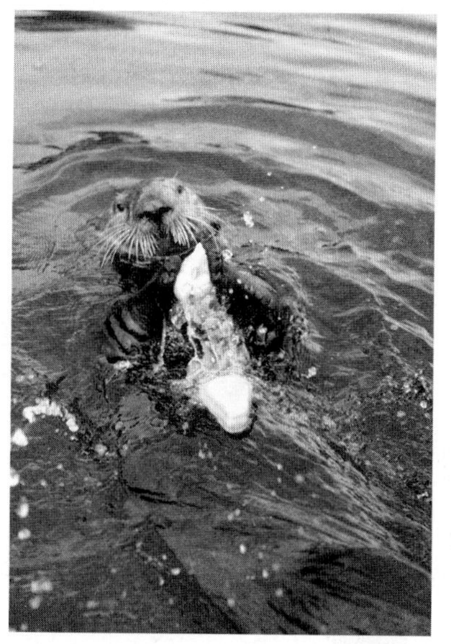

A sea otter

Tools

Anthropologists used to distinguish humans from other animals as tool users, and there is no doubt that *Homo* does employ tools much more than any other animal does. However, tool use also appears among several nonhuman species. For example, in the Galapagos Islands off western South America, there is a woodpecker finch that selects twigs to dig out insects and grubs from tree bark. Sea otters use rocks to break open mollusks, which are important in their diet. Beavers are famous for dam construction.

When it became obvious that people weren't the only tool users, anthropologists started contending that only humans make tools with foresight, that is, with a specific purpose in mind. Chimpanzees show that this, too, is debatable. In 1960, Jane Goodall began observing wild chimps—including their tool use and hunting behavior—at Gombe Stream National Park in Tanzania, East Africa. From the work of Goodall and many other researchers, we know that chimps in the wild regularly make tools. To get water from places their mouths can't reach, thirsty chimps pick leaves, chew and crumple them, and then dip them into the water. Thus, with a specific purpose in mind, they devise primitive "sponges."

Jane Goodall

The best-studied form of tool making by chimps involves "termiting." Chimps make tools to probe[2] termite hills. They choose twigs, from which they remove leaves and peel off bark[3] to expose the sticky surface beneath. They carry the twigs to termite hills, dig holes with their

[2]**probe:** to search with a thin tool
[3]**bark:** the outer covering of tree trunks and branches; the tree's "skin"

A chimp in the wild termiting

fingers, and insert the twigs. Finally, they pull out the twigs and dine on termites that were attracted to the sticky surface.

Termiting isn't as easy as it might seem. Learning to termite takes time, and many Gombe chimps never learn to do it well. Twigs with certain characteristics must be chosen. Furthermore, once the twig is in the hill and the chimp judges that termites are crawling on its surface, the chimp must quickly flip the twig as it pulls it out so that the termites are on top. Otherwise, they fall off as the twig comes out of the hole. This is an elaborate skill that neither all chimps nor human observers have been able to master.

Communication Systems

Only humans speak. No other animal has anything approaching the complexity of language. However, evidence is accumulating that linguistic ability is also a quantitative rather than a qualitative difference between humans and other primates, especially gorillas and chimps.

Chimps in the wild communicate through gestures and calls. Goodall (1968a) identified 25 distinct calls used by Gombe chimps. Each had a distinct meaning and was used only in particular situations. Like people, chimps also communicate through facial expressions, noises, and body movements. Other primates also use calls to communicate messages to other members of the group. African vervet monkeys, for example, have three slightly different calls (grunts) that they use to communicate danger from leopards, eagles, and snakes (Seyfarth, Cheney, and Marlker, 1980).

Although wild primates use call systems, the vocal tract[4] of apes is not suitable for speech. Until the 1960s, attempts to teach spoken language to apes suggested that they lacked linguistic abilities. However, recent experiments have shown that apes in captivity can learn to use, if not speak, true language (Miles, 1983). Several apes have learned to converse with people through means of American Sign Language, or Ameslan, which is widely used by deaf and mute Americans. Ameslan employs a limited number of basic gesture units that are analogous to (represent) sounds in spoken language. These combine to form words and larger units of meaning.

The first chimpanzee to learn Ameslan was Washoe, a female. Captured in West Africa, Washoe was acquired by R. Allen Gardner and Beatrice Gardner, scientists at the University of Nevada in Reno, in 1966. Washoe lived in a trailer and heard no spoken English. The researchers always used Ameslan to communicate with each other in her presence. The chimp gradually acquired an expressive vocabulary of 132 signs representing English words (Gardner, Gardner, and Van Cantfort, 1989). At the age of two, Washoe began to combine as many as five signs into rudimentary[5] sentences such as "you, me, go out, hurry." During her first few years learning Ameslan, she varied

[4]**vocal tract:** the parts of the mouth and throat used for producing speech, such as the tongue, lips, and larynx
[5]**rudimentary:** basic; simple

the order of her gestures. She would as easily say "Tickle Washoe" as "Washoe tickle." However, work with other chimps, along with Washoe's later progress, showed that apes can distinguish between subject and object.

Human-Primate Differences

The preceding material emphasized similarities between humans and other primates. However, a unique concentration and combination of characteristics make humans distinct. These distinctions lie mainly in the areas of sharing, cooperation and the division of labor, and in mating, exogamy (marrying outside one's group), and kinship.

Sharing and Cooperation

Early humans lived in small social groups called bands, with economies based on hunting and gathering (foraging). Until fairly recently (12,000 to 10,000 years ago), all humans lived this way. Some such societies even managed to survive into the modern world, and ethnographers have studied them. From those studies, we can conclude that in such societies, the strongest and most aggressive members do not dominate, as they do in a troop of terrestrial monkeys, monkeys that live on the ground. Sharing and curbing of aggression are as basic to technologically simple humans as dominance and threats are to baboons.

Humans appear to be the most cooperative of the primates—in the food quest and other social activities. Except for meat sharing by chimps, the ape tendency is to forage individually. Monkeys also fend for[6] themselves in getting food. Among human foragers, men generally hunt and women gather. Men and women bring resources back to the camp and share them. Older people who did not engage in the food quest get food from younger adults. Everyone shares the meat from a large animal. Nourished and protected by younger band members, elders live past the reproductive age. They

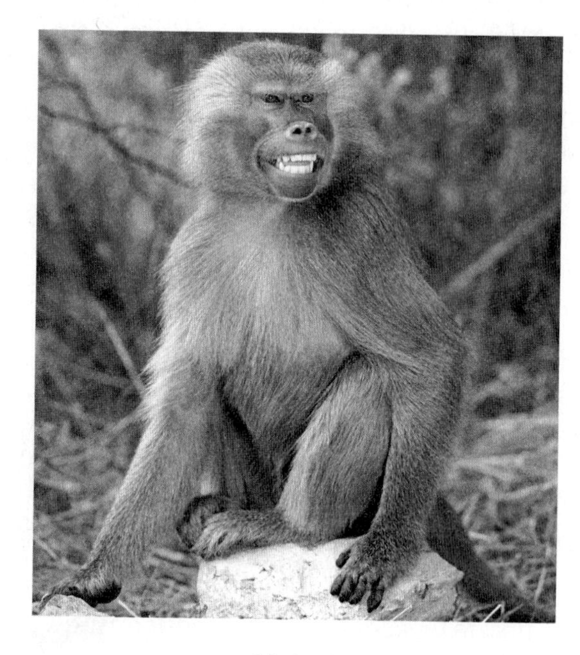

A baboon

A bonobo

[6]**fend for:** to take care of without help from others, usually in a difficult situation

receive respect for their knowledge and experience. The amount of information stored in a human band is far greater than that in any other primate society. Sharing, cooperation, and language are intrinsic to information storage. Through millions of
140 years of adaptation to an omnivorous diet—a diet of both plants and animals—hominids have come to rely, more than any other primate, on hunting, food sharing, and cooperative behavior. These are universal features in human adaptive strategies.

Mating and Kinship

Another difference between humans and other primates involves mating. Among baboons, chimpanzees, and bonobos, most mating occurs when females enter estrus,
145 the period in which they ovulate. Receptive females form temporary bonds with, and mate with, males. Human females, by contrast, lack a visible estrus cycle, and their ovulation is concealed. Neither a woman's sexual receptivity nor her readiness to conceive is physically evident, as it is in chimps and bonobos. Not knowing when ovulation is occurring, humans maximize their reproductive success by mating
150 throughout the year. Human pair-bonds for mating tend to be more exclusive and longer lasting than are those of chimps or bonobos. Related to our more constant sexuality, all human societies have some form of marriage. Marriage gives mating a reliable basis and grants to each spouse special, though not always exclusive, sexual rights.

155 Marriage creates another major contrast between humans and nonhumans: exogamy and kinship systems. Most cultures have rules of exogamy requiring marriage outside one's kin or local group. Coupled with the recognition of kinship, exogamy has adaptive advantages. It creates ties between the spouses' groups of origin. Their children have relatives, and therefore allies, in two kin groups rather than just one. The
160 key point here is that ties of affection and mutual support between members of different local groups tend to be absent among primates other than *Homo*. There is a *tendency* among primates to leave the group at adolescence. Among chimps and gorillas, females tend to migrate, seeking mates in other groups. Both male and female gibbons leave home when they become sexually mature. Once they find mates and
165 establish their own territories, ties with their native groups cease. Among terrestrial monkeys, males leave the troop at adolescence, eventually finding places elsewhere. The troop's core members are females. They sometimes form groups made up of mothers, sisters, daughters, and sons that have not yet left the troop. Females mate with males born elsewhere, which join the troop at adolescence. Although kin ties are
170 maintained between female monkeys, no close lifelong links are preserved through males.

Humans choose mates from outside the native group, and usually at least one spouse moves. However, *most humans maintain lifelong ties with sons and daughters.* The systems of kinship and marriage that preserve these links provide a
175 major contrast between humans and other primates.

Source: *Anthropology: The Exploration of Human Diversity* (Kottak)

AFTER READING

A. COMPREHENSION CHECK In small groups, discuss these questions about the lines you highlighted in the reading.

1. When researchers compare humans and other primates, do they talk about *kinds* of difference, or *degrees* of difference? What does this mean? What examples in the reading illustrate this?

2. Fill in the chart to answer these questions:
   - What are the five main areas of similarities and differences between humans and nonhuman primates?
   - For each of the five areas, were more similarities or differences mentioned in the reading? Check (✓) the correct boxes.
   - What are some examples from the reading of the category you checked?

Areas	More Similarities or Differences?	Examples
Learning	☑ Similarities ☐ Differences	• From captivity: Harlow's macaques • From the wild: Japanese macaques (washing sweet potatoes and eating wheat)
	☐ Similarities ☐ Differences	
	☐ Similarities ☐ Differences	
	☐ Similarities ☐ Differences	
	☐ Similarities ☐ Differences	

B. NOTICING PHRASES Look back at the reading on pages 53–57 to find phrases for each definition below. Then decide which type of phrase it is (noun phrase = NP, prepositional phrase = PP, verb phrase = VP, or adjective phrase = AP).

Definitions	Phrases	Types
1. having grown up alone (Lines 20–25)	raised in isolation	AP
2. from the leader to the follower (Lines 35–40)	______	______
3. from the follower to the leader (Lines 35–40)	______	______
4. in a natural habitat (Lines 55–60)	______	______
5. in a zoo (Lines 100–105)	______	______
6. in the present time (Lines 120–125)	______	______
7. eating both plants and animals (Lines 140–145)	______	______
8. to have children (Lines 145–150)	______	______
9. the most important idea (Lines 160–165)	______	______
10. grow up and live on one's own (Lines 160–165)	______	______

C. VOCABULARY CHECK Look back at the reading to find words and phrases that match the definitions below. Don't use a dictionary.

1. compete to control other group members (Lines 20–25) ______
2. a group of animals that live together (Lines 25–30) ______
3. a communication system widely used by deaf and mute Americans (Lines 100–105) ______
4. controlling; limiting (Lines 125–130) ______

5. marriage outside one's kin or local group (Lines 155–160) ______________________

6. people who help or support you, such as friends and family (Lines 155–160) ______________________

7. the period before adulthood (Lines 160–165) ______________________

D. MAKING INFERENCES Discuss these questions with a partner.

1. You read about two different troops of macaques in the wild. What did each learn to do (Line 30)? Which troop learned more quickly? Why?
2. What does the following sentence from Lines 127–129 mean?

   "Sharing and curbing of aggression are as basic to technologically simple humans as dominance and threats are to baboons."
3. What is exogamy? How is it different from a "tendency to leave the group"?
4. Look back at the reading on pages 53–57. Find words in quotation marks in the article. What is the reason for the quotation marks? Find uses of italics. What is the reason for the italics?

Reading Strategy

Understanding Pronoun References

Instead of using the same noun over and over in a reading, writers use pronouns to avoid repetition. Good readers keep the referent–the original noun–in mind when they encounter the pronoun that refers to it. This helps them read faster and with better understanding. One strategy that good readers use is paying attention to whether the pronoun is singular or plural.

Example: Harry Harlow (1966) demonstrated that many aspects of monkey behavior once thought to be instinctive are not. Rather, **they** depend on social interaction.

What does the pronoun *they* refer to? Does it refer to *monkey* or *monkey behavior*? It doesn't refer to either; you know because *they* is plural. To understand what the pronoun refers to, look for a plural noun in the first sentence. (The correct referent is *aspects*.)

If there are several singular or plural nouns, you need to use logic to decide which one is the referent.

Example: Harlow discovered that macaques raised in isolation didn't form dominance hierarchies when **they** were brought together as young adults.

You can logically guess that *they* refers to *macaques*, not *hierarchies* since hierarchies cannot be "young adults".

E. UNDERSTANDING PRONOUN REFERENCES Identify the referent for the pronouns in orange. First, decide whether the pronoun is singular or plural. Then highlight the referent.

1. In one group of Japanese macaques, a three-year-old female monkey started washing dirt off sweet potatoes before **she** ate them.

   The pronoun is: ☑ **singular** ☐ **plural**

2. Anthropologists started contending that only humans manufacture tools with foresight, that is, with a specific purpose in mind. Chimpanzees show that **this**, too, is debatable.

   The pronoun is: ☐ **singular** ☐ **plural**

3. To get water from places their mouths can't reach, thirsty chimps pick leaves, chew and crumple them, and then dip **them** into water.

   The pronoun is: ☐ **singular** ☐ **plural**

4. Until the 1960s, attempts to teach spoken language to apes suggested that **they** lacked linguistic abilities.

   The pronoun is: ☐ **singular** ☐ **plural**

5. Nourished and protected by younger band members, elders live past their reproductive age. **They** receive special respect for their age and knowledge.

   The pronoun is: ☐ **singular** ☐ **plural**

F. IN YOUR OWN WORDS: SUMMARIZING Choose one of the five sections of the reading. Fill in the first blank with the topic of the section. Use a noun or noun phrase. Fill in the second blank with the main idea. Complete the sentence with an independent clause.

1. The section is about ______________________________.

2. The author says that ______________________________.

G. WORD JOURNAL Go back to the readings in Part 1 and Part 2. Which new words are important for *you* to remember? Write them in your Word Journal.

PART 3 ACADEMIC READING Modern Stone Age Humans

BEFORE READING

A. THINKING AHEAD In small groups, discuss these questions.

1. Paleolithic ("Stone Age") humans lived between 40,000 and 10,000 years ago. What do you know about Paleolithic humans? What were their daily lives like? What kind of tools did they use?
2. Besides tools, what other evidence do we have of the culture of Paleolithic people?

B. VOCABULARY PREPARATION Read the sentences below. The words in orange are from the next reading. Guess their meanings from the context.

- First, circle the part of speech—noun (n), verb (v), or adjective (adj).
- Then write your guess.
- If you are very unsure of your guess, check with a dictionary to see if your guess was close. To save time, do the third step with a small group. Divide the group of words; each person will look up several words and then share the answers

Parts of Speech

1. Because animals are sometimes shown with spears in their bodies, cave paintings might have been attempts to **ensure** success in hunting. n v adj

   Guess: ______________________

   Dictionary Definition: secure, guarantee, make sure of

2. Some see cave painting as a magical human attempt to control animal reproduction. Something **analogous** was done by Native Australian hunters and gatherers, who held annual ceremonies to honor and promote the fertility of animals. n v adj

   Guess: ______________________

   Dictionary Definition: Similar, comparable

3. Paintings often occur in **clusters**. In some caves, as many as three paintings have been drawn over the original. n v adj

   Guess: ______________________

   Dictionary Definition: group or bunch

4. Perhaps Upper Paleolithic people were, through their drawings, **reenacting** the hunt after it took place. n v adj

   Guess: act again

   Dictionary Definition: ______________________

5. Why would artists **obliterate** someone else's work by painting over it? n (v) adj

Guess: ______

Dictionary Definition: destroy/remove

6. To be considered a man, an adolescent male had to withdraw temporarily from normal social life and go into the wilderness, where he sought contact with an animal spirit, which would become his personal guardian spirit. If mere **seclusion** didn't bring the desired spirit, the boy tried to reach a state of spiritual receptivity by fasting, taking drugs, or inflicting pain on himself. (n) v adj

Guess: ______

Dictionary Definition: being alone

7. In some caves, as many as three paintings have been drawn over the original, yet next to these **superimposed** paintings are blank walls never used for painting. n v (adj)

Guess: ______

Dictionary Definition: one on top of another

8. There is reason to doubt that cave paintings were simply expressions of individual artistic temperament—that is, **art for art's sake.** (n) v adj

Guess: ______

Dictionary Definition: ______

Reading Strategy

Previewing: Using Pictures and Captions

Looking at the pictures and captions before you read a passage will often give you a good idea of what the passage is about. Before you read a new passage, take a look at any accompanying art and make predictions about the passage based on what you see.

Example: You see: A picture of an orangutan painting.
You think: This passage might be about apes that create art.

C. PREVIEWING: USING PICTURES AND CAPTIONS Look at the pictures on pages 65 and 67. Read the captions. Discuss these questions with a partner:

- What did Paleolithic humans show in cave paintings?
- What kinds of tools did Mesolithic people use?
- How did the pictures and captions help you preview the reading?

D. PREVIEWING: USING HEADINGS Preview the reading on pages 64–68. Look at the headings. What are the two main topics of the reading?

Reading Strategy

Having Questions in Mind

Good readers ask themselves questions about what they are reading as they are reading it. Sometimes good writers even supply questions to help their readers become more engaged in what they are reading. The author of the textbook passage "Modern Stone Age Humans" asks several of these questions.

Example: Some of the animals in the cave murals are pregnant, and some are copulating. Did Upper Paleolithic people believe they could influence the sexual behavior or reproduction of their prey by drawing them? Or did they perhaps think that animals would return each year to the place where their souls had been captured pictorially?

If there are questions in the reading, answer them as you read. Ask and answer your own questions, too.

E. HAVING QUESTIONS IN MIND Practice asking questions to become more engaged in your reading.

- Write three questions that you have about humans in the Paleolithic and Mesolithic ages. Try to answer them as you read.

1. ______________________________

2. ______________________________

3. ______________________________

READING

Read the passage without using a dictionary. As you read, highlight main ideas, important details, and important vocabulary with three different colors. Think about these questions:

- What might cave paintings tell us about the lives of Paleolithic humans?
- What kind of economy did the people of the Mesolithic period have?

Note: There are many new words in this reading. Some of them are glossed; that is, they are defined in footnotes at the bottom of each page.

Modern Stone Age Humans

The Paleolithic, or Old Stone Age, has three divisions: Lower (early), Middle, and Upper (late). Each part is roughly associated with a particular stage in human evolution. The Lower Paleolithic is roughly associated with *H. erectus* (*Homo erectus*); the Middle Paleolithic with archaic *H. sapiens*, including the Neanderthals of Western Europe and the
5 Middle East; and the Upper Paleolithic with early members of our own subspecies, *H. sapiens sapiens*, anatomically modern humans. We refer to the period after the Paleolithic Age as the Mesolithic, or Middle Stone Age.

Upper Paleolithic

It isn't the tools or the skeletons of Upper Paleolithic people but their art that has made them most familiar to us. Most extraordinary are the cave paintings, the earliest of which dates back some 30,000 years. More than a hundred cave painting sites are known, mainly from a limited area of southwestern France and adjacent northeastern Spain. The most famous site is Lascaux, found in 1940 in southwestern France by a dog and his young human companions.

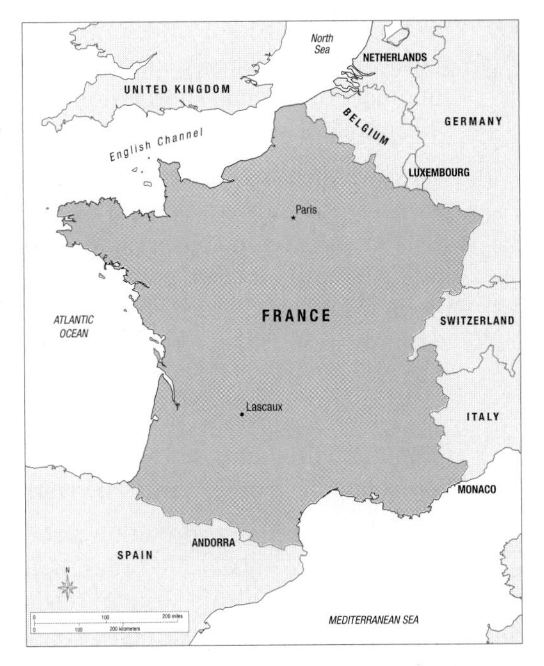

Location of Lascaux

The paintings adorn limestone walls of true caves located deep in the earth. Over time, the paintings have been absorbed by the limestone and thus preserved. Prehistoric big-game hunters painted their prey: woolly mammoths, wild cattle and horses, deer and reindeer. The largest animal image is eighteen feet long.

Most interpretations associate cave painting with magic and ritual surrounding the hunt. For example, because animals are sometimes depicted with spears in their bodies, the paintings might have been attempts to ensure success in hunting. Artists might have believed that by capturing the animal's image in paint and predicting the kill, they could influence the hunt's outcome[1].

Another interpretation sees cave painting as a magical human attempt to control animal reproduction. Something similar was done by Native Australian hunters and gatherers, who held annual *ceremonies of increase* to honor and to promote, magically, the fertility[2] of the plants and animals that shared their homeland. Australians believed that ceremonies were necessary to keep alive the species on which humans depended. Similarly, cave paintings might have been part of annual ceremonies of increase. Some of the animals in the cave murals are pregnant, and some are copulating. Did Upper Paleolithic people believe they could influence the sexual behavior or reproduction of their prey by drawing them? Or did they perhaps think that animals would return each year to the place where their souls had been captured pictorially?

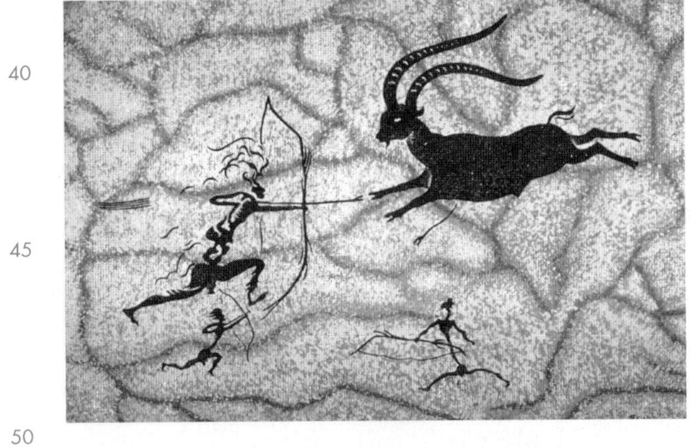

Cave painting, c. 15,000–10,000 B.P.

Paintings often occur in clusters. In some caves, as many as three paintings have been drawn over the original, yet next to these superimposed paintings are blank walls never used for painting. It seems reasonable to speculate that an

[1]**outcome:** result
[2]**fertility:** ability to reproduce

event in the outside world sometimes reinforced a painter's choice of a given spot. Perhaps there was an especially successful hunt soon after the painting had been done. Perhaps members of a social subdivision significant in Upper Paleolithic society customarily used a given area of wall for their drawings.

Cave paintings also might have been a kind of pictorial history. Perhaps Upper Paleolithic people were, through their drawings, reenacting the hunt after it took place, as hunters of the Kalahari Desert in southern Africa still do today. Designs and markings on animal bones may indicate that Upper Paleolithic people had developed a calendar based on the phases of the moon (Marshack, 1972). If this is so, it seems possible that late Stone Age hunters, who were certainly as intelligent as we are, would have been interested in recording important events in their lives.

There is reason to doubt that cave paintings were simply expressions of individual artistic temperament, that is, art for art's sake. Why would artists choose remote locales where few could appreciate their work? And why would artists obliterate someone else's work by painting over it?

Still another interpretation associates cave paintings with initiation rites. Examples of initiation rites—also called rites of passage—in our own society include fraternity hazing and the process by which a woman retreats from secular life and gradually becomes a Roman Catholic nun. Other examples are boot-camp training prior to full-fledged military service and training camp prior to sports season.

Considering other cultures, some of the best-known initiation rites are associated with the quest for a guardian spirit in certain Native American (North American Indian) cultures. To be considered a man, an adolescent male had to temporarily withdraw from normal social life and go into the wilderness, where he sought contact with an animal spirit, which would become his personal guardian spirit. If mere seclusion didn't bring the desired spirit, the boy tried to reach a state of spiritual receptivity by fasting, taking drugs, or inflicting pain on himself. After the vision appeared, the young man returned home, told of his experience, and was reintegrated into his group with adult status. Dark and remote cave passages and interior caverns would be appropriate places for similar rites of passage (Pfeiffer, 1985).

Associated with initiation rites in West Africa and northern Australia are so-called bush schools, which are located far from residential areas. Young people go there when they reach puberty, to be instructed by an older person in tribal lore—knowledge viewed as essential to adult status. On the floor of one European cavern, several small heel prints have been fossilized. Could this cave have been the site of an Upper Paleolithic bush school, a place where the young were instructed by specialists in tribal lore? Were there such specialists? Again, Upper Paleolithic cave paintings offer a hint. Humans are shown in about 50 cave paintings, usually in animal skins. Sometimes they seem to be dancing. It has been suggested that these were the shamans, the religious specialists, of Upper Paleolithic society.

It is worth noting that the *late* Upper Paleolithic, when many of the most spectacular multicolored cave paintings were done and Paleolithic artistic techniques were perfected, coincides with[4] the period when the glaciers were melting. An intensification of cave painting for

Time Abbreviations

B.P. = Before the Present

Abbreviations for time periods before the Year 1 in the Western calendar include these:

B.C.E. = Before the Common Era
B.C. = Before Christ

Abbreviations for time periods from the Year 1 to the present include these:

C.E. = Common Era
A.D. = Anno Domini (Latin: Year of our Lord)

[4]**coincides with:** happens at the same time

any of the reasons connected with hunting magic could have been caused by concern about decreases in herds as the open lands of southwestern Europe were being replaced by forests.

A glacier

The Mesolithic

The broad-spectrum revolution in Europe includes the late Upper Paleolithic and the Mesolithic, which followed it. Again, because of the long history of European archeology, our knowledge of the Mesolithic (particularly in southwestern Europe and the British Isles) is extensive. According to the traditional typology that distinguishes between Old, Middle, and New Stone Ages, the Middle Stone Age—the Mesolithic—had a characteristic tool type—the *microlith* (Greek for "small stone"). Of interest to us is what an abundant inventory of small and delicately shaped stone tools can tell us about the total economy and way of life of the people who made them.

By 12,000 B.P., there were no longer subarctic animals in southwestern Europe. By 10,000 B.P., the glaciers had retreated to such a point that the range of hunting, gathering, and fishing populations in Europe extended to the formerly glaciated British Isles and Scandinavia. The reindeer herds had gradually retreated to the far north, with some human groups following (and ultimately domesticating) them. Europe around 10,000 B.P. was forest rather than treeless steppe and tundra. Europeans were exploiting a wider variety of resources and gearing their lives to the seasonal appearance of particular plants and animals.

People still hunted, but their prey were solitary forest animals, such as the roe deer, the wild ox, and the wild pig, rather than herd species. This led to new hunting techniques: solitary stalking and trapping, similar to more recent practices of many American Indian groups. The coasts and lakes of Europe and the Middle East were fished intensively. Some important Mesolithic sites are Scandinavian shell mounds—the garbage dumps of prehistoric oyster collectors. Microliths were used as fishhooks and in harpoons. Dugout canoes were used for fishing and travel. The process of preserving meat and fish by smoking and salting grew increasingly important. (Meat preservation had been less of a problem in a subarctic environment, since winter snow and ice, often on the ground nine months of the year, offered convenient refrigeration.) The bow and arrow became essential for hunting water fowl in swamps and marshes. Dogs were domesticated as retrievers by Mesolithic people (Champion and Gambel, 1984). Woodworking was important in the forested environment of northern and western Europe. Tools used by Mesolithic carpenters appear in the archeological record: new kinds of axes, chisels, and gouges.

A harpoon from the Mesolithic period

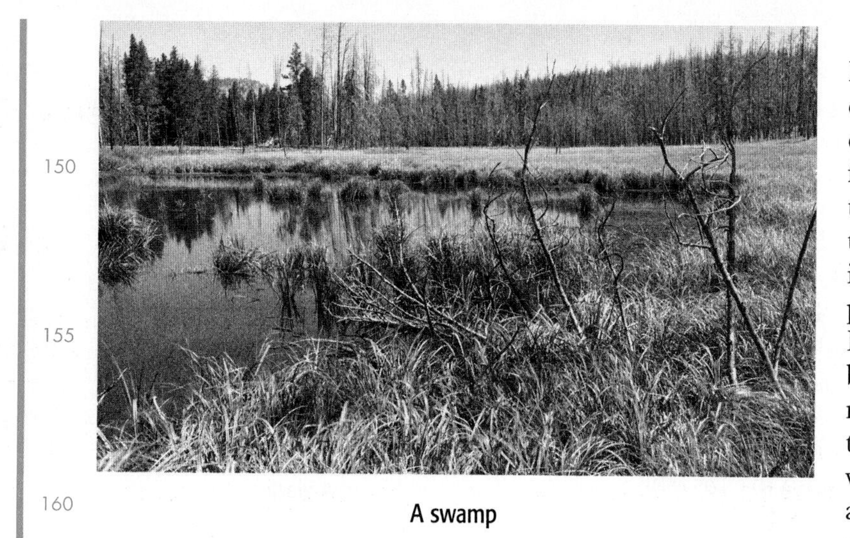

A swamp

150 The decline of big-game hunting probably brought a change in the gender-based division of labor. Hunting and fishing, usually male tasks, tend to be more important in temperate areas than they are in warmer climates, 155 particularly the tropics. In Europe, male dominance of big-game hunting gave way to more equal economic roles for the sexes. On the basis of what 160 we know ethnographically about temperate zone foragers, although Mesolithic men still hunted and fished, women gathered wild plants, small animals, insects, and shellfish. Women probably contributed more to subsistence during the Mesolithic than they had during the Upper Paleolithic.

165 Big-game hunting and, thereafter, Mesolithic hunting and fishing were important in Europe, but other foraging strategies were used by prehistoric humans in Africa and Asia. Among modern-day foragers in the tropics, gathering is an important source of food (Lee, 1968/1974). Although herds of big-game animals were more abundant in the tropics in prehistory than they are today, gathering has probably always been at least as important as 170 hunting for tropical foragers. Wherever gathering contributes more to the diet than hunting, women's economic labor is highly valued and social status discrimination based on gender is rudimentary (Draper, 1975).

Generalized, broad-spectrum economies persisted about 5,000 years longer in Europe than in the Middle East. Whereas Middle Easterners had begun to cultivate plants and breed 175 animals by 10,000 B.P., food production came to Western Europe only around 5,000 B.P. and to northern Europe 500 years later.

Source: *Anthropology: The Exploration of Human Diversity* (Kottak)

AFTER READING

A. COMPREHENSION CHECK Use the information you highlighted in the reading to discuss these questions with a partner.

1. What might cave paintings tell us about the lives of Paleolithic humans?
2. What kind of economy did the people of the Mesolithic period have?

B. COMPREHENSION CHECK Complete the graphic organizers (below and on page 70) with answers to the following questions.

1. What are some of the possible motives that Paleolithic people had for creating cave art? Write them in the chart. Then give an example for each.

Motives	Examples
To ensure success in hunting	Animals are depicted with spears in their bodies.

2. How did climate change lead to changes in the Mesolithic economy? To show this, put the events in the correct order:

- new tools and techniques were invented
- glaciers melted
- big-game hunting declined
- ✓ climate change
- ✓ economic roles of the sexes became more equal
- more plant and animal resources appeared
- gender–based division of labor

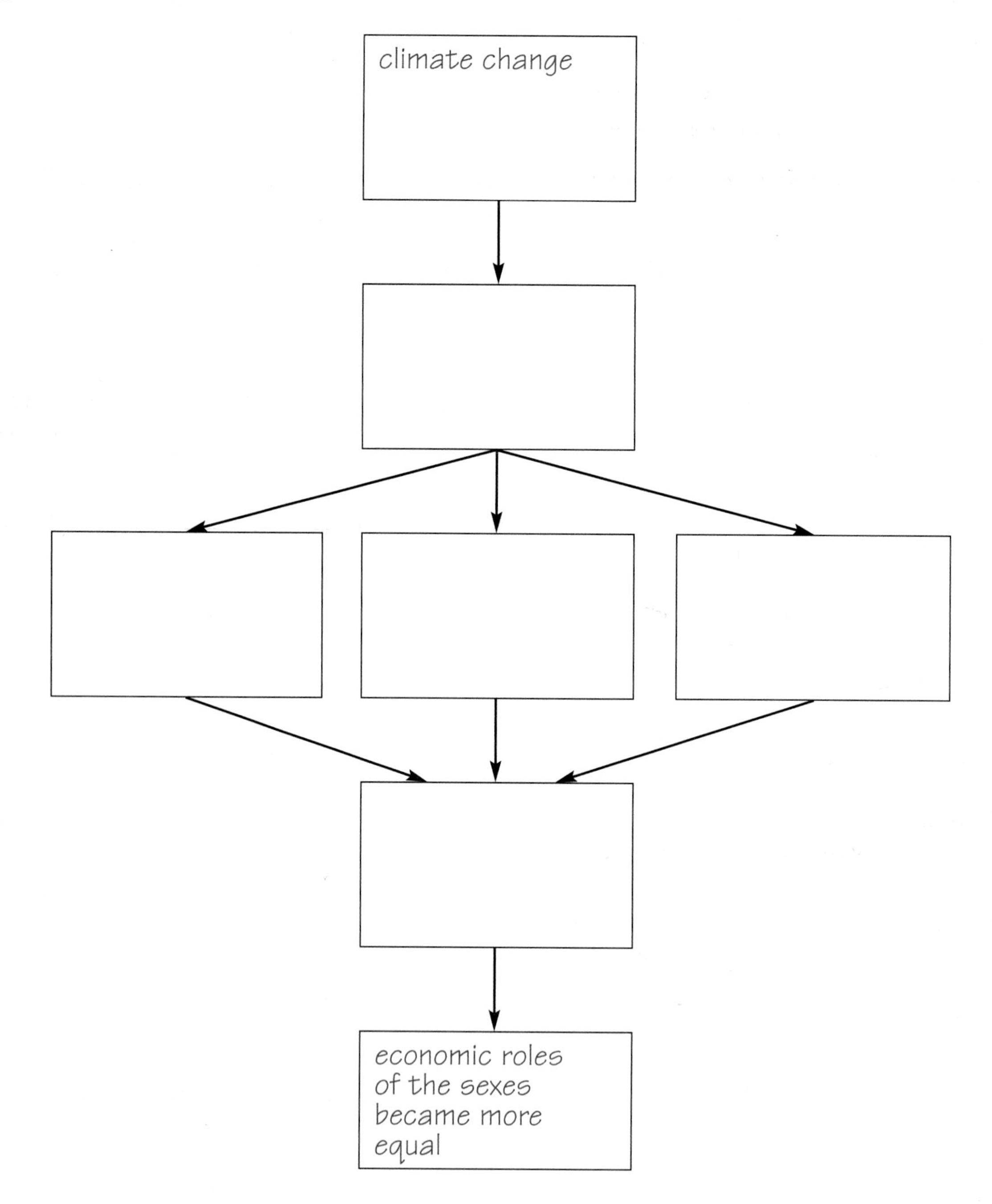

C. VERB PHRASES WITH PREPOSITIONS Look back at the reading on pages 64–68 to find prepositions that complete the phrases in orange.

1. The Lower, Middle, and Upper Paleolithic periods **are associated** ____________ particular stages in human development. (Lines 1–5)
2. Some cave paintings **have been drawn** ____________ others. (Lines 45–50)
3. Upper Paleolithic people may have developed a calendar **based** ____________ the phases of the moon. (Lines 60–65)
4. And why would artists obliterate someone else's work by **painting** ____________ it? (Lines 65–70)
5. In some Native-American cultures, a young man must **withdraw** ____________ normal social life and go into the wilderness. (Lines 70–75)
6. As part of this ritual, the young man may have to **inflict pain** ____________ himself. (Lines 75–80)
7. The most interesting cave paintings **coincide** ____________ the melting of the glaciers. (Lines 95–100)
8. Due to glacial melting, open lands were **being replaced** ____________ forests. (Lines 100–105)
9. The abundance of forest animals **led** ____________ new hunting techniques. (Lines 125–130)
10. Male dominance **gave way** ____________ new roles between the sexes. (Lines 155–160)

D. VOCABULARY CHECK Look back at the reading to find words and phrases that match the definitions below. Don't use a dictionary.

1. animals that are hunted (Lines 20–25) ____________________
2. ceremonies to help keep animals alive (Lines 35–40) ____________________
3. placed on top of (Lines 45–50) ____________________
4. rituals that mark when a person moves from one group or place in society to another (Lines 65–70) ____________________
5. the knowledge that a group of people shares and teaches to younger members (Lines 80–85) ____________________
6. Greek for "small stone" (Lines 115–120) ____________________
7. using (Lines 120–125) ____________________

E. WORD JOURNAL Go back to the readings in Parts 1 and 2. Which new words are important for *you* to remember? Write them in your Word Journal.

F. MAKING CONNECTIONS You know that climate change brought about major changes in the economy of modern humans. In the chart below, write information about the "broad-spectrum economy" of the Mesolithic compared to the relatively simple Paleolithic economy. In other words, how did Mesolithic humans differ from Paleolithic humans?

Paleolithic Economy	Mesolithic Economy
✓ big game hunting	✓ hunting • solitary animals • new solitary hunting methods • fishing + oysters
✓ no need for techniques to preserve meat • plenty of ice	✓ preserving meat • smoking + salting • warmer climate → more important
	✓ tools for hunting and fishing • bow and arrow: birds • dogs: retrieving • fish-hooks, harpoons, canoes • wood tools: axes, chisels
	✓ gathering • done mainly by women • more important as big game declined • as imp. as hunting • women's work ↑ value

G. RESPONSE WRITING In your journal, write about *one* of the topics below for 15 minutes. Don't worry about grammar and don't stop writing to use a dictionary.

- your opinion about animals in captivity producing art
- your ideas about the different motives for creating art
- something that you learned about the similarities between humans and other primates
- something that you learned about Paleolithic or Mesolithic cultures

PART 4 THE MECHANICS OF WRITING

In Part 4, you will learn to use comparison language, complex sentences using subordinating conjunctions, and language of contrast. You will use this knowledge in Part 5 to write a paragraph of comparison.

Review: Adverbial Conjunctions to Show Similarities and Differences

In Chapter 1 (page 35), you learned how to use adverbial conjunctions, including *however* and *in contrast*. These conjunctions, along with *similarly* and *in a similar way*, are used to tell the reader whether the writer is writing about similarities or differences between two groups.

Examples: Adolescent monkeys tend to leave the troop. **In contrast,** human adolescents usually stay close to home until they have grown up.

Adolescent monkeys tend to leave the troop; **however,** human adolescents usually stay close to home until they have grown up.

Humans learn from experience. **Similarly,** monkeys will adapt their behavior as a result of social interaction.

Humans learn from experience; **in a similar way,** monkeys will adapt their behavior as a result of social interaction.

However and *in contrast* tell you that the writer is introducing a difference; *similarly* and *in a similar way* introduce similarities.

Note: These adverbial conjunctions can follow either a period or a semicolon.

A. ADVERBIAL CONJUNCTIONS TO SHOW SIMILARITIES AND DIFFERENCES

Combine the pairs of sentences using *in contrast*, *however*, *similarly*, or *in a similar way*.

1. Human behavior depends extensively on learning. Monkeys and apes profit from experience.

____

____

2. Tool use appears among several nonhuman species. *Homo* employs tools more often than any other animal does.

____

____

3. People communicate nonlinguistically (without words). Chimps communicate through facial expressions, noises, and body movements.

____

____

4. Monkeys fend for themselves in the quest for food. People bring resources back to camp and share them.

____

____

5. Baboons and chimpanzees mate only when females go into heat. Among humans, sexual activity occurs throughout the year.

____

____

Complex Sentences: Subordinating Conjunctions

There are three types of **conjunctions**: adverbial, coordinating, and subordinating. In Chapter 1 (pages 33 and 35), you learned about coordinating and adverbial conjunctions. Here are some subordinating conjunctions:

because	when	by the time
although (= but)	whenever	as soon as (= immediately after)
as (= because)	before	until
since (= because)	after	as (= while; when)
even though	while (= when)	
while (= although)		if
whereas (= although)		unless (= if not)
		in case

Examples: **Since** winter snow and ice were often on the ground nine months of the year, meat preservation was less of a problem in a subarctic environment.

Harlow learned that macaques that grew up away from the group didn't form dominance relationships **when** they rejoined their peers as young adults.

If mere seclusion didn't bring the desired spirit, the boy tried to reach a state of spiritual receptivity by fasting, taking drugs, or inflicting pain on himself.

Punctuation of subordinating conjunctions:

1. There is a comma after the first clause if the sentence begins with the subordinating conjunction.
2. There is no comma if the subordinating conjunction is in the middle.

A sentence with a subordinating conjunction must have two clauses, or it is a fragment and therefore incorrect.

B. SUBORDINATING CONJUNCTIONS Combine the pairs of sentences using the conjunction in orange. Decide where to use the conjunction—at the beginning or in the middle of the sentence—and use appropriate punctuation.

1. Apes' artwork is never representational. Apes are not able to draw forms and figures. **(since)**

   ____

   ____

2. The dominant male first tried the new kind of food. The whole troop soon began to eat it. **(after)**

   ____

   ____

3. A low-ranking macaque began to wash sweet potatoes. It took the rest of the troop a long time to learn from her. **(when)**

   ____

   ____

4. Paleolithic artists created art simply for the sake of beauty. It seems strange that it was hidden in such remote caves. **(if)**

   ____

   ____

5. Humans needed to develop new methods of hunting. Their environment was changing. **(because)**

   ____

   ____

Subordinating Conjunctions to Show Differences

You can use the following subordinating conjunctions to show differences: *while*, *whereas*, and *although*.

The use of these subordinating conjunctions is the same as for all subordinating conjunctions. However, when a subordinating conjunction of contrast is *in the middle,* a comma is frequently used.

Examples: **While** humans share food, monkeys fend for themselves.

Humans share food, **while** monkeys fend for themselves.

C. SUBORDINATING CONJUNCTIONS TO SHOW DIFFERENCES Combine each pair of sentences twice. Use the subordinating conjunction in orange in a different position in each sentence.

Example: Kalimantan orangutans are reddish-brown in color. Their Sumatran cousins are a paler, ginger color. **(while)**

While Kalimantan orangutans are reddish-brown in color, their Sumatran cousins are a paler ginger color.

Kalimantan orangutans are reddish-brown in color, **while** their Sumatran cousins are a paler ginger color.

1. Male orangutans travel on the ground to search for food. Females never leave the trees. **(although)**

   ___

   ___

2. Orangutans have a solitary lifestyle. Other primates live in groups. **(whereas)**

   ___

   ___

3. Orangutans forage for food primarily by moving about in the canopy. Males sometimes descend to the ground to travel long distances in search of food. **(while)**

   ___

   ___

D. ERROR ANALYSIS/EDITING Find and correct the error in each sentence. It is either an error with adverbial conjunctions to show similarities and differences or subordinating conjunctions to show differences.

1. Some nonhuman primates can learn to communicate; however, only humans can speak.
2. Humans learn from experience. In contrast, chimps can learn new behavior by watching other chimps.
3. Most primates live in groups. Whereas orangutans tend to have a solitary lifestyle.
4. While humans use tools tool use is also common among nonhuman primates.
5. Men played the most important role in getting food in the Paleolithic period, however, men and women shared that role more equally in the Mesolithic period.
6. The artist Jeff Koons creates art in order to earn money, in contrast, Paleolithic artists painted because they believed it was necessary for their survival.

Test-Taking Strategy

Taking a Closed-Book Essay Exam

As you saw in Chapter 1 (page 38), there are three types of essay exams. For all three, you need to answer one or more questions in complete paragraphs. Your job is to show that you have understood the class material.

On a closed-book essay, you cannot use any notes. Therefore, when you study for this type of exam, you need to anticipate (predict) what you think you will be asked to write about. Brainstorm for possible types of questions that you might be asked.

Once you have anticipated some questions, you will need to remember and memorize important information for the exam. You need to remember the main concepts of the course material and important facts. You will paraphrase–discuss in your own words–these key concepts in your essay exam. However, you will need to memorize key words and phrases such as:

- names
- **academic buzzwords** (words and phrases that are used in the field that you are studying)
- collocations
- dates
- spellings of words that you can expect to use

Knowing and correctly using key words and phrases will show the instructor that you really understand the topic. For example, for an essay exam based on the reading in Part 2, you might memorize things such as specific primate names (*macaques* instead of *monkeys*) and collocations such as *nonhuman primates, in the wild,* or *reproductive success.* You should try to remember examples of chimpanzee tool use and be able to explain these examples in your own words.

TAKING A CLOSED-BOOK ESSAY EXAM Before doing your writing assignment for this chapter, complete these two activities.

A. ANTICIPATING THE QUESTION Imagine that you are going to have a closed-book essay exam on the material that you read in Parts 2 and 3. Try to anticipate the types of essay questions you might be asked. Write the questions on the lines.

Part 2: ______________________________

____

____

Part 3: ______________________________

____

____

B. WHAT TO STUDY Based on the type (or types) of questions you anticipated in Activity A on page 77, go back to the readings on pages 53–57 and 64–68 and make a list of things to remember and things to memorize for the essay exam in the chart.

	What to Remember	What to Memorize
Part 2		
Part 3		

WRITING ASSIGNMENT

Write one paragraph of comparison. Use information from the reading in Part 2 or 3.

STEP A. CHOOSING A TOPIC Choose one of the following topics to compare in your paragraph.

- Compare human and nonhuman primates in *one* of these areas: learning, use of tools, communication, cooperation and sharing, or mating and kinship.
- Compare how humans lived in the Paleolithic period with how they lived in the Mesolithic period.

Writing Strategy

Getting Started by Brainstorming

Brainstorming helps you get started when you have a writing assignment. It helps you discover not only what you may already know or remember about the topic but also what you need to find out in order to cover the topic completely. Brainstorming can also help you decide which topic seems the most interesting to you when you have a choice. It's always easier to write about a topic that interests you.

You can brainstorm alone by making a list of ideas you want to include in your essay. You can also brainstorm with a partner or in small groups by having everyone contribute ideas about what to include.

BRAINSTORMING In small groups, choose one of the writing topics on page 78. Then list each of the possible points of comparison for your topic on a separate piece of paper. To do this, compare the information you've highlighted in this chapter and all the charts and graphic organizers you've completed. Are you missing anything? Is there anything you don't understand?

Now write here who and/or what you have decided to compare and the points of comparison (if applicable):

___

___

Writing Strategy

Paraphrasing

Unless you are quoting a source, all the information in an essay must be in your own words. This means you must paraphrase the key points in the material from which you get your information. It's a good idea to start paraphrasing early, in the information-gathering stage.

Here are some techniques for paraphrasing the ideas of others. Try to combine two or more of these techniques when paraphrasing.

1. Use synonyms and synonymous phrases that mean the same thing as the original. However, you don't use synonyms for names of things or for academic buzzwords and collocations.

   Example: **Original:** Harlow **discovered** that macaques (a kind of monkey) **raised in isolation** didn't form dominance relationships when **brought together** as young adults.
   Paraphrase: Harlow **learned** that macaques that **grew up away from the group** didn't form dominance relationships when they **rejoined** their peers as young adults.

2. Change the parts of speech. For example, change nouns to verbs, verbs to nouns, nouns to adjectives, adjectives to nouns, or adjectives to adverbs.

   Example: **Original:** Another example is that chimpanzees and orangutans make tools for specific tasks, but human **reliance on tools is much greater**.
   Paraphrase: Humans **rely on tools to a much greater extent** than chimpanzees and orangutans do.

3. Change the sentence structure. For example, change the passive voice to active, active to passive, direct quotes to indirect speech, or reverse clauses.

   Example: **Original:** Tools used by Mesolithic carpenters appear in the archeological record: new kinds of axes, chisels, and gouges.
   Paraphrase: **We have archeological evidence that Mesolithic people began using new kinds of axes, chisels, and gouges.**

STEP B. GATHERING INFORMATION AND PARAPHRASING Go back to the readings in Part 2 (pages 53–57) or Part 3 (pages 64–68). Find information about the topic that you chose. Paraphrase it below. (You don't have to write in complete sentences.)

1. Who and/or what you are going to compare:

____

____

2. Examples of similarities or differences:

____

____

____

____

Writing Strategy

Writing a Paragraph of Comparison

When you write a single comparison paragraph, you usually focus on similarities or differences. Your topic sentence states who or what you are comparing, the point(s) of comparison, and whether you are going to discuss similarities or differences. The rest of the paragraph includes ideas, examples and details that support your topic sentence. It should include at least one example of how the two individuals, groups, or ideas are similar or different.

Example:

Human and nonhuman primates create art for different reasons. While a primate might have very uncomplicated motives for painting a picture, humans often produce art as a result of very strong needs. For example, Nonja, the orangutan at the Schönbrunn Zoo, probably paints to pass the time or because she was trained to do so at an early age, and she knows that it pleases her caretaker. Humans, on the other hand, may paint for many reasons: to earn a living, to communicate cultural values or deep and intense feelings such as love or hate, or, as in the case of Mesolithic cave painters, to ensure their very survival. Nonja's work is just pretty splatters on a piece of paper; there is no message in her work. A pregnant ox painted deep inside a cave, however, can tell us a great deal about the artist's values and way of life.

Analysis: In the example paragraph above, find one subordinating conjunction and three adverbial conjunctions. Why are they used?

STEP C. ORGANIZING YOUR MATERIAL First, write your topic sentence. Then choose which information from Step B to include as supporting information. (You probably won't use all of it.)

STEP D. WRITING THE PARAGRAPH Write complete sentences in paragraph form. Be sure to include at least one example for each of the things that you are comparing. You might make some mistakes, but don't worry about them at this point.

STEP E. EDITING Read your paragraph and answer these questions.

1. Is the paragraph form correct (indentation, margins)?
2. Does your topic sentence state who or what you are comparing and whether you are discussing similarities or differences?
3. Is there at least one example of how the two individuals, groups, or things are similar or different?
4. Is there correct use of adverbial conjunctions to show similarities and differences?
5. If there are subordinating conjunctions to show differences, are they used correctly?
6. Is sentence structure correct (no fragments)?

STEP F. REWRITING Write your paragraph again. This time, try to write with no mistakes.

IT 1 VOCABULARY WORKSHOP

…ocabulary items that you learned in Chapters 1 and 2.

A. MATCHING Match the definitions to the words. Write the letters on the lines.

Words	**Definitions**
______ **1.** acquaintances	~~**a.**~~ ability to think ahead
______ **2.** adolescence	**b.** difference
______ **3.** allies	**c.** kings and queens
______ **4.** analogous	**d.** not important
______ **5.** foresight	**e.** organization into a system of ranks (low to high)
______ **6.** gap	**f.** people who help or support you
______ **7.** hierarchy	**g.** people whom you know but not well
______ **8.** a quest	**h.** period of life between childhood and adulthood
______ **9.** royalty	**i.** a search
______**10.** trivial	**j.** similar to; in an equal situation

B. COLLOCATIONS Write the correct prepositions on the lines.

1. an array ______________forms

2. focus ______________ this

3. a combination ______________ a priest and physician

4. based ______________ different theories

5. differ ______________ one religion ______________ another

6. raised ______________ isolation

7. ______________ the top down

8. chimps ______________ the wild

9. withdraw ______________ the group

10. coincided ______________ the melting of the glaciers

Stems and Affixes

Parts of words, usually from Greek or Latin, will help you to guess the meaning of many new words. These word parts are prefixes (at the beginning of a word), stems (the main part of a word), and suffixes (the ending of a word): Prefixes and suffixes = affixes. Here are some from this unit.

Prefixes	**Meaning**
con-	with, together
exo-	out, away
im-	in, on, *or* not
non-	not
pre-	before
re-	new, again
super-	above

Stems	**Meaning**
-anthro-	man (human)
-archae-	ancient
-dict-	say, speak
-gam-	marriage
-lith-	stone
-med/mes-	middle
-micro-	small
-mit-	send
-mono-	one
-morph-	form, shape
-omni-	all

Stems	**Meaning**
-paleo-	old
-poly-	many
-pose-	place, put
-spec-	see, look at
-tempo-	time
-terr-	earth
-the-	god
-trans-	across
-vor-	eat
-zoo-	animal

Suffixes	**Meaning**
-able	capable of
-ate	(indicates a verb)
-ism	belief in
-ist	person who (believes in or studies)

Example: mono the ism (mono = one, the = god, ism = belief in)

Monotheism is the belief in one god.

C. STEMS AND AFFIXES What do you know about these words? With a partner, use stems and affixes in the box to guess the meanings of the words below.

1. contemporary
2. polytheist
3. zoomorphic
4. nonindustrial
5. anthropomorphic
6. polygamist
7. transmit
8. speculate
9. supernatural
10. predate
11. archaeologist
12. Paleolithic
13. superimpose
14. terrestrial
15. predict
16. exogamy
17. Mesolithic
18. omnivorous

D. THE ACADEMIC WORD LIST The words in the boxes below are from the Academic Word List (Appendix 3, pages 313–316). They are some of the most common *academic* words in English. Write the words from the boxes on the correct lines. When you finish, check your answers in the readings on page 13 (for items 1–5) and page 56 (for items 6–11).

aspect	consumption	~~cultural~~	links	nuclear

Cultural (1) rules determine every ______ (2) of food ______ (3). Who eats together defines social units. For example, in our society, the ______ (4) family is the unit that regularly eats together. The anthropologist Mary Douglas (1972) has pointed out that, for the English, the kind of meal and the kind of food that is served relate to the kinds of social ______ (5) between people who are eating together.

adults	cooperation	~~cooperative~~	individually	intrinsic	resources

Humans appear to be the most cooperative (6) of the primates—in the food quest and other social activities. Except for meat sharing by chimps, the ape tendency is to forage ______ (7). Monkeys also fend for themselves in getting food. Among human foragers, men generally hunt and women gather. Men and women bring ______ (8) back to the camp and share them. Older people who did not engage in the food quest get food from younger ______ (9). Everyone shares the meat from a large animal. Nourished and protected by younger band members, elders live past the reproductive age. They receive respect for their knowledge and experience. The amount of information stored in a human band is far greater than that in any other primate society. Sharing, ______ (10), and language are ______ (11) to information storage.

UNIT 2

ECONOMICS

Chapter 3
Developing Nations

Chapter 4
The Global Economy

CHAPTER 3

Developing Nations

Discuss these questions:

- Did you have a job when you were this child's age (12)?
- What does a person need in order to start a business?
- How can we make sure that everyone has the same opportunity to succeed?

PART 1 INTRODUCTION What Can One Person Do about Poverty?

BEFORE READING

Bono, leader of the band U2, at work

One of over 2,000 stores in The Body Shop chain

THINKING AHEAD In small groups, look at the pictures and discuss these questions.

1. Do you know anything about the singer Bono? What do you think his life is like?
2. Have you ever been in a Body Shop store? What kinds of products do they sell?
3. Read the following quotations. Look up any words that you don't know in a dictionary. Is there one quotation that you especially like? Which one? Why?

   The greatest of evils and the worst of crimes is poverty.
   —George Bernard Shaw

   A decent provision for the poor is the true test of civilization.
   —Samuel Johnson, quoted in Boswell's *Life of Johnson*, 1770

   Anticipate charity by preventing poverty.
   —Maimonides

   If a free society cannot help the many who are poor, it cannot save the few who are rich.
   —John F. Kennedy, Inaugural Address, 1961

   The truth is we are all caught in a great economic system which is heartless.
   —Woodrow Wilson, *The New Freedom*

4. In your culture, are there any famous sayings or proverbs about poverty?

READING

Read about Bono and Anita Roddick. As you read, think about this question:

- What are these people doing to solve the problem of poverty?

The War on Poverty: Two People's Stories

Bono, Africa, and AIDS

In 2004, Bono, lead singer for the rock group U2, joined with several others to launch a project called the ONE Campaign (www.theonecampaign.org). 5 Their hope is to build support for attacking the AIDS epidemic and other ills that accompany extreme poverty. This battle has several fronts:

- Start with a more vigorous fight against 10 HIV/AIDS, which has taken an unmatched toll on sub-Saharan Africa's social and economic structure. Last year, 26.6 million people in that region had HIV, the virus that causes HIV/AIDS; 15 about 2.3 million people died of AIDS in 2003. The plague has left untold numbers of children without parents, households without income earners, nations without able-bodied workforces.
- 20 Go next to debt relief, so that these nations can address their domestic problems without having to use an enormous chunk of limited national assets to pay off debts.
- Follow up, then, with greater foreign aid, more strategically aimed, in nations that have vowed to use foreign aid in ways that guard against corruption.

Source: *The Philadelphia Inquirer*

> When Bono and his wife Ali first went to Africa, they worked in a refugee camp for a month. On the day they were leaving, a man approached him carrying a baby. "This is my son," the man said. "Please take him with you when you leave. If you do, he will live. Otherwise he will die."
>
> I have heard Bono tell that story several times. Each time, I think he is haunted by the unacceptable fact that any father should be faced with such a choice and by the horror that this unjust moment is repeated every day across Africa. He has dedicated his life to making sure that such extreme poverty comes to an end.
>
> **Source:** *Time* (Shriver)

Anita Roddick Has Changed Business

25 Anita Roddick started The Body Shop in 1976. Her intention was just to support herself and her daughters while her husband was traveling in the Americas. She didn't have training or experience in business. Nevertheless, the shop that sold beauty and health products was successful and multiplied into a chain of what is now more than 2,000 shops in over fifty countries. It made its founder into a 30 multimillionaire.

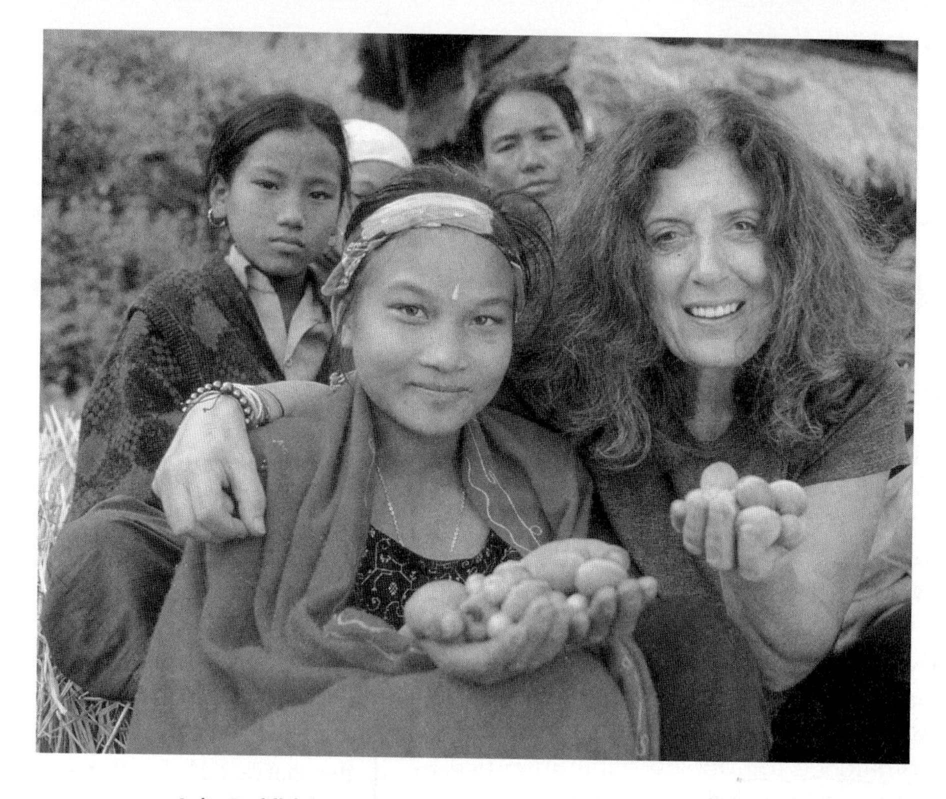

Anita Roddick in one community with which she does business

What made The Body Shop different from other beauty supply shops was Roddick's social consciousness. As a child, Anita Roddick was influenced by her mother's frugality and learned not to be wasteful. She learned to reuse, refill, and recycle. As a young woman, Anita Roddick traveled extensively and spent time in 35 many rural communities, where she learned about women's beauty rituals all over the world. These ideas formed the foundation of The Body Shop's environmental and social activism. Since the beginning, Roddick's business has been deeply involved in the Community Trade program.

What is the Body Shop's Community Trade program?

- It is aimed at small communities worldwide that supply the stores with natural ingredients.
- It pays fair prices to producers of ingredients and materials.
- It helps these producers to support their families.
- It allows money to go back into the community.
- It makes it possible for such communities to better supply the people with basic needs such as water, health, and education.

AFTER READING

A. COMPREHENSION CHECK In small groups, look back at the reading. When you find the answers to these questions, highlight them.

1. Both Bono and Anita Roddick are very rich. What are the sources of their wealth?
2. How are Bono and Anita Roddick similar?
3. In what ways is HIV/AIDS affecting Africa economically?
4. In what ways is The Body Shop benefiting small rural communities?

B. VOCABULARY CHECK Look back at the reading to find the words and phrases that match these definitions. Don't use a dictionary.

1. begin (Lines 1–5) ______________________
2. problems (Lines 5–10) ______________________
3. areas where fighting takes place (Lines 5–10) ______________________
4. has cost a terrible amount in terms of human health and life (Lines 10–15) ______________________
5. things that have value and can be sold (Lines 20–25) ______________________
6. promised (Lines 20–25) ______________________
7. carefulness with money (Lines 30–35) ______________________

Reading Strategy

Finding the Meaning of Words with Multiple Definitions

Many words in English have multiple meanings. When you use a dictionary, it is important to choose the definition that fits your context. To do this, first figure out the word's part of speech (noun, verb, adjective, etc.) *in the context* of what you are reading. Look back and forth from the context in your reading to the dictionary until you find a match.

Examples: She needs to **address** the envelope.

The president **addressed** the graduating class.

ad • dress \ă` drĕs\ *n.* [Middle English *addressen*, from Latin *addirectiare*] **1 a :** a description of the location of a person or organization, as written or printed on mail as directions for delivery **b :** the location at which a particular organization or person may be found or reached **2 a :** in computer science, a name or number used in information storage or retrieval that is assigned to a specific memory location **b :** the memory location identified by the name or number **c :** a name or sequence of characters that designates an email account or a specific site on the Internet or other network **3 :** a formal spoken or written communication **4 :** a formal speech **5 :** courteous attentions (often used in the plural) **6 a :** the manner or bearing of a person, esp. in conversation **b :** skill, deftness, and grace in dealing with people or situations **7 :** the act of dispatching or consigning a ship, as to an agent or a factor

\ə drĕs`\ *v.* **1 :** to speak to **2 :** to make a formal speech to **3 :** to direct (a spoken or written message) to the attention of **4 :** to write a name and address on

In the first example, *address* means "to write a name and address on" something. In the second, it means "to make a formal speech."

C. FINDING THE MEANING OF WORDS WITH MULTIPLE DEFINITIONS For each word in orange below, choose the appropriate dictionary definition. Write the number of the definition on the line.

> **rich** \ritsh\ *adj.* [Middle English *rîche* from Old English *rīce*] **1 :** having abundant possessions and esp. material wealth **2 a :** having high value or quality **b :** well supplied **3 :** magnificently impressive : sumptuous **4 a :** vivid and deep in color *a rich red* **b :** full and mellow in tone and quality *a rich voice* **c :** pungent *rich odors* **5 :** highly productive or remunerative *a rich mine* **6 a :** having abundant plant nutrients *rich soil* **b :** highly seasoned, fatty, oily, or sweet *rich foods* **c :** high in the combustible component *a rich fuel mixture* **7 a :** amusing; also laughable **b :** meaningful, significant *rich allusions* **c :** lush *rich meadows* **8 :** pure or nearly pure *rich lime* **—richness** *n*
>
> ***syn*** RICH, WEALTHY, AFFLUENT, WELL-OFF, WELL-TO-DO, OPULENT *shared meaning element* : having goods, property, and money in abundance ***ant*** POOR

__6b__ **1.** This dessert is fabulous, but it's so **rich** that I can eat only a little.

__1__ **2.** If I could invest in that company, I'd soon be **rich**.

__4b__ **3.** Taylor's **rich** baritone voice filled the theater.

__7a__ **4.** Ashley's joke made me laugh until my stomach hurt. "Oh, that's **rich**," I said, shaking with laughter.

__2b__ **5.** The library is a **rich** source of information.

__4a__ **6.** The sunset splashed **rich** purples, reds, and yellows across the western sky.

D. IN YOUR OWN WORDS: SUMMARIZING Choose either the section on Bono or the one on Anita Roddick. Fill in the first blank with the topic of the section. Use a noun or noun phrase. Fill in the second blank with the main idea. Complete the sentence with an independent clause.

1. The section is about ____

2. The author says that ____

____

PART 2 GENERAL INTEREST READING
A Bank for the Down and Out

BEFORE READING

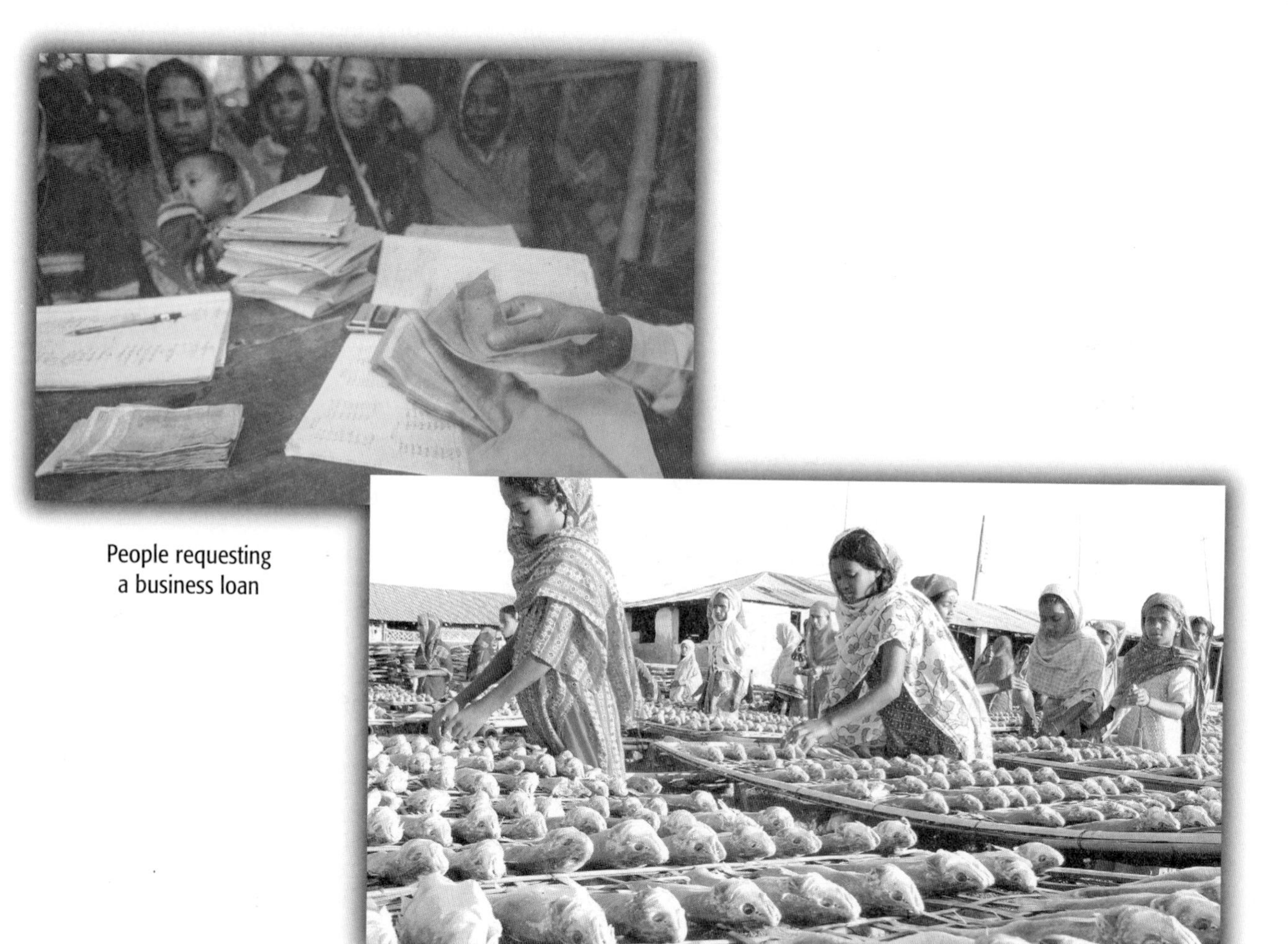

People requesting a business loan

Workers drying fish

THINKING AHEAD In small groups, look at the pictures and discuss these questions.

1. Where might these photos have been taken? Explain your answer.
2. Imagine the lives of the people in each photo. What adjectives can you think of to describe their lives?
3. What kind of **collateral** (a car? a house?) is usually necessary in order to receive a business loan from a bank?

READING

Read about the Grameen Bank. As you read, think about this question:
• How is the Grameen Bank different from most banks?

A Bank for the Down and Out

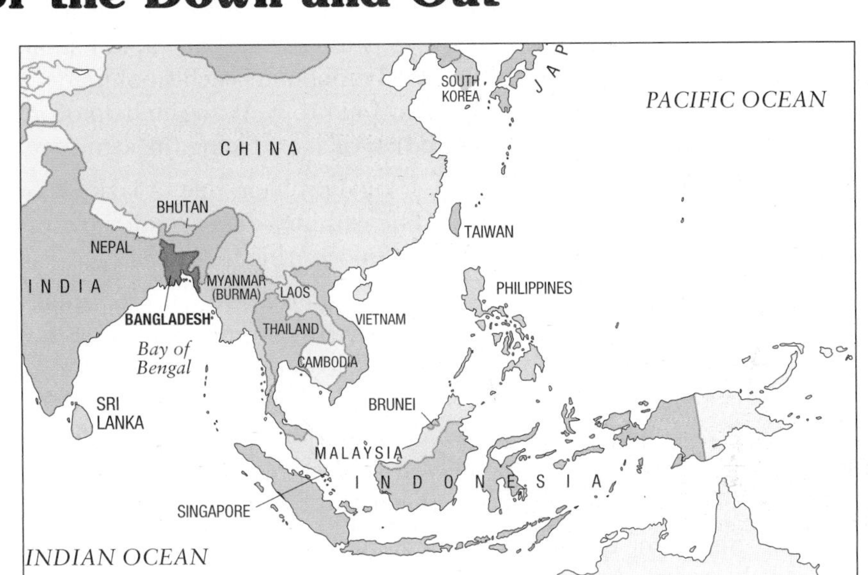

Bangladesh and the surrounding area

Mohammud Yunus, a banker from Bangladesh, is that rare thing: a bona fide visionary. His dream is the total eradication of poverty from the world. "One day," he says confidently, "our grandchildren will go to museums to see what poverty was like."

What this man has invented is called micro-credit. It is both terribly simple and, in the field of development and aid, completely revolutionary. Yunus' bank gives loans of as little as $30 to the destitute. A typical borrower would be a Bangladeshi woman (96 percent of the bank's borrowers are women) who has never touched money before. All her life, her father and husband will have told her she is useless and a burden to the family; finally, widowed or divorced, she will have been forced to beg to feed her children. Yunus' bank lends her money—and doesn't regret it. She uses the loan to buy an asset that can immediately start paying income—such as cotton to weave, or raw materials for bracelets to sell, or a cow she can milk. She repays the loan in tiny installments until she becomes self-sufficient. Then if she wants, she can take out a new, larger loan. Either way, she is no longer poor.

Mohammud Yunus, founder of Grameen Bank

The Grameen Bank ("rural bank" in Bengali), which Yunus has built over the last 30 years, has more than 3.7 million borrowers in 46,000 villages throughout Bangladesh. In 2004, it made loans of more than $473.78 million. The bank actively seeks out the most deprived of Bangladeshi society: beggars, illiterates, and widows. Yet, it claims a loan repayment rate of 99 percent. Most Western banks would be delighted with such a small ration of bad debts.

Born in Chittagong, the business center of what was then Eastern Bengal, Yunus studied at Vanderbilt University in

Nashville, Tennessee, before becoming head of the Economics Department at Chittagong University. The terrible manmade famine of 1974, which by some estimates killed 1.5 million Bangladeshis, changed his life forever. "While people were dying of hunger on the streets, I 45 was teaching elegant theories of economics. I started hating myself for the arrogance of pretending I had the answers. Why did people who worked 12 hours a day, seven days a week, not have enough food to eat? I decided that the poor themselves would be my teachers. I began to study them and question them on their lives."

Then he made his big discovery. One day, when he was interviewing a woman who made 50 bamboo stools, he learned that, because she had no capital of her own, she had to borrow the equivalent of 23 cents to buy raw bamboo for each stool made. After repaying the middleman, she kept only 1.5 cents in profit. With the help of graduate students, Yunus discovered that there were 42 other villagers facing the same predicament.

"Their poverty was not a personal problem due to laziness or lack of intelligence, but a 55 structural one: lack of capital. The existing system made it certain that the poor could not save a penny and could not invest in bettering themselves."

Borrowers who are not destitute are excluded, and so, usually, are men. Yunus soon discovered that lending to women was much more beneficial to whole families—and that women were more careful about their debts. To be eligible for a loan, a person must prove she 60 understands how Grameen works. Borrowers promise to abide by "the 16 decisions," a set of personal commitments. The most important is to join with four fellow borrowers, none of whom can be a family member, to form a "group." The group provides a borrower with self-discipline and courage. Peer pressure and peer support effectively replace collateral.

Studies of the Grameen method suggest that after a wife joins the bank, her husband is 65 likely to show her more tenderness and respect. Divorce rates drop among Grameen borrowers, as do birth rates.

Yunus' method works well wherever the social life of the poor is tightly knit. But in many urban settings, the lack of community has been the greatest stumbling block. However, Yunus does not pretend to have solutions for all problems.

70 "People say I am crazy, but no one can achieve anything without a dream," he says. "If one is going to make headway against poverty, one cannot do business as usual. One must be revolutionary and think the unthinkable."

Source: *The Independent on Sunday* (Jolis)

AFTER READING

A. COMPREHENSION CHECK With a partner, look back at the reading. When you find the answers to these questions, highlight them.

1. What has Mohammud Yunus invented?
2. How is Grameen Bank different from most banks?
3. To whom does the bank lend money? What *doesn't* the bank require of borrowers?
4. What must borrowers promise to do?
5. What is the repayment rate?

B. VOCABULARY CHECK Match the words and phrases on the left with the definitions on the right. Don't use a dictionary, but look back at the reading on pages 95–96 if necessary. Write the correct letters on the lines.

a 1. beg	a. ask for money from strangers on the street
g 2. bona fide	b. complete removal
h 3. burden	c. a difficult situation
d 4. capital	d. money to begin a business
k 5. destitute	e. an obstacle; something that prevents action or causes worry
b 6. eradication	f. people who can't read or write
i 7. headway	g. authentic, genuine
f 8. illiterates	h. something heavy that must be carried
c 9. predicament	i. progress
j 10. tightly knit	j. very close (family or community)
e 11. stumbling block	k. very, very poor

C. EXPANSION In small groups, explore the website of the Grameen Bank (www.grameen-info.org/bank/index.html). Find the list of "16 decisions." What are they? Which ones might you expect in any country? Which ones surprise you or are specific to a Bangladeshi village?

PART 3 ACADEMIC READING Developing Countries

BEFORE READING

"It looks like we're beginning to hold the line against inflation."

A. THINKING AHEAD In small groups, discuss these questions.

1. According to the next reading, there is an enormous gap between rich and poor nations. Why do people in poor countries want to close this gap? Why do people in rich countries want to close it?
2. Make a list of **obstacles** to economic development in poor countries. In other words, what are problems or stumbling blocks that stand in the way of development?
3. In your opinion, how can rich countries help poorer ones to develop? How can poor countries help themselves?
4. What are some examples of countries that used to be poor but are now economically successful?
5. The topic of the cartoon above is **inflation**. Why are these men happy?

+ parts of speech

B. VOCABULARY PREPARATION Read the sentences below. The words in orange are from the next reading. Try to guess their meanings from the context.

- First, circle the part of speech—noun (n), verb (v), or adjective (adj).
- Then write your guess.
- If you are very unsure of your guess, check a dictionary to see if your guess was close. To save time, do the third step with a small group. Divide the group of words; each person will look up several words and then share the answers.

Parts of Speech

1. The United Nations and many non-governmental organizations are searching for solutions to the **plight** of developing countries. — n v adj

   Guess: ____________________

   Dictionary Definition: ____________________

2. An obstacle such as the lack of natural resources can **hinder** economic growth. — n v adj

   Guess: ____________________

   Dictionary Definition: ____________________

3. Countries such as Bolivia and Mongolia are **landlocked** and depend on agreements with other countries to give them access to an ocean. — n v adj

   Guess: ____________________

   Dictionary Definition: ____________________

4. Many Buddhists believe that it is important to **extinguish** all desires as one would extinguish a fire. — n v adj

   Guess: ____________________

   Dictionary Definition: ____________________

5. The people were full of fear when it was clear that their country was on the **brink** of war. — n v adj

   Guess: ____________________

   Dictionary Definition: ____________________

6. Although it is illegal, government officials in some countries accept **bribes** in exchange for granting people certain favors. — n v adj

   Guess: ____________________

   Dictionary Definition: ____________________

Parts of Speech

7. Many countries have **barriers** to trade—i.e., laws that prevent people from doing business with certain other countries. Economists usually say that these barriers should be reduced or even completely **eliminated**.

n v adj

n v adj

Guess: ______

Dictionary Definition: ______

Guess: ______

Dictionary Definition: ______

8. There are great **fluctuations** in the temperature at this time of year. One day, it's cold, and the next day, it's hot. Nobody knows what to expect.

n v adj

Guess: ______

Dictionary Definition: ______

9. When the state of Alaska began to profit from the sale of oil, there was a yearly **allocation** of money to every resident of the state.

n v adj

Guess: ______

Dictionary Definition: ______

10. The possibility of a bonus salary payment gave the workers an **incentive** to work harder.

n v adj

Guess: ______

Dictionary Definition: ______

Reading Strategy

Dealing with Too Much Material: Divide and Conquer

In school, you will often need to read hundreds of pages a week. You need to acquire strategies for dealing with this. You have already used two of these strategies: 1) marking up a text with different colors signifying different levels of importance and 2) putting information into graphic organizers.

Another strategy is to form a study group with other students in class and divide responsibility for different parts of the reading. All group members should scan the entire reading, but each student is responsible for reading one part of it *in depth*. Reading in depth means:

- Make a list of important new vocabulary terms.
- Find good examples for the concepts.
- Create a graphic organizer to make clear the main ideas and important details.

When the study group meets, each student in the group explains his or her section of the reading, becoming a sort of teacher for the rest of the group.

C. DEALING WITH TOO MUCH MATERIAL The reading that follows might seem long and difficult. (However, it is much shorter than most homework assignments in a college class.) Your classmates and you will help each other understand the reading in greater depth. Follow these steps:

- Read the entire passage to become generally acquainted with it.
- Read the introduction again. You will discuss this later.
- Join either Group A or Group B.
- Group A is responsible for reading the section "Obstacles to Economic Development" in depth. Group B is responsible for the section "A Framework for Development."
- As you read, highlight main ideas, important details, and examples.

READING

Developing Countries

Section 1: Economic Development

Most people in the world today live in **developing countries**—countries whose average per capita GNP* is a fraction of that in more industrialized countries. In many ways, developing economies are similar to other economies of the world. The major difference is that their problems are much greater.

Obstacles to Economic Development

5 Before examining some of the possible solutions to the plight of developing countries, we need to take a closer look at some common problems and challenges.

*GNP is a measure of income

POPULATION GROWTH

One obstacle to economic development is population growth. The populations of most developing countries grow at a rate much faster than those of industrialized countries. One reason for this growth is the high **crude birthrate**—the number of live births per 1,000
10 people.

People in many developing countries are also experiencing an increasing **life expectancy**—the average remaining lifetime in years for persons who reach a certain age. Longer life expectancies, coupled with a high crude birthrate, make it difficult to increase per capita GNP.

15 Some countries, like China, have encouraged lower birth rates and smaller families. Some people even feel that societies should work for **zero population growth (ZPG)**—the condition in which the average number of births and deaths balance. Others feel efforts to disrupt population growth are wrong from both moral and religious perspectives.

NATURAL RESOURCES AND GEOGRAPHY

Another obstacle to economic growth is limited natural resources, which includes
20 unproductive land and harsh climates. A shortage of natural and energy sources needed for industry also hinders growth.

In some cases, countries with limited natural resources can make up for the deficiency by engaging in international trade, as Japan has done. However, if a country is landlocked, trade is much more difficult. It is no accident that all of the major economic powers today have
25 long had coastal cities with access to major trade routes.

EDUCATION AND TECHNOLOGY

Still another obstacle to economic development is a lack of appropriate education and technology. Many developing countries do not have a highly literate population or the high level of technical skills needed to build an industrial society. In addition, most do not have money to train engineers and scientists.

30 Many developing countries cannot afford to provide free public education for school-age children. In those that can, not everyone is able to take advantage of it because children must work to help feed their families.

RELIGION

Religious beliefs may also stand in the way of economic development. While almost everyone realizes that capital investment and new technologies can help economic growth,
35 some people may not be interested for religious reasons.

In Asia, most Hindus and Buddhists believe that life is governed by a fate called *karma*; they believe that people are part of an eternal cycle of life, death, and rebirth. Many Hindus believe that the eternal cycle can be broken, in part, by purifying the mind and body through living a simple lifestyle. Many Buddhists believe that the way to break the cycle is to extinguish
40 desire and reject the temptations of the material world. Consequently, some Hindus and Buddhists have little motivation to improve their material well-being. However, other Hindus and Buddhists embrace Western concepts of economic growth.

The teachings of Catholicism, Protestantism, and Judaism are much more compatible with the concept of economic growth and material improvement, while the Islamic world is in
45 between the Christians and the Hindus. We must realize, however, that some cultures may not be as interested in the Western concept of economic growth and development as we imagine.

EXTERNAL DEBT

Another major problem facing the developing nations today is the size of their **external debt**—money borrowed from foreign banks and governments. Some nations have borrowed so much that they may never be able to repay loans.

Today a number of developing countries—Bulgaria, Cameroon, the Ivory Coast, Ethiopia, Honduras, Jordan, Madagascar, Syria, and Tanzania—all have external debts larger than their GNP.

When debts get this large, countries have trouble even paying interest on the loans. As a result, some developing nations are on the brink of **default**, or not repaying borrowed money. Even this strategy is dangerous, however, because a country that defaults on its loans may not be able to borrow again.

CAPITAL FLIGHT

Another problem for developing nations is **capital flight**—the legal or illegal export of a nation's currency and foreign exchange. Capital flight occurs because people lose faith in their government or in the future of their economy. When capital flight occurs, businesses and even the government often face a cash shortage. At a minimum, it limits the funds available for domestic capital investment.

CORRUPTION

Corruption at any level of government is an obstacle to economic development. Sometimes corruption takes the form of minor officials requiring modest bribes to get even the smallest things done. At other times, corruption occurs on a massive scale.

When Ferdinand Marcos was president of the Philippines, foreign investors poured billions into the country's economy. Years later, however, the majority of Filipinos still lived in poverty. Officials later charged that Marcos had stolen at least $500 million from the nation and deposited the money in personal Swiss bank accounts.

Section 2: A Framework for Development

Priorities for Industrialized Nations

Assistance to developing countries helps assure the industrial nations of a stable supply of critical raw materials. Developing countries also provide markets for the products of industrial nations.

The World Bank has become a powerful force in economic development because it often requires that countries actually make market reforms as a condition for obtaining a loan. Because of its considerable experience with developing nations, the World Bank has a list of recommendations for both developing and industrialized countries.

Reduce Trade Barriers. **Trade barriers** need to be reduced or eliminated. The World Bank has estimated that eliminating trade barriers would generate as much as $50 billion annually in export earnings for the developing countries.

Reform Macroeconomic Policy. Industrialized countries need to implement **macroeconomic policies** that reduce budget deficits, lower interest rates, and stabilize inflation and foreign currency fluctuations. This would help the economic development of all types of economies. When industrialized economies grow, their increased international trade often includes, and benefits, the developing economies.

Increase Financial Support. The industrialized nations need to provide more external financing to the developing countries. This financing could be direct aid, or it could be indirect aid to international agencies.

Support Policy Reform. The industrial economies need to support the economic development of developing countries. Traditionally, the majority of United States foreign aid has been granted to achieve political aims.

Priorities for the Developing Countries

The World Bank also has a list of recommendations for the developing countries. The developing countries face the responsibility for directing their own economic development and future.

Invest in People. Governments in developing countries need to invest more in education, family planning, nutrition, and basic health care. The wealth of any nation, as Adam Smith wrote, resides in the strength and vitality of its people.

Improve the Climate for ***Free Enterprise***. Many of the price controls and other regulations that restrict the free development of markets should be removed. The World Bank suggests that competitive markets—not politicians—make the allocation decisions.

Open Economies to International Trade. Many developing economies have quotas, tariffs, and other barriers to trade that are used to protect domestic jobs and infant industries. At the same time, however, the trade barriers protect inefficient industries and hold down a country's standard of living. Countries that open their markets to the world will benefit from comparative advantage and will ultimately develop competitive specialties of their own.

Revise Macroeconomic Policies. Developing countries, like the industrialized ones, need to follow policies that curb inflation, reduce borrowing, and decrease deficits. Their policies also must allow market incentives such as profits, so that the economies can begin to sustain their own growth.

The South Korean Success Story

One of the most successful developing nations is South Korea. In the early 1950s, South Korea was one of the poorest nations in Asia. It had the highest **population density**—number of people per square mile of land area—in the world. It also had a war-torn economy that had to be rebuilt.

The South Korean government opened its markets to world trade. In addition, the government focused only on a few industries so that its people could gain experience producing and exporting for world markets. Businesses in the South Korean economy first began to produce inexpensive toys and consumer goods for the world market. Next, they moved into textiles such as shirts, dresses, and sweaters. Then they invested in heavy industry, such as shipbuilding and steel manufacturing. Later, South Korea produced consumer and electronic goods such as radios, televisions, microwave ovens, and home computers. Most recently, the country has become a leading producer of automobiles. The South Korean experience shows that a country can change a war-damaged economy to a well-developed, highly industrial one.

Source: *Economics: Principles and Practices* (Clayton)

AFTER READING

A. VOCABULARY CHECK Before discussing *ideas* in economics, it is essential to have a common vocabulary. Textbooks often highlight important new words for you. For the section your group was responsible for, go back and scan the reading for vocabulary in **bold** print. Find a bold word or phrase for the definitions below. Then share this vocabulary with a person from the other group.

Vocabulary from Section 1 (Group A)

1. the number of live births per 1,000 people ____________________
2. the average remaining lifetime in years ____________________
3. the condition in which the average number of births and deaths balance ____________________
4. money borrowed from foreign banks and governments ____________________
5. the legal or illegal export of a nation's currency and foreign exchange ____________________

Vocabulary from Section 2 (Group B)

1. important things that need to be done before other things ____________________
2. obstacles to foreign exchange ____________________
3. plans for the economy of whole countries ____________________
4. the free development of markets ____________________
5. number of people per square mile of land area ____________________

 **B. COMPREHENSION CHECK** Use your highlighted information from the reading to complete the chart for your group below. When you finish, share your information with a person from the other group. Fill in the other chart with their notes.

Ideas from Section 1 (Group A)

	Obstacles	Examples
1.		
2.		
3.		
4.		
5.		
6.		
7.		

Ideas from Section 2 (Group B)

Priorities for Industrialized Nations
1.
2.
3.
4.
Priorities for Developing Countries
1.
2.
3.
4.

Reading Strategy

Using a Table to Find Information

In some classes, such as economics, textbooks are full of tables. Often, these make clear *graphically* information that is written in the text. However, sometimes they give information that is not elsewhere in the text. You need to pay close attention to these. You may need to make inferences based on them.

C. USING A TABLE TO FIND INFORMATION The table gives two pieces of information about each country on it. Study it and then discuss the questions below with a partner.

Note: *GDP* means Gross Domestic Product. It is similar to GNP, but it includes only goods, services, and structures produced *inside* a country's borders within one year. *Per capita* means per person.

Country	GDP Per Capita	Crude Birthrate	Country	GDP Per Capita	Crude Birthrate
Luxembourg	$55,100	12.21	Angola	$1,900	45.14
Norway	37,800	11.89	Uganda	1,400	46.31
United States	37,800	14.13	Chad	1,200	46.50
Bermuda	36,000	11.83	Burkina Faso	1,100	44.46
Cayman Islands	35,000	13.11	Liberia	1,000	44.81
San Marino	34,600	10.31	Mali	900	47.29
Switzerland	32,700	9.83	Niger	800	48.91
Denmark	31,100	11.59	Afghanistan	700	47.27
Iceland	30,900	13.83	Congo, Dem. Rep	700	44.73
Austria	30,000	8.9	Somalia	500	46.04

Source: *The World Factbook* online, 2004

1. What is the crude birthrate (i.e., live births per 1,000 people) in Luxembourg? In Angola?
2. What is the GDP per person in Luxembourg? In Angola?
3. In what areas of the world are the countries with the highest GDP per capita?
4. In what area of the world are the countries with the lowest GDP per capita?
5. Which country has the lowest crude birthrate? Which has the highest?
6. Which country has the highest GDP per capita? Which has the lowest?
7. What inferences can you make from this table?

Critical Thinking Strategy

Synthesizing

Students frequently need to **synthesize** information—that is, put together information from different sources. As you read, you need to *make logical connections* with other material that you already know from your own experience, have read, or have learned from lectures in the class.

D. SYNTHESIZING In small groups, use the readings in Parts 1, 2, and 3 to answer these questions.

1. What recommendation from the World Bank did South Korea follow in order to improve its economy? (Synthesize two pieces of information from Part 3.) (2 sections, p. 104)
2. In Part 1, what obstacles is Bono trying to overcome?
3. In Part 1, what priority for developing countries is Anita Roddick focusing on?
4. What priority for developing countries is Mohammud Yunus (Part 2) focusing on in his use of microcredit?

E. PHRASES WITH PREPOSITIONS Complete the phrases in orange with prepositions. Look back at the reading on pages 101–104 to check your answers. This will help you to begin noticing phrases as you read. As you find these phrases in the reading, highlight them in the color that you use for important vocabulary.

1. Developing economies are similar __________ other economies. (Lines 1–5)
2. One obstacle __________ economic development is population growth. (Lines 5–10)
3. A shortage __________ natural and energy resources hinders growth. (Lines 20–25)
4. Not everyone is able to take advantage __________ free public education. (Lines 30–35)
5. Religious beliefs may also stand __________ the way __________ economic development. (Lines 30–35)
6. The teachings of Catholicism, Protestantism, and Judaism are much more compatible __________ the concept __________ economic growth. (Lines 40–45)
7. Some developing nations are __________ the brink __________ default. (Lines 50–55)
8. Capital flight occurs because people lose faith __________ their government. (Lines 55–60)
9. The Koreans invested __________ heavy industry. (Lines 115–119)

F. WORD JOURNAL Study the vocabulary sections before and after the readings in this chapter. Also, review the words that you highlighted in the readings. Which new words are important for *you* to remember? Write them in your Word Journal.

G. RESPONSE WRITING In your journal, write about *one* of the topics below for 15 minutes. Don't worry about grammar and don't stop writing to use a dictionary.

- your reaction to Bono's or Anita Roddick's efforts
- your reaction to the idea of microlending
- your ideas on how to eradicate poverty
- something that you learned about economics
- an obstacle to economic progress in one country that you know about
- something that one country is doing (or has done) to make economic progress

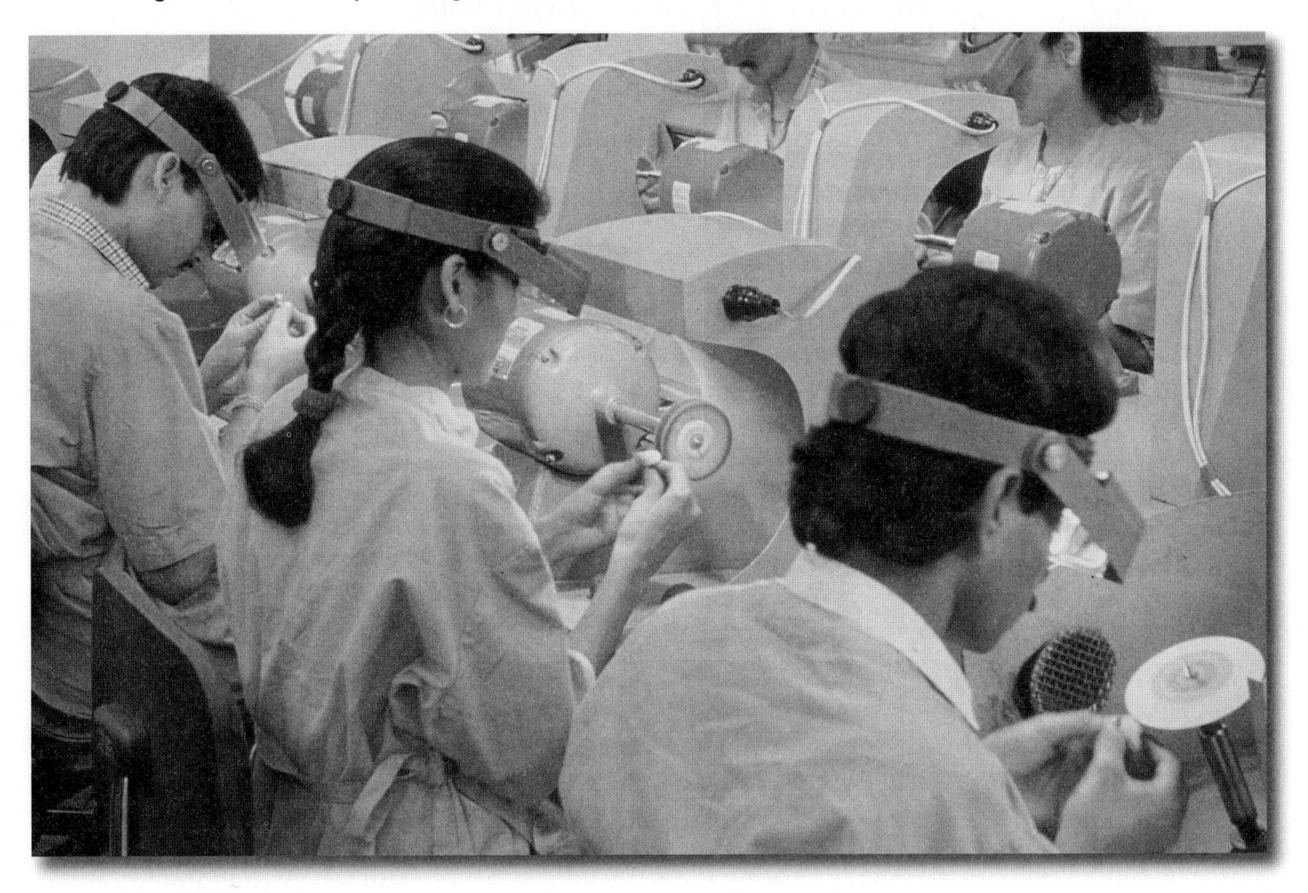

Workers in Bangalore, India

PART 4 THE MECHANICS OF WRITING

In Part 4, you will learn to use source material, find support in a source, and introduce a citation. You will also learn to quote and paraphrase, to choose the right reporting verb, and to weave in quotations. You will use this knowledge in Part 5 to write a paragraph of argument.

Using Source Material

Whenever you use the exact words or the ideas of another person in your writing, it is important to **cite** your source–in other words, to give credit to the person who first said or wrote it. If you do not cite your source, you are **plagiarizing** (stealing words or ideas), and this is a serious offense. If you use three or more consecutive words (words together) from a source, enclose them in **quotation marks**.

Example: According to the *Philadelphia Inquirer*, the disease that "has taken an unmatched toll on sub-Saharan Africa" is HIV/AIDS.

If you paraphrase, do not use quotation marks. However, you must still cite your source.

Finding Supporting Information

In most academic writing–but especially in argument or persuasive writing–it is necessary to support or give reasons for any opinion that you state. The first step is simply beginning to *notice* appropriate support in a text. As you read, highlight reasons when you find them.

A. FINDING SUPPORTING INFORMATION For each of the statements below, go to the page indicated and find a sentence that *supports* the statement. At this point, simply highlight this supporting sentence in the reading. Don't write anything.

1. It is unconscionable—and barbaric—for us to live in comfort without doing something to lift others out of poverty. (p. 89)

   ____

   ____

2. In addition to pulling hundreds of thousands of people out of poverty, the lending practices of the Grameen Bank are beginning to bring about changes in Bangladeshi family relationships. (p. 96)

   ____

   ____

3. It seems that the "usual" way of doing things hasn't done much to solve the problem of poverty; we may need to try a radical solution. (p. 96)

   ____

   ____

4. Population growth rate is related to the economic condition of a country. (p. 102)

____

____

5. Religion can play a role in a country's development—or lack of development. (p. 102)

____

____

6. Corruption among government officials contributes to slow economic development. (p. 103)

____

____

7. In their own interest, it is important for industrialized countries to help close the gap between them and the developing countries. (p. 103)

____

____

8. The World Bank recommends investing in the people in developing countries. (p. 104)

____

____

Introducing Citations

One common way to cite a quoted *sentence* of support (or a paraphrase of it) is to use one of these expressions:

According to Smith, "Nothing is possible without investment in education."

As Smith | **says,** / **points out,** / **explains,** "Nothing is possible without investment in education."

Smith | **says** / **points out** / **explains** **that** "Nothing is possible without investment in education."

Smith says that it is essential for schools to receive financial support.

In the examples above, which structures need a comma? Is there a comma after the word *that*? Which example above is a paraphrase? (How do you know?) What tense is used in the citations that have verbs?

Note on *as*: The word *as* is a subordinating conjunction. (See page 74 for the rules on how to use these conjunctions.) Do not use the word *that* in a citation with *as*. A quote or paraphrase that begins with the word *as* can only support a previous sentence.

Note on tenses: Although the present tense is most often used in citations, the *past* tense is used if the quote is a famous one, such as those on page 88.

Example: Maimonides once said that the solution was to "anticipate charity by preventing poverty."

B. INTRODUCING CITATIONS Go back to Activity A on pages 110–111. Copy the sentences of support that you highlighted from the passage. Introduce each sentence with an expression of citation from the box on page 111. Be sure to use quotation marks around words that you copy exactly.

Knowing When to Quote and When to Paraphrase

It is often a good idea to begin by *trying* to put much of your source material in your own words–that is, by paraphrasing. However, there will be many times when you think, "But these words are so *good*! It's exactly what I want to say, and I can't imagine how to put this in my own words." *This* is when you quote. In other words, quote when your source's language is distinctive or unique.

In addition, as you saw in Chapter 2 (page 79), there are some words and phrases that must be quoted because there are no good synonyms.

When you paraphrase, you still need to cite the source of the ideas.

Example: **Original:** "Yunus' method works well wherever the social life of the poor is tightly knit."

Paraphrase: Jolis explains that Yunus' microlending programs are successful in poor communities with close relationships.

C. NOTICING QUOTED MATERIAL Look back at the reading in Part 2 on pages 95–96. This was written by Alan Jolis, but he quotes from Mohammud Yunus. Find the sentences and phrases that Jolis quotes. In each case, why does Jolis quote–because Yunus' choice of vocabulary is so good (that is, his language is distinctive), because of Yunus' clarity of expression–or both?

D. USING SYNONYMS Think of other ways to express the words and phrases in orange. Share your ideas with a partner.

1. Start with a **more vigorous fight** against HIV/AIDS, which has **taken an unmatched toll on** sub-Saharan Africa's social and economic structure. The epidemic has left **untold numbers** of children without parents, households without income earners, nations without **an able-bodied workforce**. (**Source:** *The Philadelphia Inquirer*)

2. Mohammud Yunus, a 56-year-old banker from Bangladesh, is **that rare thing**: a **bona fide** visionary. His dream is the **total eradication** of poverty from the world. (**Source:** *The Independent on Sunday*, Jolis)

E. CHOOSING LANGUAGE TO QUOTE In the following excerpt from the reading on pages 101–104, highlight phrases or sentences that are special enough to quote. Also, highlight technical terms for which there are no synonyms. Do not highlight important information that you can imagine putting in your own words. Then in small groups, compare what you highlighted.

One obstacle to economic development is population growth. The populations of most developing countries grow at a rate much faster than those of industrialized countries. One reason for this growth is the high crude birthrate—the number of live births per 1,000 people.

People in many developing countries are also experiencing an increasing life expectancy—the average remaining lifetime in years for persons who reach a certain age. Longer life expectancies, coupled with a high crude birthrate, make it difficult to increase per capita GNP.

Some countries, like China, have encouraged lower birth rates and smaller families. Some people even feel that societies should work for zero population growth (ZPG)—the condition in which the average number of births and deaths balance. Others feel efforts to disrupt population growth are wrong from both moral and religious perspectives.

Source: Economics: *Principles and Practices* (Clayton)

Choosing the Right Reporting Verb

When you cite your source, there are many ways to express the verb "*says.*" The most common, other than *says*, is probably "*according to.*" You need to begin to notice these as you read academic material and include them in your own writing. Here are some other words for *says.*

acknowledge	determine	mention	recommend	urge
admit	discuss	note	remark	warn
argue	emphasize	point out	specify	wonder
ask	encourage	predict	speculate	write
assert	explain	propose	state	
conclude	express	question	stress	
deny	indicate	quote	suggest	

Examples: Perez **argues that** "something must be done–and soon."

Wong **stresses that** government policies have been insufficient.

Kim **concludes**, "Microlending has begun to change the social structures as well as the economic structures within the village."

The verbs above have slightly different meanings. As a general rule, when in doubt, use the verb *according to* or *says.* This is better than choosing an inappropriate verb.

Are there verbs on this list that you don't understand? If so, check their meaning with a dictionary.

F. CHOOSING THE RIGHT REPORTING VERB Match the situations on the left and reporting verbs on the right. Write the correct letters on the lines.

_______ **1.** a point of great importance

_______ **2.** a strong claim by the person whom you are quoting

_______ **3.** an unproven idea of the author

_______ **4.** a point of less importance

_______ **5.** a question in the mind of the author

_______ **6.** advice from the author

_______ **7.** a situation that the author accepts (but might not want to)

a. acknowledge, admit

b. argue, assert

c. ask, question, wonder

d. emphasize, stress

e. mention, note, remark

f. recommend, suggest, urge

g. speculate

G. CHOOSING THE RIGHT REPORTING VERB Circle the letters for the appropriate verbs for each item below.

1. In "A Bank for the Down and Out," Jolis ______ that the typical borrower is a woman "who has never touched money before" and who has heard throughout her life that "she is useless and a burden to the family."

Which three verbs are appropriate?

A. discusses B. explains C. points out D. notes

2. Jolis ______ that Mohammud Yunus is "a soft-spoken former professor."

Which one verb is the best in this case?

A. asserts B. emphasizes C. mentions D. stresses

3. There are actions that can be taken without simply handing out money to the poor. As Maimonides once ______, we should "anticipate charity by preventing poverty."

Which two verbs are best? (Also, why are they in the past tense?)

A. discussed B. mentioned C. recommended D. suggested

4. Many people believe that charity is the answer to poverty. However, Alan Doss, of the United Nations Development Program, ______ that handouts are *not* the answer.

Which two verbs express his strong opinion?

A. determines B. argues C. mentions D. warns

5. The economist Amartya Sen ______ that famine, the most extreme form of poverty, has never occurred in a democratic country with a free press.

Which three verbs are appropriate?

A. argues B. asserts C. concludes D. expresses

Weaving in Quotations

You will very often have to "weave" quotations into your academic writing.

Think of how a weaver includes some blue and green thread in a piece of cloth, basket, or carpet that is mainly beige. The blue and green are *woven* in. Similarly, in academic writing, the quotations are woven in. You will use your own words, a quotation, your own words, a quotation, and so on. It is almost an art form. You need to choose the right "thread" (which words to quote). Then you need to figure out how to weave this "thread" into your own words. How can you do this?

Women weaving

1. Begin by paraphrasing.
2. When there is a perfect *phrase* from your source—usually two or more words—or a *sentence*, copy it. Be sure to put quotation marks around your copied material and add the source.

Important suggestion: to make sure that your grammar and style are good, try this:

- Take out the quote marks (temporarily). Read your sentence. Is it logical and grammatical? If not, fix it. Then check the source again and *put the quote marks back in*.

The exception is on in-class essay exams. On these exams, you do not usually have access to your sources (such as your textbook), so you cannot copy anything exactly. You can only paraphrase and summarize. However, weaving in quotes is essential elsewhere.

H. ERROR ANALYSIS/EDITING Check the grammar, style, and citation of the following quotations by answering these questions. One quotation is correct. The other four are not. Find and fix the errors.

- Which one has no citation?
- Which one has an inappropriate reporting verb?
- Which one has incorrect use of the word *as*?
- Which one has a quote that doesn't really support the sentence before it?
- Which one is correct?

1. Jolis explains that unlike most banks in any country, the Grameen Bank "actively seeks out the most deprived of Bangladeshi society: beggars, illiterates, and widows."
2. The Grameen Bank is trying to address the problem of poverty by using a system of micro-credit, which "is both terribly simple and, in the field of development and aid, completely revolutionary."
3. A woman who borrows from the Grameen Bank pays the loan back in small installments. Jolis says, "She repays the loan in tiny installments."
4. Grameen Bank borrowers are not able to put up collateral for their loans. Jolis expresses that "peer pressure and peer support effectively replace collateral."
5. When people feel hopeless, the consequences can be serious. As Clayton argues that "the result can be revolution, social upheaval, and even war."

Test-Taking Strategy

Summarizing

The most common type of writing in college is probably **summarizing**. By writing a good summary of source material, you prove that you truly understand that material. You will frequently be required to summarize material on essay exams and in research papers.

Summarizing is similar to paraphrasing in that you need to rephrase information *in your own words.* The difference is that a summary is *shorter* than the original. Follow these steps to summarize written material:

1. Read the material and make sure that you understand it well.
2. Highlight the main ideas.
3. Highlight *important* details and examples in different colors.
4. Decide which details and examples are *not* important enough to include.
5. Use the same techniques that you learned on page 79; e.g., change sentence structure and find synonyms but do not change technical terms that have no synonyms.
6. If the source material includes lists of related items, think of one word or term that can substitute for the whole list.

Examples:

Instead of:		Substitute:
houses, cars, land, jewelry, art	→	assets
cows, horses, chickens, donkeys	→	farm animals

7. Take notes or make a graphic organizer.
8. As you write your summary, *do not look* at the original material. There is too much temptation to copy.
9. Write your summary in your own words.
   Your summary should be *25% of the length of the original.*

SUMMARIZING Follow the steps in the box on page 116. On another piece of paper, summarize each of the passages. The first two are from Clayton's book (Part 3). The third is from Jolis' article (Part 2).

1. Mohammud Yunus, a 56-year-old banker from Bangladesh, is that rare thing: a bona fide visionary. His dream is the total eradication of poverty from the world. "One day," he says confidently, "our grandchildren will go to museums to see what poverty was like."

   What this man has invented is called micro-credit. It is both terribly simple and, in the field of development and aid, completely revolutionary. Yunus gives loans of as little as $30 to the destitute. A typical borrower from his bank would be a Bangladeshi woman (94 percent of the bank's borrowers are women) who has never touched money before. All her life, her father and husband will have told her she is useless and a burden to the family; finally, widowed or divorced, she will have been forced to beg to feed her children. Yunus lends her money— and doesn't regret it. She uses the loan to buy an asset that can immediately start paying income—such as cotton to weave, or raw materials for bangles to sell, or a cow she can milk. She repays the loan in tiny installments until she becomes self-sufficient. Then if she wants, she can take out a new, larger loan. Either way, she is no longer poor.

2. One obstacle to economic development is population growth. The populations of most developing countries grow at a rate much faster than those of industrialized countries. One reason for this growth is the high crude birthrate—the number of live births per 1,000 people.

   People in many developing countries are also experiencing an increasing life expectancy—the average remaining lifetime in years for persons who reach a certain age. Longer life expectancies, coupled with a high crude birthrate, make it difficult to increase per capita GNP.

   Some countries, like China, have encouraged lower birth rates and smaller families. Some people even feel that societies should work for zero population growth (ZPG)—the condition in which the average number of births and deaths balance. Others feel efforts to disrupt population growth are wrong from both moral and religious perspectives.

3. Religious beliefs may also stand in the way of economic development. While almost everyone realizes that capital investment and new technologies can help economic growth, some people may not be interested for religious reasons.

   In Asia, most Hindus and Buddhists believe that life is governed by a fate called *karma*; they believe that people are caught up in an eternal cycle of life, death, and rebirth. Many Hindus believe that the eternal cycle can be broken, in part, by purifying the mind and body through living a simple lifestyle. Many Buddhists believe that the way to break the cycle is to extinguish desire and reject the temptations of the material world. Consequently, some Hindus and Buddhists have little motivation to improve their material well-being. However, other Hindus and Buddhists embrace Western concepts of economic growth.

   The teachings of Catholicism, Protestantism, and Judaism are much more compatible with the concept of economic growth and material improvement, while the Islamic world is in between the Christians and the Hindus. We must realize, however, that some cultures may not be as interested in the Western concept of economic growth and development as we imagine.

Writing Strategy

Writing a Paragraph of Argument: Cause/Effect

Many paragraphs of persuasion are also cause/effect paragraphs. That is, there are several *causes* or reasons and one effect of these. Or there are several *effects* and one cause. Look back at Chapter 1 (page 7) to review.

Exam questions that require this type of paragraph are often not in the form of a question; instead, they are frequently in the form of directions or commands.

Examples: **Explain why . . .**
Trace the causes of . . .
Give three reasons for . . .
Identify the major effects of . . .
What were four results of . . .

In your topic sentence, express your **opinion**. In the rest of the paragraph, it is important to use solid **evidence**: examples, facts, statistics, and/or the opinion of experts.

Find this evidence in sources from your class, such as your textbook or lecture notes. (Later, when you write a research paper, you will need to find sources from the library or online.) **Paraphrase** and **quote** from your sources. If the source material is long, you will also **summarize it**.

Example:

A belief in Hinduism is one cause of the slow economic development in Xenrovia. In Hinduism, some believers attempt to live simply and, as Clayton says, "extinguish desire and reject the temptations of the material world." A rejection of these temptations leads to less consumption of consumer goods. In addition, at the core of Hinduism is a belief in *karma*, or fate. Because people believe that everything in life is governed by fate, and not their own efforts, there is not much incentive to strive to overcome economic difficulties. Western economists see this as an obstacle. However, Clayton points out that "some cultures may not be as interested in the Western concept of economic development as we imagine."

Analysis: Compare the example paragraph above to the section on religion on page 102. What is quoted? What is paraphrased? Who is the source of the quotes? Why isn't the evidence summarized?

WRITING ASSIGNMENT

Write one paragraph of argument (specifically, of cause/effect) on the eradication of poverty.

STEP A. CHOOSING A TOPIC Choose *one* country, *one* of the questions below, and *one* specific topic from the bulleted list following the question.

1. What are the economic (or social) effects of:
   - microlending?
   - one person's efforts to eradicate poverty?
   - capital flight?
   - external debt?
2. What are the causes of:
   - the success of microlending?
   - economic success in one country?
   - the problem of overpopulation in many developing nations?

CHAPTER 4

The Global Economy

Discuss these questions:

- The people in the picture work for an international company. Would you like to work for an international company? Why or why not?
- What international companies are you familiar with?
- How do you think international companies help or hurt countries?

PART 1 INTRODUCTION The Global Marketplace

BEFORE READING

THINKING AHEAD In small groups, look at the **logos** (designs that represent a company, a brand, or a product) and discuss these questions.

1. Which of these logos do you recognize?
2. Have you seen an advertisement for any of these companies? If yes, was it a **print advertisement** (in a magazine or newspaper)? Was it a commercial on television? What do you remember about it? Did the advertisement have famous actors in it? Was there a special **slogan**—a saying that encourages people to remember the product—in the advertisement? Did the television commercial have a **jingle**—a song about the product? Was there any other music in the advertisement?
3. Have you seen any of these companies advertised in different countries or in different languages? If yes, how do the advertisements differ from country to country or language to language?

B. DISCUSSION In small groups, complete the chart with details of advertisements that you've seen from these companies. If you remember the advertisement in a language other than English, you can write the slogans in that language, but try to translate them into English for your group members.

Companies/ Products	Slogans	Jingles or Other Music	Famous People	Differences in Another Country or Language
McDonald's/ fast food	"I'm lovin' it."	Yes: hip-hop version of "I'm lovin' it."	Serena Williams	Yao Ming appears in ad in China
Coca-Cola/ soft drinks				
Toyota/ cars and trucks				
Nokia/ cell phones				

READING

In the following reading, don't worry about words that are new to you. Instead, try to understand the main ideas. As you read, think about the answer to this question:

• What should companies do when they want to sell products in different countries?

Lost in Translation

When companies want to sell their products globally, they must take into consideration the languages and the cultures in which they want to do business. For example, when translating product names and slogans, companies need to understand the **nuances** (slight differences in meaning) of other languages; otherwise, they risk offending potential consumers, or worse, creating a bad image for themselves. Take a look at what happens when companies *don't* do this before advertising a product in another country or culture:

Bottle of Schweppes tonic water

- The Scandinavian vacuum manufacturer Electrolux tried to sell its goods in America but didn't help itself with this slogan: "Nothing sucks like an Electrolux."
- When the Pope visited Miami, Florida, an American T-shirt maker printed shirts in both English and Spanish. But instead of "I saw the Pope," the Spanish shirts said: "I saw the potato."
- Parker Pen tried an ad campaign in Mexico that was meant to say, "It won't leak in your pocket and embarrass you." But instead—because the company mistakenly used the word "embarazar" for "embarrass"—the ads said, "It won't leak in your pocket and make you pregnant."
- In Italy, a campaign for Schweppes Tonic Water, a British soft drink, translated the name as "Schweppes Toilet Water."
- A Japanese company wanted to import the sports drink called "Pocari Sweat" to the United States, but quickly realized that it had to remove the second word from the name.
- A French company sold one of its products, a perfume called "Opium," in the United States. Some American **consumers** (customers) were offended by the product name.

Source: "You Say Potato" from *The San Francisco Chronicle* and Global Software (Taylor)

AFTER READING

A. COMPREHENSION CHECK Look back at the reading. When you find the answers to these questions, highlight them.

1. What should companies do when they want to sell products in different countries? Why?
2. Which problems resulted from not understanding the language of the country that the company wanted to market in? Which one resulted from not understanding the culture?
3. What happens when companies make mistakes such as these? Find at least one example to support your answer.
4. Compare your answers with a partner's answers. Did you highlight the same sentences?

B. VOCABULARY CHECK Look back at the reading to find the words and phrases that match these definitions. Don't use a dictionary. Numbers in parentheses refer to line numbers in the reading.

1. think about (Lines 1–5) ____________________
2. possible in the future (Lines 5–10) ____________________
3. appearance or reputation (Lines 5–10) ____________________
4. products (Lines 10–15) ____________________
5. an advertising project (Lines 15–20) ____________________
6. perspiration (Lines 20–25) ____________________
7. an addictive substance (Lines 25–28) ____________________

C. UNDERSTANDING DETAILS In small groups, discuss problems with examples of mistranslated slogans or product names in the reading. Use the graphic organizer to record your ideas.

Slogans/Products | **Problems**

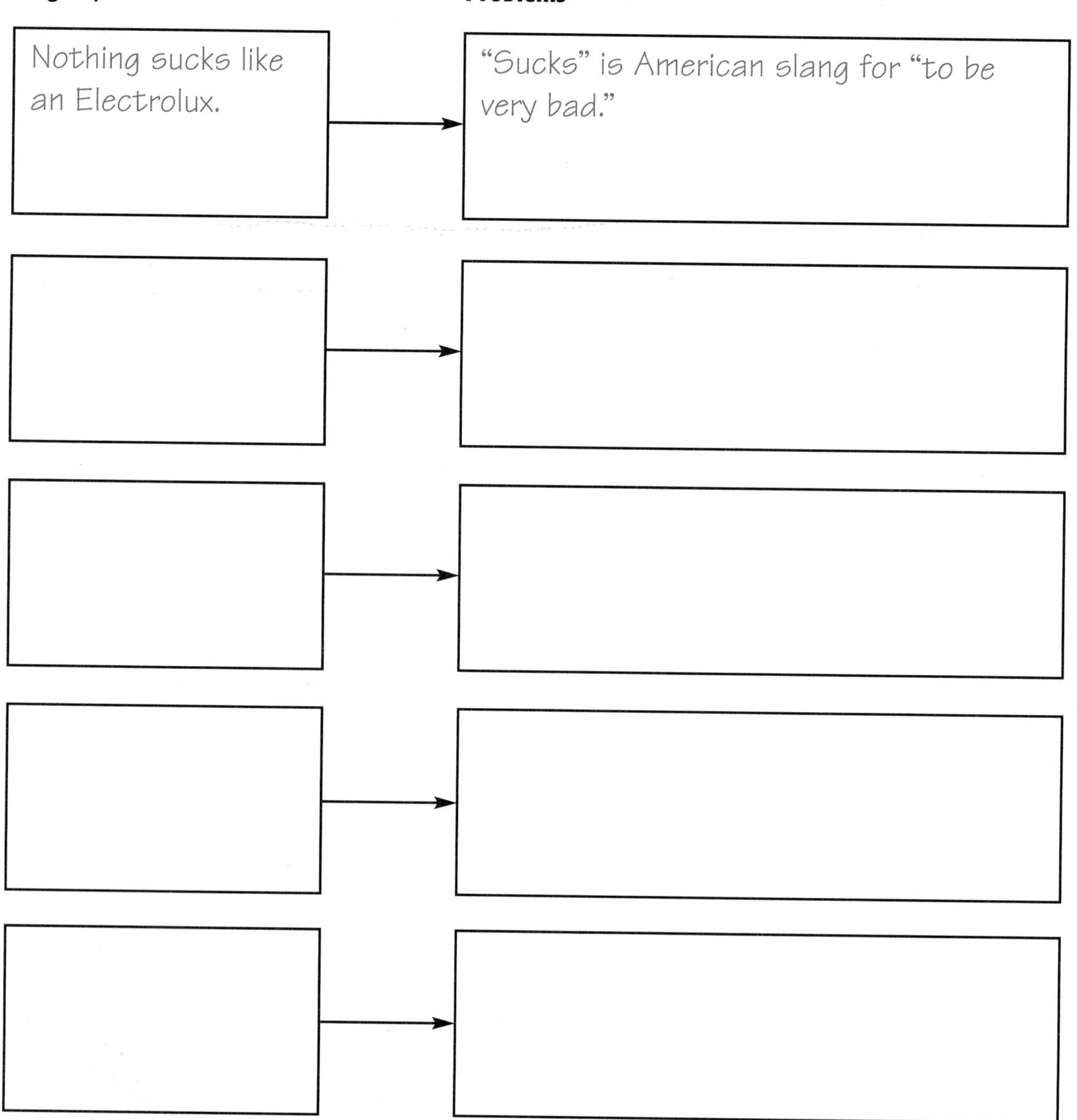

D. DISCUSSION In small groups, discuss these questions.

1. How could the companies in the reading have avoided problems that they had with ad slogans and product names?
2. Has an ad slogan ever made you want to buy a product? If yes, which one and why? Has a slogan ever made you *not* want to buy a product? If yes, which one and why?
3. How do you make buying decisions?
4. Do you think about where a product is manufactured before you buy it? Does the **country of origin** (the country from which it came) make any difference to you?

PART 2 GENERAL INTEREST READING
Skills for the Global Marketplace

BEFORE READING

THINKING AHEAD In small groups, discuss these questions.

1. What are the most important skills to have if you want to work for an international company?
2. How important are language skills in the global marketplace? What languages are important to know for today's global marketplace?

READING

Read the passage without using a dictionary. As you read, highlight main ideas with one color, important details with another, and examples with a third. Highlight important vocabulary with a fourth color. As you read, think about the answer to this question.

- For what two reasons might companies want employees who are **bilingual** (speak two languages)?

Skills for the Global Marketplace

More Companies Recruit Bilingual Employees

Whether it's *parlez-vous français, habla español,* or *você fala português,* more American companies want to recruit and hire bilingual employees. Several factors contribute to this trend, but there are two primary reasons for the increased need to recruit multilingual employees. There is a growing immigrant population in the 5 United States that is not fluent in English, and American companies are becoming more global—expanding their operations overseas, which requires employees to speak another language.

"Over the past two to three years, we have seen an increase in companies asking us for employees that have a language besides English," says Teresa Setting, vice 10 president, recruiting and retention, at Troy, Michigan-based Kelly Services, a temporary employment and staffing firm. "We're finding that more companies are becoming global, and, as the U.S. population diversifies, companies want to market to these ethnic groups."

As requests for bilingual employees grow, demand is primarily increasing within 15 the pharmaceutical, life sciences, technology, and financial services sectors for managerial candidates with bilingual skills, according to Chris van Someren, president of global markets at Los Angeles-based Korn/Ferry International, which specializes in executive recruitment. This need can be attributed to the increasing global presence of U.S. companies. More American firms have divisions or 20 manufacturing facilities overseas.

In the United States, the greatest need for bilingual employees is occurring in the consumer services sector in such areas as banking, retailing, and telecommunications.

Within these industries, bilingual employees are needed to fill positions such as call or customer service center personnel, receptionists and secretaries, and medical and legal administrative staff.

A call center

Customer Assistance Employees

"The majority of our bilingual staffing needs are for customer call centers," says Jeanne Pardo, regional director for south Florida at Atlanta-based Randstad North America, an employment services firm. "Depending on the call center, 15 to 20 percent of a center's staff is working in a bilingual capacity."

The need for bilingual customer assistance workers in the United States can vary depending on what area of the country a company serves. In general, Spanish is the most highly requested language, due to the 40 million-plus Latino population, which is still growing. However, there is an increasing need for Chinese and Vietnamese on the West Coast. In addition, there's an increased need for French and Portuguese on the East Coast, due to increasing populations of Haitians and many African immigrants (who speak French) and Brazilians (who speak Portuguese). At the managerial level, if a company requests that a candidate have foreign language skills, Western European languages, such as French and German, still remain desirable, van Someren says. Japanese also is requested at times.

"[However,] Spanish is usually the first choice for companies requesting a bilingual employee," says Luis Rodriguez, branch manager at Manpower, Inc. "And as the Hispanic population grows, there is, and will continue to be, a need for Spanish-speaking employees."

Source: *Employment Management Today* (Teixeira)

Microsoft's Call-center Business in India Gets an American Accent

BANGALORE, India — Indians working at Microsoft's new call center in Bangalore may sound a bit like they're from Seattle.

For the past year, the center's 350 employees have been taught to speak more like Americans by Seattleite (a person who lives in Seattle) Andrea Koehler, a former University of Washington language instructor, who is part of Microsoft's training team.

During a six-week language program, Koehler teaches the "technical-support professionals" to speak in a way that's clearer and easier to understand by U.S. customers who call for help with their Microsoft products.

India and the surrounding area

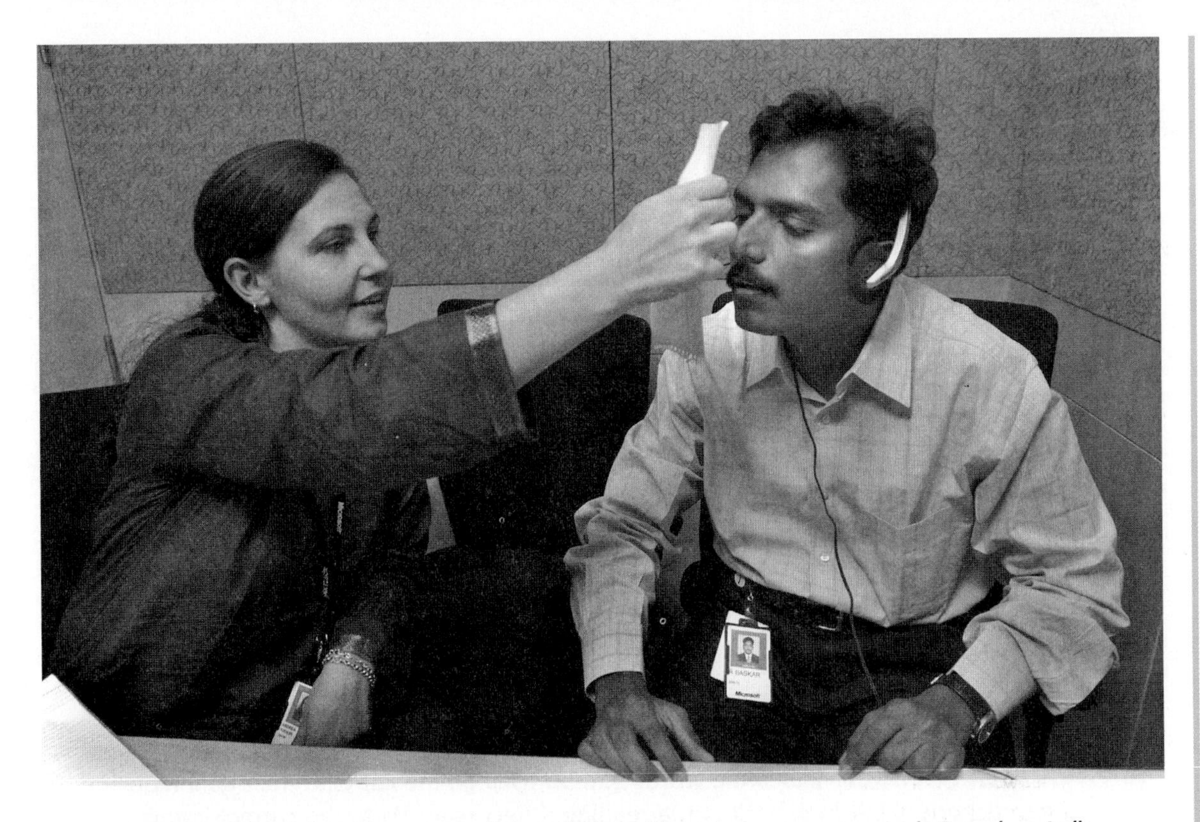

Andrea Koehler works with a new employee at Microsoft's customer support center in Bangalore, India

They also receive training in popular culture and current events to improve their
65 conversational skills.

Koehler likes the workers to listen to National Public Radio (NPR) and watch Ken Burns documentaries. But the workers prefer to get their U.S. culture from action movies such as *Independence Day* and sitcoms like *Friends*. In the end, they get a mix of things they'll enjoy watching and things that Koehler and Microsoft want them to
70 learn.

"It comes out more even, so somebody in North America is able to easily understand them," she said. "In the language group, our goal customer is the person in middle America that's never really spoken to anyone with an accent before. As long as they can understand them and deal with them without having any problem, we're O.K."

75 Koehler, who received a master's degree in linguistics from the UW in 1999, previously worked with Microsoft immigrant employees in Redmond (Washington) who took night classes to improve their English-speaking skills.

Koehler said the workers' Indian accent never goes away, but she does hear echoes of NPR in their language sometimes. "What you end up hearing is they're given the
80 tools to turn the accent on and turn it off, which is a really wonderful skill because they get on the phone and put their phone voice on," she said. "They're able to interact that way."

Source: *The Seattle Times Online* (Dudley)

AFTER READING

A. COMPREHENSION CHECK Discuss the questions with a partner. Refer to your highlighted words and sentences.

1. What are two reasons that U.S. companies might want employees who are bilingual?
2. According to the first section, which kinds of companies operating overseas have an increased need for employees with bilingual skills?
3. Which kinds of companies operating *within* the United States need employees with bilingual skills, according to the first section?
4. What is the most highly requested language for call center employees in the United States, according to the first section?
5. According to the second section, what are four ways that employees in Microsoft's Bangalore call center learn about U.S. culture?
6. Why do employees in Microsoft's Bangalore call center need to improve their speaking skills? Describe a typical call center customer.

B. VOCABULARY CHECK Match the words and phrases on the left with their definitions on the right. Don't use a dictionary, but look back at the reading if necessary. Write the correct letters on the lines.

______	**1.** be attributed to	**a.** communicate with
______	**2.** deal with	**b.** do and then stop doing
______	**3.** diversifies	**c.** people who are being considered for jobs as managers
______	**4.** interact	**d.** people who give help with technical problems
______	**5.** managerial candidates	**e.** be a result of
______	**6.** multilingual	**f.** supplying employees
______	**7.** recruit	**g.** work with
______	**8.** retention	**h.** parts; segments
______	**9.** sectors	**i.** look for in order to hire
______	**10.** staffing	**j.** keeping employees at a company
______	**11.** technical support professionals	**k.** speaking several languages
______	**12.** turn (something) on and off	**l.** varies; includes a variety

C. WORDS WITH MULTIPLE DEFINITIONS Read the sentences below. For each word in orange, choose the appropriate dictionary definition. Write the number of the definition on each line.

cul • ture \kŭl` tshər\ *n.* [Middle English, from Latin *cultura*] **1 :** cultivation, tillage **2** the act of developing intellectual and moral faculties, especially by education **3 :** expert care and training <*beauty* ~> **4 a :** enlightenment and excellence of taste acquired by intellectual and aesthetic training **b :** acquaintance with and taste in fine arts, humanities, and broader aspects of science **5 a :** the customary beliefs, social forms, and material traits of a racial, religious or social group **b :** the set of shared attitudes, values, goals, and practices that characterizes a company or corporation **6 a :** a cultivation of living material in prepared nutrient media **b :** a product of such cultivation

_______ **1.** Employees at Microsoft's Bangalore call center enjoy their work because of the opportunities offered by the corporate **culture**.

_______ **2.** The **culture** of roses requires time and patience to get the best results.

_______ **3.** Brad studied early Mayan **culture** in his anthropology course last semester.

_______ **4.** One of the technician's duties in the lab was the **culture** of cells in a Petri dish.

Critical Thinking Strategy

Evaluating Sources

Journalists (magazine and newspaper writers) quote and paraphrase people they've interviewed for a story in order to make the story more believable. These people are called "sources." When journalists mention sources, they include the sources' name and facts about their background.

Sources' background information (for example, their profession, the company they work for, or their educational background) should indicate that they are qualified to support the reporter's story.

When you find sources in an article, notice their qualifications and the facts or ideas that their words support. This helps you decide if the information in the article is valid.

D. EVALUATING SOURCES Answer these questions about the sources in the first section of the reading (pages 127–128).

1. What are Teresa Setting's qualifications (Lines 5–15)? ______________________________

____

What fact in the article does Teresa Setting's quote support? (Lines 1–5) ______________

____

2. Who is Chris van Someren (Lines 15–20)? ______________________________

____

What fact does the reporter attribute to this source? (Lines 15–20) ______________

____

3. What are Jeanne Pardo's qualifications (Lines 30–35)? ______________________________

____

Why did the reporter quote her? ______________________________

____

E. CITING SOURCES Look back at the second section of the reading. Which sources are quoted directly? Which source's words are paraphrased? Which reporting verbs has the writer used?

F. IN YOUR OWN WORDS: SUMMARIZING Choose one of the sections of the reading. Fill in the first blank with the topic of the section. Use a noun or noun phrase. Fill in the second blank with the main idea. Complete the sentence with an independent clause.

1. The article is about ____.
2. The author says that ____

____.

G. APPLICATION Imagine that you have hired a group of Indian call center employees to work with customers from your native language or culture. What should they know about your culture? What TV shows or movies should they see? What radio programs should they listen to? What should they read? In small groups, brainstorm a list of things they should know and ways that they can acquire this knowledge. Share your ideas with your class.

H. MAKING CONNECTIONS In small groups, use the reading in Parts 1 and 2 to discuss these questions.

- Are you planning a career in international business?
- If yes, how might your knowledge of a second language help you in your career?
- If no, how might knowledge of a second language help you in other ways?

PART 3 ACADEMIC READING International Trade

BEFORE READING

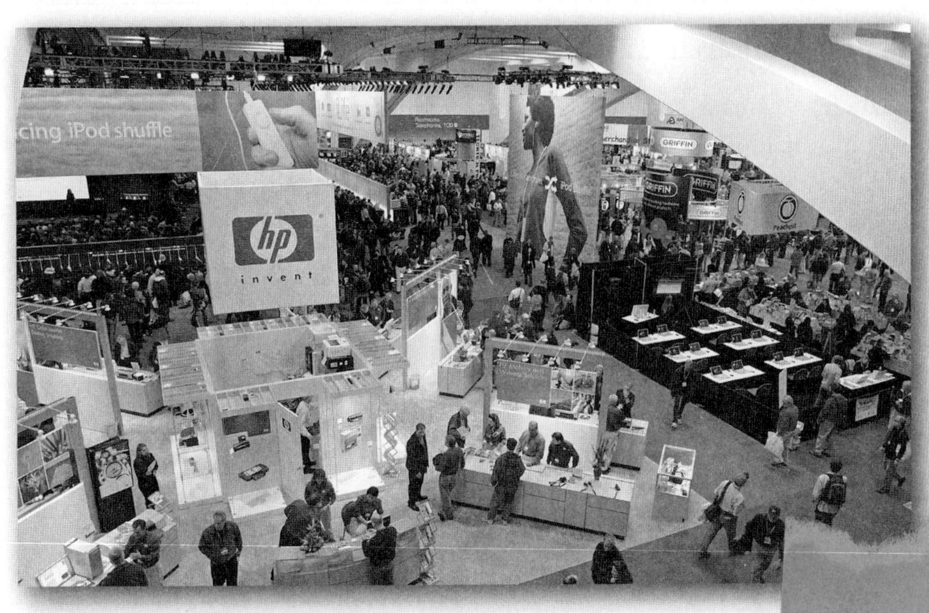

At this international trade show, various countries display their consumer electr

A. THINKING AHEAD In small groups, discuss these questions.

1. What would life be like if we did not have international trade? Would you miss anything? What are some necessary materials a country couldn't survive without?
2. What are some products countries specialize in producing? Why do they specialize in these products?
3. Why do some people object to international trade? What is your opinion?
4. In your opinion, is it good or bad for countries to be dependent on each other for supplies such as food, oil, and weapons?
5. Do you think any industries should be protected from foreign competition? Why or why not?
6. What is your opinion of a company moving its factories to another country because workers in that country earn less? (In other words, manufacturing expenses are lower.)

B. VOCABULARY PREPARATION Read the sentences on pages 134 and 135. The words in orange are from the next reading. Try to guess their meanings from the context.

- First, circle the part of speech—noun (n), verb (v), or adjective (adj). If it is a phrase, is it a *noun* phrase, *verb* phrase, or *adjective* phrase.
- Then write your guess.
- If you are very unsure of your guess, check a dictionary to see if your guess was close. To save time, do the third step with a small group. Divide the group of words; each person will look up several words and then share the answers.

Parts of Speech

1. Without international trade, Americans wouldn't be able to buy **exotic** products such as Chinese herbs. n v adj

   Guess: ______________________________

   Dictionary Definition: ______________________________

2. Without trade, **essential raw materials** such as industrial diamonds wouldn't be available to tool manufacturers. n v adj

   Guess: ______________________________

   Dictionary Definition: ______________________________

3. Some countries have **revenue** taxes—taxes intended to increase their income. n v adj

   Guess: ______________________________

   Dictionary Definition: ______________________________

4. For many years, Xenrovia **undersold** Rexnovia in the automobile industry. This ruined the car industry in Rexnovia because consumers preferred the lower-priced Xenrovian models. n v adj

   Guess: ______________________________

   Dictionary Definition: ______________________________

5. Xenrovia **levied** a tax on all cheese that was imported into the country. Xenrovia charged this fee in order to help protect its own cheese-producing industries. n v adj

   Guess: ______________________________

   Dictionary Definition: ______________________________

6. Some countries have developed large **armament** industries so that they will have enough weapons if war breaks out. n v adj

   Guess: ______________________________

   Dictionary Definition: ______________________________

7. The electronics industry is **crucial** to national defense; without it, a country wouldn't be able to develop effective weapons. n v adj

   Guess: ______________________________

   Dictionary Definition: ______________________________

8. Although international trade has many benefits, some people object to it because it can **displace** groups of workers. It is not unusual to hear workers in one country say they lost their jobs due to unfair foreign competition. n v adj

Guess: ____________________

Dictionary Definition: ____________________

9. There is an enormous **volume** of trade between the United States and Xenrovia. The amount indicates that trade between the two countries is beneficial. n v adj

Guess: ____________________

Dictionary Definition: ____________________

10. In the 1990s, limits **were imposed on** steel imports in Xenrovia. They placed these limits in order to protect jobs in the steel industry. n v adj

Guess: ____________________

Dictionary Definition: ____________________

C. PREVIEWING: USING HEADINGS Look over the reading on pages 136–141 very quickly. Notice that it has headings that are in three different sizes. There are two sections, and each section has two headings, one larger and one smaller. On a separate piece of paper, answer the questions about the headings.

1. What are the two sections?
2. What are the two larger-sized headings in Section 1?
3. How many smaller-sized headings are there in Section 1?
4. What are the two larger-sized headings in Section 2?
5. How many smaller-sized headings are there in Section 2?
6. Now, make a guess about the information that the reading might contain.

READING

The textbook passage in this chapter may seem very long to you, but it is just part of one chapter from a textbook. It is short in comparison to the amount of reading that you will need to do in school. Most college students are required to read several hundred pages each week. This reading will give you a preview of a typical assignment. The reading should be done for homework—not in class.

Read through the passage without using a dictionary. As you read, highlight main ideas with one color, important details with another, and important vocabulary with a third.

As you read, think about the answers to these questions:

- Why is international trade necessary?
- What are some of the pros and cons of international trade?
- This reading was written for students in one particular country. What country is it?

International Trade

SECTION 1—ABSOLUTE AND COMPARATIVE ADVANTAGE

The key to trade—whether among people, states, or countries—is specialization.

Some people specialize in cutting hair. Others specialize in fixing computers. These people exchange their services for money, which they then use to buy the specialized goods and services they need from others.

Different regions of a country specialize in certain economic activities in much the same way. New York, for example, is the center of the U.S. financial industry, and Detroit specializes in automobiles. The Midwest and High Plains areas are known for wheat farming. Texas is recognized for oil and cattle, while Florida and California are famous for citrus fruit. All of these states trade with one another so that people in one area can consume the goods and services that workers in other areas offer.

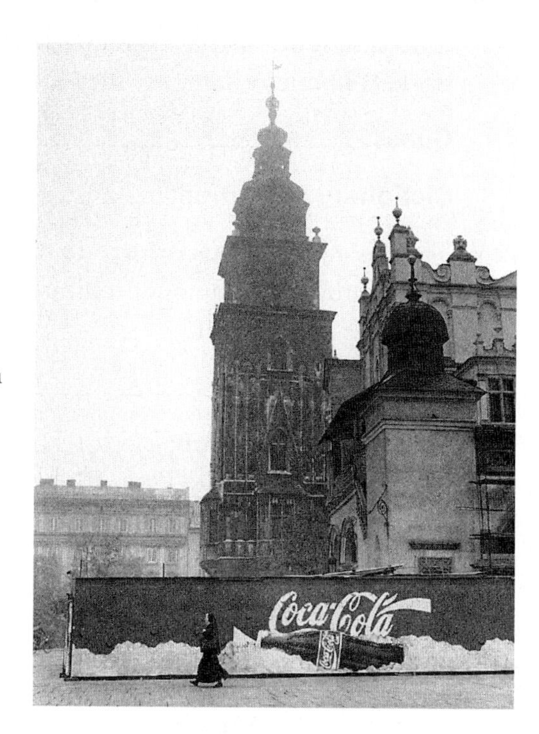

Coca-Cola ad in Moscow, Russia

If you want to find out what a country specializes in, look at its **exports**—the goods and services that it produces and then sells to other nations.

The U.S. and International Trade

International trade is important to all nations. Most of the products exchanged are goods, although services, such as insurance and banking, are being bought and sold in increasing numbers.

In the United States for example, **imports**—goods and services that one country buys from other countries—amounted to about $1,590 billion in 2003. This number corresponds to nearly $5,460 for every person in the country, and it has grown steadily over the years. Figure 4.1 shows the merchandise trade patterns for the United States and the rest of the world. As large as these numbers are, they would be even bigger if we counted the values of services in addition to the **merchandise**, or goods, shown in the figure. The sheer volume of trade between nations of such different geographic, political, and religious characteristics is proof that trade is beneficial.

In fact, nations trade for the same reasons that individuals do—they trade because they believe that the products they receive are worth more than the products they give up.

The United States exports merchandise all over the world. The biggest trade imbalance for the U.S. is with Japan, followed by Western Europe and Canada.

Without international trade, many products would not be available on the world market. Bananas, for example, would not leave Honduras, nor would coffee beans leave Colombia or Brazil. Some people think of international trade as a way to obtain exotic products, but trade

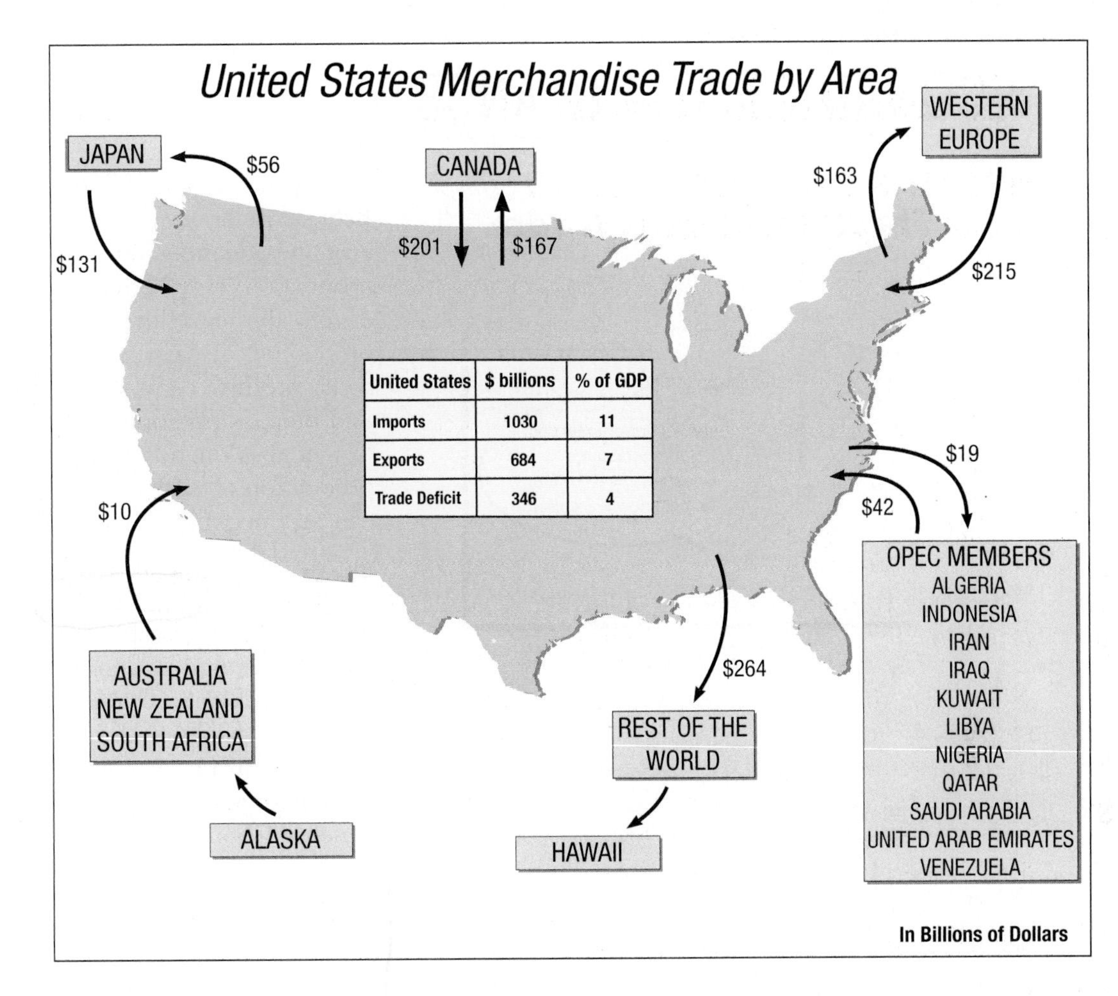

Figure 4.1: United States Merchandise Trade by Area

is much more than that. Many imports are necessities such as crude oil, clothing, and shoes. In the United States, many minerals, metals, and raw materials that are not available must be imported.

The Basis for Trade

In many cases, it may be cheaper for a country to import a product than to manufacture it. This becomes clear when we examine the differences between absolute and comparative advantage.

ABSOLUTE ADVANTAGE

A country has an **absolute advantage** when it can produce a product more efficiently (i.e., with greater output per unit of input) than can another country. Consider, for example, the case of two countries—Alpha and Beta—which are the same size in terms of area, population, and capital stock. Only their climate and soil fertilities differ. In each country, only two crops can be grown—coffee and cashew nuts.

If Alpha and Beta each specializes in the product it can produce relatively more efficiently, total output for both countries goes up. After specialization, each country would trade its surplus production with its neighbor.

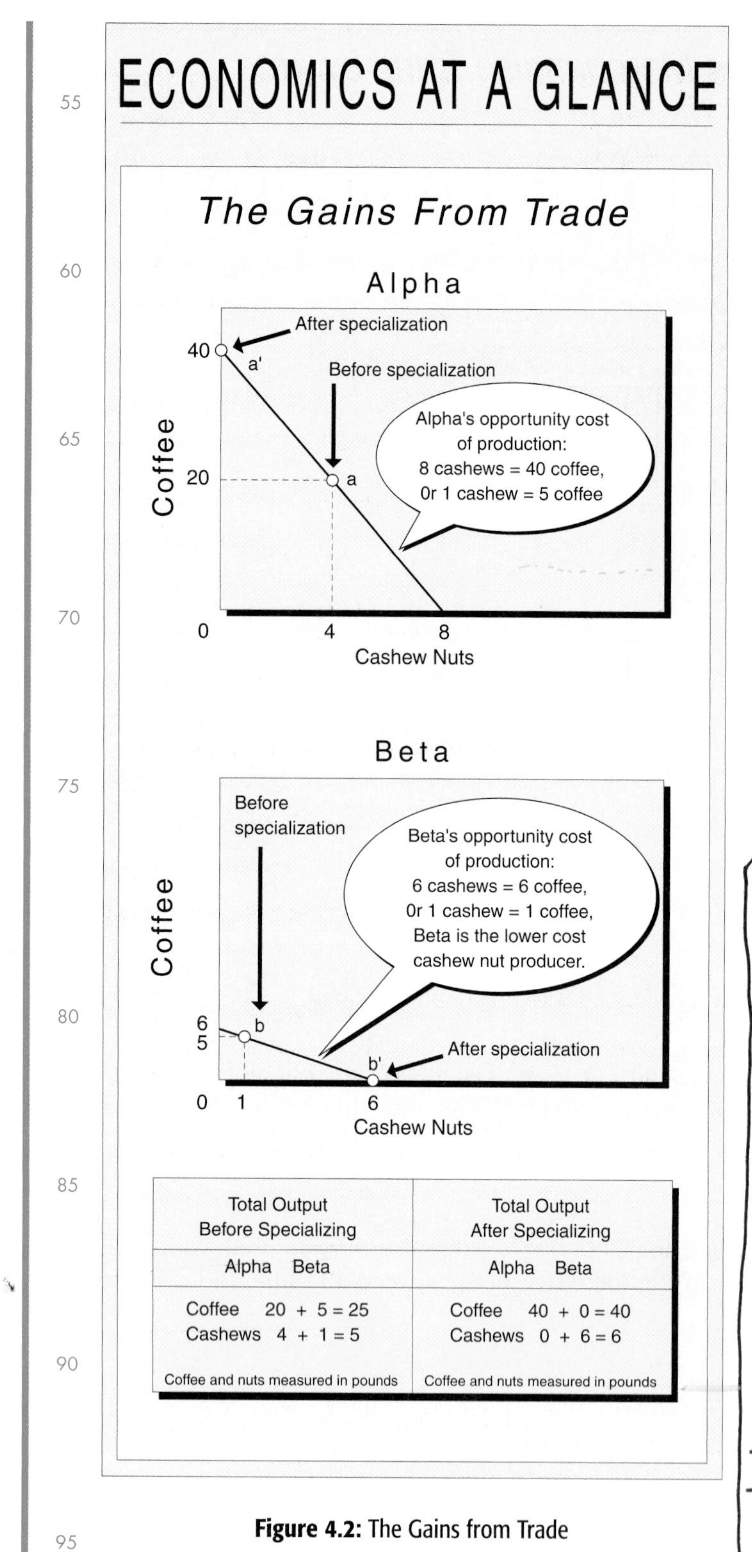

Total Output Before Specializing	Total Output After Specializing
Alpha Beta	Alpha Beta
Coffee 20 + 5 = 25 Cashews 4 + 1 = 5	Coffee 40 + 0 = 40 Cashews 0 + 6 = 6
Coffee and nuts measured in pounds	Coffee and nuts measured in pounds

Figure 4.2: The Gains from Trade

Figure 4.2 shows the production possibilities for Alpha and Beta. Note that if both countries devote all of their efforts to producing coffee, Alpha could produce 40 million pounds and Beta six million—giving Alpha an absolute advantage in the coffee production. However, if both countries devote all their efforts to the production of cashew nuts, Alpha could produce eight million pounds and Beta six million. Alpha, then, also has an absolute advantage in the production of cashew nuts because it can produce more than Beta.

For years, people thought that absolute advantage was the basis for trade because it enabled a country to produce enough of a good to consume domestically as well as to export. The theory of absolute advantage did not explain how a large country could trade with a small country to the benefit of both.

COMPARATIVE ADVANTAGE

Even when one country enjoys an absolute advantage in the production of all goods, trade between it and another country is still beneficial if one country can produce a product relatively more efficiently. The more efficient country has a **comparative advantage** in the production of a good if it can produce that good at a relatively lower opportunity cost.

Alpha, for example, has a comparative advantage in the production of coffee. Given a fixed amount of resources, it can produce relatively more coffee than nuts. If Alpha were to specialize in the production of one good, it would choose coffee beans.

Beta, however, does a relatively better job of producing cashew nuts. Its comparative advantage in cashew nuts would lead Beta to specialize in their production.

THE GAINS FROM TRADE

100 The concept of comparative advantage is based on the assumption that everyone will be better off producing the products they produce relatively best.

This concept applies to individuals, companies, states, and regions as well as to nations. The final result is that specialization and trade increase total world output, just as in the case of Alpha and Beta.

105 This explains the nature of trade between the United States and a country such as Colombia. The United States has excellent supplies of iron and coal. It also has the capital and the labor that are needed to produce tractors and farm machinery efficiently. Colombia, in contrast, does not have as much capital or skilled labor. It does, however, have the land, labor, and climate to produce coffee efficiently. Because the United States has a comparative 110 advantage in the production of farm machinery, it will trade these products for Colombian coffee. Because Colombia has a comparative advantage in the production of coffee, it will export coffee and import farm equipment.

SECTION 2—BARRIERS TO INTERNATIONAL TRADE

Although international trade can bring many benefits, some people object to it because it can displace selected industries and groups of workers in the United States.

Restricting International Trade

115 Historically, trade has been restricted in two major ways. One is through a **tariff**—a tax placed on imports to increase their price in the domestic market. The other is through a **quota**—a limit placed on the quantities of a product that can be imported.

TARIFFS

Governments levy two kinds of tariffs—protective and revenue. A **protective tariff** is a tariff high enough to protect less-efficient domestic industries. Suppose, for example, that it 120 costs $1 to produce a mechanical pencil in the United States. The exact same product, however, can be imported for 35 cents from another country. If a tariff of 95 cents is placed on each imported pencil, the cost climbs to $1.30—more than the cost of the American-made one. The result is that a domestic industry is protected from being undersold by a foreign one.

The **revenue tariff** is a tariff high enough to generate revenue for the government 125 without actually prohibiting imports. If the tariff on imported mechanical pencils were 40 cents, the price of the imports would be 75 cents, or 25 cents less than the American-made ones. As long as the two products are identical, people would prefer the imported one because it was less expensive—so the tariff would raise revenue rather than protect domestic producers from foreign competition.

QUOTAS

130 Foreign goods sometimes cost so little that even a high tariff on them may not protect the domestic market. In such cases, the government can use a quota to keep foreign goods out of the country. Quotas can even be set as low as zero to keep a product from entering the country. More typically, quotas are used to reduce the total supply of a product to keep prices high for domestic producers.

135 In 1981, for example, domestic automobile producers faced intense competition from lower-priced Japanese automobiles. Rather than lower their own prices, domestic manufacturers wanted President Ronald Reagan to establish import quotas on Japanese cars. The Reagan administration told the Japanese to voluntarily restrict auto exports, and they

reluctantly agreed. As a result, Americans had fewer cars from which to choose, and the prices of all cars were higher than they would otherwise have been.

During the Bush administration in the early 90s, "voluntary" import quotas were imposed on steel. The quotas protected jobs in the domestic steel industry, but at the cost of higher steel prices for the rest of the country. A trade crisis emerged in mid-1977 when charges of **dumping**, or selling products abroad at less than it cost to produce them at home, were levied against Russia and Japan.

Arguments for Protection

Freer international trade has been a subject of debate for many years. Some people, known as **protectionists**, favor trade barriers that protect domestic industries. Others, known as **free traders**, favor fewer or even no trade restrictions. The debate between the two groups usually centers on the five arguments for protection discussed below.

NATIONAL DEFENSE

The first argument for trade barriers centers on national defense. Protectionists argue that without trade barriers, a country could become so specialized that it would end up too dependent on other countries.

During wartime, protectionists argue, a country might not be able to get critical supplies such as oil and weapons. As a result, even some smaller countries such as Israel and South Africa have developed large armament industries for such crises. They want to be sure they will have a domestic supply if hostilities break out or other countries impose economic boycotts.

Free traders admit that national security is a compelling argument for trade barriers. They believe, however, that the advantages of having a reliable source of domestic supply must be weighed against the disadvantages that the supply will be smaller and possibly less efficient than it would be with free trade. The political problem of deciding which industries are crucial to national defense and which are not must also be considered. At one time, the steel, auto, ceramic, and electronics industries all have argued that they are critical to national defense and so should receive protection.

INFANT INDUSTRIES

The **infant industries argument**—the belief that new or emerging industries should be protected from foreign competition—is also used to justify trade barriers. Protectionists claim that these industries need to gain strength and experience before they can compete against developed industries in other countries. Trade barriers would give them the time they need to develop. If infant industries compete against foreign industries too soon, they argue, they might fail.

Many people are willing to accept the infant industries argument only if protection will eventually be removed so that the industry is forced to compete on its own. The problem is that industries used to having some protection are normally unwilling to give it up—making for difficult political decisions later on.

To illustrate, some Latin American countries have used tariffs to protect their own infant automobile industries, with tariffs as high as several hundred percent. In some cases, the tariff raised the price of used American-made cars to more than double the cost of new ones in the United States. In spite of this protection, no country in Latin America has been able to produce a competitive product on its own.

PROTECTING DOMESTIC JOBS

A third argument—the one used most often—is that tariffs and quotas protect domestic jobs from cheap foreign labor. Workers in the shoe industry, for example, have protested the import of lower-cost Italian, Spanish, and Brazilian shoes. Garment workers have opposed the import of lower-cost Korean, Chinese, and Indian clothing. Steelworkers have blocked foreign-made cars from company parking lots to show their displeasure with the foreign-made steel used in producing the cars.

In the short run, protective measures provide temporary protection for domestic jobs. This is especially attractive to people who want to work in the communities where they grew up. In the long run, however, industries that find it hard to compete today will find it even harder to compete in the future unless they change the way they are doing things. As a result, most free traders believe that it is best not to interfere, and thereby keep pressure on threatened industries to modernize and improve.

When inefficient industries are protected, the economy produces less and the standard of living goes down. Because of unnecessarily high prices, people buy less of everything, including those goods produced by protected industries. If prices get too high, substitute products will be found and protected jobs will be lost. Free traders argue that the profit-and-loss system is one of the major features of the American economy. Profits reward the efficient and hard-working, while losses eliminate the inefficient and weak.

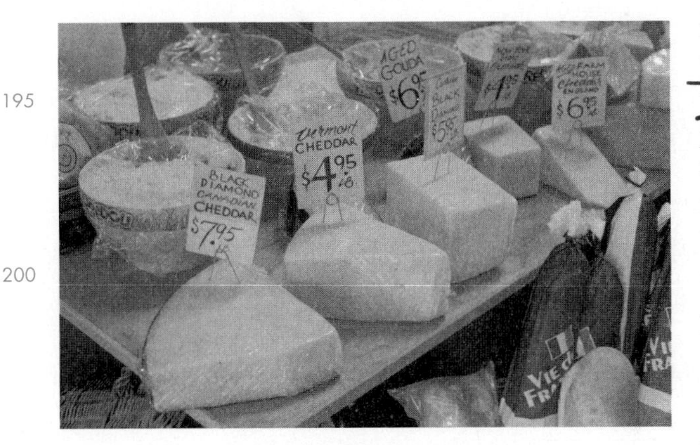

Protectionism vs. Free Trade
Free Traders argue that reducing tariffs and quotas allows consumers to choose from a variety of both domestic and foreign products.

KEEP THE MONEY AT HOME

Another argument for trade barriers claims that limiting imports will keep American money in the United States instead of allowing it to go abroad.

Free traders, however, point out that the American dollars that go abroad generally come back again. The Japanese, for example, use the dollars they receive for their automobiles to buy American cotton, soybeans, and airplanes.

These purchases benefit American workers in those industries. The same is true of the dollars used to buy oil from the Middle East. The money comes back to the United States when oil-wealthy foreigners buy American-made oil technology. Keeping the money home hurts those American industries that depend on exports for their jobs.

HELPING THE BALANCE OF PAYMENTS

Another argument involves the **balance of payments**—the difference between the money a country pays out to, and receives from, other nations when it engages in international trade. Protectionists argue that restrictions on imports help the balance of payments by restricting the amount of imports.

What protectionists overlook, however, is that the dollars return to the United States to stimulate employment in other industries. As a result, most economists do not believe that interfering with free trade can be justified on the grounds of helping the balance of payments.

Source: *Economics: Principles and Practices* (Clayton)

AFTER READING

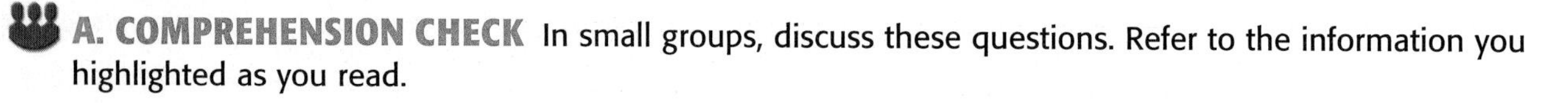

A. COMPREHENSION CHECK In small groups, discuss these questions. Refer to the information you highlighted as you read.

1. Why is international trade necessary?
2. What are some of the pros and cons of international trade?

B. VOCABULARY CHECK Textbooks often highlight important new words for you. Look back and scan the reading on pages 136–141 for economics vocabulary in bold. Find a word or phrase for each definition below.

1. what a country has when it can produce a given product more efficiently than another country can

   ____

2. what a country has if it can produce a good at a relatively lower cost than another country

   ____

3. a tax placed on imports to increase their price in the domestic market

   ____

4. limits placed on the quantities of a product that can be imported

   ____

5. a tariff that is high enough to protect domestic industries that are less efficient than others

   ____

6. a tariff that is designed to raise money

   ____

7. selling products abroad at less than it costs to produce them at home

   ____

8. people who favor trade barriers that protect domestic industries

   ____

9. people who favor fewer or even no restrictions on trade

   ____

10. the belief that new or emerging industries should be protected from foreign competition

    ____

11. the difference between the money paid to and received from other nations

    ____

Reading Strategy

Providing Definitions and Examples to Check Understanding

A good way to check your understanding of new concepts as you read is to define them in your own words and to provide examples for them. The examples can be from the text or from your own experience. Graphic organizers are one way to record your definitions and examples.

Example:

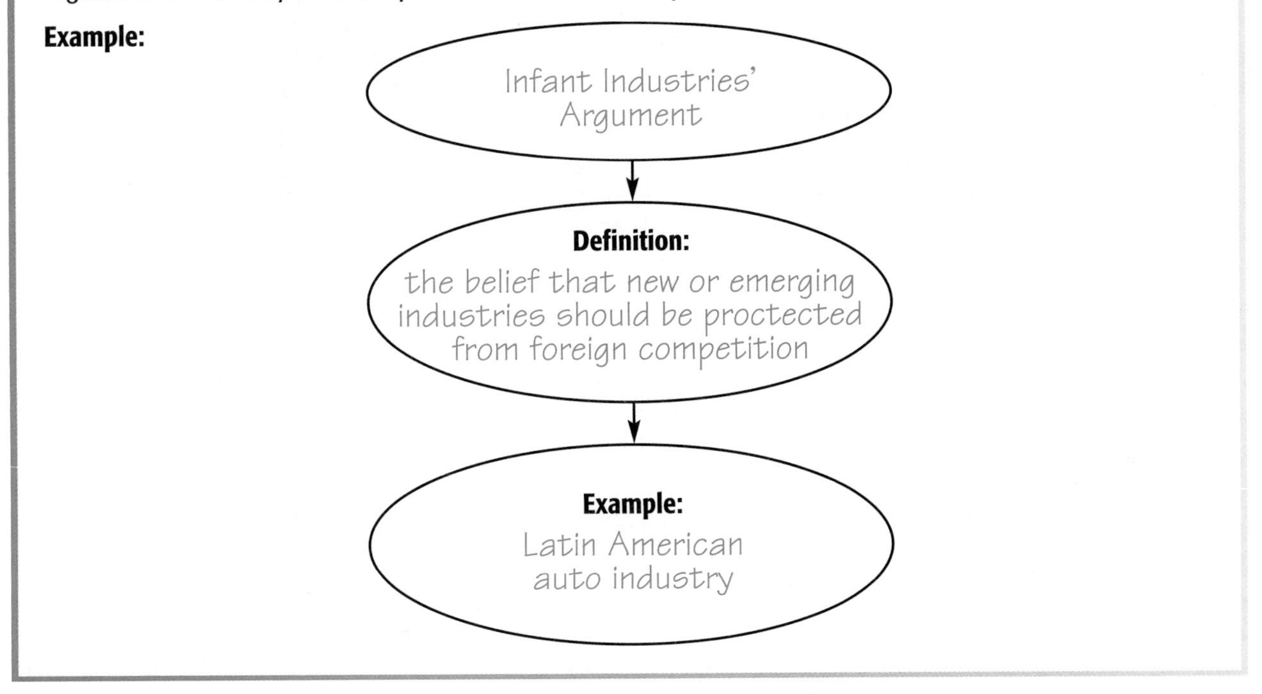

C. PROVIDING DEFINITIONS AND EXAMPLES TO CHECK UNDERSTANDING Complete the graphic organizers to explain the difference between **absolute** and **comparative advantage**.

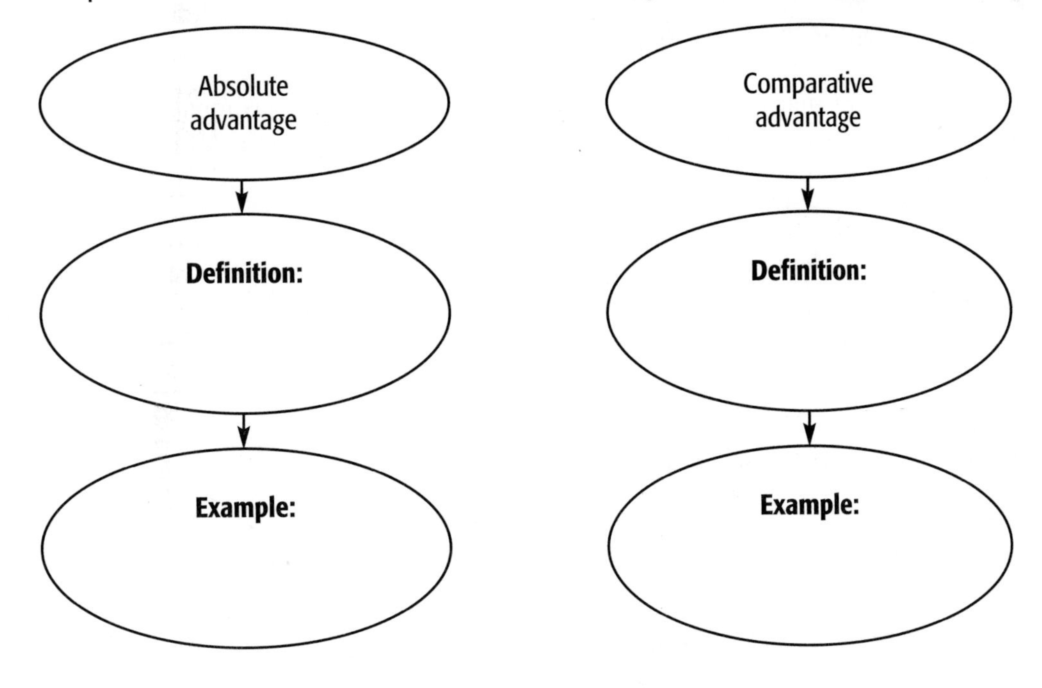

D. DISCUSSION In small groups, discuss these questions.

1. How involved in world trade is the United States? Give examples.
2. Describe a situation in which a country that you are familiar with might have an absolute advantage over another country in the production of a good.
3. Explain how comparative advantage can make trade possible between countries of different sizes.
4. Name three barriers to international trade.
5. Paraphrase the five protectionist arguments.

Reading Strategy

Summarizing Your Reading

In Chapter 3, you learned how to write a summary. You will often be required to summarize material on essay exams and in research papers. However, writing summaries for yourself is also an excellent way to understand and retain the ideas in the material. You may want to summarize an entire chapter, or just parts that you think you will need to use later. Summarizing is also a good way to collect information that you may need for a writing assignment because it allows you to paraphrase someone else's ideas.

To write you own summaries on material that you are reading, follow the same steps that you learned on page 116 in Chapter 3.

E. SUMMARIZING YOUR READING On a piece of paper, write a summary of the section "Arguments for Protection" on pages 140–141. Follow the steps outlined on page 116 of Chapter 3.

Note: This will help you with your writing assignment in Part 5.

F. APPLICATION In small groups, discuss these questions.

1. Think of a project that you recently completed with a friend or classmate. How could you have completed the project more efficiently by applying the principle of comparative advantage? Explain.
2. You have just started a business manufacturing toothbrushes. Would you favor a quota on imported toothbrushes? Why or why not?

G. PHRASES WITH PREPOSITIONS Complete the phrases in orange with prepositions. Look back at the reading on pages 136–141 to check your answers. As you find these phrases in the reading, highlight them in the color that you use for important vocabulary.

1. Different regions of a country **specialize** ____________ **certain economic activities.** (Lines 5–10)
2. For years, people thought that absolute advantage was **the basis** ____________ **trade.** (Lines 65–70)
3. A large country can trade with a small one ____________ **the benefit** ____________ **both.** (Lines 75–80)
4. Some people **object** ____________ **international trade** because it can displace workers. (Lines 110–115)
5. Historically, trade has been **restricted** ____________ **two major ways.** (Lines 115–120)
6. A quota is a limit **placed** ____________ **the quantities** ____________ **a product** that can be imported. (Lines 115–120)
7. Governments can use quotas **to keep foreign goods** ____________ ____________ **the country.** (Lines 130–135)
8. The first argument for trade barriers **centers** ____________ **national defense.** (Lines 145–150)
9. Sometimes **the advantages must be weighed** ____________ **the disadvantages.** (Lines 155–160)
10. Keeping the money home hurts those industries that **depend** ____________ **exports** ____________ **their jobs.** (Lines 210–215)

H. WORD JOURNAL Study the vocabulary sections before and after the readings in this chapter. Also, review the words that you highlighted in the readings. Which new words are important for *you* to remember? Write them in your Word Journal.

I. RESPONSE WRITING In your journal, write about *one* of the topics below for 15 minutes. Don't worry about grammar and don't stop writing to use a dictionary.

- Describe your favorite imported products. Why do you like them? (Is it because the country you live in doesn't produce them as well as other countries? Is it because it doesn't produce them at all?)
- Does it matter to you where products come from? Why or why not?
- Should a country be able to sell its products wherever it wants? Why or why not?

PART 4 THE MECHANICS OF WRITING

In Part 4, you will learn to use present unreal conditionals, conditionals with *without*, and transitions of cause and effect. You will use this knowledge in Part 5 to write a paragraph of argument about free trade.

Present Unreal Conditional

You can express a present unreal conditional to tell a reader *what would happen* if a certain condition existed. A conditional statement consists of an *if*-clause and a main clause.

Examples: **If** international trade **didn't exist**, many products **wouldn't be** available on the world market. (= International trade exists, so many products are available on the world market.)

If Xenrovia **had** an agreement with its neighbor, the two countries **could trade** goods and services. (= Xenrovia doesn't have an agreement with its neighbor, so the two countries can't trade goods and services.)

The formula for this kind of sentence is:

If-clause in the past tense + main clause with *would/could* (*not*) + simple form of the verb.

You can switch the order of the two clauses.

Examples: Many products **wouldn't be** available on the world market **if** international trade **didn't exist**.

Xenrovia and its neighbors **could** trade goods and services if the two countries **had** an agreement.

A sentence in the present unreal conditional appears to be in the past tense, but the meaning is present. Notice that the conditional is opposite the real situation. In other words, a negative clause in the conditional indicates an affirmative meaning in the real situation; an affirmative conditional clause indicates a negative meaning in reality.

A. PRESENT UNREAL CONDITIONAL Complete the following sentences to create present unreal conditionals. Use general knowledge, personal opinion, or information from the readings in this chapter.

1. If international trade didn't exist, I could not buy strawberries in the middle of winter.
____.

2. If war broke out in my country, ____
____.

3. Selling products overseas would be easy if ____
____.

4. If I spoke ____________________ [fill in the blank with a language that you do not speak],
____
____.

5. I could get a job with an international corporation if ____

____.

6. If companies learned about the nuances of the culture in which they want to sell products, ________

____

____.

7. If Nike manufactured shoes in the United States instead of in Vietnam, ________________________

____

____.

8. If Xenrovia didn't have a revenue tariff on imported tomatoes, ______________________________

____.

9. According to protectionists, if we didn't have trade barriers, _______________________________

____.

10. Infant industries wouldn't be able to compete against developed industries if ________________

____

____.

Conditionals with *Without*

Another way to express a present unreal conditional is to replace a negative *if*-clause with a *without*-clause.

Examples: *If* international trade **did not exist**, many products **would not be** available on the world market. =

Without international trade, many products **would not be** available on the world market.

If the concept of comparative advantage **did not exist**, countries of different sizes **couldn't trade** with each other. = *Without* comparative advantage, countries of different sizes **couldn't trade** with each other.

Notice that the *if*-clauses in both examples are negative; you use *without* with only a negative condition.

Notice that the main clause structure is the same, but in the *without*-clause, there is a phrase instead of a clause. That is, there is no verb in a phrase, so you don't have to worry about the tense.

B. CONDITIONALS WITH *WITHOUT* You can transform many negative *if*-clause statements into *without* statements to vary your writing. Practice this by transforming the following sentences. Rewrite each sentence so that it begins with a *without* + noun phrase. To do so, you may have to add or take away words from the *if*-clause.

1. If we didn't have trade barriers, a country could become too specialized and dependent on other countries.

   Without trade barriers, a country could become too specialized and dependent on other countries.

2. If we didn't have a revenue tariff on imported tomatoes, we couldn't protect domestic producers from foreign competition.

   ____

3. If we didn't have quotas on steel imports, domestic steelworkers would lose their jobs.

   ____

4. If we didn't have intense competition, prices would be much higher.

   ____

5. If the advertising agency didn't have multilingual employees, the agency wouldn't be able to produce ads that work in different countries.

   ____

6. If we didn't protect infant industries, they wouldn't be able to compete against foreign imports.

   ____

Transition Expressions of Cause and Effect: Review of Coordinating, Adverbial, and Subordinating Conjunctions

In Chapter 1 (pages 33 and 35), you learned how to use coordinating and adverbial conjunctions. Here are those conjunctions that express a cause and effect relationship.

Coordinating	**Adverbial**	
so (= that's why)	therefore	
for (= because)	consequently	
	as a result	(= so)
	for this reason	
	thus	

Examples: Historically in Xenrovia, inefficient industries were protected, **so** the economy produced less and the standard of living went down.

Historically in Xenrovia, inefficient industries were protected; **thus,** the economy produced less and the standard of living went down.

In Chapter 2 (pages 73–74) there was an explanation of subordinating conjunctions of contrast. Here are subordinating conjunctions that express a cause and effect relationship. Notice the punctuation in the examples.

Subordinating

because

since

as

Examples: Xenrovia's economy produced less and the standard of living went down **because** infant industries were protected.

Because infant industries were protected, Xenrovia's economy produced less and the standard of living went down.

Transitions Followed by Phrases

If the cause or reason is a noun or noun phrase (instead of a clause as in the examples above), use *due to*, *because of*, or *as a result of*.

cause

Examples: **Due to** negative reactions from consumers, *Pocari Sweat* changed its name in the United States.

Pocari Sweat changed its name in the United States **due to** negative reactions from consumers.

cause

C. TRANSITION EXPRESSIONS OF CAUSE AND EFFECT Fill in the blanks with some of the transition conjunctions from the box. Don't use the same expression more than once.

Note: This activity will give you additional information on international trade.

Subordinating Conjunctions		Adverbial Conjunctions	
as	due to	as a result	for this reason
because	since	as a result of	therefore
because of		consequently	thus

Tariffs During the Great Depression

In 1930, the United States passed the Smoot-Hawley Tariff, one of the highest in history. It set import duties so high that the price of many imported goods rose nearly 70 percent. Because (1) other countries did the same, international trade nearly came to a halt.

Before long, most countries realized that high tariffs hurt more than they helped. for this reason (2), in 1934, the United States passed the Reciprocal Trade Agreements Act, which allowed it to reduce tariffs up to 50 percent if other countries agreed to do the same. The act also contained a **most favored nation clause**—a provision allowing a country with such an agreement to receive the same tariff reduction that the United States negotiates with a third country.

Suppose, for example, that the United States and China have a trade agreement with a most favored nation clause. If the United States then negotiates a tariff reduction with a third country, the reduction would also apply to China. This clause is very important to a foreign country because (3) its goods will then sell at a lower price in the American market.

The World Trade Organization

In 1947, 23 countries signed the General Agreement on Tariffs and Trade (GATT). The GATT extended tariff concessions and worked to do away with import quotas. Later, the Trade Expansion Act of 1962 gave the President of the United States the power to negotiate further tariff reductions. As a result of (4) this legislation, more than 100 countries had agreed to reduce the average level of tariffs by the early 1990s.

Most recently, the GATT was replaced by the **World Trade Organization (WTO)**—an international agency that administers previous GATT trade agreements, settles trade disputes between governments, organizes trade negotiations, and provides technical assistance and training for developing nations.

________________ (5) the fact that so many countries have been willing to reduce tariffs and quotas under GATT and the WTO, international trade is flourishing. Tariffs that once nearly doubled the price of many goods now increase prices by a small percentage, while other tariffs have been dropped altogether. ________________ (6), stores are able to offer a wide variety of industrial and consumer goods from all over the world.

Source: *Economics: Principles and Practices* (Clayton)

D. ERROR ANALYSIS/EDITING Find and correct the error in each sentence. It is either an error with the present unreal conditional, conditionals with *without*, or with a transition expression of cause and effect.

1. If we don't have intense competition, prices would be much higher.
2. Indian call center employees could get a higher salary if they study American culture and conversation techniques.
3. Because of American TV programs such as *Friends* contain a lot of cultural information, some call center employee-training courses in India use them.
4. Without international trade did not exist, many products would not be available on the world market.
5. The manufacturers of *Opium* perfume did not adequately analyze American culture. As a result of they offended some American consumers.
6. James can get a job with Electrolux if he spoke Swedish.

Writing Strategy

Writing a Paragraph of Argument: Inductive Reasoning

One way to organize a paragraph of argument in a way that will appeal to and convince your readers is to use **inductive** reasoning.

With inductive reasoning, you start with the specific and move to the general. You begin with specific examples or observations—evidence—regarding your topic, and then draw a conclusion from them. The statement of your conclusion becomes your topic sentence. It is the *last* sentence in your paragraph.

One way to work through the inductive process is to ask yourself a question (which will not appear in your paragraph), answer the question with your evidence—several specific examples or observations—and then reach a conclusion based on the evidence.

Example: Question: Is it important to know a second language if you're considering a career in business?

Evidence: Example 1: InterMedia interviewed two prospective employees with the same qualifications; the one who spoke a second language was hired.

Example 2: Studies show that at companies with global operations, managers who speak a second language are paid on average 15 percent more than monolingual managers at the same level.

Example 3: According to Bob Grabowski of Sunnyside Staffing in Denver, CO, there has been a 10 percent jump in requests from corporations for bilingual staff in the last year.

Conclusion: It's important to know a second language if you're considering a career in business.

Note: You can further convince your readers by citing reliable sources in your examples.

Your topic sentence must:

- be an opinion, not a fact
- be arguable (an idea that you can support with reasons)
- be limited enough to deal with in a single paragraph
- deal with a single point

Example:

Earlier this year, InterMedia Corporation interviewed two candidates for the position of global marketing manager. Both candidates had identical qualifications: MBAs and at least five years' experience in the field. However, one was bilingual and the other wasn't. InterMedia hired the bilingual candidate. A recent survey of companies with global operations such as InterMedia revealed that managers who speak a second language are paid an average of 15 percent more than monolingual managers at the same level. In addition, Bob Grabowski of Sunnyside Staffing in Denver, CO, reported in the March 2007 issue of *Staffing Magazine* that his company has received a 10 percent jump in requests from corporations for bilingual staff just in the last year. These examples show that now more than ever, it's important to be able to speak and read a second language if you're considering a career in business.

Analyze the example paragraph. Does it move from general to specific or specific to general evidence? What source does the writer cite? What is the topic sentence?

WRITING ASSIGNMENT

Write one paragraph of argument either for or against free trade. Use inductive reasoning.

STEP A. CHOOSING A TOPIC First, decide if you are a protectionist (against free trade) or a free trader (for free trade).

Next, choose one of the five arguments from the reading that you will use to support your position:

- national defense
- infant industries
- protecting domestic jobs
- keeping the money at home
- helping the balance of payments

Test-Taking Strategy

Taking a Side

In academic writing in English, you often have to take a side or a position on an arguable issue. When you take an essay exam, you need to decide your position quickly and under pressure. In this case, it's a good idea to choose the side that is the easiest to argue. The side that is easiest to argue may be the one for which you can remember the most evidence, the more popular side, or the side that you've recently read about. This means that you won't necessarily choose the side that you truly believe in. This will help you save valuable time in a test-taking situation.

TAKING A SIDE Choose sides on the following issues. Time yourself: take one minute or less for each choice. For each statement, circle *Agree* or *Disagree*. Then working with a partner, explain why you chose the side that you did and how you might argue it.

1. Companies should not have overseas call centers.

   Agree **Disagree**

2. College students should be required to prove that they can speak at least one foreign language in order to graduate.

   Agree **Disagree**

3. Watching television is the best way to learn a second language.

   Agree **Disagree**

4. Controlling population growth in order to end poverty is wrong.

   Agree **Disagree**

5. Poor nations should not be relieved of their debts to foreign banks and governments.

   Agree **Disagree**

STEP B. GATHERING MATERIAL For this assignment, you will gather material from two sources—the readings in Parts 1, 2, and 3 and your own experience. In small groups, list the arguments for or against international trade. Fill in the chart below. Refer to the reading on pages 136–141 and your own background knowledge. Then with your group members, try to think of a real-life example for each argument. This makes your argument more convincing. Think of examples from your country or any country that you are familiar with.

HW: info from readings

Arguments	Examples: In Favor of Free Trade	Examples: Against Free Trade
Protecting Domestic Jobs	Car prices in Xenrovia went down in the 1990s.	In the 1980s, Xenrovian autoworkers lost their jobs because of car imports.

Now that you've looked at the arguments on both sides, what is your opinion of free trade? Has it changed? Discuss your before and after opinions with the group and talk about why your opinion has or hasn't changed.

Writing Strategy

Providing Evidence

In any argument paragraph, you must support your position with evidence, or proof. Evidence can be facts, statistics, or examples; you've used these in previous assignments. Evidence can also take the form of a narrative, or story, that illustrates your position. You can also use a combination of evidence types.

Always choose evidence from reliable, authoritative sources. For example, which of the following statements is more believable? Why?

- Companies that spend money on culture and language training for call center employees have higher revenues than those that don't.
- Bernadette Schwartz, a professor of business at Harper University, concluded from her 2007 study of Internet service providers that those who invested in language and culture training for their call center employees had 32 percent higher revenues than those providers who did not.

Regardless of type or source, evidence must always be accurate, up to date, and typical—that is, it is found in a variety of circumstances, not just one.

STEP C. ORGANIZING YOUR INFORMATION Now that you have a position, an argument, and have discussed several examples, choose the evidence that will work best for your paragraph. On a separate piece of paper, write notes (not complete sentences) on the evidence that you will use to support your position. Make sure that your evidence follows the guidelines in the box above.

STEP D. WRITING THE PARAGRAPH Write complete sentences in paragraph form. Use inductive reasoning. If you copy anything, be sure to quote and cite your source. Be as specific as possible. You might make some mistakes, but don't worry about them at this point.

STEP E. EDITING Read your paragraph and answer these questions.

1. Is the paragraph form correct (indentation, margins)?
2. Have you used inductive reasoning? That is, have you started with specific examples and concluded with a statement of your opinion?
3. Is the topic sentence the last one? Is it an opinion? Does it deal with a single point?
4. Have you provided good evidence?
5. If anything is copied, is the source cited correctly? Is the punctuation correct? Is the reporting verb an appropriate one?
6. If anything is quoted, was it well chosen (in other words, difficult to paraphrase well)?
7. Is sentence structure correct (no fragments)?

STEP F. REWRITING Write your paragraph again. This time, try to write without the mistakes.

UNIT 2 VOCABULARY WORKSHOP

Review vocabulary items that you learned in Chapters 3 and 4.

A. MATCHING Match the definitions to the words. Write the letters on the lines.

Words	**Definitions**
______ **1.** burden	**a.** a time in which many people die of hunger
______ **2.** capital	**b.** number of live births per 1,000 people
______ **3.** crude birthrate	**c.** not repay borrowed money
______ **4.** default	**d.** a tax on imports
______ **5.** destitute	**e.** remove completely
______ **6.** diversifies	**f.** money to begin a business
______ **7.** eradication	**g.** complete removal
______ **8.** extinguish	**h.** people who favor few or no trade restrictions
______ **9.** famine	**i.** very, very poor
______ **10.** free traders	**j.** varies; includes a variety
______ **11.** revenue	**k.** something heavy that must be carried
______ **12.** tariff	**l.** income

B. PHRASES USING PREPOSITIONS Write the correct prepositions.

1. an obstacle ____________ economic development

2. a shortage ____________ natural and energy resources

3. stand ____________ the way ____________ economic development

4. compatible ____________ the concept ____________ economic growth

5. ____________ the brink ____________ default

6. specialize ____________ certain economic activities

7. object ____________ international trade

8. ____________ the benefit ____________ both

9. centers ____________ national defense

10. depend ____________ exports ____________ their jobs

C. THE ACADEMIC WORD LIST The words in the box below are from the Academic Word List (Appendix 3, pages 313–316). They are some of the most common *academic* words in English. Write the words from the box on the correct lines. When you finish, check your answers in the readings on the page numbers in parentheses.

attributed	**crucial**	**fluctuations**	**interact**	**sectors**
barriers	**displace**	**imposed**	**quota**	**volume**

1. ____________________ in a person's income can be a problem because if it's high one year and low the next, it's difficult to make a budget.

2. A government is imposing a ____________________ when it places a limit on the quantities of a product that can be imported.

3. If Xenrovia allows steel imports, it may ____________________ many workers in that industry.

4. There is a large ____________________ of trade between the two countries; the amount indicates that both countries are benefiting.

5. Protectionists want limits to be ____________________ on trade, while free traders are against putting restrictions on trade.

6. Many experts believe that ____________________ to trade should be lifted because they believe that economies are healthier when there are no restrictions.

7. In the past, steel was ____________________ to Xenrovia's defense industry; today, it is less critical and therefore is no longer protected.

8. Call center employees need to learn how to ____________________ over the phone because it's quite different from face-to-face communication.

9. In the financial and technical ____________________ of the economy, one finds a lot of bilingual workers because businesses in these areas tend to deal more with international customers.

10. The need for bilingual workers can be ____________________ to the globalization of business.

D. VOCABULARY EXPANSION Your vocabulary will grow faster if you learn different parts of speech when you learn a new word. Use a dictionary to find the different parts of speech for each word in the chart.

	Verbs	Nouns	Adjectives
1.	eradicate	eradication	eradicated
2.	stabilize	(2 possible)	
3.		fluctuation	
4.			displaced
5.	recruit		
6.		allocation	
7.			imposed
8.	purify		

UNIT 3

LITERATURE

Chapter 5
The Nature of Poetry

Chapter 6
Heroes in Literature

CHAPTER 5

The Nature of Poetry

Discuss these questions:

- This man is a poet. How might he get his ideas?
- What makes a poem good?
- Do you like poetry? Why or why not?

PART 1 INTRODUCTION Poetry Lessons

BEFORE READING

A. THINKING AHEAD In small groups, look at the pictures and discuss these questions.

1. From the students' body language, can you tell which students seem interested and which seem bored?
2. In the second picture, how might the teaching methods differ from those of the first picture?
3. What kind of class is most difficult for you—a science class or a humanities class (art, literature, philosophy, etc.)?
4. Have you ever taken a poetry class? If so, how did the instructor teach the class? Did you have to memorize and **recite** poetry out loud? Did you have to study and **analyze** poetry?
5. Why might science classes be difficult for many humanities students?
6. Why might humanities classes be difficult for many science students?
7. If you enjoy poetry, what do you like about it? If you don't enjoy poetry, what don't you like about it?

Reading Strategy

Choosing the Correct Dictionary Definition: Using Parts of Speech

Many words in English have more than one part of speech and more than one meaning. Frequently, as you are reading, you'll find a word that you know, but it doesn't seem to make sense. In such a case, the word probably has a meaning that you don't know. If you can't figure out the meaning from the context, you'll need to use a dictionary. However, the dictionary may have several definitions for one word. How do you know which definition is the one you are looking for? One way to choose the correct definition is to match the part of speech of the unknown word and the definition.

B. CHOOSING THE CORRECT DICTIONARY DEFINITION Read the sentences below. Decide if each word in orange is a noun or a verb. Write the part of speech on the line. Then use the dictionary entries to choose the best definition for the context.

paper *n* **1** material made from wood, used for writing on **2** a newspaper **3** a report or long piece of writing done for school

paper *v* to cover walls with wallpaper

1. The president's speech is in all the **papers** today.

Part of Speech: ______________________________

Definition: ______________________________

2. We **papered** the room in light yellow.

Part of Speech: ______________________________

Definition: ______________________________

3. I had to write three **papers** for my poetry class.

Part of Speech: ______________________________

Definition: ______________________________

course *n* **1** direction or movement **2** a set of lessons; a class

course *v* (of liquid) to move quickly

4. They took a literature **course**.

Part of Speech: ______________________________

Definition: ______________________________

5. A river **coursed** through the town.

Part of Speech: ______________________________

Definition: ______________________________

6. We couldn't predict the **course** of the discussion.

Part of Speech: ______________________________

Definition: ______________________________

7. Jill has a lovely face.

Part of Speech: ______________________

Definition: ______________________

8. I get nervous when I have to face a blank page.

Part of Speech: ______________________

Definition: ______________________

face *n* **1** the front of the head **2** the top of most important part of something *(the face of a clock)*

face *v* **1** to point forward **2** to meet something difficult

9. Linda fielded several questions.

Part of Speech: ______________________

Definition: ______________________

10. Steve's field is engineering, but he also likes the humanities.

Part of Speech: ______________________

Definition: ______________________

field *n* **1** land on a farm **2** a branch of knowledge or study

field *v* **1** to catch or stop a ball **2** to answer questions successfully

READING

In the reading, try to guess the meaning of new words. The reading is about an experiment in which science and engineering professors spent a week taking poetry classes taught by English professors. As you read, highlight the answer to this question:

• What did the science and engineering professors learn about teaching?

Poetry Lessons

There were familiar sounds the first day of class: nervous coughs, creaking chairs, shuffling feet, scratching pens, and crackling notebook pages. Unspoken questions hung in the air: What am I doing here? What does the professor expect? How much time will this take?

5 But this was no ordinary class. The 14 students who came together were all science or engineering professors at Cornell University (in New York). They had interrupted their research to accept an invitation to participate in an unusual experiment: "an interesting week of poetry." This class was part of a study to answer several questions: Why is science difficult for many non-science students? Why do physical science and 10 engineering students have trouble with literature courses? What can teachers learn about teaching if they take a class that is not in their field?

The students in the poetry class listened to lectures and took notes. They had reading assignments and had to write three short papers. They also took notes on things that they enjoyed, things that were difficult, and the teaching style. All students noticed one 15 thing—the importance of spoken words. In science and engineering classes, the instructors put tables, diagrams, and mathematical formulas on the blackboard. But in this poetry class, the instructors just *talked*. They didn't write anything on the board. Also, discussions in the poetry class followed unpredictable courses.

Initially, the scientists and engineers "seemed bewildered . . . by the variety of responses you can make to a poem," says Stephen Parrish (one of the instructors, a member of Cornell's English Department). "It isn't like using a formula. You can look in various places for the essential statement a poem makes, or you can be persuaded that it doesn't make a statement at all or that it makes contradictory statements." The apparent lack of focus and the absence of clear-cut answers was frustrating for some participants.

Then the day came when the students had to face a blank sheet of paper and write their first essay. It was difficult and took a lot of time. It also took a lot of time for the instructors to correct the papers. In science classes, the instructors usually just circle right answers or make Xs. But the poetry instructors wrote detailed notes and opinions.

The scientists and engineers noticed one similarity between science and poetry. In both subjects, students need to find layers of meaning. Some layers are simple, clear, and on the surface; other layers are deeper and more difficult. This search for different levels of meaning doesn't happen much in *undergraduate* science classes, but it is important later, in graduate school. And it is always important in literature.

Both the poetry instructors and their students—the scientists and engineers—learned something about teaching from this experience. One poetry instructor, for example, now sees the importance of using careful, clear definitions when he explains a poem. He also plans to be more precisely informative about social and linguistic history as he teaches. Most of the scientists agreed on several points. First, humanities classes might help science students to see patterns and decide which information is important and which isn't important. Second, the poetry class was *fun*. One engineer decided, "We need to change the way we teach engineering to make it an enjoyable experience for students."

But perhaps the most important result of the experience was this: All of the professors began to think about how they teach and how they can teach *better*.

Source: "Poetry Lessons" *Science News* (Peterson)

AFTER READING

A. COMPREHENSION CHECK Discuss these questions with a partner.

1. What did all students in the class notice?
2. What made them uncomfortable?
3. What was one similarity between science and poetry classes?
4. What did the poetry instructors learn about teaching?
5. What did the scientists and engineers learn about teaching?

B. GUESSING THE MEANING FROM THE CONTEXT Look back at the reading on pages 164–165. The first paragraph describes the classroom by using images of sound. In small groups, analyze these images by doing the following.

1. Find four adjectives of sound.
2. Notice the nouns that these adjectives modify. What are they?
3. Without a dictionary, guess what these adjectives might mean.

C. VOCABULARY CHECK Look back at the reading to find the words and phrases that match these definitions. Don't use a dictionary.

1. rules (in science or mathematics) in the form of numbers, letters, and signs (Lines 15–20) ______________
2. confused (especially by a large variety of considerations) (Lines 15–20) ______________
3. absolute; certain (Lines 20–25) ______________
4. composition (Lines 25–30) ______________
5. levels (Lines 30–35) ______________
6. the top or outside part (Lines 30–35) ______________
7. the action of studying and looking for (Lines 30–35) ______________
8. regular, repeated ordering (Lines 40–45) ______________

D. PRONOUN REFERENCE What does each pronoun in orange mean in each sentence? Highlight the noun that it refers to.

1. The students in the poetry class listened to lectures and took notes. **They** had reading assignments and had to write three short papers.
2. You can look in various places for the essential statement a poem makes, or you can be persuaded that **it** doesn't make a statement at all or that it makes contradictory statements.
3. This search for different levels of meaning doesn't happen much in undergraduate classes [classes taken during the first four years of college], but it is important later, in graduate school. And **it** is always important in literature.

E. MAKING INFERENCES The ability to analyze a poem can help you in classes other than literature courses. What is one way this ability can help you in other classes? Make an inference based on the reading. Share your inference with a partner.

BEFORE READING

A. THINKING AHEAD Think about the questions below. Then in small groups, write as many answers as possible in the T-charts.

1. How is poetry different from prose (for example, short stories, novels, and articles)?

Poetry	Prose

2. In your native language, what are some differences between poetry of the past (perhaps one hundred years ago) and modern poetry?

Poetry in the past	Poetry today

B. PREVIEWING Look over the reading on pages 168–170 very quickly. What four main subtopics does it contain? Write them on the lines.

____________________ ____________________

____________________ ____________________

READING

Read about how to appreciate poetry. As you read, highlight the elements of poetry. In other words, highlight the basic characteristics of poetry. (You'll find these in the four subsections.)

Appreciating Poetry

Did you ever have an emotion or an idea that you knew was important, but you couldn't put it into words? Poetry is one kind of writing that can catch such emotions and ideas and give them form.

A poet's purpose is different from other kinds of writers'. Imagine a scientist 5 writing about ice cream. The scientist might discuss the amount of milk fat in the ice cream or its temperature. A historian might write about how Marco Polo brought the idea for the frozen dessert to Europe from China. A businessperson might write about the numbers of gallons of ice cream that people buy every month. But the poet will try to create an "ice cream experience."

10 A poem is not just the work and joy of the poet. You, the reader, must participate. Your ear must hear the poem's "music." Your eye must see how the poem looks on the page. Your mind must find images and meaning in the poem.

The Sound of Poetry

Rhyme occurs when stressed vowel sounds (*a, e, i, o, u*) and the consonants (*b, c, d, f, g*, etc.) after them sound the same in two or more words. For example, 15 the words *sweetly* and *neatly* rhyme because the stressed vowels and all of the consonants that follow them sound the same.

When rhyming words are at the ends of lines, they are called **end rhymes**. End rhymes often fall into a repeating pattern called a rhyme scheme. We can show the rhyme scheme of a poem by giving a different letter of the alphabet to each end 20 rhyme. For example, the rhyme scheme of the following poem by Edgar Allen Poe is a /b /a /b /c /b:

It was many and many a year ago, (a)
In a kingdom by the sea, (b)
That a maiden there lived whom you may know (a)
25 By the name of Annabel Lee; (b)
And this maiden she lived with no other thought (c)
Than to love and be loved by me. (b)

Rhythm is the order of stressed and unstressed syllables. In poetry, rhythm can be shown with stress marks (ʹ) over stressed syllables and rounded (˘) marks over 30 unstressed syllables. For example, in the word *poetry* (pó-ĕ-trў] the first syllable is stressed, and the second two are not.

Sometimes the rhythm is regular and predictable. In Robert Frost's poem "Stopping by Woods on a Snowy Evening," for example, the rhythm is regular:

My little horse must think it queer

35 To stop without a farmhouse near

Between the woods and frozen lake

The darkest evening of the year.

Sometimes the rhythm is irregular and not very predictable (as you'll see on pages 172 and 173).

The Language of Poetry

40 Poetry has been called "the best words in the best order." Poets choose words carefully and put them in specific relationships to each other. Every word in a poem is an important part of the whole design.

As you've seen before, one type of language is **imagery**. Images help us to see, hear, feel, taste, and smell the world that poets describe in their poems.

45 **Figurative language** is also very important in poetry. Figurative language is not factually true; instead, it helps us to see in new ways. The most common forms of figurative language are **similes** and **metaphors**. A simile is a comparison that often uses the words *like* or *as*: "She runs like a deer" or "His skin was as tough as leather." A metaphor also compares two different things but does not use *like* or *as*: "His skin 50 was leather."

Poets often use **symbols**—objects, people, places, or experiences that mean more than they are. For example, a young tree in a garden may be a symbol of growth, of hope for the future, or of the power of nature.

The Form of Poetry

The **form** of a poem is its organization of sounds, images, and ideas and the way 55 the words are placed on the page. Often, a poem has several **stanzas**, groups of lines together—usually between two and eight lines, although more are possible. There is a space between each stanza. Each stanza may be like a paragraph in a composition, with a change of subject, time, or speaker.

Poems with a **closed form** follow traditional rules of rhythm, rhyme, number of 60 syllables, number of lines, and so on. For example, in a **couplet**, each stanza has two lines and usually rhymes, as in this couplet by Robert Frost:

And of course there must be something wrong

In wanting to silence any song.

A **quatrain** is a four-line stanza, as in Frost's "Stopping by Woods on a Snowy 65 Evening" [Lines 34–37]. Poems with an **open form** have no formal groupings. In **free verse**, the poem seldom rhymes, and it has irregular rhythms. It does not have a specific number of lines in a stanza and is similar to the way that we speak.

The Meaning of Poetry

The **title** of a poem is a kind of introduction. It can suggest the poem's main idea and is sometimes especially important because we can't understand the poem without it, as in this very short poem by E.V. Rieu:

Night Thought of a Tortoise Suffering from Insomnia[1] on a Lawn

70 The world is very flat—

There is no doubt of that.

A tortoise

The **speaker** is the voice that you "hear" when you read a poem. A poem may have several speakers. Sometimes the speaker is 75 not the poet at all. Instead, the speaker is another person, animal, or even a thing (in the poem above, the speaker is the tortoise).

The **theme** is the meaning of a poem, the main idea. A poet can state the theme 80 directly or indirectly. In a **narrative poem**, the poet tells a story. In a **lyric poem**, the poet expresses personal thoughts and emotions.

All of these elements—sound, language, form, and meaning—work together to create the **total effect** of a poem.

[1]**insomnia:** the inability to sleep

Source: *Appreciating Poetry* (Glencoe)

AFTER READING

A. PREPARING TO ANALYZE POEMS What are some themes (topics) that poets often explore? In small groups, brainstorm a list of as many themes as you can think of.

Reading Strategy

Analyzing Poems

When you read a poem simply for pleasure, you might just read it several times, get whatever you can from it, and then move on to another poem.

However, when you read a poem in a literature course, you will need to analyze its elements. To analyze a poem's elements, follow these steps.

1. Read the poem silently. If possible, also listen to the poem being read aloud by someone who truly understands it. This will help you to understand it better.
2. Try to figure out what the poem is about in general–its topic or theme–and get an immediate impression of it.
3. When you finish reading the poem, make sure that you understand all the words. In poetry, unlike prose, it is usually not possible to figure out the meaning of new words from the context, so you *need to use a dictionary* for new words that aren't glossed (explained on the side or at the bottom). You can probably get the main idea of a poem without knowing every word, but to understand the deeper layers, you need to know all the words.

4. Check for the various elements of the poem:
- **sound:** rhyme, rhythm (or their absence)
- **language:** imagery, similes, metaphors, symbols
- **form:** closed/open, free verse
- **meaning:** title, speaker(s), narrative/lyric, theme

In any poem, *some of these elements are more important than others.* For example, one poem might have an important central simile or metaphor or be full of symbols. Another might have no figurative language but, instead, have an important speaker. For some poems, the title is almost unnecessary. For others, it's impossible to get the meaning of the poem without the title.

B. ANALYZING POEMS: THEMES Read the three poems on pages 171–174. (New vocabulary is defined in boxes to the right of the poems.)

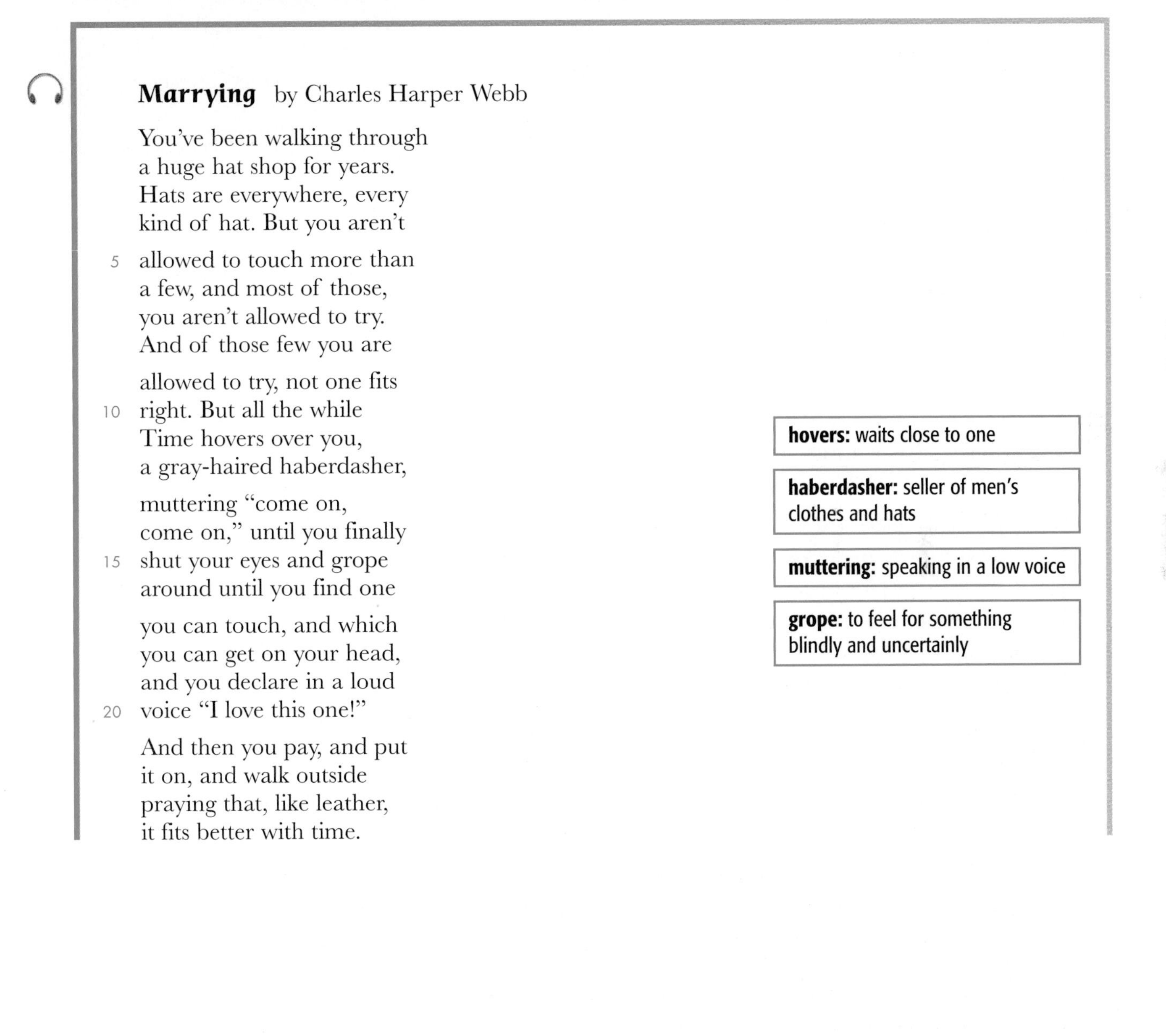

Marrying by Charles Harper Webb

You've been walking through
a huge hat shop for years.
Hats are everywhere, every
kind of hat. But you aren't

5 allowed to touch more than
a few, and most of those,
you aren't allowed to try.
And of those few you are

allowed to try, not one fits
10 right. But all the while
Time hovers over you,
a gray-haired haberdasher,

muttering "come on,
come on," until you finally
15 shut your eyes and grope
around until you find one

you can touch, and which
you can get on your head,
and you declare in a loud
20 voice "I love this one!"

And then you pay, and put
it on, and walk outside
praying that, like leather,
it fits better with time.

hovers: waits close to one

haberdasher: seller of men's clothes and hats

muttering: speaking in a low voice

grope: to feel for something blindly and uncertainly

Going to Norway by Jack Anderson

I asked my parents,
"Have you ever thought
of going to Norway?
You are Andersons
5 and deserve to know
Norway, where we all began.
Do you not wonder
how things are in Norway?
I know that I wonder."
10 And my parents said,
"Yes,
we shall go to Norway,
we are Andersons
and want to see where
15 our people began.
We are growing old:
we must go now."
Yet they stayed
on the dock, staring
20 at the water
as ship after ship
sailed toward the north,
toward Norway.
So I said
25 to my parents, "Now,
you must leave now.
These are the boats
that are leaving for Norway.
It is not long
30 or far."
Then my parents said,
"Yes, we want to see
Norway: we are Andersons.
But it is so far."
35 They stayed
where they were, watching
the boats leave for Norway
and trying to picture it,
even testing a few words
40 of that dear language
on their tongues
—but standing

A boat "leaving for Norway"

still, never moving,
never climbing aboard,
45 though I kept pleading,
"Please, now, you must leave now
if you want to see Norway."
"Norway?" they murmured,
"Norway? Ah, where is that?"
50 They stood very still,
grayness crept through their hair;
it frightened me to see them
growing so old,
for I had not thought
55 such a thing possible.
At last I said,
"I must go
to Norway. I am
an Anderson
60 and want to know
where all of us began.
I must go now."
They stood
on the dock, waving
65 out at the water, and I
waved back over the water
which darkened between us
with distance and tears.

pleading: begging

murmured: said in a soft voice

Richard Cory by Edwin Arlington Robinson

Whenever Richard Cory went down town,
We people on the pavement looked at him:
He was a gentleman from sole to crown,
Clean favored, and imperially slim.
5 And he was always quietly arrayed,
And he was always human when he talked;
But still he fluttered pulses when he said,
"Good morning," and he glittered when he walked.
And he was rich—yes, richer than a king—
10 And admirably schooled in every grace:
In fine, we thought that he was everything
To make us wish that we were in his place.
So on we worked, and waited for the light,
And went without the meat, and cursed the bread;
15 And Richard Cory, one calm summer night,
Went home and put a bullet through his head.

pavement: street

from sole to crown: from his feet to his head

arrayed: dressed

fluttered pulses: caused people to be excited

glittered: shone

grace: charming characteristic

Source: *Stand Up Poetry* (Webb); *Collected Poems* (Robinson)

C. FINDING TOPICS Match the title of each poem on the left to its topic on the right. Write the correct letters on the lines.

_______ "Marrying" — **a.** postponing a dream until it is too late

_______ "Going to Norway" — **b.** choosing a person to live with for life

_______ "Richard Cory" — **b.** envy of a person who is not truly known

D. RECOGNIZING OTHER ELEMENTS Check (✓) your answers to these questions. For some questions, you'll check more than one poem.

Which poem . . .	"Marrying"	"Going to Norway"	"Richard Cory"
has end rhymes?			
has a rhyme scheme?			
has regular, predictable rhythm?			
has closed form?			
can you *not* understand without its title?			
has a speaker who is probably the poet?			
is a narrative?			

E. FIGURATIVE LANGUAGE Discuss the questions below with a partner. If you have trouble with any of them, don't worry about it. You'll learn more about figurative language in Part 3.

1. In "Marrying," what is a metaphor for time? What are the hats symbolic of? (How do you know?)
2. In "Richard Cory," the speaker says, "So on we worked, and waited for the light." What do you think the "light" is a metaphor for?

Reading Strategy

Stating the Theme of a Poem: The Topic and Main Idea

In poetry, the word ***theme*** can refer to both the topic and the main idea of a poem. The **topic** is a noun or noun phrase. To state the **main idea** of a poem, take the topic and extend it into a complete sentence. In stating the main idea, you tell *what the poet says about the topic*. Here are examples of how you might begin a statement of the theme:

Examples: "Marrying" **is about . . .**

In "Marrying," **the poet compares . . .**

In 'Marrying," **the speaker chooses . . .**

In "Marrying," **Webb says that . . .**

In "Marrying," **Webb explores . . .**

F. STATING THE THEME In Activity C on page 174, you identified the topic of each poem. Now take each topic and extend it into a main idea. In other words, what does the poet say about the topic?

Note: Do not assume that the speaker is the same as the poet.

1. "Marrying" ______________________________

____

2. "Going to Norway" ______________________________

____

3. "Richard Cory" ______________________________

____

PART 3 ACADEMIC READING Three More Poems

BEFORE READING

A. THINKING AHEAD You're going to read three poems. To understand one of them, you'll need to know something about events in world history. Four of these events are explained in the chart below. The first two rows are left blank. In small groups, discuss what you know about these two periods from Chapter 2 (pages 64–68).

Periods and Events	Years	Explanations
Ice Age		
Stone Age		
War of the Roses	1455–1487	a bloody civil war in England; it was called "the War of the Roses" because the emblem (symbol) of each side in the war was a rose—one red, one white
Spanish Inquisition	1478–1834	a period in Spain when the Catholic church and state either killed non-Catholics or made them leave the country
Boer War	1899–1902	a war in South Africa between the British army and white farmers who were descendants of Dutch and German settlers; *Boer* means "farmer" in Dutch
Enola Gay	1945	the name of the American plane that dropped the first atomic bomb on Hiroshima, Japan, at the end of World War II; between 130,000 and 150,000 people died

B. DISCUSSION In small groups, discuss these questions.

1. What are some things that people want (or want to *do*) when they are teenagers? Young adults? Middle-aged? Old?
2. What are the most important decisions that people have to make at different times in their lives? (Think of decisions that can affect the rest of a person's life.)

C. VOCABULARY PREPARATION The three poems have a number of new words and phrases. Some words are glossed in the margin. Some others are in orange in the sentences below. Guess their meanings from the context. Write your guesses on the lines.

1. There was a sudden **outbreak** of violence.

   Guess: ______________________________

2. In a nightmare I had last night, these horrible monsters **tormented** me until I finally forced myself to wake up.

   Guess: ______________________________

3. I had just walked out of the hair salon when a strong wind came up and completely **mussed up** my hair.

   Guess: ______________________________

4. When Michael's family moved to a new city, his new school **put him back** from the third grade to the second grade.

   Guess: ______________________________

5. Someday I want to study Latin. I know! **It doesn't make any sense**. Nobody speaks the language these days, so I can't really use it. It just seems interesting to me.

   Guess: ______________________________

6. I wanted to start college right after high school, but I didn't have enough money, so I **deferred** college for a few years and got a job.

   Guess: ______________________________

7. When the road **diverged**, we weren't sure which way to go—right or left.

   Guess: ______________________________

8. I took a long walk through a beautiful **wood**. It was lovely and green and quiet, except for the sound of wind in the trees and a few bird songs.

   Guess: ______________________________

Now compare your answers with a partner's answers.

READING

Read the poems silently as the teacher reads them aloud or plays the audio. Don't worry about understanding everything. Just get an initial impression. As with all poems, keep these questions in mind:

- What is the poem about?
- What is the poet telling me?

The History Teacher by Billy Collins

Trying to protect his students' innocence
he told them the Ice Age was really just
the Chilly Age, a period of a million years
when everyone had to wear sweaters.
5 And the Stone Age became the Gravel Age,
named after the long driveways of the time.
The Spanish Inquisition was nothing more
than an outbreak of questions such as
"How far is it from here to Madrid?"
10 "What do you call the matador's hat?"
The War of the Roses took place in a garden,
and the Enola Gay dropped one tiny atom
on Japan.
The children would leave his classroom
15 for the playground to torment the weak
and the smart,
mussing up their hair and breaking their glasses,
while he gathered up his notes and walked home
past flower beds and white picket fences,
20 wondering if they would believe that soldiers
in the Boer War told long, rambling stories
designed to make the enemy nod off.

chilly: cool

gravel: small stones used to make a road or driveway (from the road to a garage)

matador: bullfighter

rambling: long and boring

nod off: go to sleep

Deferred by Langston Hughes

This year, maybe, do you think I can graduate?
I'm already two years late.
Dropped out six months when I was seven,
a year when I was eleven,
5 *then got put back when we come North.*
To get through high school at twenty's kind of late—
But maybe this year I can graduate.

Maybe now I can have that white enamel stove
I dreamed about when we first fell in love
10 eighteen years ago.
But you know,
rooming and everything
then kids,
cold-water flat and all that.
15 But now my daughter's married
And my boy's most grown—
quit school to work—
and where we're moving
there ain't no stove—
20 Maybe I can buy that white enamel stove!

get through: finish

rooming: renting a cheap room

cold-water flat: a cheap apartment

ain't no: isn't any

Me, I always did want to study French.
It don't make sense—
I'll never go to France,
but night schools teach French.
25 *Now at last I've got a job*
where I get off at five,
in time to wash and dress,
so, s'il-vous plait, *I'll study French!*

Someday,
30 I'm gonna buy two new suits
at once!

All I want is
one more bottle of gin.

All I want is to see
35 my furniture paid for.

All I want is a wife who will
work with me and not against me. Say,
baby, could you see your way clear?

Heaven, heaven is my home!
40 This world I'll leave behind.
When I set my feet in glory
I'll have a throne for mine!

I want to pass the civil service.

I want a television set.

45 *You know, as old as I am,*
I ain't never
owned a decent radio yet?

I'd like to take up Bach.

Montage
50 *of a dream*
deferred.

Buddy, have you heard?

get off: finish

s'il-vous plait: please (in French)

at once: at the same time

gin: a kind of liquor

set my feet in glory: walk into heaven (when I die)

throne: chair for a king or queen

civil service: a test for people who want a job in the post office, for example

ain't never: haven't ever

decent: good

take up: begin to study

Bach: famous European composer of Baroque music

montage: a picture that is made up of many smaller pictures

The Road Not Taken by Robert Frost

Two roads diverged in a yellow wood,
And sorry I could not travel both
And be one traveler, long I stood
And looked down one as far as I could
5 To where it bent in the undergrowth;

Then took the other, as just as fair,
And having perhaps the better claim,
Because it was grassy and wanted wear;
Though as for that the passing there
10 Had worn them really about the same,

And both that morning equally lay
In leaves no step had trodden black.
Oh, I kept the other for another day!
Yet knowing how way leads on to way,
15 I doubted if I should ever come back.

I shall be telling this with a sigh
Somewhere ages and ages hence:
Two roads diverged in a wood, and I—
I took the one less traveled by,
20 And that has made all the difference.

undergrowth: small, thick plants

fair: good

wanted wear: most people didn't go that way

had trodden black: had walked on

yet: but

ages and ages hence: far in the future

Sources: *Stand Up Poetry* (Webb); *Collected Poems of Langston Hughes* (Rampersad); *The Poetry of Robert Frost* (Lathem)

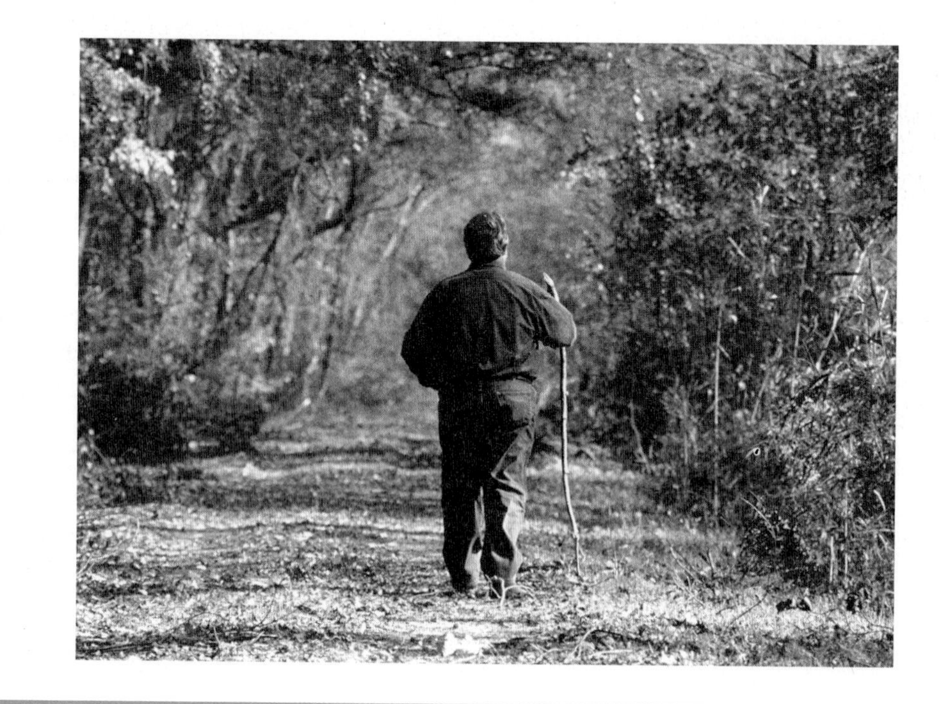

AFTER READING

A. SOUND AND FORM Before analyzing the poems for their meaning, which is more difficult, answer these questions about their sound and form with a partner. Use the vocabulary for poetry that you have learned in Part 2 (pages 168–170).

1. How many stanzas are in each poem?
2. Which poem is the most traditional—in other words, has closed form? What is its rhyme scheme? Which words rhyme in it?
3. Which poem seems to have language that is old-fashioned?
4. Is open form used in any poem? Which one(s)?
5. In your opinion, which poem is in free verse—is the most similar to the way we speak? Explain your answer.

Critical Thinking Strategy

Discovering the Meaning of a Poem

A well-written poem is possible to understand. However, as you saw in Part 1, there are often *layers* of meaning, and you need to dig deep to reach them. You often need to read a poem many times in order to discover the clues to meaning–like a detective. Here are some clues to look for.

Symbolism: Some poems are not symbolic, but many *are*. Look for metaphors and similes. Sometimes there is one central symbol–something concrete, physical, literal–that represents something else.

Example: In "Marrying," the gray-haired haberdasher symbolizes time.

Juxtaposition: Some poems include juxtaposition–an unexpected combination of ideas, words, or actions. Juxtaposition is always surprising, but after you think about it for a while, it seems *right* and *true*.

Example: In "Richard Cory," there is a juxtaposition between the people's *image* of Richard Cory's life and its *reality*.

Ambiguity: Some poems include a bit of ambiguity–something that can be understood in more than one way. If there is too much ambiguity, it's not possible to understand the poem. This is a sign that the poem is not well written. However, a small amount of ambiguous material makes the poem richer and gives the reader something to think about.

Example: In "Deferred," we aren't always sure if a certain speaker is a man or a woman.

Speakers: It helps to figure out who the speaker is. The speaker and the poet are often the same, but frequently the speaker is someone else–another "character" in the "story" of the poem. Sometimes there are multiple speakers.

Example: In "Night Thought of a Tortoise Suffering from Insomnia on a Lawn," the speaker is a tortoise.

In analyzing poetry in an academic class, *you always need to justify (explain) your interpretation with evidence from the poem.*

B. LANGUAGE AND MEANING Read the three poems silently again, or several times if necessary. Look for clues to help you answer these questions. Then, in small groups, discuss your answers.

"The History Teacher"

1. List five lies that the history teacher told the children in his class.
2. What was another lie that the teacher considered telling the children about the Boer War? **Note:** The poet is playing with words. Say "*Boer*" out loud. What word does it sound like?
3. Why did the teacher tell these lies?
4. What did the children do when they left the classroom?
5. Find the juxtaposition between what the teacher thinks about the children and what the children are really like.

"Deferred"

6. There are several speakers in "Deferred." Look for clues to identify some of them from their own words. Find stanzas written by
   - an elderly man or woman
   - a young person (20 years old)
   - a middle-aged man
   - a middle-aged woman
   - the poet
7. How do you know that these people were the speakers in those stanzas? (Find evidence in the stanzas to justify your answers.)
8. How is the eighth stanza different in sound and form from the other stanzas? What might this tell you about this speaker?
9. The speakers in "Deferred" use some grammar that is not standard in academic English. Find four examples of this. Why does the poet use this nonstandard grammar in the poem? (What does their use of English tell you about the speakers?)
10. What does each of the following symbolize to the speaker who dreams of it?
    - the white enamel stove
    - studying French and Bach
    - the bottle of gin
11. Have the speakers in "Deferred" achieved their dreams? What has happened to their dreams?

"The Road Not Taken"

12. What is the speaker sorry about in the first stanza of "The Road Not Taken"?
13. This poem is probably not actually about a walk through a forest. What does each of the following symbolize?
    - the diverging roads
    - the yellow wood
    - the place where one road "bent in the undergrowth"

- the road that "was grassy and wanted wear"
- the "way" that "leads on to way"
- the road "less traveled"
- the "road not taken"

14. In your opinion, does the speaker of "The Road Not Taken" think that he made a good choice? Support your answer with evidence from the last stanza.

C. IN YOUR OWN WORDS: SUMMARIZING On a separate piece of paper, write the themes of "Deferred" and "The Road Not Taken." ("The History Teacher" is done for you, as an example.) Write one sentence about the topic—a noun or noun phrase—of each poem. Write another about the main idea of each; use complete sentences.

Example:
Topic: "The History Teacher" **is about a naive teacher's belief in his students' innocence.**

Main idea: Collins is saying that **children are not always the sweet, innocent beings that adults imagine.**

D. MAKING CONNECTIONS: COMPARING THEMES Look back at three poems in Part 2. What is similar about their themes and the themes of the poems in Part 3? Write your answers in the chart below.

Poems from Part 2	Poems from Part 3	Themes: What are the poems about? Write one sentence that is general enough to cover both poems.
"Marrying" (page 171)	**"The Road Not Taken"** (page 180)	
"Going to Norway" (page 172)	**"Deferred"** (page 178)	
"Richard Cory" (page 174)	**"The History Teacher"** (page 178)	Both "Richard Cory" and "The History Teacher" are about . . .

E. WORD JOURNAL Go back to the poems in Parts 2 and 3. Which new words are important for *you* to remember? Write them in your Word Journal.

F. RESPONSE WRITING "The Road Not Taken" explores the importance—and difficulty—of making a choice at a place where a path or road divides into two. Literally, such a place is called a "fork in the road." Figuratively, it is a "turning point." Think about important turning points in your life. What is a major decision that you have made—or will have to make in the near future? Choose a turning point that will make "all the difference" in your life.

In your journal, write about your topic for 15 minutes. Don't worry about grammar and don't stop writing to use a dictionary.

PART 4 THE MECHANICS OF WRITING

In Part 4, you will learn to use expressions of possibility and probability, collocations for symbols, and similes with *as . . . as*. You will use this knowledge in Part 5 to write a paragraph of analysis.

Expressing Possibility and Probability

There are several ways to express possibility: with the words *possibly, possible,* or *likely* (= possible) and the clauses *It seems that, It appears that . . . .* You can also use a modal. The modals of possibility are:

may	+	(not)	+	the simple form of the verb = present or future
might				
could*	+	(not)	+	*have* + past participle = past

*In the negative, *couldn't* doesn't mean "maybe not," as the others do. It means "absolutely for certain not."

To express probability, use the modal **must**.

Examples: **It appears that** Richard Cory was basically a good person, in addition to being handsome and rich.

The poet's parents in "Going to Norway" **may have regretted** the postponement of their trip to Norway.

The speaker in "Richard Cory" **might not know** why he killed himself.

The speaker in "The Road Not Taken" **could be** the poet himself.

The children **couldn't be** as innocent as their teacher thinks they are.

A. EXPRESSING POSSIBILITY AND PROBABILITY Write your answer to each question. Use an expression of possibility or probability in each and use the same tense (present or past) as in the question. Numbers in parentheses indicate pages where you can find the answers.

1. What kind of person is the speaker in "The History Teacher"? (Page 178)

   ____

2. What does the "white enamel stove" symbolize to the speaker in the second stanza of "Deferred"? (Page 178)

   ____

3. In "Deferred," what kind of job did the speaker of the third stanza have until recently? (Page 179)

   ____

4. In "Deferred," where did the speaker of the eighth stanza ("Heaven, heaven is my home! . . .") probably learn these four lines? (Page 179)

   ____

5. In what season of the year does "The Road Not Taken" take place? (Hints: Look in the first stanza. You also need to know that most of Frost's poems are set in the northeast United States, which has a four-season climate.) (Page 180)

____

6. In "The Road Not Taken," why was the road in the second stanza "grassy"? (Page 180)

____

Using Phrases for Symbols

Many poems include symbols. A symbol is a thing that represents an idea, person, or another thing. Here are six phrases for symbols.

Noun (or Noun Phrase)		Noun (or Noun Phrase)
A flag	symbolizes	a country.
Buying a new house	is a symbol of	economic success.
Two roads going different ways	are symbolic of	choices in life.
Champagne	is associated with	celebration.
A need for alcohol	might indicate	sadness or desperation.
A new purchase	may represent	hope for the future.

Notice that only nouns or noun phrases can be used before and after the verb phrases for symbols. Do not use a clause before or after a phrase for symbols.

INCORRECT: Buying a new house can be a symbol of **they are successful.**
CORRECT: Buying a new house can be a symbol of **success.**

B. USING PHRASES FOR SYMBOLS What do the things below symbolize to you? (There are no "right" or "wrong" answers. Just write your opinions.) Finish each sentence with an expression from the box above and a noun (or noun phrase).

1. A suitcase ______________________________
2. The sky ______________________________
3. An empty wallet ______________________________
4. A bird ______________________________
5. A classroom ______________________________
6. A tenement in a bad neighborhood ______________________________
7. A road that many people are taking ______________________________
8. A road that other people aren't taking ______________________________

Using Similes with *as . . . as*

You can compare two things with this structure: *as* + adjective + *as* + noun.

Example: Kate's skin was **as soft as a peach**.

In every language there are traditional similes—expressions of comparison. Below are some in English.

Examples: My love is **as deep as the ocean**.
Lara's boyfriend is **as stubborn as a mule**.

These can be fun to learn in a new language, but don't expect to see them in poetry! Poets try to use comparisons that are new and fresh. These similes are also not used in academic writing because they are too casual. However, they are common in conversation.

C. USING SIMILES WITH *AS . . . AS* On the chart are the beginnings of some traditional expressions in English. How do you think they end? Write a noun for each one. Then stand up, take your book and a pencil and move around the room. Ask two other classmates for their answers.

Meanings	My Nouns	Classmate 1's Nouns	Classmate 2's Nouns
1. as wise as . . .			
2. as happy as . . .			
3. as busy as . . .			
4. as strong as . . .			
5. as pretty as . . .			
6. as red as . . .			
7. as old as . . .			
8. as free as . . .			
9. as clear as . . .			
10. as flat as . . .			
11. as cute as . . .			
12. as neat as . . .			

Note: You can find out how to say these in English on page 192.

Avoiding and Repairing Problems with Sentence Structure

A common error in written English is the incorrect combination of two sentences.

INCORRECT: Robert Frost used traditional New England characters and settings he was actually writing about universal experiences.

This is incorrect because two independent clauses are combined with no punctuation. The error is between "settings" and "he," where the first independent clause ends and the next begins. This error is called a **run-on sentence** because it runs on when it should stop. Sometimes a student tries to "fix" a run-on sentence with a comma.

INCORRECT: Robert Frost used traditional New England characters and settings, he was actually writing about universal experiences.

This does not improve the sentence. It simply replaces one mistake with another. A comma cannot hold two independent clauses together. This mistake is called a **comma splice**.

There are several ways to fix a run-on sentence or comma splice.

1. Put a period between the two clauses and change the next letter to a capital, or put a semicolon between the two clauses.

   CORRECT: Robert Frost used traditional New England characters and settings. He was actually writing about universal experiences.

2. Use a coordinating conjunction. (For a list of coordinating conjunctions, see page 306.) In many cases–especially if there is contradiction, cause and effect, or an example–it is more logical and better style to use a conjunction.

   CORRECT: Robert Frost used traditional New England characters and settings, but he was actually writing about universal experiences.

3. Use a period or semicolon and an adverbial conjunction with a comma after it. (For a list, see page 308.)

   CORRECT: Robert Frost used traditional New England characters and settings; however, he was actually writing about universal experiences.

4. Use a subordinating conjunction. (For a list, see page 307.)

   CORRECT: Although Robert Frost used traditional New England characters and settings, he was actually writing about universal experiences.

   Robert Frost was actually writing about universal experiences, although he used traditional New England characters and settings.

When you weave quotations into your writing, you also need to be careful to avoid run-on sentences and comma

D. AVOIDING AND REPAIRING PROBLEMS WITH SENTENCE STRUCTURE Identify each item as a run-on (R), comma splice (CS), fragment (F), or good sentence (OK). Then correct the errors. Do not change the good sentences.

______ **1.** Frost spent two years at Harvard he didn't enjoy his time there.

______ **2.** Problems with health and business and grief over the death of two of his children caused Frost to turn more to poetry.

______ **3.** As he says "imperially slim."

______ **4.** In 1912, Frost sold his farm, his family went to England.

______ **5.** Richard Cory appears to have a perfect life, but clearly this isn't the case. "Went home and put a bullet through his head."

______ **6.** We don't know if the speaker is wistful or not for "the road not taken."

______ **7.** The family had financial needs Frost began to give public readings and lectures.

______ **8.** Hughes tells us that this has been a "montage of a dream deferred."

______ **9.** Frost had weak lungs, therefore, his doctor ordered him to spend winters in a warmer climate.

______ **10.** Robert Frost suffered tragedy and sorrow however he was also one of the most beloved, greatly honored poets of the United States.

PART 5 ACADEMIC WRITING

WRITING ASSIGNMENT

Write one paragraph of analysis about the meaning of one poem. Follow these steps.

STEP A. CHOOSING A TOPIC Choose one of these topics.

- the juxtaposition in "The History Teacher"
- the speakers of "Deferred"
- the symbols of "The Road Not Taken"

STEP B. WRITING THE THEME OF THE POEM Write one sentence with the topic of the poem you chose.

STEP C. FINDING SUPPORT Go through the poem and highlight all of the evidence that supports the theme.

Writing Strategy

Planning a Paragraph of Analysis: Idea Mapping

One way to begin organizing information for a paragraph of analysis is to gather your evidence and put it on an idea map (a type of graphic organizer) that shows connections between ideas.

Example: This is a possible map of the poem "Richard Cory."

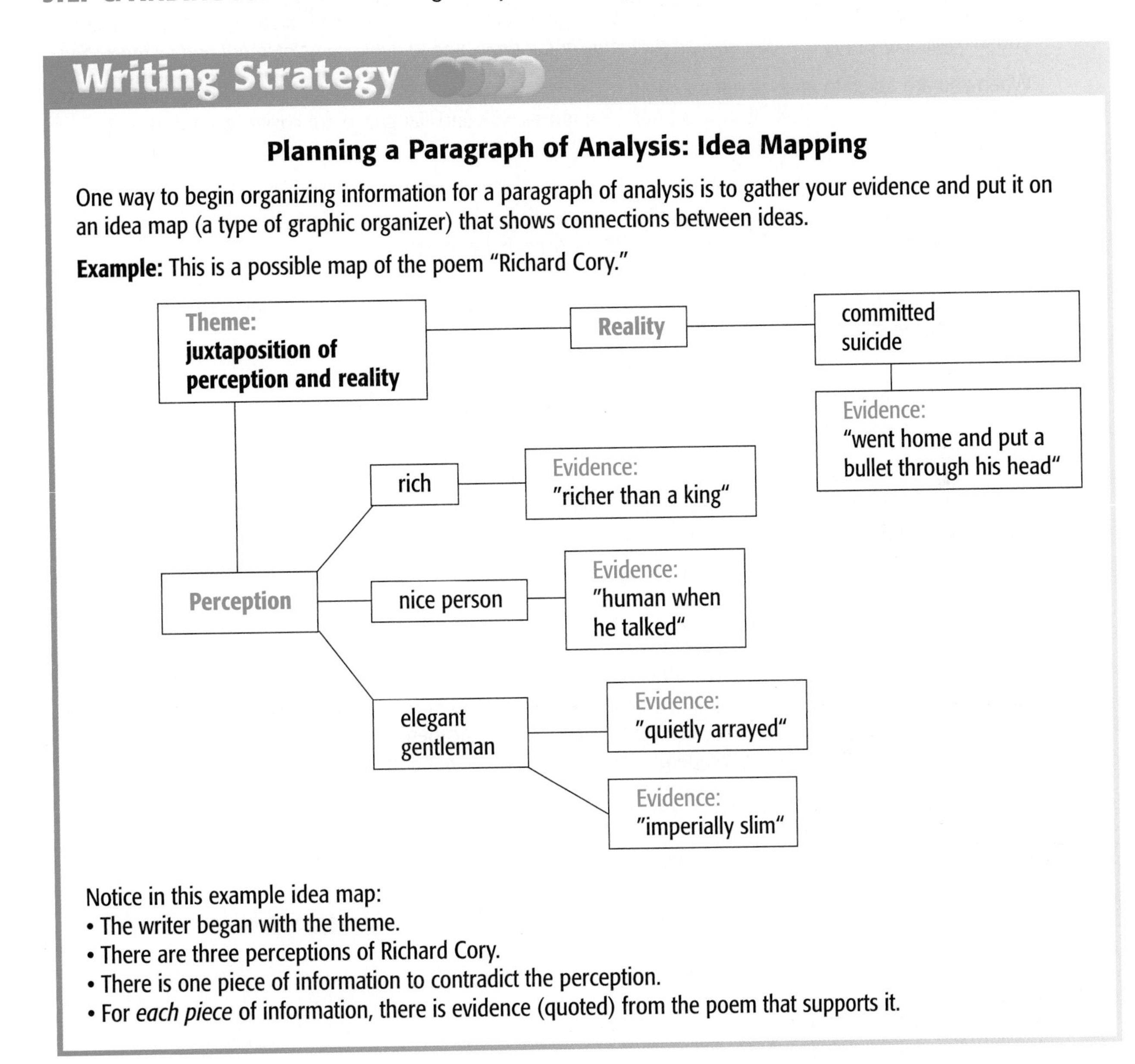

Notice in this example idea map:

- The writer began with the theme.
- There are three perceptions of Richard Cory.
- There is one piece of information to contradict the perception.
- For *each piece* of information, there is evidence (quoted) from the poem that supports it.

STEP D. CHOOSING AND ORDERING YOUR MATERIAL Take your theme from Step B and the material that you highlighted in Step C and move this information onto an idea map.

Test-Taking Strategy

Hedging and Avoiding Overstatement

In academic writing, it is essential to be able to **hedge**. In other words, you need to choose words that allow you to *avoid expressing a strong opinion that you cannot prove* and to *avoid overstatement and exaggeration.*

When you are asked to analyze poetry on an essay exam, it is often necessary to express uncertainty. This is especially true if there is ambiguity in a poem. Sentences with such language are easier to support than sentences without hedging.

Here are some ways to **express uncertainty** in academic writing:

1. Use a modal of possibility *(may, might, could)* or probability (*must*).
2. Use another expression such as

probably	possibly	suggests
It is probable that . . .	likely that . . .	It is possible that . . .
It appears that . . .	seems that . . .	

Examples: The poem **suggests, indicates, tends to suggest . . .**
The poet **appears to be saying** that . . .

In conversational English, **overstatement** and **exaggeration** are common, and the listener understands that they are probably not meant literally.

Examples: The candidate I vote for **never** wins.
My job **is killing me**.
This poem is **absolutely impossible** to understand.

However, overstatement and exaggeration are not commonly used in academic English. In academic English, you need to stay away from words such as *all, every, always,* and *never,* as well as **definite adverbs** such as *extremely, really, strongly, absolutely,* and *completely*. Instead, academic English makes liberal use of **indefinite adverbs** such as *often, frequently, almost,* and *somewhat* and other cautious use of language.

Examples: It **seems** that the candidate I vote for doesn't **usually** win.
My job **tends** to be stressful.
This poem is **somewhat** challenging.

Here are some words and expressions to help you avoid overstatement and exaggeration:
frequently, often, generally, usually, most of the time
occasionally, sometimes, from time to time
rarely, almost never, seldom

most, many, a great many, a good deal of
few, not many, little, not much

HEDGING AND AVOIDING OVERSTATEMENT In each sentence, cross out language that is too certain or too strong and replace it with more careful hedging.

1. The "people on the pavement" ~~were~~ must have been poor in spirit, too, for they "waited for the light."
2. The history teacher was absolutely naive.

3. The speaker in the second stanza in "Deferred" associates the "white enamel stove" with a comfortable, secure life.

4. The speaker in the eighth stanza is an elderly person who learned these lines in a hymn in church.

5. The speaker in "The Road Not Taken" regrets his choice.

6. The speaker in "The Road Not Taken" is content with his choice.

Writing Strategy

Writing a Paragraph of Analysis

In your paragraph of analysis about poetry, your topic sentence (the first) should include the title of the poem, the name of the poet, and the theme of the poem. The rest of the poem has evidence that supports the topic sentence.

For each element of the poem that you interpret, you must include a supporting quotation from the poem. Weave these quotes into your own sentences. There are two ways to do this:
1. Begin with your interpretation and then support it with a quote.
2. Begin with a quote and then explain it in your own words.

Example: What is the meaning of the poem "Richard Cory"?

In "Richard Cory," Edwin Arlington Robinson explores the juxtaposition between perception and reality. He describes Richard Cory as a "gentleman from sole to crown" who was "imperially slim" and "quietly arrayed"—well dressed but not in a way that flaunted the quality of his clothing. He seems to have been kind to other people because the speaker tells us that he was "human when he talked." More than that, he was "richer than a king," and "we people on the pavement" (that is, the people of the town) "thought that he was everything/To make us wish that we were in his place"; in other words, we envied him. Clearly, the speaker and other townspeople were poor. They "went without the meat, and cursed the bread." However, they must have been poor in spirit, too, for they "waited for the light." There is a great contrast between them and Richard Cory, which is why, like the reader of the poem, they must have been shocked when "Richard Cory, one calm summer night/Went home and put a bullet through his head." Why would a person with such an apparently perfect life commit suicide? The speaker can't imagine. The reader probably can't either, because the poet doesn't explain it. Robinson simply wants us to understand that people are not always what they seem to be.

Analysis Look back at the example paragraph to answer these questions.
- Notice how the quotes are woven in. What are ways in which the writer explains the meaning of three of them?
- What are ways in which the writer uses quotes to support an interpretation?
- What are four examples of hedging?
- Notice that the writer does not mention the rhyme scheme or rhythm because it would not answer the question.

STEP E. WRITING THE PARAGRAPH Write your paragraph based on your idea map from Step D (page 189). Be sure to weave in quotations and use hedging. You might make some mistakes, but don't worry about them now.

STEP F. EDITING Read your paragraph and answer these questions.

1. Is the paragraph form correct (indentation, margins)?
2. Does the topic sentence include the title of the poem, the poet, and the theme?
3. Is there good evidence from the poem?
4. Are the quotes either explained or used as support for interpretations?
5. Are the quotes woven in well?
6. Is there use of hedging?
7. Is sentence structure correct (no run-ons, comma splices, or fragments)?

STEP G. REWRITING Write your paragraph again. This time, try to write without the mistakes.

Answers to Activity C on page 186, as most people would say them in English:

1. as wise as an owl
2. as happy as a clam
3. as busy as a bee
4. as strong as an ox
5. as pretty as a picture
6. as red as a lobster
7. as old as the hills
8. as free as a bird
9. as clear as a bell
10. as flat as a pancake
11. as cute as a button
12. as neat as a pin

CHAPTER 6

Heroes in Literature

Discuss these questions:

- Who were your heroes when you were a child?
- How have your ideas of heroism changed since then?
- What qualities make someone a hero?

PART 1 INTRODUCTION
Old Country Advice to the American Traveler

BEFORE READING

THINKING AHEAD In small groups, discuss these questions.

1. Have you ever taken a long train trip? If yes, describe the train cars, the other passengers, and what you did during the trip. If you haven't taken a long train trip, describe any long trip that you have taken.
2. Do older friends or family members like to give you advice? Do they ever give you advice about what to do in new situations such as going on a trip by yourself for the first time, starting a new job, or leaving home to go to school? Do you follow the advice or do you ignore it? Why?
3. How do young people in your culture regard older people? For example, if you disagree with an older person, how do you behave toward him or her?
4. Did anyone from your family immigate to a different country? What is their story?

READING

You are going to read a short story by William Saroyan. Saroyan wrote stories about Armenian immigrants in California. The "old country" in the title is Armenia, the place that Saroyan's family came from. Many of his stories are about these immigrants adjusting to life in a new country.

William Saroyan

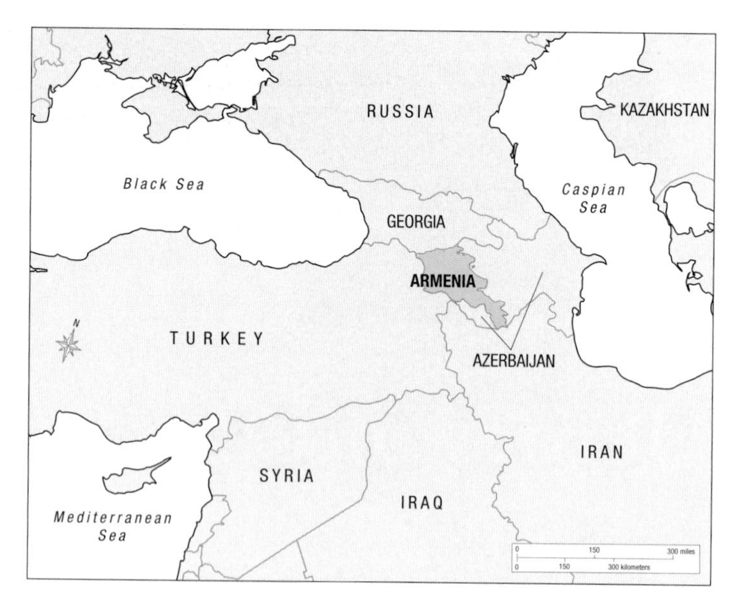

Armenia and the surrounding area

In this story, the narrator, Aram, is describing two of his family members. As you read, think about this question.
• Does Melik learn anything from Garro? If so, what?

Old Country Advice to the American Traveler

One year my uncle Melik traveled from Fresno[1] to New York. Before he got aboard the train, his uncle Garro paid him a visit and told him about the dangers of travel.

When you get on the train, the old man said, choose your seat carefully, sit
5 down, and do not look about.

Yes, sir, my uncle said.

Several moments after the train begins to move, the old man said, two men wearing uniforms will come down the aisle and ask you for your ticket. Ignore them. They will be impostors.[2]

10 How will I know? my uncle said.

You will know, the old man said. You are no longer a child.

Yes, sir, my uncle said.

Before you have traveled 20 miles, an amiable[3] young man will come to you and offer you a cigarette. Tell him you don't smoke. The cigarette will be doped.[4]

15 Yes, sir, said my uncle.

On your way to the diner,[5] a very beautiful young woman will bump into you intentionally and almost embrace you, the old man said. She will be extremely apologetic and attractive, and your natural impulse will be to cultivate her friendship. Dismiss[6] your natural impulse and go on in and eat. The woman will be an adventuress.

20 A what? my uncle said.

A whore[7], the old man shouted. Go on in and eat. Order the best food, and if the diner is crowded, and the beautiful young woman sits across the table from you, do not look into her eyes. If she speaks, pretend to be deaf.

Yes, sir, my uncle said.

25 Pretend to be deaf, the old man said. That is the only way out of it.

Out of what? my uncle said.

Out of the whole ungodly mess, the old man said. I have traveled. I know what I'm talking about.

Yes, sir, my uncle said.

30 Let's say no more about it, the old man said.

---

1 **Fresno:** a city in California

2 **imposters**: fakes; not who they pretend to be

3 **amiable**: friendly

4 **be doped**: have an illegal drug in it

5 **diner**: the restaurant car on a train

6 **dismiss**: forget about; ignore

7 **whore**: prostitute

Yes, sir, my uncle said.

Let's not speak of the matter again, the old man said. It's finished. I have seven children. My life has been a full and righteous one. Let's not give it another thought. I have land, vines, trees, cattle, and money. One cannot have everything—except for a 35 day or two at a time.

Yes, sir, my uncle said.

On your way back to your seat from the diner, the old man said, you will pass through the smoker.[8] There you will find a game of cards in progress. The players will be three middle-aged men with expensive-looking rings on their fingers. They will nod at you 40 pleasantly and one of them will invite you to join the game. Tell them: No speak English.

Yes, sir, my uncle said.

That is all, the old man said.

Thank you very much, my uncle said.

One thing more, the old man said. When you go to bed at night, take your money 45 out of your pocket and put it in your shoe. Put your shoe under your pillow, keep your head on the pillow all night, *and don't sleep.*

Yes, sir, my uncle said.

That is all, the old man said.

The old man went away and the next day my uncle Melik got aboard the train and 50 traveled straight across America to New York. The two men in uniforms were not impostors, the young man with the doped cigarette did not arrive, the beautiful young woman did not sit across the table from my uncle in the diner, and there was no card game in progress in the smoker. My uncle put his money in his shoe and put his shoe under his pillow and put his head on the pillow and didn't sleep all night the first night, 55 but the second night he abandoned the whole ritual.

The second day he *himself* offered another young man a cigarette which the other young man accepted. In the diner, my uncle went out of his way to sit at a table with a young lady. He started a poker game in the smoker, and long before the train ever got to New York, my uncle knew everybody aboard the train and everybody knew him. 60 Once, while the train was traveling through Ohio, my uncle and the young man who had accepted the cigarette and two young ladies on their way to Vassar formed a quartette[9] and sang *The Wabash Blues.*

The journey was a very pleasant one.

When my uncle Melik came back from New York, his old uncle Garro visited him again.

65 I see you are looking all right, he said. Did you follow my instructions?

Yes, sir, my uncle said.

The old man looked far away in space.

I am pleased that *someone* has profited by my experience, he said.

Source: *My Name is Aram* (Saroyan).

[8] **smoker**: the smoking car on trains of the past (similar to a bar car)

[9] **quartette**: old-fashioned singing group with four people

AFTER READING

A. COMPREHENSION CHECK Discuss these questions about the reading with a partner.

1. Who are the main characters in the story?
2. Who is the hero?
3. What advice does Garro give?
4. What kind of person is Garro? How does he describe himself? Find examples in the story that support your answer.
5. Use the T-chart to compare Garro's predictions of Melik's trip with the actual events of Melik's trip.

Garro's Predictions	Melik's Trip

6. What do you think Melik might have learned on his trip?

B. VOCABULARY CHECK Look back at the reading on pages 195–196 to find the words and phrases that match these definitions. Don't use a dictionary.

1. got onto the train (Lines 1–5) ______________________
2. came to see him (Lines 1–5) ______________________
3. look around (Lines 1–5) ______________________
4. walk so close that she touches you (Lines 15–20) ______________________
5. what you will want to do without thinking about it (Lines 15–20) ______________________
6. the (only) way to escape (Lines 20–25) ______________________
7. made a special effort (Lines 55–60) ______________________
8. learned from (Lines 65–68) ______________________

Reading Strategy

Recognizing Euphemisms

A euphemism is a positive or neutral-sounding word or phrase that is used to express a negative or unpleasant idea. A common example that many English speakers use is, "He is no longer with us" instead of "He died." Another example is that people in the United States often say *bathroom* or *restroom* instead of *toilet*. Recognizing euphemisms is fun and makes you enjoy your reading more as you realize what the speaker or writer *really* means.

C. RECOGNIZING EUPHEMISMS In the story, Garro uses some euphemisms when giving advice to Melik. With a partner, try to guess the meanings of the euphemisms below.

1. cultivate her friendship = ______________________________________
2. dismiss your natural impulse = ______________________________________

D. MAKING INFERENCES Where might Garro have gotten his ideas about travel? In other words, why are his warnings so specific? Also, do many people listen to Garro's advice? In small groups, make inferences based on the reading.

E. DISCUSSION In small groups, discuss these questions.

1. In what ways can another person's experience teach you something about life? Give an example of a time you learned from someone else's experiences.
2. Was there a time when someone's experience was not like your own? Explain your answer.
3. What role do older friends and relatives play in your life?
4. Go back to the reading and look at Saroyan's use of punctuation. For example, how do you know when people are speaking? Why do you think he does this?
   Note: Incorrect use of punctuation is acceptable in a story but not in an essay.

PART 2 GENERAL INTEREST READING The Hero's Journey

BEFORE READING

Luke Skywalker of *Star Wars*

Han Solo of *Star Wars*

A. THINKING AHEAD In small groups, discuss these questions.

1. What is your definition of a *hero*? How is a hero different from the average person? How is a hero similar to the average person? List the characteristics of a hero.
2. Give examples of heroes either in real life or in movies you have seen or stories you have read. Why are they heroes?

B. VOCABULARY PREPARATION Read the sentences below. The words in orange are from the next reading. Guess their meanings from the context.

- First, circle the part of speech (noun, verb, or adjective).
- Then write your guess.
- If you are very unsure of your guess, check a dictionary to see if your guess was close. To save time, do the third step with a small group. Divide the group of words; each person will look up several words and then share the answers.

	Parts of Speech		
1. A hero often does a good **deed**—for example, saving someone's life.	n	v	adj

Guess: ______________________________

Dictionary Definition: ______________________________

2. Kirk was **compelled** to participate in a rite of passage. He had no choice in the matter.	n	v	adj

Guess: ______________________________

Dictionary Definition: ______________________________

3. Nowadays, the term *hero* is used for both a man and a woman, but some people still use the term **heroine** to describe a women.	n	v	adj

Guess: ______________________________

Dictionary Definition: ______________________________

4. There are many definitions of *hero*, but most people would agree that bravery is a **fundamental** quality that all heroes share.	n	v	adj

Guess: ______________________________

Dictionary Definition: ______________________________

5. In some cultures, young people must **undergo** a rite of passage to determine if they are ready to become adults.	n	v	adj

Guess: ______________________________

Dictionary Definition: ______________________________

6. The rite of passage helps the young person **evolve** into a new person. When the rite is over, the young person has gone from being a child to an adult.	n	v	adj

Guess: ______________________________

Dictionary Definition: ______________________________

7. A rite of passage is often a symbolic death and **resurrection**: the death of the child and the re-birth of the person as an adult. n v adj

Guess: ______________________________

Dictionary Definition: ______________________________

8. A hero is not primarily concerned with **self-preservation**; she is more concerned about the welfare of others than about herself. n v adj

Guess: ______________________________

Dictionary Definition: ______________________________

9. A key concept in many stories about heroes is the idea of **redemption**—that people can change and become better. n v adj

Guess: ______________________________

Dictionary Definition: ______________________________

10. In *Star Wars*, Han Solo is a **compassionate** character because he makes a sacrifice to help others. n v adj

Guess: ______________________________

Dictionary Definition: ______________________________

11. I visited my hometown after being away for many years. The experience **evoked** memories that I thought I had forgotten. n v adj

Guess: ______________________________

Dictionary Definition: ______________________________

C. CHOOSING THE CORRECT DICTIONARY DEFINITION Read the sentences below. Use the dictionary entries to choose the best definitions of the words in orange for the context. Write the correct numbers of the definitions on the lines.

1. Karen was sick, but she'll **recover** soon.

   Definition: __________

2. Josh is going to **recover** the money he lost last year.

   Definition: __________

3. Maggie plans to **recover** the couch with nicer material.

   Definition: __________

> **recover** *v* **1** become well again **2** replace the cover on an object **3** get back

4. Kevin has a very sweet **nature**.

Definition: ___________

5. Robyn and John like to spend time exploring **nature**, so they go hiking in the woods every weekend.

Definition: ___________

nature *n* **1** the natural environment such as plants, animals, and landscapes **2** qualities or characteristics

6. After a long **trial**, the thief went to prison.

Definition: ___________

7. In order to become a man, Jeff experienced a **trial** in the wilderness.

Definition: ___________

trial *n* **1** a test **2** a legal process in which a judge and jury decide a person's guilt or innocence

8. The football **match** was exciting to watch.

Definition: ___________

9. I am not Jennifer's **match**. She's much stronger than I am!

Definition: ___________

10. Amber lit the candles with a **match**.

Definition: ___________

match *n* **1** an object used to light a fire **2** a contest between two teams or players **3** a thing or person that is equal to another

READING

The reading is a transcription—a written version—of a television interview with Joseph Campbell, an American professor and writer who specialized in mythology. The interviewer is Bill Moyers, an American journalist. Moyers asks Campbell to discuss the characteristics of heroes in **mythology** (the study of myths—collections of stories associated with a culture or society).

As you read, think about the answer to this question:
- What are the characteristics of a hero, according to Campbell?

The Hero's Journey

Moyers: Why are there so many stories about the hero in mythology?

Campbell: Because that's what's worth writing about. Even in popular novels, the main character is a hero or heroine who has found or done something beyond the normal range of achievement and experience. A hero is someone who has given his or her life to something bigger than oneself. 5

Moyers: So in all of these cultures, whatever the local costume the hero might be wearing, what is the deed?

Campbell: Well, there are two types of deed. One is the physical deed, in which the hero performs a courageous act in battle or saves a life. The other kind is the
10 spiritual[1] deed, in which the hero learns to experience the supernormal range of human spiritual life and then comes back with a message.

The usual hero adventure begins with someone from whom something has been taken, or who feels there's something lacking in[2] the normal experiences available or permitted to the members of society. This person then takes off on a series of
15 adventures beyond the ordinary, either to recover what has been lost or to discover some life-giving elixir[3]. It's usually a cycle, a going and a returning.

But the structure and something of the spiritual sense of this adventure can be seen already anticipated in the puberty[4] or initiation rituals of early tribal societies, through which a child is compelled to give up its* childhood and become an adult—to
20 die, you might say, to its infantile personality and psyche[5] and come back as a responsible adult. This is a fundamental psychological transformation that everyone has to undergo. We are in childhood in a condition of dependency under someone's protection and supervision for some 14 to 21 years—and if you're going for your Ph.D., this may continue to perhaps 35. You are in no way a self-responsible, free
25 agent[6], but an obedient dependent, expecting and receiving punishments and rewards. To evolve out of this position of psychological immaturity to the courage of self-responsibility and assurance requires a death and a resurrection. That's the basic motif[7] of the universal hero's journey—leaving one condition and finding the source of life to bring you forth into a richer or mature condition.
30 [. . .]

Moyers: What's the significance of the trials, and tests, and ordeals of a hero?

Campbell: If you want to put it in terms of intentions, the trials are designed to see to it that the intending hero should be really a hero. Is he really a match for this task? Can he overcome the dangers? Does he have the courage, the knowledge, the
35 capacity, to enable him to serve?

[. . .]

If you realize what the real problem is—losing yourself, giving yourself to some higher end, or to another—you realize that this itself is the ultimate trial. When we quit thinking primarily about ourselves and our own self-preservation, we undergo a
40 truly heroic transformation of consciousness.

And what all the myths have to deal with is transformation of consciousness of one kind or another. You have been thinking one way, now you have to think a different way.

**his* or *her* (using the pronoun *it* or *its* to refer to people is a typical error that even well-educated native English speakers sometimes make in spoken English).

---

[1] **spiritual**: having to do with religion
[2] **lacking in**: not having
[3] **elixir**: a liquid medicine; often, a magical drink that gives special powers
[4] **puberty**: adolescence; the age between childhood and adulthood
[5] **psyche**: mind
[6] **free agent**: someone who can do whatever he or she wants to do
[7] **motif**: subject

Moyers: How is consciousness transformed?

45 **Campbell:** Either by the trials themselves or by illuminating revelations[8]. Trial and revelations are what it's all about.

Moyers: Isn't there a moment of redemption in all of these stories? The woman is saved from the dragon, the city is spared from obliteration, the hero is snatched[9] from danger in the nick of time.

50 **Campbell:** Well, yes. There would be no hero deed unless there were an achievement. We can have the hero who fails, but he's usually represented as a kind of clown, someone pretending to more than he can achieve.
[. . .]

Moyers: In George Lucas' *Star Wars*, [Han] Solo begins as a mercenary[10] and ends
55 up a hero, coming in at the last to save Luke Skywalker.

Campbell: Yes, there Solo has done the hero act of sacrificing himself for another.

Moyers: Do you think that a hero is created out of guilt? Was Solo guilty because he had abandoned Skywalker?

Campbell: It depends on what system of ideas you want to apply. Solo was a very
60 practical guy, at least as he thought of himself, a materialist[11]. But he was a compassionate human being at the same time and didn't know it. The adventure evoked a quality of his character that he hadn't known he possessed.

Moyers: So perhaps the hero lurks[12] in each one of us when we don't know it?

Campbell: Our life evokes our character. You find out more about yourself as you go
65 on. That's why it's good to be able to put yourself in situations that will evoke your higher nature rather than your lower.

---

[8] **illuminating revelations**: information that increases understanding
[9] **snatched**: grabbed, removed, saved
[10] **mercenary**: usually, a person who fights in wars for money rather than for his or her political beliefs
[11] **materialist**: someone concerned with money and objects as opposed to spiritual matters
[12] **lurks**: hides

Source: "The Hero's Journey" *The Power of Myth* (Campbell)

AFTER READING

A. COMPREHENSION CHECK Discuss these questions with a partner.

1. What are the characteristics of a hero, according to Campbell? Highlight them in the reading. Then compare these to what you listed in Activity A, page 199.
2. How else does Campbell describe the hero? What does the hero do?
3. How is Han Solo a hero?

B. CHECKING DETAILS In small groups, discuss these questions about the hero's journey.

1. What are the two types of heroic deeds? Complete the flow chart, a type of graphic organizer, to answer this question.

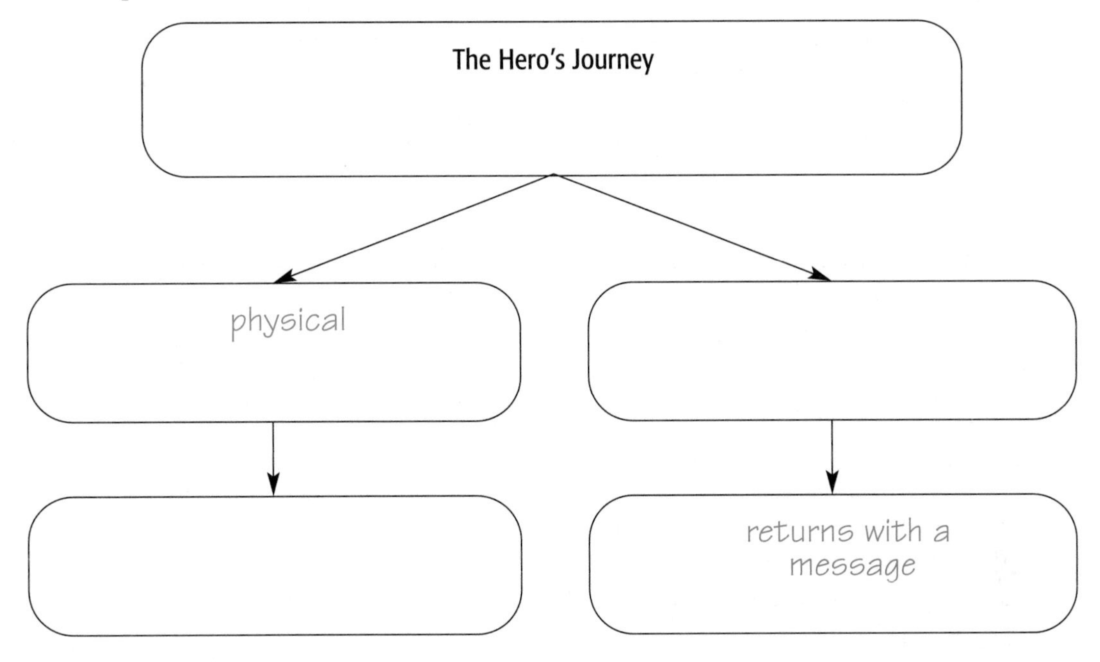

2. What is the purpose of the hero's ordeal? What must the hero prove?
3. How does Campbell describe the hero who fails the test?
4. How are puberty rites similar to the hero's journey?

C. PHRASES WITH PREPOSITIONS First, do this activity as a pre-test to find out what you already know. Complete the phrases in orange with prepositions.

Then look back at the reading on pages 202–204 to check your answers. This will help you to begin noticing collocations as you read. As you find these phrases in the passage, highlight them in the color that you use for important vocabulary.

1. The person **takes** ____________ ____________ **a series of adventures** beyond the ordinary. (Lines 10–15)
2. In puberty rituals, a child is compelled **to give** ____________ its childhood. (Lines 15–20)
3. **To evolve** ____________ ____________ **this position** of psychological immaturity, the person must die and be reborn. (Lines 25–30)
4. Losing yourself, **giving yourself** ____________ **some higher end** is the ultimate trial. (Lines 35–40)
5. There is usually **a moment** ____________ **redemption** in the stories about heroic deeds. (Lines 45–50)

6. In some stories, a person **is saved** ____________ a dangerous situation. (Lines 45–50)

7. In other stories, the hero saves a city ____________ **the nick** ____________ **time**, just at the last moment. (Lines 45–50)

8. In *Star Wars*, Han Solo starts out as a mercenary, but **ends** ____________ a hero. (Lines 50–55)

9. **Sacrificing himself** ____________ **another** makes Solo a hero. (Lines 55–60)

10. **As you go** ____________, you learn more about yourself. (Lines 60–65)

Critical Thinking Strategy

Interpreting

The skill of interpreting often involves understanding information and explaining its patterns. It is very useful in discussing and writing about literature. It also helps you summarize information and use it in new contexts.

Example: One way to interpret is to take ideas from a literary expert such as Joseph Campbell and use those ideas to explain a work of literature. For example, Campbell uses his ideas about the hero's journey to interpret the movie *Star Wars*. He interprets *Star Wars* as a hero-type story by comparing the film hero to the mythical hero. Campbell explains how the behavior and characteristics of the film hero are examples of this kind of story.

D. INTERPRETING Re-read the story "Alone on a Hilltop" (Chapter 1, page 29), about Lame Deer's puberty ritual. Find details in the story that are examples of the hero's adventure.

E. AVOIDING SEXISM In academic English, writers try to avoid the use of sexist language whenever possible. In other words, they try not to use masculine words like *he/his/him* when they mean "people in general." There are two ways to avoid sexist language: use both genders (*he or she*) or use the plural.

Rewrite line 19 of Campbell's interview twice. Change the pronoun in two different ways to make the sentence correct while avoiding sexism.

____

____

____

____

PART 3 ACADEMIC READING Ta-Na-E-Ka

BEFORE READING

La fiesta de quinceañera

A *bar mitzvah*

A debutante ball

A. THINKING AHEAD In small groups, look at the pictures and answer these questions.

1. Are you familiar with any of the rituals in these pictures? If yes, tell your group members about them.
2. Does your culture or religion have a special ceremony for young people who are becoming adults?

B. VOCABULARY PREPARATION The story that follows is about a Native-American girl named Mary. The story has many new words and phrases. Some words are glossed. Some others are in orange in the sentences below. Guess their meanings from the context.

- First, circle the part of speech noun (n), verb (v), or adjective (adj). (If it is a phrase, is it a *noun* phrase, *verb* phrase, or *adjective* phrase?)
- Then write your guess.
- If you are very unsure of your guess, check a dictionary to see if your guess was close. To save time, do the third step with a small group. Divide the group of words; each person will look up several words and then share the answers.

Parts of Speech

1. Many years ago, Mary's grandfather fought in a **skirmish** between his Native-American tribe and the United States army. n v adj

   Guess: ______________________________

   Dictionary Definition: ______________________________

2. Young Native Americans had to prove that they could **endure** difficult times. Staying alive during times when there was war or not enough food was very important in their culture. n v adj

   Guess: ______________________________

   Dictionary Definition: ______________________________

3. Many of the stories of Mary's tribe **revolve around** a special character called Good Woman, a strong woman who helps men win battles. n v adj

   Guess: ______________________________

   Dictionary Definition: ______________________________

4. Mary proved that she was a very **shrewd** person: she thought of an easy way to do a difficult thing. n v adj

   Guess: ______________________________

   Dictionary Definition: ______________________________

5. Mary's parents agreed with her grandfather about most of the ritual, but they absolutely **put their foot down** when he suggested she do the endurance ritual with no clothes on. n v adj

   Guess: ______________________________

   Dictionary Definition: ______________________________

6. Today is February 9. I was born on February 11, so my birthday is **drawing close**. n v adj

Guess: ____

Dictionary Definition: ____

7. Ta-Na-E-Ka was an **endurance ritual**. It was a series of difficult activities that helped children prove they could be strong adults. n v adj

Guess: ____

Dictionary Definition: ____

8. The Ta-Na-E-Ka ritual was part of Mary's **heritage**. It was an important part of the traditions and beliefs of her culture. n v adj

Guess: ____

Dictionary Definition: ____

Reading Strategy

Understanding Italics for Foreign Words

Writers use italics to indicate foreign words and phrases. They usually give the English translation in a nearby sentence. As you read, pay close attention to the italicized words. If you don't know their meanings, look for a definition in the next sentence.

Example: "*N'ko-n'ta,*" I said. It was the Kaw word for courage.

READING

"Ta-Na-E-Ka" is the story of a rite of passage of a Native-American girl, Mary. As you read, highlight the answers to these questions.

- What lesson is Mary supposed to learn?
- Does she learn it?

Ta-Na-E-Ka

Four generations of Sioux women

As my birthday drew closer, I had awful nightmares about it. I was reaching the age at which all Kaw Indians[1] had to participate in Ta-Na-E-Ka. Well, not all Kaws. Many of the younger families on the reservation were beginning to give up the old customs. But my grandfather, Amos Deer Leg, was devoted to[2] tradition. He still wore handmade beaded moccasins[3] instead of shoes, and kept his iron gray hair in tight braids. He could speak English, but he spoke it only with white men. With his family, he used a Sioux dialect.[4]

Grandfather was one of the last living Indians (he died in 1953 when he was 81) who actually fought against the U.S. Cavalry.[5] Not only did he fight, he was wounded in a skirmish at Rose Creek—a famous encounter in which the celebrated Kaw chief Flat Nose lost his life. At the time, my grandfather was only 11 years old.

Eleven was a magic word among the Kaws. It was the time of Ta-Na-E-Ka, the "flowering of adulthood." It was the age, my grandfather informed us hundreds of times, "When a boy could prove himself to be a warrior and a girl took the first steps to womanhood."

"I don't want to be a warrior," my cousin, Roger Deer Leg, confided to me. "I'm going to be an accountant."

"None of the other tribes make girls go through the endurance ritual," I complained to my mother.

"It won't be as bad as you think, Mary," my mother said, ignoring my protests. "Once you've gone through[7] it, you'll certainly never forget it. You'll be proud."

I even complained to my teacher, Mrs. Richardson, feeling that, as a white woman, she would side with[8] me. She didn't. "All of us have rituals of one kind or another," Mrs. Richardson said. "And look at it this way: how many girls have the opportunity to compete on equal terms with boys? Don't look down on[9] your heritage."

Heritage, indeed! I had no intention of living on a reservation for the rest of my life. I was a good student. I loved school. My fantasies were about knights in armor and fair ladies

[1] **Kaw Indians**: North American Indian (Native American) tribe that lived along the Kansas River in eastern Kansas
[2] **devoted to**: cared about very much
[3] **moccasins**: soft shoes made from animal skin
[4] **Sioux dialect**: The Sioux are a nation of North American Indian tribes. (The Kaw are a subtribe of the Sioux.) "Dialect" is a variety of a language that they spoke.
[5] **Cavalry**: soldiers who fought on horseback
[7] **gone through**: experienced
[8] **side with**: agree with
[9] **look down on**: criticize

in flowing gowns being saved from dragons. It never once occurred to me that being Indian was exciting.

35 But I've always thought that the Kaw were the originators of the women's liberation movement. No other Indian tribe—and I've spent half a lifetime researching the subject—treated women more "equally" than the Kaw. Unlike most of the subtribes of the Sioux Nation, the Kaw allowed men and women to eat together. And hundreds of years before we were "acculturated,"[10] a Kaw woman had the right to refuse a prospective husband even if 40 her father arranged the match.

The wisest women (generally wisdom was equated with age) often sat in tribal councils. Furthermore, most Kaw legends revolve around "Good Woman," a kind of supersquaw, a Joan of Arc[11] of the high plains. Good Woman led Kaw warriors into battle after battle from which they always seemed to emerge victorious.

45 And girls as well as boys were required to undergo[12] Ta-Na-E-Ka. The actual ceremony varied from tribe to tribe, but since the Indian's life on the plains was dedicated to survival, Ta-Na-E-Ka was a test of survival.

"Endurance is the loftiest[13] virtue of the Indian," my grandfather explained. "To survive, we must endure. When I was a boy, Ta-Na-E-Ka was more than the mere symbol it is now. 50 We were painted white with the juice of a sacred herb and sent naked into the wilderness without as much as a knife. We couldn't return until the white had worn off. It wouldn't wash off. It took almost eighteen days, and during that time we had to stay alive, trapping food, eating insects and roots and berries, and watching out for enemies. And we did have enemies—both the white soldiers and the Omaha[14] warriors, who were always trying to 55 capture Kaw boys and girls undergoing their endurance test. It was an exciting time."

"What happened if you couldn't make it?"[15] Roger asked. He was born only three days after I was, and we were being trained for Ta-Na-E-Ka together. I was happy to know he was frightened too.

"Many didn't return," Grandfather said. "Only the strongest and shrewdest. Mothers 60 were not allowed to weep[16] over those who didn't return. If a Kaw couldn't survive, he or she wasn't worth weeping over. It was our way."

"What a lot of hooey,"[17] Roger whispered. "I'd give anything to get out of it."

"I don't see how we have any choice," I replied.

Roger gave my arm a little squeeze. "Well, it's only five days."

65 Five days! Maybe it was better than being painted white and sent out naked for eighteen days. But not much better.

We were to be sent, barefoot and in bathing suits, into the woods. Even our very traditional parents put their foot down when Grandfather suggested we go naked. For five

---

[10] **acculturated**: mixed with another culture, and took the other culture's customs and qualities instead of one's own

[11] **Joan of Arc**: French national heroine born 1412, died 1431. She helped French troops win a battle against the English but was executed

[12] **undergo:** endure

[13] **loftiest**: highest (most important; best)

[14] **Omaha**: North American Indian tribe, part of the Sioux Nation

[15] **make it**: survive

[16] **weep**: cry

[17] **hooey**: slang from the past for ideas that are exaggerated or untrue

days we'd have to live off the land,[18] keeping warm as best we could, getting food where we could. It was May, but on the northernmost reaches[19] of the Missouri River the days were still chilly and the nights were fiercely cold.

Grandfather was in charge of the month's training for Ta-Na-E-Ka. One day he caught a grasshopper and demonstrated how to pull its legs and wings off on one flick of the fingers and how to swallow it.

I felt sick, and Roger turned green.[20] "It's a darn good thing it's 1947," I told Roger teasingly. "You'd make a terrible warrior." Roger just grimaced.

I knew one thing. This particular Kaw Indian girl wasn't going to swallow a grasshopper, no matter how hungry she got. And then I had an idea. Why hadn't I thought of it before? It would have saved nights of bad dreams about squooshy grasshoppers. I headed straight for my teacher's house. "Mrs. Richardson," I said, "would you lend me five dollars?"

"Five dollars!" she exclaimed. "What for?"

"You remember the ceremony I talked about?"

"Ta-Na-E-Ka. Of course. Your parents have written me and asked me to excuse you from school so you can participate in it."

"Well, I need some things for the ceremony," I replied, in half-truth. "I don't want to ask my parents for the money."

"It's not a crime to borrow money, Mary. But how can you pay it back?"

"I'll baby-sit for you ten times."

"That's more than fair," she said, going to her purse and handing me a crisp new five-dollar bill. I'd never had that much money at once.

"I'm happy to know the money's going to be put to a good use," Mrs. Richardson said.

A few days later, the ritual began with a long speech from my grandfather about how we now had to fend for ourselves and prove that we could survive the most horrendous of ordeals. All the friends and relatives who had gathered at our house for dinner made jokes about their own Ta-Na-E-Ka experiences.

They all advised us to fill up now, since for the next five days we'd be gorging ourselves on[21] crickets. Neither Roger nor I was very hungry. "I'll probably laugh about this when I'm an accountant," Roger said, trembling.[22]

"Are you trembling?" I asked.

"What do you think?"

"I'm happy to know boys tremble too," I said.

At six the next morning we kissed our parents and went off to the woods.

"Which side do you want?" Roger asked. According to the rules, Roger and I would stake out "territories" in separate areas of the woods, and we weren't to communicate during the entire ordeal.

"I'll go toward the river, if it's okay with you," I said.

---

[18] **live off the land**: survive by eating plants and animals

[19] **northernmost reaches**: regions that are the farthest north

[20] **turned green**: his face looked pale, as though he felt sick

[21] **gorging ourselves on**: eating large amounts of

[22] **trembling**: shaking

"Sure," Roger answered. "What difference does it make?"

To me, it made a lot of difference. There was a marina a few miles up the river and there were boats moored there. At least, I hoped so. I figured that a boat was a better place to sleep than under a pile of leaves.

The Kansas River valley as it looks today.

"Why do you keep holding your head?" Roger asked.

"Oh, nothing. Just nervous," I told him. Actually, I was afraid I'd lose the five-dollar bill, which I had tucked into my hair with a bobby pin. As we came to a fork in the trail, Roger shook my hand. "Good luck, Mary."

"*N'ko-n'ta*" I said. It was the Kaw word for courage.

The sun was shining and it was warm, but my bare feet began to hurt immediately. I spied[23] one of the berry bushes Grandfather had told us about.

"You're lucky," he had said. "The berries are ripe in the spring, and they are delicious and nourishing." They were orange and fat and I popped one into my mouth.

Argh! I spat it out. It was awful and bitter, and even grasshoppers were probably better tasting, although I never intended to find out. I sat down to rest my feet. A rabbit hopped out from under the berry bush. He nuzzled the berry I'd spat out and ate it. He picked another one and ate that too. He liked them. He looked at me, twitching his nose. I watched a redheaded woodpecker[24] bore into an elm tree and I caught a glimpse of a civet cat[25] waddling through some twigs. All of a sudden I realized I was no longer frightened. Ta-Na-E-Ka might be more fun than I'd anticipated. I got up and headed toward the marina.

"Not one boat," I said to myself dejectedly. But the restaurant on the shore, "Ernie's Riverside," was open. I walked in, feeling silly in my bathing suit. The man at the counter was big and tough-looking. He wore a sweat shirt with the words "Fort Sheridan, 1944," and he had only three fingers on one of his hands. He asked me what I wanted.

"A hamburger and a milkshake," I said, holding the five-dollar bill in my hand so he'd know I had money.

"That's a pretty heavy breakfast, honey," he murmured.

"That's what I always have for breakfast," I lied.

"Forty-five cents," he said, bringing me the food. (Back in 1947, hamburgers were twenty-five cents and milk shakes were twenty cents.) "Delicious," I thought. "Better'n grasshoppers—and Grandfather never once mentioned that I couldn't eat hamburgers."

While I was eating, I had a grand idea. Why not sleep in the restaurant?

[23] **spied**: saw
[24] **woodpecker**: a kind of bird
[25] **civet cat**: a kind of skunk–a small, furry animal

I went to the ladies' room and made sure the window was unlocked. Then I went back outside and played along the riverbank, watching the water birds and trying to identify each one. I planned to look for a beaver dam the next day.

The restaurant closed at sunset, and I watched the three-fingered man drive away. Then I climbed in the unlocked window. There was a night light on, so I didn't turn on any lights. But there was a radio on the counter. I turned it on to a music program. It was warm in the restaurant, and I was hungry. I helped myself to a glass of milk and a piece of pie, intending to keep a list of what I'd eaten so I could leave money. I also planned to get up early, sneak out through the window, and head for the woods before the three-fingered man returned. I turned off the radio, wrapped myself in the man's apron, and, in spite of the hardness of the floor, fell asleep.

"What the heck are you doing here, kid?"

It was the man's voice. It was morning. I'd overslept. I was scared.

"Hold it, kid. I just wanna know what you're doing here. You lost? You must be from the reservation. Your folks must be worried sick about you. Do they have a phone?"

"Yes, yes," I answered. "But don't call them."

I was shivering. The man, who told me his name was Ernie, made me a cup of hot chocolate while I explained about Ta-Na-E-Ka.

"Darndest thing I ever heard," he said, when I was through. "Lived next to the reservation all of my life and this is the first I've heard of Ta-Na-whatever-you-call-it." He looked at me, all goosebumps in my bathing suit. "Pretty silly thing to do to a kid," he muttered.

That was just what I'd been thinking for months, but when Ernie said it, I became angry. "No, it isn't silly. It's a custom of the Kaw. We've been doing this for hundreds of years. My mother and my grandfather and everybody in my family went through this ceremony. It's why the Kaw are great warriors."

"Okay, great warrior," Ernie chuckled, "suit yourself. And, if you want to stick around,[26] it's okay with me." Ernie went to the broom closet and tossed me a bundle. "That's the lost-and-found closet," he said. "Stuff people left on boats. Maybe there's something to keep you warm."

The sweater fitted loosely, but it felt good. And I'd found a new friend. Most important, I was surviving Ta-Na-E-Ka.

My grandfather had said the experience would be filled with adventure, and I was having my fill.[27] And Grandfather had never said we couldn't accept hospitality.

I stayed at Ernie's Riverside for the entire period. In the mornings I went into the woods and watched the animals and picked flowers for each of the tables at Ernie's. I had never felt better. I was up early enough to watch the sun rise on the Missouri, and went to bed after it set. I ate everything I wanted—insisting that Ernie take all my money for the food. "I'll keep this in trust for you, Mary," Ernie promised, "in case you are ever desperate for five dollars."

I was sorry when the five days were over. I'd enjoyed every minute with Ernie. He taught me how to make western omelets and to make Chili Ernie Style (still one of my favorite dishes). And I told Ernie all about the legends of the Kaw. I hadn't realized I knew so much about my people.

[26] **stick around**: stay

[27] **having my fill**: having enough of something

But Ta-Na-E-Ka was over, and as I approached my house at about nine-thirty in the evening, I became nervous all over again. What if Grandfather asked me about the berries and the grasshoppers? And my feet were hardly cut.

195 I hadn't lost a pound and my hair was combed.

"They'll be so happy to see me," I told myself hopefully, "that they won't ask too many questions.

I opened the door. My grandfather was in the front room. He was wearing the ceremonial beaded deerskin shirt which had belonged to his grandfather.

200 "*N'g'da'ma,*" he said. "Welcome back."

I embraced my parents warmly, letting go only when I saw my cousin Roger sprawled on the couch. His eyes were red and swollen. He'd lost weight. His feet were an unsightly mass of blood and blisters, and he was moaning, "I made it, see. I made it. I'm a warrior. A warrior."

My grandfather looked at me strangely. I was clean, obviously well-fed, and radiantly 205 healthy. My parents got the message. My uncle and aunt gazed at me with hostility.

Finally my grandfather asked, "What did you eat to keep you so well?"

I sucked in my breath and blurted out[28] the truth: "Hamburgers and milk shakes."

"Hamburgers!" my grandfather growled.

"Milk shakes!" Roger moaned.

210 "You didn't say we had to eat grasshoppers," I said sheepishly.[29]

"Tell us about your Ta-Na-E-Ka," my grandfather commanded.

I told them everything, from borrowing the five dollars, to Ernie's kindness, to observing the beaver.

"That's not what I trained you for," my grandfather said sadly.

215 I stood up. "Grandfather, I learned that Ta-Na-E-Ka *is* important. I didn't think so during training. I was scared stiff of it. I handled it my way. And I learned I had nothing to be afraid of. There's no reason in 1947 to eat grasshoppers when you can eat a hamburger."

I was inwardly shocked at my own audacity.[30] But I liked it. "Grandfather, I'll bet you never ate one of those rotten berries yourself."

220 Grandfather laughed! He laughed aloud! My mother and father and aunt and uncle were all dumbfounded.[31] Grandfather never laughed. Never.

"Those berries—they are terrible," Grandfather admitted. "I could never swallow them. I found a dead deer on the first day of my Ta-Na-E-Ka—shot by a soldier, probably—and he kept my belly full for the entire period of the test!"

225 Grandfather stopped laughing. "We should send you out again," he said.

I looked at Roger. "You're pretty smart, Mary," Roger groaned. "I'd never have thought of what you did."

"Accountants just have to be good at arithmetic," I said comfortingly. "I'm terrible at arithmetic."

---

[28] **blurted out**: said quickly
[29] **sheepishly**: with embarrassment
[30] **audacity**: state of being brave
[31] **dumbfounded**: surprised

230 Roger tried to smile, but couldn't. My grandfather called me to him. "You should have done what your cousin did. But I think you are more alert to what is happening to our people today than we are. I think you would have passed the test under any circumstances, in any time. Somehow, you know how to exist in a world that wasn't made for Indians. I don't think you're going to have any trouble surviving."

235 Grandfather wasn't entirely right. But I'll tell about that another time.

Source: "Ta-Na-E-Ka," *Scholastic Voice* (Whitebird)

AFTER READING

A. MAIN IDEAS Discuss these questions about the story with a partner.

1. What does Grandfather say is "the loftiest virtue of the Indian"?
2. List at least three examples of equal treatment of men and women in the Kaw tribe.
3. Does Grandfather think Mary will survive in the world? What reason does he give?

B. REVIEW: MAKING INFERENCES In small groups, make inferences to answer these questions. Find evidence in the reading to support your answers.

1. Why do you think Mary becomes angry when Ernie criticizes the Kaw ritual?
2. How does Mary feel about her culture?
3. Will Mary have any trouble surviving in the future?

C. VOCABULARY CHECK Reread the part of the story that describes how Roger and Mary looked after the ritual (lines 201–205). How does Roger look after Ta-Na-E-Ka? How does Mary look after Ta-Na-E-Ka? Write the meanings of these words on the lines. They describe physical and emotional feelings. Don't use a dictionary. Guess the definition from sentences in the reading.

blisters: ______________________________

____

unsightly: ______________________________

____

well-fed: ______________________________

____

radiantly healthy: ______________________________

____

Reading Strategy

Finding the Theme of a Story

A theme is the main idea of a story. Sometimes an author tells you what the theme is. This is a *stated* theme. The author might state the theme at the end of the story, or a character might state it.

Other times, the theme is *unstated*, but the details in the story support it. For example, the theme of "Old Country Advice to the American Traveler" might be that sometimes it's better to learn from experience than from the advice of others. The theme isn't stated, but all of the events in the story support this idea.

D. FINDING THE THEME Discuss these questions with a partner.

1. What is the theme of Ta-Na-E-Ka?
2. Is it a stated theme? If so, where is it stated?

E. MAKING CONNECTIONS In small groups, discuss these questions.

1. Do you think Mary is brave? Does she fit into Joseph Campbell's definition of the hero?
2. Compare Mary's coming-of-age with that of Lame Deer in Chapter 1, page 29.

F. IN YOUR OWN WORDS: SUMMARIZING Choose one of the paragraphs in the reading (pages 210–216). Fill in the first blank with the topic of the paragraph. Use a noun or noun phrase. Fill in the second blank with the main idea. Complete the sentence with an independent clause.

1. The paragraph is about ____.
2. The author says that ____

____.

G. WORD JOURNAL Which new words from Parts 2 and 3 are important for *you* to remember? Write them in your Word Journal.

H. RESPONSE WRITING Choose one of the following topics and write for 15 minutes. Don't worry about grammar or spelling. Don't stop writing to use a dictionary.

- Who are your heroes? Why do you admire them?
- In what ways are *you* a hero/heroine?

PART 4 THE MECHANICS OF WRITING

In Part 4, you will learn to use parallelism, strong arguments, and synonyms. You will use this knowledge in Part 5 to write a persuasive essay.

Parallelism

In parallelism, two or more similar elements with the same grammatical structure are joined with a coordinating conjunction. These parallel elements might be:

nouns	verbs
adjectives	gerunds
adjective clauses	prepositional phrases
infinitives	noun phrases or verb phrases

Faulty (incorrect) parallelism occurs when a writer uses elements with *different* grammatical structures.

Examples:

INCORRECT: Uncle Melik **put his money in his shoe**, **put his shoe under his pillow**, and **he stayed awake** all night.

CORRECT: Uncle Melik **put his money in his shoe**, **put his shoe under his pillow**, and **stayed awake** all night.

INCORRECT: Roger was **tired**, **hungry**, and **he was covered** with insect bites.

CORRECT: Roger was **tired**, **hungry**, and **covered** with insect bites.

INCORRECT: In *Star Wars*, Han Solo starts out **working as a mercenary**, and **he hangs out** in alien bars.

CORRECT: In *Star Wars*, Han Solo starts out **working as a mercenary** and **hanging out** in alien bars.

INCORRECT: Mrs. Richardson knew **that Mary was trustworthy** and **she would pay back** the loan.

CORRECT: Mrs. Richardson knew **that Mary was trustworthy** and **that she would pay back** the loan.

A. PARALLELISM The sentences below contain incorrect parallelism. Circle the incorrect element and write the correct element on the line.

1. Many of Saroyan's characters were Californian or they came from Armenia.

   Many of Saroyan's characters were Californian or Armenian.

2. Uncle Melik spent most of his trip meeting nice people, playing cards, and he sang in a quartette.

   ____

3. Sioux men are not afraid to endure hunger, thirst, and they are sometimes lonely.

   ____

4. Mary realized that she didn't have to eat grasshoppers and she could eat hamburgers if she wanted to.

   ____

5. Grandfather demonstrated how to pull off the legs of a grasshopper and swallowing it.

____

6. Mary succeeded due to her intelligence, creativity, and she was lucky.

____

Making a Strong Argument: *Should, Ought to,* and *Must*

When you write a persuasive essay, modals such as *should*, *ought to*, and *must* help you make strong statements. You use *should* and *ought to* to make a strong suggestion; *must* expresses a demand.

You should use these modals in the active voice wherever possible; sometimes, however, the agent (the person or thing causing the action) is not important enough to state. In that case, you can use the passive voice. Here are the affirmative and negative forms of these modals in both the active and passive voice, where appropriate.

Examples: Parents **should not allow** children to watch MTV. **(Active)**
Children **should not be allowed** to watch MTV. **(Passive)**
The tribal elders **must discontinue** Ta-Na-E-Ka because it is dangerous for children. **(Active)**
Ta-Na-E-Ka **must be discontinued** because it is dangerous for children. **(Passive)**
Acupuncture **ought to be outlawed** because there's no scientific evidence that it works. **(Passive)**

Note: The passive voice works better in the last sentence because the agent is not important.

B. MAKING A STRONG ARGUMENT React to the following facts. What do you think *should*, *ought to*, or *must* be done in the following cases?

1. The religion of Santeria allows animal sacrifice.

____

2. Surveys show that 30 percent of computer game players are under the age of 10.

____

3. American children watch an average of 21 hours and 42 minutes of television each week.

____

4. Some companies have call centers that are located in foreign countries.

____

5. Orangutans are an endangered species.

____

6. Some nonhuman primates in captivity (such as orangutans) produce art that is often exhibited and sold.

____

7. Some foreign products have insulting advertising campaigns.

____

8. A certain cigarette manufacturer uses a cartoon character in its advertising.

____

Using Synonyms

Synonyms are useful when you need to paraphrase someone else's material. As you improve your ability in English, you will build your own **repertoire** (collection) of synonyms to use when you write. You can also find synonyms in a thesaurus.

In a thesaurus, the entries are alphabetical, like those in a dictionary. Each entry lists all of the synonyms in order of most direct, or most common, first. Often a group of related synonyms will be set off by semicolons (;). If applicable, an entry will also have the following items:

- part of speech
- words related to it that you can look up elsewhere in the thesaurus (in small capital letters)
- its antonym–opposite (Ant.)
- colloquial–slang or informal–synonyms for the word (Colloq.)

The word you choose from the synonym list depends on the context of the word you started with.

Look at this example from *Roget's Thesaurus*:

> **original** *adj.* **1 :** novel, unique (DIFFERENCE); **2 :** creative, inventive (IMAGINATION); **3 :** earliest, primal, aboriginal; initial, (BEGINNING)

Which synonym is the best choice for "original" in the following sentence?

Some people think the filmmaker George Lucas isn't very **original** because the plot of his *Star Wars* series is based on old cowboy movies.

____

Other ways to use synonyms for paraphrasing are **condensing** and **expanding**. Condensing is using one word for a phrase or collocation; expanding is the opposite: using a collocation or phrase in place of a word. Look at these examples:

Condensing: Mary's grandfather admitted that she had devised a **well-thought-out** plan. → Mary's grandfather admitted that she had devised a **clever** plan.

Expanding: Mary devised a **simple** plan. → Mary devised a strategy **that was straightforward**.

C. USING SYNONYMS Study the following sentence from "The Hero's Journey" and the thesaurus entry with a partner. Then answer the questions.

One is the physical deed, in which the hero performs a courageous act in battle or saves a life.

> **act** *n.* **1 :** deed, exploit, action, step (ACTION); **1 :** ordnance, edict, mandate (COMMAND); **3 :** performance, impersonation, impression, presentation (DRAMA); **4 :** measure, statute, bill (LAW).

1. What part of speech is *act*?
2. How many synonyms are there in the thesaurus entry?
3. If you wanted a synonym for *act* in the sentence from "The Hero's Journey," which group of synonyms (1, 2, 3, or 4) would you choose from?
4. Which synonym works best for the meaning of *act* in the sentence?

D. CONDENSING Match the phrases in orange with the one-word condensed versions in the box that mean about the same thing. Write the correct letters on the lines.

a. about	**c.** ate	**e.** saw
b. at	**d.** eating	**f.** stay

1. ______ Grandfather died **when he was** 81.
2. ______ There is a Kaw legend **that revolves around** the "Good Woman."
3. ______ We'll be **gorging ourselves on** grasshoppers.
4. ______ I **popped** a berry **into my mouth.**
5. ______ I **caught a glimpse of** a civet cat.
6. ______ You can **stick around** if you want.

E. EXPANDING Match the words in orange with the expanded versions in the box that mean about the same thing. Write the correct letters on the lines.

a. came back	**c.** in progress	**e.** thought it would be
b. ends up	**d.** staying alive	

1. ______ Ta-Na-E-Ka might be more fun than I **anticipated.**
2. ______ There was no card game **happening** in the smoker.
3. ______ When my Uncle Melik **returned** from New York, his uncle visited him again.
4. ______ Han Solo eventually **becomes** a hero.
5. ______ Grandfather said, "I don't think you are going to have any trouble **surviving.**"

Review: Paraphrasing

Paraphrasing is restating information in different words. There are many ways to put original material into your own words. There are two main rules to follow:

1. Read the original carefully and make sure you understand the main ideas and how they are organized.
2. Put the original away—don't look at it again. Then quickly write the main ideas as you remember them, in the order they were presented.

As you write the main ideas, try these different ways of putting the original material into your own words:

- use synonyms (There are some words you should not use synonyms for, however, such as technical terms.)
- condense and expand
- change parts of speech (For example, change nouns to verbs, verbs to nouns, nouns to adjectives, adjectives to nouns, or adjectives to verbs.)
- change the sentence structure (For example, change passive voice to active, active to passive, or direct quotes to indirect speech.)

Example: Original: The Kaws were **the originators** of the women's liberation movement.
Paraphrase: The Kaws **originated** the women's liberation movement.

Notice that the paraphrase has the same meaning. The noun phrase *the originators*, however, becomes a verb (*to originate*) in the paraphrase. You can paraphrase the original even more by using synonyms.

Example: Paraphrase: The Kaws **started the feminist movement**.

originated → started
the women's liberation movement → the feminist movement

Here's another example:

Example: Original: Mary fell asleep **in spite of** the **hardness** of the floor.
Paraphrase: **Even though** the floor was **hard**, Mary fell asleep.

in spite of → even though
hardness → hard

F. PARAPHRASING Paraphrase these statements. Combine as many of the techniques as possible (using synonyms, condensing, expanding, changing the part of speech, and changing sentence structure). Make sure that you do not repeat the words and phrases in orange in your paraphrases.

1. During Ta-Na-E-Ka, **communication was forbidden** between Roger and Mary.
Roger and Mary were not allowed to speak to each other during Ta-Na-E-Ka.

2. Grandfather **gave a demonstration of** how to eat insects.

3. Mary spent a lot of time **researching** the Kaws' **treatment** of women.

____

____

4. Even grasshoppers **were better tasting** than the berries.

____

____

5. "I'm **happy** to know the money's going to **be put to a good use**," Mrs. Richardson said to Mary.

____

____

6. Roger **squeezed** my arm.

____

____

7. Grandfather **was in charge of** our *Ta-Na-E-Ka* training.

____

____

PART 5 ACADEMIC WRITING

WRITING ASSIGNMENT

Write a persuasive essay about an issue suggested by "Ta-Na-E-Ka" or "The Hero's Journey."

STEP A. CHOOSING A TOPIC Answer one of the following questions in your argument essay.

1. Choose any rite of passage or traditional belief. Does this have value in today's society?
2. Choose a person, famous or not famous, alive or dead, fictional or real. Is he or she a hero?

STEP B. GATHERING IDEAS You're going to write an essay about an issue suggested by "Ta-Na-E-Ka" or "The Hero's Journey." The purpose of an argument is to persuade the reader that your position on an issue is correct. To do this, you must support your position with convincing evidence.

To begin gathering evidence—supporting ideas for your paragraph—read the w. If you chose Topic 1 on page 223, read Question 1. If you chose Topic 2, read Question our answer. Then share your opinions in small groups of students who have selected th s you listen to other students, take notes on ideas different from yours.

1. Do traditional beliefs and rituals have any place in the modern world abandon them? Choose a tradition from your culture or another, and argue for or aga it. Traditions might include rites of passage, magic and good luck rituals, and tradi practices such as the use of herbs and acupuncture.

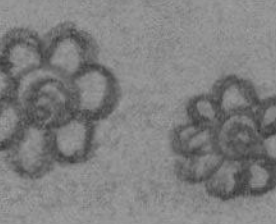

2. Describe someone who is or is not a hero. It can be someone alive today, the past. It can be someone from your culture or from any culture or country. It can be sor any people think is a hero, but you do not. Use the qualities of the hero described by Campbell to support your choice.

Writing Strategy

Understanding the Organization of an Essay

In a single paragraph, you develop one main idea. In an essay, you develop several main ideas. The first paragraph is the **introduction**. The last paragraph is the **conclusion**. The paragraphs between are called **body paragraphs**.

Here is an outline of a typical five-paragraph essay.

Paragraph 1: Introduction

1. information (also called the **opener**) to catch the attention of the reader
2. a **thesis statement**—a sentence including:
   - the main idea of the entire essay
   - a "map" or plan of what the reader can expect in the body paragraphs

Paragraph 2: First Body Paragraph

1. a topic sentence (as in any single paragraph)
2. supporting material

Paragraph 3: Second Body Paragraph

1. a topic sentence (as in any single paragraph)
2. supporting material

Paragraph 4: Third Body Paragraph

1. a topic sentence (as in any single paragraph)
2. supporting material

Paragraph 5: Concluding Paragraph

a summary of the main ideas of the essay

Introductory Paragraph

This is, perhaps, the most difficult paragraph to write. (Although this is the first paragraph in the essay, you will probably write it *last*.) To catch the reader's attention, you might include one or more of the following in your opener:

- a surprising or interesting fact
- a quotation
- a definition
- a question
- background information

The **thesis statement** is usually the last sentence in the introductory paragraph. In a five-paragraph persuasive essay, it presents the writer's point of view and includes the three ideas that the writer will explore. Each idea introduces one of the body paragraphs, in the order in which they appear in the essay. These parts are parallel; that is, they all have the same structure. The thesis statement is for an essay what the topic sentence is for a paragraph.

Body Paragraphs

Each body paragraph discusses one of the supporting ideas for the thesis statement. These paragraphs follow the same guidelines that you have studied in previous chapters. Some possible types of paragraphs are these: definition, comparison, cause/effect, argument, or analysis. The topic for Body Paragraph 1 comes from the first of the three parts in your thesis statement. The topic for Body Paragraph 2 comes from the second part of your thesis statement. The topic for Body Paragraph 3 comes from the third part of your thesis statement.

Concluding Paragraph

A good conclusion usually restates the main ideas of the essay–in different words. It might also suggest some new information on the topic but shouldn't appear to be a thesis statement for a new essay!

Remember to indent each new paragraph.

Example:

Rite of Passage

Thirteen-year old Aaron H. has returned from a two-week wilderness trip in the Sierra mountains. He's tired, dirty, and hungry. However, even though he missed his usual comforts—he slept outside, caught his own food, and built fires without matches—Aaron gained a lot more than he lost. Asked how he feels about the trip, he'll tell you he now knows what to do if he ever gets lost. In addition, he feels strong and confident. Aaron's wilderness experience is a new trend in upper-middle class American culture: a rite of passage for the non-religious, in a modern, urban society. The modern rite of passage movement typically involves a wilderness experience. It helps teenagers experience independence and self-reliance as they begin the rocky transition to adulthood. This movement is gaining popularity in many parts of the United States because it addresses some of the major challenges that face adolescents today: the hectic pace of life, a lack of community, and the lure of risky behavior.

American culture moves at a faster pace than ever before and has become increasingly competitive. As a result, American teens are under intense pressure from parents and society as a whole to succeed. Pushed to prepare for exams, take special classes, and excel in extracurricular activities such as sports, they have little time for themselves. Many experts predict that this may someday backfire, that these overscheduled teens will someday simply drop out, or worse, suffer lifelong physical and emotional problems from unnecessary competition and the pressure to succeed. The modern rite of passage movement, such as the wilderness trip that Aaron experienced, allows teens to retreat from their normal lives and spend time thinking about who they are and what their own goals are. This can help them become better adults by giving them a sense of purpose in life, one that comes from reflecting on their inner desires, rather than what society wants for them.

Many modern American adolescents experience the lack of a strong cultural or religious identity. In addition, overworked, absent, or divorced parents intensify the natural disconnection from the family that many adolescents go through. Teens therefore are missing a community that acknowledges who they are and what they are becoming. There's no tribe or village to give them an identity and help them deal with the world. The modern rite of passage movement provides teens with a sense of belonging to a group led by adults who serve as role models. Also, many rite of passage organizations work with young people in their early teens and follow them as they grow into young adults and prepare to leave home. In this way, they can provide teens with a solid springboard from which they launch into adult life.

Many experts agree that the desire for risk and challenge is an innate human need. A brush with danger and even the possibility of death connects many people with something beyond themselves, giving them a real sense of what it means to be alive. Unfortunately, however, many teens express this need in risky, self-destructive behavior such as driving too fast, experimenting with sex and drugs, and joining gangs. This behavior can be dangerous not only for themselves, but for society in general. The modern rite of passage movement recognizes that accomplishing a dangerous task to become an adult is the hallmark of rites of passage in many parts of the world. Therefore, modern rites of passage such as the wilderness experience provide teens with survival challenges that address the need for risk. As a result, teens who participate in these programs develop a strong sense of accomplishment and self-reliance; feelings that can help them become happy, productive adults.

Beyond getting a driver's license and graduating from high school, American culture has few rituals that mark the passage to adulthood. In addition, the few that do exist don't really help young people deal with the world they will inhabit as adults. The modern rite of passage movement, however, takes its inspiration from the adulthood rituals of traditional societies and provides teens in today's world with structures, challenges, and models that can truly help them make the transition to maturity.

ANALYZING Use these questions to analyze the example paragraph above.

1. In the opener, what catches the attention of the reader—a quotation, a question, a surprising fact, or background information?
2. Which sentence is the thesis statement? What are the three parts that "map" the rest of the essay? What type of parallelism is used?
3. What is the topic sentence of the first body paragraph? In which paragraph does the author begin to discuss the second supporting idea? What is the topic sentence for this paragraph? In which paragraph does the author begin the discussion of the third supporting idea? What is the topic sentence for this paragraph?
4. How do you know where each new paragraph begins?
5. Are the body paragraphs in the same order in which they were introduced in the thesis statement?
6. What type of support is given in the body paragraphs?
7. What does the conclusion do to give the reader a sense of completion?

Writing Strategy

Writing a Thesis Statement

The thesis statement is probably the most important sentence in your essay. This sentence:

- gives the main idea of the entire essay
- suggests the topic of each body paragraph
- commonly has three parts (for a five-paragraph essay)
- has parallel structures
- is strongest if it is arguable

Example: This movement is gaining popularity in many parts of the United States because it addresses some of the major challenges that face adolescents today: the hectic pace of life, a lack of community, and the lure of risky behavior.

WRITING A THESIS STATEMENT On the lines below, write a thesis sentence for the writing assignment you chose. **Note:** Use your notes from Step B on pages 223–224, to help you with this.)

____

____

____

____

____

Writing Strategy

Writing Topic Sentences in an Essay

In previous chapters, you studied topic sentences for different types of paragraphs. In an essay, each body paragraph has a topic sentence that was suggested in the thesis statement.

WRITING TOPIC SENTENCES IN AN ESSAY Using the thesis statement that you wrote above as a basis, write three topic sentences, one for each body paragraph. These should be mentioned in the same order they were mentioned in the thesis statement.

1. ____

____

____

____

2. ____

____

____

____

3. ____

____

____

____

Test-Taking Strategy

Writing Supporting Material in an Essay

In an essay, you will support each topic sentence with evidence just as you do when you write a single paragraph.

Use one or more of these types of evidence:

- examples
- reasons
- facts
- statistics
- the opinion of experts

Example: Unfortunately, however, many teens express this need in risky, self-destructive behavior such as driving too fast, experimenting with sex and drugs, and joining gangs.

If you use ideas, information, or exact words from another source such as an article, story, or interview, *make sure to cite that source* (see pages 111–112).

STEP C. ORGANIZING YOUR INFORMATION Think of as much support as possible for each of the body paragraphs in your essay. To do this:

- Use your notes from Step B on pages 223–224.
- Use information or direct quotations from the readings in this chapter.

STEP D. WRITING YOUR ESSAY Using the thesis statement, the topic sentences, and the supporting material you gathered in this section, write a five-paragraph argument essay on the topic that you chose.

STEP E. EDITING Read your essay and answer these questions.

1. Is the essay form correct (indentation, margins)?
2. How does the introduction catch the reader's attention?
3. Does the thesis statement include the main idea of the essay?
4. Does the thesis statement include a three-part "map" of the body paragraphs?
5. Are the three parts in the thesis statement parallel?
6. Are there three body paragraphs?
7. Do the body paragraphs follow the order in the thesis statement?
8. Is there strong evidence for each topic sentence?
9. Have sources been cited?
10. Is the evidence well organized?
11. Is there a one-paragraph conclusion?
12. Does the conclusion restate the main idea of the essay?
13. Is the restatement in different words?
14. Is sentence structure correct (no run-ons, comma splices, or fragments)?

STEP F. REWRITING Write your essay again. This time, try to write with no mistakes.

UNIT 3 VOCABULARY WORKSHOP

Review vocabulary items that you learned in Chapters 5 and 6.

A. CHOOSING THE CORRECT DICTIONARY DEFINITION Write the part of speech (noun or verb) of each word. Then use the dictionary entries and choose the best definition for the context. Write the number of the definition on the lines.

wood *n* **1** the hard substance under the bark of trees **2** area where a large number of trees grow together **3** a musical instrument in which sound is produced by a vibrating column of air **4** a golf club with a heavy wooden head

1. Britney wanted to play in the orchestra, so I suggested she learn a **wood** instrument such as the flute.

   Definition: __________

2. For her last shot, the golfer chose a **wood** because she had to hit the ball a great distance.

   Definition: __________

3. Instead of spending her rite of passage in a deep **wood**, she stayed at a café by the lake.

   Definition: __________

4. A house made of **wood** is more earthquake-proof than one made of bricks.

   Definition: __________

heritage *n* **1** the customs and beliefs of a cultural group **2** property that can be inherited

5. The family's **heritage** included a great deal of land in the country.

   Definition: __________

6. Participating in a rite of passage was an important part of Mary's Kaw **heritage**.

   Definition: __________

B. MATCHING Match the definitions to the words. Write the correct letters on the lines.

Words	Definitions
______ **1.** bewildered	**a.** got on a train
______ **2.** chaos	**b.** absolute; certain
______ **3.** clear-cut	**c.** composition
______ **4.** essay	**d.** confused
______ **5.** got aboard	**e.** disorder
______ **6.** paid a visit	**f.** came to see
______ **7.** patterns	**g.** test
______ **8.** recover	**h.** get well
______ **9.** surface	**i.** repeated ordering
______ **10.** trial	**j.** the top or outside part

C. COLLOCATIONS Check your knowledge of some common collocations from this unit. Fill in each blank with the missing words.

1. he mussed ____________ my hair

2. dropped ____________ of school

3. put him ____________ a year

4. get ____________ work at 6:00 P.M.

5. talk ____________ once

6. got ____________ the train

7. paid him a ____________

8. bump ____________ you

9. your ____________ impulse

10. he went out ____________ his way

11. they put their foot ____________

12. stories revolve ____________ the culture's myths

13. descended ____________ escaped animals

14. an endurance ____________

15. the day is ____________ close

D. VOCABULARY EXPANSION Your vocabulary will grow faster if you learn different parts of speech when you learn a new word. Use a dictionary to find the different parts of speech for each word in the chart.

	Verbs	Nouns	Adjectives
1.	defer		
2.		endurance	
3.			profitable
4.	torment		
5.	diverge		
6.			prospering; prosperous

E. THE ACADEMIC WORD LIST The words in the box below are from the Academic Word List (Appendix 3, pages 313–316). They are some of the most common *academic* words in English. Write the words from the box on the correct lines. When you finish, check your answers in the reading on pages 164–165.

apparent	**focus**	**initially**	**participants**
contradictory	**formula**	**instructors**	**responses**

__________ (1), the scientists and engineers "seemed bewildered . . . by the variety of __________ (2) you can make to a poem," says Stephen Parrish (one of the __________ (3), a member of Cornell's English Department). "It isn't like using a __________ (4). You can look in various places for the essential statement a poem makes, or you can be persuaded that it doesn't make a statement at all or that it makes __________ (5) statements. The __________ (6) lack of __________ (7) and the absence of clear-cut answers was frustrating for some __________ (8)."

UNIT 4

ECOLOGY

Chapter 7
Endangered Species

Chapter 8
Human Ecology

CHAPTER 7

Endangered Species

Discuss these questions:

- This type of animal in the picture is endangered. What does *endangered* mean?
- What other endangered animals can you think of?
- What can people do to save endangered animal species?

PART 1 INTRODUCTION
A Dutch Scientist Teaches Indians to Hunt

BEFORE READING

A Xavante (Brazilian Indian) hunter from the village at Pimental Barbosa Reserve, Matto Grosso, Brazil

A. THINKING AHEAD In small groups, discuss these questions.

1. Do you know about changes in the culture of South American Indians? In other words, how might their lives be different from one hundred years ago?
2. In the past, when nomadic hunting people could not find **game** (animals hunted for meat) in one area, what do you imagine they did?
3. When nomadic hunting tribes become **sedentary** (i.e., settle down in one place), how does this affect their lifestyle? How do they get food? How does it affect the wildlife, such as game, in their environment?

READING

The reading, adapted from a *Bangkok Post* newspaper article, is about one scientist's effort to reteach the Xavantes, a Brazilian Indian tribe, their lost hunting traditions. As you read, think about the answers to these questions.

- What problems resulted when the Xavantes became sedentary?
- What is Frans Leeuwenberg's role in Xavante society?

A Dutch Scientist Teaches Indians to Hunt

Fearing that they have lost their traditional hunting methods, Brazil's Xavante Indians asked a Dutch biologist to help them.

When going out to hunt, Brazilian Indians from the Xavante tribe follow a complex hierarchy, which specifies the tasks the old and the young should do when capturing animals. Three years ago, however, this tradition was broken to include a white man, who was accepted as a "hunting apprentice."

Dutch biologist Frans Leeuwenberg does not actually hunt. His task is much more difficult: retrieving ancient Indian hunting techniques. The wildlife where the Xavantes live has substantially declined in the last decades and the Xavantes needed to relearn sustainable techniques[1].

A survey of hunting techniques and the stories told by older Indians showed that the problem was caused by the Xavantes' adoption of sedentary life-styles, which occurred after contact with white men. "A long time ago, the Xavantes spent some time in one place and then moved to another. The hunting area changed continuously. At the present time, the Indians have settled down [onto their own reserve] and the wildlife is increasingly scarce[2]," said Leeuwenberg.

The Dutch biologist was working for IBAMA—Brazil's Federal Environment Agency—when he first met the Xavantes. The idea of inviting the researcher to study the loss of fauna—wildlife—came from the local Indian tribes who established a game research center. The project is being developed with financial support from WWF—World Wide Fund for Nature—and Wildlife Conservation International (WCI).

Until the 1940s, the Xavantes were a seminomadic tribe, isolated from modern civilization. There was enough land to migrate to whenever game decreased. This system allowed for the recovery of animal populations and lasted until the 1960s when contact with outsiders increased substantially.

With the increased contact, the Indians were encouraged to settle down. At the same time, the boundaries of the tribe's reserve were drawn by the Brazilian

[1]**sustainable techniques** – hunting techniques that allow hunters to capture enough animals so that no one goes hungry but that allow the wildlife population to remain about the same.

[2]**scarce** – small in number

government. Since then, it has been easier for the Xavantes to defend themselves against invasions by cattle ranchers and farmers, but it has been increasingly difficult for them to live from nature.

For the Xavantes, decisions on what and how to hunt take into account cultural factors which lessen the pressure on wildlife. Young people, for instance, prefer hunting deer, which requires speed from hunters. Other Xavantes appreciate the risks of hunting the white-lipped peccary (*Tayassu pecari*), a wild boar[3]. The variety of hunting styles means that no single animal species becomes overhunted.

Although the Xavantes still follow some of these practices, many other practices have been set aside because of their new sedentary lifestyle. According to Leeuwenberg, "The Xavantes have lost their instinct of what and where to hunt." At the Pimentel Barbosa settlement, the Indians live in a 65,000 hectare[4] area, leaving the remaining 155,000 hectares untouched.

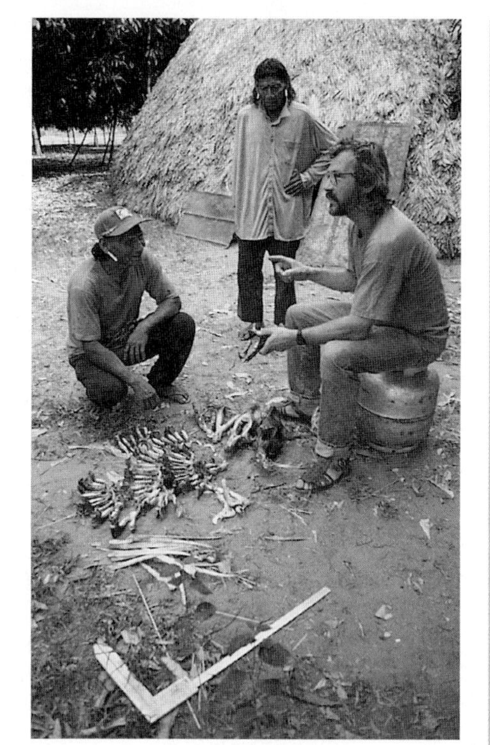

Researcher Frans Leeuwenberg and Xavante staff examining bones from hunting

Family hunting trips, whose purpose is to teach hunting and fishing techniques, are less frequent nowadays. On such trips, young people also learn to identify edible fruit and to fashion bows, arrows, and cudgels [short, heavy clubs]. The loss of this tradition and the drop in game have led a growing number of Indians to hunt with guns, thus increasing the pressure on wildlife populations.

If successful, wildlife management by the Xavantes could provide valuable lessons for other tribes. The Xavantes have been affected more than other tribes who have settled down because game meat accounts for more than 90 percent of the protein they consume, and they farm only for immediate consumption.

Leeuwenberg has commanded the respect of the 315-member tribe and the confidence of the Council of Elders, the local parliament, which meets after sunset, when the members lie down in a circle and talk.

His intimacy with the tribe permits the researcher to speak in a straightforward manner, like the Indians. He is allowed to say things that would sound offensive to white men. "You are lazy. You do not know how to hunt anymore," he said at one time. "Jaguars are smart. They use a rotational hunting system and change their area when they realize that it is taking them more time to hunt."

The forceful arguments of Leeuwenberg have hit their target. The Council of Elders decided to support the project and assigned three Xavante youths to help in the present data-gathering phase. The youths have a variety of tasks: cleaning and storing bones, determining the age and sex of the animals, and recording the number of animals killed.

[3]**boar** – a wild pig
[4] **hectare** – 10,000 square meters

The tasks are rotated, so that all three Indian youths learn and master the techniques. The idea is that, in the future, all Xavantes will be able to combine ancestral techniques with the new knowledge acquired. Thus, they will be able to better 85 manage the wildlife.

There are natural difficulties. For example, the Xavante's language does not have specific numbers for anything over five. Any number higher than five is "many." "It was practically impossible to explain that only a given number of animals could be hunted in a 1,000-hectare area," says Leeuwenberg.

90 But there is constant progress. The tribe agreed to adopt the "jaguar system" and are now changing the hunting areas when needed. They use a satellite-based technology called GPS (geographic positioning system), to choose hunting areas. In 1992, it was decided that hunting would no longer be permitted in the 65,000 hectares of the reserve most frequently used. In the second half of the second year, 95 however, the Xavantes began to hunt again in that area.

"When the cultural-ecological behavior of a people is so heavily impacted, it is impossible to go back to the old patterns in a short period of time," said Leeuwenberg.

Source: *Bangkok Post* (Fernandes)

AFTER READING

A. COMPREHENSION CHECK In small groups, discuss these questions.

1. What is Frans Leeuwenberg's role in Xavante society?
2. What is one obstacle that Leeuwenberg has faced in explaining his ideas to the Xavantes?
3. What is the "jaguar system" of hunting?
4. What did you learn about the Xavantes' hunting practices from this article? Fill in the chart in note form. In other words, don't write complete sentences. Use mostly verb phrases.

Traditional Hunting Practices
identify edible fruit
How a Sedentary Lifestyle Changed These Practices

Critical Thinking Strategy

Understanding Irony

An **ironic** situation is the opposite of what people might expect. A writer might explicitly point out irony (e.g., "It is ironic to note that . . .") or include an ironic word or phrase in quote marks. Frequently, a writer does not point out an obvious piece of irony, in which case the reader needs to infer what it is.

B. UNDERSTANDING IRONY Finish the sentences below. Then in small groups, compare your sentences.

The irony of "A Dutch Scientist Teaches Indians to Hunt" is that the Xavante Indians need

____

____. This is

ironic because ____

____

____

____.

C. IN YOUR OWN WORDS: SUMMARIZING Fill in the first blank with the topic of the reading. Use a noun or noun phrase. Fill in the second blank with the main idea. Complete the sentence with an independent clause.

1. The reading is about ____.
2. The author says that ____

   ____.

PART 2 GENERAL INTEREST READING The Human Factor

BEFORE READING

A. THINKING AHEAD In small groups, discuss these questions.

4/26

1. Read the sentence below and answer the questions without a dictionary.

   "Faster than any other biomes, the world's forests are disappearing."

   - What does *bio-* mean?
   - According to this sentence, what is one example of a biome?
   - What might be some other biomes?

2. Why do you think people are cutting down forests? Give as many reasons as possible.
3. What are some possible problems that are the result of disappearing forests?
4. What do you think caused dinosaurs to become **extinct** (completely die out)? How are more recent extinctions the result of human activity?
5. What does the word *chain* mean? What is a *food chain*? Give an example.
6. How do **indigenous** (original or native) people protect the environment? How do "advanced civilizations" protect the environment?
7. Why are zoos important?
8. In some countries there is a movement against wearing fur. Why?

Reading Strategy

Knowing Which New Words to Focus On

You will find many new words in academic reading assignments. Of course, you can guess the meaning of many of them. Some are defined in the reading. But what should you do with the others? You won't have time to look up all of them, so it's important to learn which words to focus on and which to ignore. Here are some guidelines for what to do with words that cannot be guessed.

- Don't begin to look up words until you have finished a reading. A new word might appear a second or third time.
- If a word appears several times in a short reading, it is important in that context. If you can't guess the meaning, you'll probably need to look it up.
- Nouns and verbs are *usually* more important than adjectives and adverbs.
- If you can guess *something* about a word but don't understand it exactly, you probably shouldn't look it up unless it is a key word (an important word).

Note: You will often find words that you already know, but they don't make sense in the new context. Sometimes they are followed by a preposition or other word that changes the meaning. Remember there is a possibility that you might *not* know a word that seems familiar.

B. VOCABULARY PREPARATION In each sentence below, highlight all key words, two-word verbs, and phrases that are new to you. Then decide which of these words you can guess, which ones aren't very important (so you don't need to look them up), and which ones you should look up.

1. Huge tracts of boreal forest in Siberia are being cleared for fuel and mining operations. In North America, there is a replanting program, but the new conifer forests are not as diverse as the ancient temperate rain forests they are replacing.
2. When huge tracts of forests are cleared, rainfall in those areas diminishes, causing the climate to become hotter and drier.
3. Animals that prey on livestock may be shot on sight. Others may behave in unusual ways that make them vulnerable.
4. Conservation is often hampered by social and economic conditions. Poor countries' priorities are often development and education—or simply food, housing, and public health.
5. In 1987, the first "debt for nature swap" was arranged. [Part of] Bolivia's national debt was written off against a 160,000-sq.-km. (61,766-sq.-mi.) area of rain forest.
6. A crop may become susceptible to a particular disease, which can wipe out an entire crop.
7. National gene banks now exist in more than 60 countries in order to preserve the genetic diversity of important food crops. However, seeds cannot be stored infinitely; they deteriorate and are vulnerable to disease.

READING

4/26 + p. 253-254 outline (thru. section 2)

Read the passage without using a dictionary. Highlight main ideas, important details, and important new vocabulary with different colors. As you read, think about the answer to this question:

- Why are so many species becoming extinct, and what can be done about it?

The Human Factor

In India, local women began a forest-protection plan called the Chipko movement (*chipko* means "to hug" or "to cling to"). As loggers arrive to clear a forest, villagers simply encircle the trees, refusing to let them be cut.

Disappearing Forests

Faster than any other biomes, the world's forests are disappearing. As much as a third of the total tree cover has been lost since agriculture began some 10,000 years ago. The remaining forests are home to more species than any other biome, making them the Earth's chief resource for the biodiversity of species.

Tropical rain forests once covered 12 percent of the land of the planet. As well as supporting at least 50 percent of the world's species of plants and animals, they are home to millions of people. But there are other demands on the rain forest: much is cut for timber, especially hardwoods such as teak and mahogany. The land is cleared for oil prospecting, road building, or cattle grazing and for growing crops such as coffee, cocoa, and bananas. Less than half of the Earth's original rain forests remain, and more than 50 million acres a year are lost.

Forests outside the tropics are suffering the same fate. Huge tracts of boreal forest in Siberia are being cleared for fuel and mining operations. In North America, there is a replanting program, but the new forests are not as diverse as the ancient temperate rain forests they are replacing. However, this does not mean that these forests are not important to the global ecology. Temperate forests are the Earth's largest land-based source of carbon. If the trees are cut down, they cease to use carbon dioxide in the atmosphere (for photosynthesis). As a result, levels of the gas increase, contributing to the global warming.

In Europe and North America, pollution is an even bigger threat than clearing. Millions of hectares of trees in 21 countries are dead or dying. The same damage is occurring in China, where 90 percent of Sichuan province's forests have died. The cause appears to be a combination of pollutants, including acid rain. Trees that do survive are more vulnerable to disease, harsh weather, and other stress.

When huge tracts of forests are cleared, rainfall in those areas diminishes, causing the climate to become hotter and drier. The soil also becomes dry and hard, making it less able to absorb rain; its fertility decreases along with its moisture. Eventually, if no restoration is attempted, the forest is transformed into desert.

Under Threat of Extinction

Dinosaurs, saber-toothed tigers, and the dodo bird are famous examples of animals that have become extinct. In the case of the dinosaurs, it seems likely that a catastrophic event (probably a meteorite strike) altered the global climate enough to lead to their disappearance. More recent extinctions and near-extinctions—such as the blue whale, tiger, panda, and North American bison—have been the direct result of human activity. Between 20,000 and 30,000 species become extinct every year, a figure quoted by the American biologist Edward O. Wilson of Harvard University, based on his most conservative estimates. This rate of extinctions carries with it some terrible consequences. Each plant that becomes extinct, for example, may take with it as many as 30 insects and animals that depend on it for food.

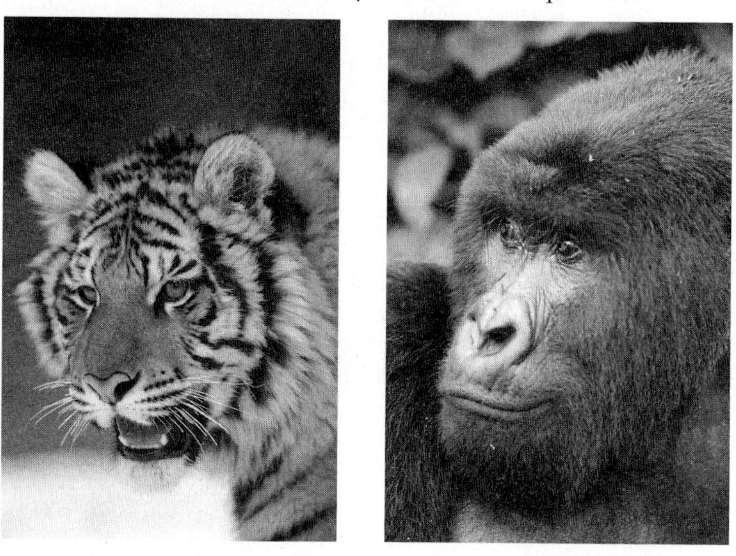

The Siberian tiger and the mountain gorilla of central Africa are among the most endangered species on Earth, as a result of forest clearance and hunting. There are thought to be fewer than 500 of each left—below the minimum figure for adequate reproduction.

Habitat loss is one of the most important causes of extinction. As rising populations in many countries lead to the clearing of more land, habitats such as rain forests and grasslands disappear. In East Africa, once renowned for its wildlife, few wild animals survive outside the boundaries of national parks and game reserves. In other parts of the world, coastal ecosystems are cleared for development. Wetland areas such as the Cota Doñana in southern Spain and the Everglades in Florida are drying out as a result of water extraction to support farming and tourism. Bird species are among the worst affected by the loss of wetlands.

Some species are more vulnerable to extinction than others. A specialized habitat or diet restricts a species to certain locations or foods, especially if it feeds at the upper levels of a food chain, as eagles do. Species with low rates of reproduction, such as blue whales, whooping cranes, and giant pandas, may not breed fast enough to keep up with any increase in their death rate, or to keep their populations large enough to avoid inbreeding, which weakens the gene pool and eventually leads to extinction. Large species, such as African lions, elephants, and grizzly bears, are often the target of commercial and sport hunters. Animals that prey on livestock or have a reputation for attacking humans, such as wolves and some crocodiles, may be killed on sight. Still others may behave in unusual ways that make them vulnerable. Redheaded woodpeckers fly in front of cars. Key deer are hit by cars as they look for cigarette butts on highways.

Alien species, such as rabbits, rats, dogs, and cats, brought by humans to new habitats have led to the disappearance of many native species. In New Zealand, flightless birds were killed by rats that escaped from ships carrying European colonists. Tourists in pursuit of the wonders of nature also endanger the balance of natural systems: on beaches in Malaya, hundreds of people wait for the endangered giant leather-backed turtle to lay eggs. Their noise and flash cameras frighten the turtles and interfere with the egg-laying. Remote areas such as the Antarctic and Mount Everest are now regularly visited by tourists who trample vegetation and disturb bird colonies.

Conserving and Restoring

In 1987, the Sierra Club of the United States sponsored a survey of the world's remaining wilderness—defined as any completely undeveloped area of at least 405,000 hectares. About 34 percent of the Earth's land meets this definition. Most of it is forest, desert, and tundra, and most is found at high latitudes. However, less than 4 percent of the Earth is protected. With ever more of the world's biomes damaged or disappearing, it is essential that what remains is conserved.

Conservation is inbuilt in the lifestyles and beliefs of most indigenous peoples. In other civilizations, conservation began when rulers of countries set aside land for hunting or other royal recreation. The first national park in the world was Yellowstone in the northwestern United States, established in 1872. As the American frontier "closed," it became apparent that the vast country's resources were not infinite, as they had seemed to the first settlers 200 years earlier. Restricted hunting seasons had been introduced in the original 13 colonies as early as 1700 to protect deer.

The Yosemite Valley in California was set aside in 1890 as a national park, one of the first in the world. National parks were created primarily to protect the landscape rather than the wildlife. Ironically, one of the greatest threats to Yosemite is posed by the 3.5 million tourists who flock there every year.

Now there are more than 3,831 national parks in 183 countries around the world, almost half of them established since 1972; new acreage is continuously being added. Many of these parks were originally introduced to preserve landscapes, but it is now recognized as more important to preserve whole ecosystems because each is important on the global scale.

There have been 1.8 million hectares of Amazonian rain forest handed over by Colombia's government to its indigenous population in recognition of their conservation skills. The local people live in and farm the forest. Their traditional shifting cultivation does not over-use local resources. If taken up elsewhere, their approach to conservation could save the world's rain forests.

Although this has been recognized, it is far from being achieved. More than half of tropical countries, whose biomes are under greatest threat, have no systematic approach to conservation. (Costa Rica and Botswana are notable exceptions.) The conservation of one biome or group of species may be emphasized over general conservation; in southern Africa, most protected areas are those that contain large numbers of mammals, while other areas—equally valuable—are ignored.

Conservation is often hampered by social and economic conditions. Poor countries' priorities are often development and education—or simply food, housing, and public health—at the expense of the environment. Their economic interests are sometimes combined with conservation programs supported by international organizations. In 1987, the first "debt for nature swap" was arranged; $650,000 worth of Bolivia's national debt was written off against a 160,000-sq-km area of rain forest and savanna. This area is now designated a biosphere reserve: a whole ecosystem with a strictly controlled central zone where no interference is allowed, surrounded by a transition zone in which research is permitted, and finally a buffer zone to protect the ecosystem from encroachment. There are now more than 436 worldwide.

Conservation sites require management in order to be successful. Careful account must be taken of what each species requires for living space and food, and how many individuals make up a viable population. The needs of any local people must also be considered. Villagers in southern Africa are being educated to realize that animal populations are a valuable tourist attraction and are learning to look after the animals that represent their future. In these areas, poaching of animals such as rhinoceroses and elephants has declined sharply, allowing controlled big-game hunting by paying tourists to be part of conservation strategy.

Preserving Diversity

As more species become extinct each year, awareness has grown of the importance of preserving wildlife. Ecologists have given a new understanding of the contribution made by most species to the ecosystems in which they live. Other scientists have discovered many benefits to humans to be derived from threatened species.

Only a fraction of the world's plants and animals have been studied for their potential value as food, medicine, or materials for industry. Many species may become extinct without revealing their potential value. Each one is a storehouse of natural genetic and biochemical resources that cannot be replaced.

As commercial agriculture spreads throughout the world, much of the traditional variety of food crops has been lost. Three types of grain—wheat, rice, and corn (maize)—make up half the world's food harvest, and many modern crops have lost their genetic diversity. A crop with nearly uniform genetic composition may become susceptible to a particular disease, which can wipe out the entire crop. The most effective way of preventing disease among such crops is to interbreed them with wild strains.

Interbreeding crops with wild plants also increases yields and expands the area suitable for cultivation. For example, 10 million square kilometers on Earth is too salty for growing the species of grain now used in intensive farming, but would be suited to the strains of wheat, rice, barley, and millet that prefer salty soil.

There are over 250.000 species of flowering plants in the world. Only 3,000 have been used by people. The great diversity among flowering plants must be preserved.

National gene banks now exist in more than 60 countries in order to attempt to preserve the genetic diversity of important food crops. Sixty thousand varieties of rice and twelve thousand types of wheat and corn from 47 countries are stored as seed samples. However, seeds cannot be stored infinitely; they deteriorate and are vulnerable to disease.

Tropical rain forests have the world's greatest biodiversity, making them a storehouse of opportunity for biotechnology, medicine, agriculture, and horticulture. More than 10 percent of all common medicines originate in tropical rain forests, and the potential for future discoveries is evident from the fact that 6,500 plants from the rain forests of southeast Asia alone are used for medicinal purposes.

As the numbers of large mammals decline, zoos take on the role of animal gene banks. When endangered species are bred in captivity, animals with the widest possible genetic makeup are used in order to keep the gene pool as large as possible. Over the next 50 to 100 years, many of the larger mammals may cease to exist in the wild. The only populations will live in zoos where they can be bred and maintained, to be appreciated and valued by future generations.

Source: *Ecology and Environment* (Morgan)

AFTER READING

A. COMPREHENSION CHECK In small groups, briefly compare the main ideas that you highlighted. Did you highlight most of the same information? (You will use this information later.)

Reading Strategy

Understanding the Passive Voice

The passive voice is often used in academic writing, especially in the sciences. It's important not to confuse the meaning of passive-voice sentences.

When the subject (of an active-voice sentence) is unknown, obvious, or not important, it is common to use the passive, instead. An active-voice sentence emphasizes the subject. The verb or object is emphasized in the passive voice.

ACTIVE: People cannot store seeds indefinitely.

PASSIVE: Seeds cannot be stored indefinitely.

What is important in the sentences above is the seeds and not the people who store the seeds. Therefore, the passive voice is more appropriate.

ACTIVE: Scientists have studied only a fraction of the world's plants and animals for their potential value as food or medicine.

PASSIVE: Only a fraction of the world's plants and animals have been studied for their potential value as food or medicine.

What is important in the sentences above is how many plants and animals have been studied and not the scientists. Therefore, the passive voice is more appropriate.

When students write, they sometimes combine passive and active in one sentence; this is not correct.

INCORRECT: People have been killed the wildlife.

CORRECT: The wildlife has been killed.

B. UNDERSTANDING THE PASSIVE VOICE With a partner, write on a separate piece of paper an active sentence for each passive-voice sentence below. Then discuss why the passive voice is more appropriate.

1. Much of the rain forest is cut for timber.
2. The land is cleared for pastureland for cattle.
3. If the trees are cut down, they cease to use carbon dioxide.
4. Animals such as wolves may be shot on sight.
5. In New Zealand, flightless birds were killed by rats from European ships.
6. Conservation is often hampered by social and economic conditions.

C. VOCABULARY CHECK Match the words and phrases on the left with their definitions on the right. Don't use a dictionary, but look back at the reading on pages 243–247 if necessary. Write the correct letters on the lines.

5|3

__H__ 1. biodiversity n.
__G__ 2. encroachment n.
__B__ 3. gene pool n.
__E__ 4. greenhouse effect n.
__F__ 5. habitat n.
__C__ 6. mammal n.
__D__ 7. soil n.
__A__ 8. wilderness n.

a. any completely undeveloped area of at least 405,000 hectares (4,050-sq.-km.)
b. all genes of all living members of a species
c. animal that has warm blood and hair and whose females produce milk for the young
d. ground; dirt
e. increase in the temperature of the Earth's atmosphere, caused by increased carbon dioxide
f. the local environment in which a plant or animal lives
g. movement or advancement beyond the usual limits (e.g., movement of people or the desert into a forested area)
h. the variety of the Earth's animal and plant species and the ecosystems that support those species

D. COLLOCATIONS In small groups, highlight the collocations in the sentences below. Look for noun phrases, adjective phrases, and prepositional phrases.

1. In India, villagers take part in the Chipko movement, which is dedicated to saving Indian forests.
2. There is a decline in species worldwide, and thousands of species are on the brink of extinction.
3. Elephants are known for their intelligence, but they are at the mercy of hunters who kill them for their tusks.
4. Protection of endangered animals requires an educated public and respect for species other than our own.

E. CATEGORIZING For each group of words, write a more general word or term from the reading on pages 243–247 for all words in the group.

5|3

1. hardwoods	2. ________	3. ________
teak mahogany cherry	coffee cocoa bananas	dinosaurs saber-toothed tigers dodo birds
4. ________	**5.** ________	**6.** ________
blue whales tigers pandas North American bison	blue whales whooping cranes giant pandas	African lions elephants grizzly bears

F. FINDING DETAILS Answer the questions below by filling in the graphic organizers with information from the reading (pages 243–247). Use note form, not complete sentences.

5/3

1. What are reasons for the clearance of forests?

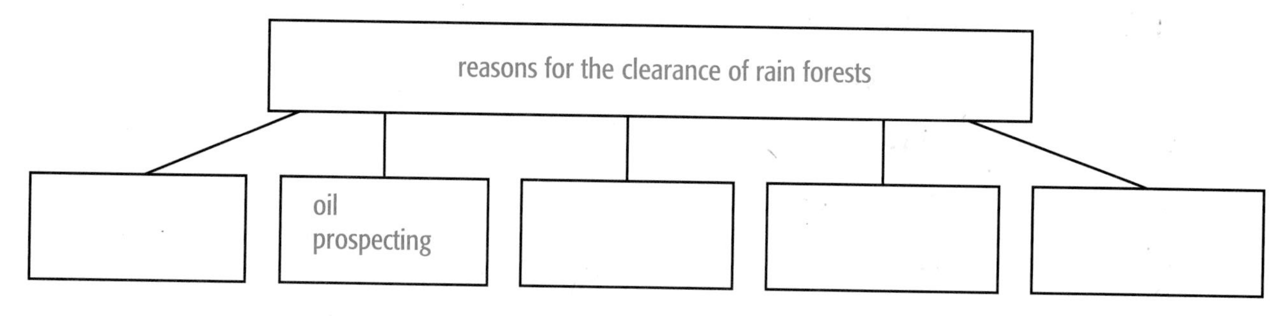

2. What are some results of the clearance of forests?

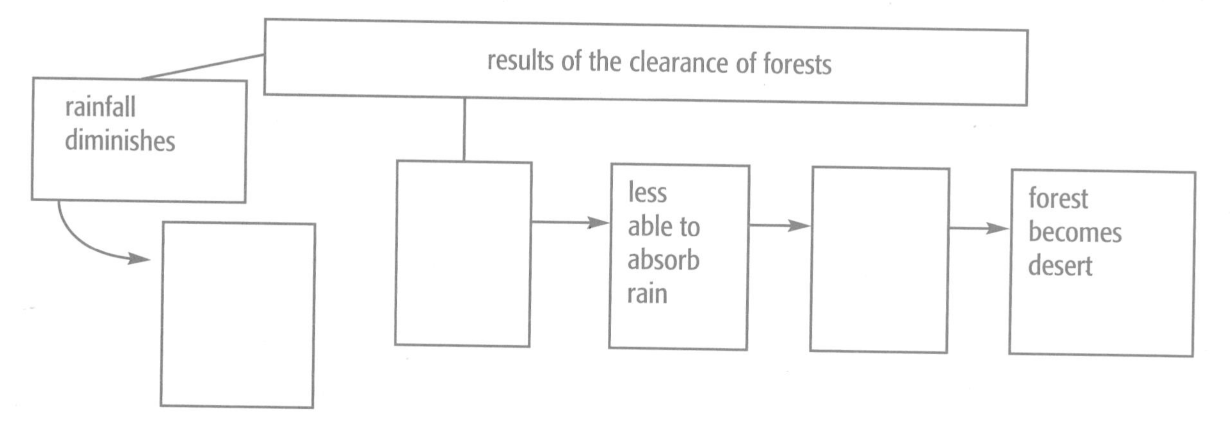

3. What are four causes of the extinction (or near extinction) of animals?

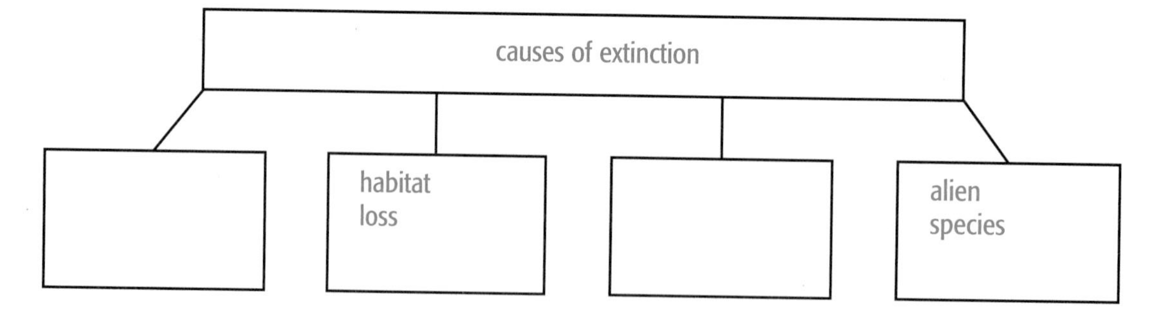

4. What is required in order for conservation sites to be successful?

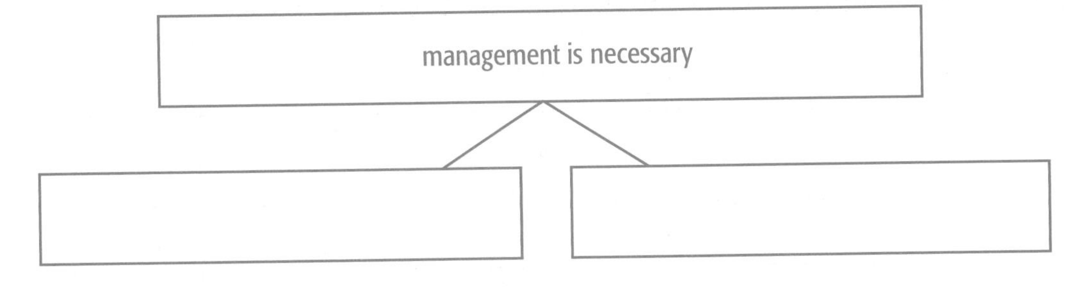

5. How is the interbreeding of crops with wild plants beneficial?

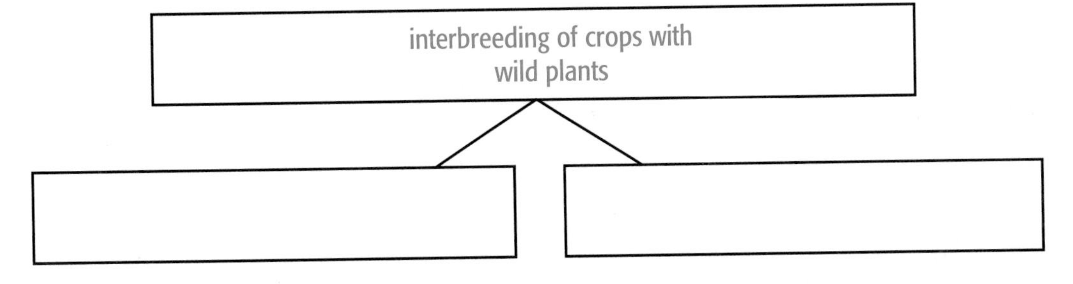

6. In what three ways are attempts being made to preserve genetic diversity?

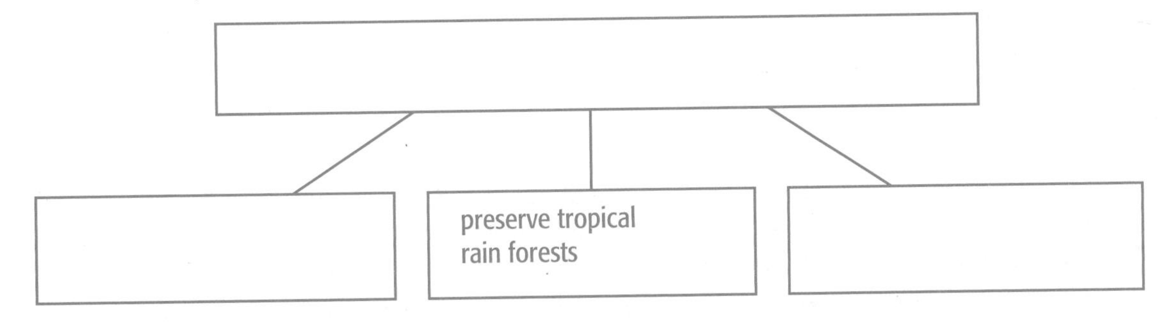

Reading Strategy

Formal Outlining

Another way to take notes on a reading is by writing a formal outline. You will not usually have time to re-read chapters before an exam, but it is possible to read over an outline. An outline is an effective study tool because it helps you see the relationship among ideas.

In an outline, the more general topics and ideas are on the left. Increasingly specific topics and ideas are indented to the right. The most general topics are indicated by Roman numerals (I, II, III, IV, etc.). More specific points have capital letters (A, B, C, D), followed by Arabic numerals (1, 2, 3, 4) and then lowercase letters (a, b, c, d).

Example:

I. Extinct animals
    A. Dinosaurs
        1. stegosaurus
        2. brontosaurus
    B. Saber-toothed tigers
    C. Dodo birds
II. Nearly extinct animals
    A. Gorillas
        1. lowland
            a. western
            b. eastern
        2. mountain
    B. Pandas

G. FORMAL OUTLINING On a separate piece of paper, organize the words in the box into one logical outline. Use only the words on this list; do not add any extra words.

birds	**eagles**	**lions**	**peacocks**	**tigers**
cats	**fish**	**mammals**	**pigeons**	**tuna**
deer	**jaguars**	**pandas**	**sharks**	**whales**

Now in small groups, compare your outlines.

H. TAKING NOTES: Below is an outline of the first two sections of the reading on pages 243–247. Use the reading to help you fill in the missing points.

4/26

I. Disappearing forests

A. Facts about forests

1. disappearing faster than any biome
2. __________
3. __________

B. Tropical rain forests

1. support at least 50% of world's species
2. are cut or cleared for
   a. __________
   b. oil prospecting
   c. __________
   d. __________
   e. __________
3. less than 1/2 of the Earth's original rain forests remain

C. Forests outside the tropics

1. are being cleared for
   a. __________
   b. __________
2. __________
3. problem: cut trees can't use carbon dioxide, so CO_2 increases, contributing to the greenhouse effect

D. Pollution

1. __________
2. China:

E. Results of the clearing of forests

1. ______________________________
2. soil becomes hard and dry
3. ______________________________
4. ______________________________
5. ______________________________
6. ______________________________

II. Under threat of extinction: causes

A. catastrophic event

B. habitat loss

1. clearance of land
2. ______________________________
   a. ______________________________
   b. ______________________________

C. ______________________________

1. specialized habitat
2. specialized diet
3. ______________________________
4. ______________________________
5. ______________________________

D. ______________________________

1. ______________________________
2. humans (tourists) disturbing endangered animals

Now compare your outline with a partner's outline.

PART 3 ACADEMIC READING The Edge of Extinction

BEFORE READING

A. THINKING AHEAD You are going to read a research paper that discusses ways to save endangered animal species. In small groups, discuss these questions.

1. Are there any environmental organizations that you know about? If so, tell your group about what they do.
2. Some people think of zoos as cruel prisons. Others think of them as **safe havens** where animals are protected. Have you ever been to a zoo? What do you think about zoos?
3. Do you know of any **nature preserves**—large areas of land protected against development or destruction by humans? If so, tell your group.

B. VOCABULARY PREPARATION In the sentences below, highlight all vocabulary that is new to you. Then decide which of these words you can guess, which ones aren't very important (so you don't need to look them up), and which ones you should look up. Then in small groups, compare your highlighted words.

5\3

1. It is possible for human beings to destroy animal life on a vast scale, for such is the case of most near-extinctions. Now is the time for humans to reverse this trend by focusing on research, breeding programs for endangered species, and safe habitats for animals in the wild, as a number of organizations are attempting to do in different but overlapping ways.
2. An organization called Earthwatch funds hundreds of research projects throughout the world, mostly by recruiting a corps of volunteers, who "have a critical job" in field projects, such as one looking into "the foraging activities and social behavior" of capuchin monkeys in Venezuela.
3. Although the "immediate benefit" of the volunteers "is to help save a generation of endangered turtles, . . . the real value is that volunteers themselves become the seed corn of the conservation movement, spreading the word when they return home."
4. Human encroachment into what used to be wilderness makes natural habitats increasingly dangerous places for wildlife, necessitating captive breeding programs to save species from extinction.
5. Safe, natural habitats are crucial to species' ultimate survival. "One of the best ways of preserving wildlife is to set aside areas where it can thrive without interference."
6. The organization admits that it can neither buy all the land nor "protect [it] single-handedly," so its method is to join "together with businesses, governments, partner organizations, indigenous people, and communities" . . .

READING

Read through the passage without using a dictionary. Highlight main ideas, important details, and important new vocabulary with different colors. As you read, think about this question:

- What three actions does the writer advocate in order to save endangered species?

The Edge of Extinction

Imagine a world without the whale, tiger, panda, or elephant; our planet without the wide-eyed lemur of Madagascar, the gentle manatee of the West Indies, or the beautiful lion tamarin of Brazil; life on Earth without thousands of the fascinating insects, reptiles, amphibians, birds, fish, and mammals that now inhabit it—some in 5 frighteningly small numbers. The famous biologist Edward O. Wilson tells us that "three [species] per hour or 27,000 every year" were becoming extinct by the early 1990s (Morgan, 1995, p. 137) and that today, "species are . . . disappearing . . . a thousand times faster than they are born, due to human activity" ("Speciation," 2002, ¶ 25). Clearly, it is possible for human beings to destroy animal life on a vast 10 scale, for such is the case of most near-extinctions. Now is the time for humans to reverse this trend by focusing on research, breeding programs for endangered species, and safe habitats for animals in the wild, as a number of organizations are attempting to do in different but overlapping ways.

Any action taken to save endangered species must be based on solid research. It 15 is research that informs scientists about the needs, habits, biology, and environment of animals in the wild, and the research, in turn, that educates the public of the need to preserve species. An organization called Earthwatch funds hundreds of research projects throughout the world, mostly by recruiting a corps of volunteers, who "have a critical job" in field projects, such as one looking into "the foraging activities and 20 social behavior" of capuchin monkeys in Venezuela (Perney & Emanoil, 1998, ¶ 21). The marine biologist who began the Earthwatch programs to study and save sea turtles, Tundi Agardy, explains that although the "immediate benefit" of the volunteers "is to help save a generation of endangered turtles, . . . the real value is that volunteers themselves become the seed corn of the conservation movement,

25 spreading the word when they return home" (Linden, 1990, ¶ 6).

Human encroachment into what used to be wilderness makes natural habitats increasingly dangerous places for wildlife, necessitating captive breeding programs to save species from extinction. The pioneer of this concept was Gerald Durrell, "the self-described 'champion of the uglies,'" who "founded Jersey Zoological Park in 1958, where he bred

30 endangered species to return to the wild" ("Died," 1995, ¶ 1). Durrell began by bringing the last few known animals of a species from their endangered habitats to this breeding zoo on the Isle of Jersey, in England. There, in this safe haven where they were protected from environmental pollution, hunters, and human destruction of their habitat, the animals successfully reproduced. The method, still used today and

35 replicated in zoos worldwide, includes providing the animals with "specially landscaped, spacious enclosures which closely resemble their natural homes . . . in the wild" (Durrell Wildlife Conservation Trust, n.d., ¶ 3). When the environment is once again safe, the animals are reintroduced to the habitat.

Safe, natural habitats are crucial to species' ultimate survival. "One of the best ways

40 of preserving wildlife is to set aside areas where it can thrive without interference" (Morgan, 1995, p. 152). Organizations such as Greenpeace, Nature Conservancy, and Pronatura are doing just that. Among others, the goals of "Greenpeace, an international group that's more than 30 years old, . . . funded mostly by contributions from its 2.5 million members . . . [is] saving ancient forests, stopping global warming, exposing toxic

45 pollutants, [and] protecting the oceans" (Vann, 2005, ¶ 5). The Nature Conservancy uses money donated by members to buy land and set it aside permanently for nature preserves where no development can take place. The organization admits that it can neither buy all the land nor "protect [it] single-handedly," so its method is to join

"together with businesses, governments, partner organizations, indigenous people, and 50 communities" to "preserve our lands and waters for future generations to use and enjoy" (The Nature Conservancy, 2005, ¶ 7). While Greenpeace and the Nature Conservancy work internationally, other groups such as the Mexican organization Pronatura work on a national level. In 2005, for example, Mexico launched "the largest conservation project in that nation's history with its plan to protect 370,000 acres of tropical forest 55 on the Yucatan Peninsula," an area that has hundreds of rare species, among them the second largest population of jaguars outside of the Amazon ("Historic land save," 2005, p. 23). The American writer Mark Twain would no doubt approve. As he once pointed out, people should buy land "because they don't make it anymore."

We humans have a history of destruction of the environment, but we needn't repeat 60 the past. By studying animals and their natural habitats, supporting captive breeding programs, and preserving habitats, there is hope that humans may be able to live in harmony with nature.

References

Died, Gerald Durrell. [Electronic version]. (1995, February 13). *Time, 145,* 23.

Durrell Wildlife Conservation Trust. (n.d.). *Jersey Zoo: A very special place*. Retrieved March 13, 2005 from http://www.durrellwildlife.org/index.cfm?a=6

Historic land save in Mexico [Electronic version]. (Winter 2005). *American Forests, 110,* 23–28.

Linden, E. (1990, April 2). Challenges for earth patriots: Stalking dwarf hamsters in Siberia [Electronic version]. *Time, 135,* 70–75.

Morgan, S. (1995). *Ecology and the environment.* New York: Oxford University Press.

The Nature Conservancy. (2005). *How we work: Our methods, tools, and techniques.* Retrieved March 13, 2005 from http://nature.org/aboutus/howwework/

Perney, L., & Emanoil, P. (1998, September–October). Where the wild things are: 25 ways to get close to nature this winter [Electronic version]. *Audubon, 100,* 82–87.

Speciation and biodiversity: Interview with Edward O. Wilson. (2002, February). Retrieved June 24, 2005 from www.actionbioscience.org/biodiversity/wilson.html

Vann, K. M. (2005, January 3). Report classifies woods as healthy [Electronic version]. *Tallahassee Democrat*, p. 5.

AFTER READING

A. ANALYSIS: ESSAY FORMAT With a partner, compare the main ideas that you highlighted in the research paper. Then use what you learned in Chapter 6 (pages 224–226) about the format of essays to discuss these questions.

1. What is the thesis statement? Where is it placed? What are the three parallel parts?
2. Where is the opener?
3. What are the three topic sentences?

4. Do the topics of the three body paragraphs follow the order of the three topics presented in the thesis statement?

5. Which part of the paper does the conclusion refer back to?

B. COMPREHENSION CHECK You have filled in many graphic organizers in this book. Now is the time for you to create your own. On a separate piece of paper, for *each* of the three body paragraphs, create a clear, logical graphic organizer that depicts main ideas, details, and the relationships among them. When you finish, compare your three graphic organizers in small groups. Are they similar?

C. IN YOUR OWN WORDS: SUMMARIZING Choose one of the three body paragraphs in the research paper. Fill in the first blank with the topic of the section. Use a noun or noun phrase. Fill in the second blank with the main idea. Complete the sentence with an independent clause.

1. The section is about ____.

2. The writer says that ____

____.

D. MAKING CONNECTIONS In small groups, discuss this question:

- Which actions advocated by the writer of the research paper in Part 3 (pages 256–259) are also explored by the author of the reading in Part 2 (pages 243–247)?

E. WORD JOURNAL Which new words from Parts 2 and 3 are important for *you* to remember? Write them in your Word Journal.

F. TAKING A SURVEY Interview two students about a country they know well. They can be in your class or another class. Try to interview students who know about different countries. Ask them the questions below and write their answers on a separate piece of paper.

1. What are some endangered animal species?

2. Why are these animals in danger of extinction? (Overhunting? Habitat loss? etc.)

3. What is being done (by the government, private organizations, or individuals) to help these endangered species?

4. Are forests being cleared? If so, for what reasons?

5. What is being done to save habitats?

6. What are some zoos? Do they have breeding programs?

G. RESPONSE WRITING Choose *one* of the following topics and write for 15 minutes. Don't worry about grammar or spelling. Don't stop writing to use a dictionary.

- one endangered species that you know about and reasons it is endangered
- reasons the Xavantes should hunt in the traditional way
- your opinion of zoos

PART 4 THE MECHANICS OF WRITING

In Part 4, you will learn to use ellipses, brackets, and source material. You will use this knowledge in Part 5 to begin a research paper.

Understanding Punctuation: Ellipses and Brackets

You know that writers must use quotation marks around any material that they copy exactly. However, sometimes, in order to weave a quote into their own words, they need to change something slightly; they may need to take out a few words or add a word. If they change *anything* within a quotation, it is necessary to indicate this change to the reader.

- To take out something within the quote, the writer uses an **ellipsis**–three periods separated by spaces.
- To add a word or two within the quote, the writer puts the added material in **brackets**–[ ].

Examples: "It is important not to . . . underestimate the problem," Rivera warns.

According to Nakamura, "Sea turtles are [further] endangered by well-intentioned tourists who come to save them."

A. PUNCTUATION: ELLIPSES AND BRACKETS Look back through the research paper on pages 256–259. Highlight six examples of ellipses and three examples of brackets.

Review: Using Source Material

As you have learned, there are several basic rules you must follow when you use material from a source such as an article or book.

1. Never copy material without:
   - putting it in quotation marks,
   - giving credit to the author, and
   - making sure that you have copied it exactly.
2. Even if you put information from sources in your own words, you must give credit to the authors for their ideas; in this case, however, do not use quotation marks.
3. When you paraphrase or summarize, change the words but not the meaning.
4. When you paraphrase or summarize, make sure that your words are different enough from the words of your source. If they are too close, it is still considered to be plagiarism (as when a person copies exact words). If you find yourself in this situation, it is better simply to quote.
5. When you weave in quotations, make sure that the sentence structure is correct and that everything is logical.

B. USING SOURCE MATERIAL Read the paragraph below.

Habitat loss is one of the most important causes of extinction. As rising populations in many countries lead to the clearing of more land, habitats such as rain forests and grasslands disappear. In East Africa, once renowned for its wildlife, few wild animals survive outside the boundaries of national parks and game reserves. In other parts of the world, coastal ecosystems are cleared for development. Wetland areas such as the Cota Doñana in southern Spain and the Everglades in Florida are drying out as a result of water extraction to support farming and tourism. Bird species are among the worst affected by the loss of wetlands.

Source: Sally Morgan, *Ecology and the Environment,* 1995

Now read how one student incorrectly used this material and how another student correctly used it.

Student A:

One of the most serious causes of extinction is habitat loss because rising populations in a lot of countries are clearing land, so habitats such as rain forests and grasslands are disappearing. East Africa was once famous for its wild animals, but very few wild animals now live outside the boundaries of national parks and game reserves. In other places, people clear coastal ecosystems to develop the land to support farming and tourism. The loss of wetlands is especially bad for bird species.

Student B:

Morgan says that the loss of "habitat . . . is one of the most important causes of extinction." This is due to population growth. Such growth results in "the clearing of more land," which, in turn, causes "habitats such as rain forests and grasslands [to] disappear." She points out that this has happened in East Africa, where most wildlife exists only within "the boundaries of national parks and game reserves." Wetland areas along the coasts are also disappearing "as a result of water extraction to support farming and tourism."

Discuss these questions with a partner.

1. Which student used the material poorly?
2. What are the student's errors?
3. Which student used it well?
4. What did this student do right?
5. What was done in the good paragraph when the student wanted to delete something in the middle of a quote? What was done to insert a word in the middle of a quote?

C. USING SOURCE MATERIAL On a separate piece of paper, use the following source material to practice summarizing, paraphrasing, quoting, and citing of sources. Write two paragraphs, one for the material in each box.

> Until the 1940s, the Xavantes were a seminomadic tribe, isolated from modern civilization. There was enough land to migrate to whenever game decreased. The system allowed for the recovery of animal populations. It lasted until the 1960s, when in one area contacts with outsiders increased substantially.
>
> With the increasing contacts, the Indians were encouraged to settle down. Sedentary habits became an unforeseen consequence of the fulfillment of a long-standing aspiration of the tribe: the demarcation of their reserve. Since then, it has been easier for the Xavantes to defend themselves against invasions by cattle ranchers and farmers, but it has been increasingly difficult to live from nature.
>
> **Source:** Adriana Fernandes, "A Dutch Scientist Teaches Indians to Hunt" from *Bangkok Post,* p. 36.

> Conservation is often hampered by social and economic conditions. Poor countries' priorities are often development and education—or simply food, housing, and public health—at the expense of the environment. Their economic interests are sometimes combined with conservation programs supported by international organizations. In 1987, the first "debt for nature swap" was arranged; $650,000 worth of Bolivia's national debt was written off against a 160,000-sq.-km. area of rain forest and savanna. This area is now designated a biosphere reserve: a whole ecosystem with a strictly controlled central zone where no interference is allowed, surrounded by a transition zone in which research is permitted, and finally a buffer zone to protect the ecosystem from encroachment. There are now more than 250 worldwide.
>
> **Source:** Sally Morgan, *Ecology and the Environment,* 1995

In small groups, compare your paragraphs and discuss these questions:

- Which language did you think was important to quote?
- Which information did you paraphrase?
- Did you delete or add words? If so, did you use ellipses or brackets?
- Did you cite the source?

PART 5 ACADEMIC WRITING

WRITING ASSIGNMENT

In Chapters 7 and 8, you are going to write a fully documented research paper. In this chapter, you will choose a topic, do research, and write a tentative list of references. In Chapter 8, you will plan and write the research paper and make changes, if necessary, to your list of references.

Your paper will have only five paragraphs and follow the same format that you learned in Chapter 6 (pages 224–226); the difference is that it will include a reference list and citations. You will need a minimum of five sources on your reference list.

Writing Strategy

Writing a Research Paper

What is a research paper?
A **research paper**—also called a **term paper** or just a **paper**—is a project required in most college classes in the social sciences and humanities and in some science classes. A professor assigns a research paper and gives certain **criteria** (guidelines), e.g., length of the paper and possible general topics. Each student then chooses a topic within the requirements and does research on the topic. In other words, the student finds information on the topic in books and periodicals (magazines, journals, newspapers) at the library or on the Internet, reads these sources, decides on a point of view, and writes the paper.

What's the difference between an essay and a research paper?
A research paper is usually longer than an essay—five to 50 pages, or more. The basic format remains the same regardless of the length. (Therefore, if you are able to write a short paper, you will also be able to write a long one.) A research paper is **documented**, that is, based on sources from which the student quotes, paraphrases, and summarizes. In a research paper, there is a list of **references** at the end (also called a "bibliography"), and there are citations of these sources in the paper. There are strict rules for the documentation of sources.

How is the research paper documented?
There are various styles of documentation. One style may be required in one class and a different style in another. Some common styles are **APA** (American Psychological Association) and **MLA** (Modern Language Association)*. Classes in social sciences usually require the APA style; classes in literature usually require MLA. If you learn to use one style, it shouldn't be very difficult to change to another style when necessary. To learn the rules for these styles, the student may use a **style sheet** given by the college department that assigns the paper. However, most students also buy a **style manual** (a book) or find information online.

*An example of MLA style is in Appendix 2 on page 309.

STEP A. CHOOSING A TOPIC Choose *one* of the following general questions on page 265, suggested by material in this book, or another suggested by your teacher. You will research this question and write your paper on it. Do not worry if you don't already know about this topic. You simply need to be curious about it. As you do research, you will learn what you need to know.

Anthropology:

- How does the social use of space reflect the culture of one country?
- How does magic function in three different religions?
- In what ways are chimpanzees (or gorillas or orangutans) similar to (or different from) humans?
- From the discovery of a Neolithic man frozen in the Alps 5,000 years ago, what do we now know about life in that period?

Economics:

- Choose one country. What should this country do to improve its economy?
- What should developed countries do to eradicate poverty in poor nations?
- Choose one trade organization such as ASEAN. What is your opinion of this organization?
- What skills will be essential for people doing international business in the future?

Ecology:

- Choose one country. In what ways are humans affecting animals' habitats in this country?
- Some people think of zoos as cruel, inhumane places where animals are kept in small, prison-like cages. Others see zoos as the only hope for animals whose environment is too dangerous. What do you believe about zoos? Explain your answer.
- Is it possible to make technological advances *and* preserve the environment and human health?
- Are humans endangering themselves? Speculate on the future of human life on this planet or propose solutions to the problem.

Writing Strategy

Evaluating Online Sources

You need to be careful in your choice of material from the Internet Because *anyone* can create a website, Internet sources vary widely in quality. Some are excellent sources. Others are useless or even give misinformation. Follow the guidelines below, based on advice from Purdue University and Cornell University (reputable institutions in the United States). For more details, you can try the Purdue website.

1. Is the webpage's author or organization clearly indicated?
2. What do you know about the author? (Hints: The author is probably reputable (well-known and with a good reputation) if your instructor has mentioned him/her, if the author is listed in bibliographies, or if the author is associated with a reputable organization or university.)
3. What do you know about the organization that sponsors the page? Go to the home page. **Note**: an address that ends in *.edu* is an educational institution; *.gov* indicates a government-sponsored site; *.org* means that it is a non-profit organization; *.com* indicates a business or company and is not likely to be used in academic research.
4. Is there documentation to indicate the source of the information? Is there a bibliography?
5. Is the information current? (Check the bottom for the most recent revision of information.)
6. What is the purpose of the site? (To persuade? To advertise? To give information?)

When you find information online, keep track of it in your own source log–a sort of journal where you collect online information. It's a good idea to keep such in a document on your computer, instead of paper, so that you can easily record long web addresses by cutting and pasting.

STEP B: EVALUATING ONLINE SOURCES Look for Internet sources and create a source log like the example below. If possible, create this on your computer.

What I Wanted to Know	How I Searched (key words)	Websites that I May Want to Use (URLs)	Why I Think These Are Good Websites

Writing Strategy

Doing Library Research

The limited space in this book does not allow for a detailed explanation on how to do library research. A librarian can help you with this. However, the information here will at least help you know what you need to ask the librarian about. Included here is general guidance in using books and periodicals.

Books

For a very short research paper (such as the one that you will write in this unit), you will probably not be able to read entire books in your research, but there may be one useful *chapter* in a book. Use the computer catalog to find books. You can search in several ways. Most frequently, you will search by the **subject** (topic). If you already know the title of a book or the name of an author on the subject–perhaps recommended by your professor–you can search by **title** or **author**. Your search will lead you to a book's **call number**–the combination of numbers and letters on the book's spine that is the "address" of the book in the library. You must know the call number in order to find the book.

Periodicals

Periodicals are newspapers, magazines, and **journals**. Journals are magazines with articles written by scholars and researchers. They are usually published by professional organizations, and the articles include bibliographies. Journals are better sources for academic research papers than magazines. How can you distinguish between journals and magazines? There is an excellent list of differences on the Cornell University website.

To find articles in periodicals, you need to use the library's online **periodicals index**. One such index found in many libraries is **Infotrac**. Using such an index is similar to an Internet search: you type in key words. If at first you find nothing, change your key words and try again. The articles will appear in chronological order, with the most recent first. For each article in the index, there is at least a **citation** (information such as the title, author, and date) and usually an **abstract** (summary). For most, however, you can find the **full text** (entire article). You can print out these articles at the library or send them to your own email address. Also, you can probably access Infotrac through your library's website; you will need a library card number for this.

Very old articles might not be in the online periodicals index. For these, use an index in book form (such as the ***Readers' Guide to Periodical Literature***). These book indexes have only citations, so you will need to find the article on **microfiche** or **microfilm**. Microfiche and microfilm are plastic film on which magazine or newspaper pages are reduced and reproduced. You must use a special machine in the library to read these.

As with Internet websites, you need to evaluate the quality of books and periodicals. Cornell University has clear guidelines.

STEP C. DOING LIBRARY RESEARCH First, collect the books and articles that you think you will use. It is wise always to find more than the minimum number of required sources because some may not contain useful information. Then, as you do with Internet sources, look over your sources and evaluate *each* of them on a source log. As you evaluate, you may decide to eliminate some of your sources.

Source Log: Books and Periodicals	
What is the title of the book or periodical? (Underline or use italics.)	
If a periodical, what is the title of the article? (Put this in quotation marks and include a subtitle, if any, after a colon.)	
If a periodical, is it a scholarly journal or a popular magazine?	
What is the author's name?	
Is the author reputable? If so, why do you think this?	
What is the date of publication?	
Is the source current? (And is a current source important for my topic?)	
What is the publisher (and is this publisher associated with a university?)	
Does the book or article include a **bibliography**—a list of sources that the author used?	
What is the purpose of the source? (To inform? Persuade? Advertise?)	
Is the information **objective** (factual) or **subjective** (opinion)?	
Is the information well researched and supported by evidence?	

STEP D: READING YOUR SOURCES IN DETAIL After you have chosen good sources, you need to read them as you have done with the textbook passages in this book. Use one of these techniques to read actively and understand what you read.

1. If you are reading photocopied pages, highlight main ideas with one color, important details with another, examples with a third, and important vocabulary with a fourth. Make notes in the margins about how you might use the information (such as "maybe quote this sentence," or "good example!"). Make sure not to highlight too much. Choose carefully what should be marked.
2. If you are using a library book and can't write in it, put the source information (title, author, date) at the top of a piece of paper. On the paper, write short summaries of important information. Also, carefully copy out material that you might want to quote. *Be sure to put it in quotation marks and include the page number* on which you found it.

Writing Strategy

Writing a Reference List

At the end of your research paper, you will have a list of all sources that you have referred to in the paper. You can write this list later, when you finish the paper, but many students prefer to do it at this point, when they finish the research. Then they are free to focus on the writing of the paper itself.

The source of every citation in your paper must appear on the reference list. On the list, each of these sources is called an **entry**. Some of the rules for writing a reference list in APA style are below. However, for a more complete list, there are several possibilities:

- ask the writing center at your college
- go online to http://valencia.cc.fl.us/lrcwest/apapaper.html
- go online to http://owl.english.purdue.edu/workshops/hypertext/apa/sources/refer
- go online to the APA website: www.apastyle.org
- check the *Publication Manual of the American Psychological Association.*

It's good to have guidelines; however, it's equally important to have examples of correct reference lists. You need to begin to notice the details in sample entries.

General Guidelines

1. The word *References* (not in italics) appears at the top of the page, centered, one inch from the top of the page. Margins are one inch from both sides of the page.
2. Double space *everything* equally on the page.
3. Begin each entry at the left margin. For entries that continue onto a second or third line, indent as you would for a new paragraph. (Hit the "tab" on your computer keyboard.)
4. Sources appear on the reference list in alphabetical order, according to the surname ("last" name) of the author.
5. If no author is given for a source, use the title in place of the author. Put this in alphabetical order by the first important word of the title; e.g., include the word *A* or *The* if it is the first word, but put this source in order by the second word. Do not put quotation marks around the title.

6. Do not use authors' first or middle names. Use only their first and middle initials. Do not include "Jr." or their degrees (e.g., Ph.D.).
7. If there are multiple authors, cite them all, in the same order in which they are listed on the book or article. Separate them with commas. Before the last one, put an **ampersand**–the symbol for the word *and* (&).
8. Put a period after the author. Space once. (Always space once after a period or comma.) Then put the publication date in parentheses, followed by a period. If the source is a book, this date will be just the year. If the source is an article, the date will be the year followed by a comma and the month (for a monthly publication) or the month and day (for a daily or weekly publication): e.g., 2005, September or 2006, January 23. Do not abbreviate months.
9. After the date, put the title of the article or the title of the book.
   - For an **article**, do not use quotation marks. Capitalize *only* the first letter of the first word, the first word in the subtitle (after a colon), and any proper nouns in the title.
   - For a **book**, the title is in italics. As with article titles, capitalize *only* the first letter of the first word, the first word in the subtitle (after a colon), and any proper nouns in the title.
10. After the title of a **book**, put a period, space, and the city of publication. (Find this on the title page or copyright page of the book.) If it is in the United States and is not a well-known city, also include the abbreviation of the state, after a comma (e.g., Springfield, MA). After the city, put a colon, space, and the name of the publishing company, followed by a period.
11. After the title of the **article** comes the title of the periodical (magazine, journal, or newspaper) in italics. Capitalize the first letter of each word (except for a preposition or article unless it is the first word). After the title of the periodical, put a comma, space, and the volume number in italics. Do not include *Vol, Volume,* or *v.*
12. After the volume number for an **article**, put a comma, space, and then the page numbers (not in italics). Do not include the words or abbreviations *page, p.,* or *pp* (except for newspaper articles).
13. For an **article** that you have viewed only **electronically** (i.e., not an actual paper periodical), after the title of the article, put [Electronic version] in brackets, followed by a period.
14. Important note: In articles that you found on Infotrac or another online periodicals index, the source information is at or near the top of the page. Use this information; however, *do not copy this format.* It is *not in APA style.*
15. For a **website**, if no date is visible, put the abbreviation meaning "no date" in parentheses: (n.d.). Also for a website, include the date that you retrieved it and the URL (web address) with no period at the end, e.g., Retrieved April 16, 2006, from http://www.apastyle.org/elecsource.html

STEP E. WRITING YOUR REFERENCE LIST Use the guidelines on pages 268–269 to write your own reference list. It might seem impossible, but do not panic. Begin by putting your sources in alphabetical order. Take them one at a time. If you cannot find an answer to a question in the guidelines, look for examples of how to do it on the three reference lists in this book: on pages 25, 259, and 290. If you still cannot find an answer to a question, try one of the online sources mentioned above or a manual in book form. **Note:** When you finish writing your research paper in Chapter 8, you might need to make a few adjustments to your reference list. All entries on your reference list must be cited in the paper, and all citations in the paper must be included on the reference list.

STEP F. EDITING YOUR REFERENCE LIST When you finish the reference list, edit in this way:

1. Join with three other classmates so that there are four people in the group.
2. Exchange reference lists with a classmate in the group.
3. Look for errors on your classmate's list. For example, look for problems with spacing, italics, capitalization, and missing information. Circle anything that you think might be a problem.
4. Hand the page back to your classmate and briefly discuss each other's papers.
5. Follow these same steps with the other two classmates in your group.
6. Rewrite your reference list.

CHAPTER 8

Human Ecology

Discuss these questions:

- What are some ways people both help and harm the environment?
- What are the effects of environmental damage on humans?
- What do you think "human ecology" means?

PART 1 INTRODUCTION Simple Solutions

BEFORE READING

Feedlot beef production

Rush hour

Agricultural pesticide spraying

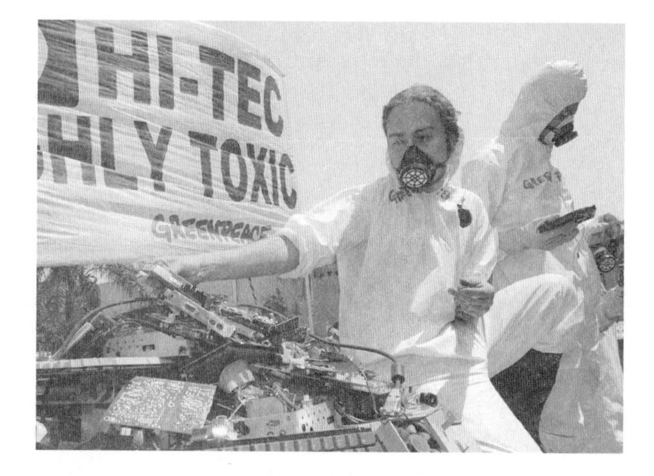

A computer-recycling center

THINKING AHEAD In small groups, look at these pictures and discuss these questions.

1. How do the activities in the photos affect the environment?
2. How might human health be affected either directly or indirectly by the activities shown in each photo?
3. How can we improve the health of the environment?

READING

Read the following excerpt from a website about an environmental organization called Turn the Tide. As you read, think about the answer to this question:

• What can individuals do to improve the environment?

Nine Steps to a Healthier Environment

Biking to work

The health of the environment directly affects human health. Air pollution can cause respiratory problems such as asthma. Chemicals such as pesticides (chemicals that kill insects) that get into drinking water can cause cancer and birth defects. In addition, the human impact on the environment is a global issue: the actions of a population in one part of the world can affect the environment of another on the other side of the globe. In fact, wealthy countries tend to use the most resources and produce the most pollution, and poorer countries tend to suffer the most. By improving the health of the environment, we can, in turn, improve human health worldwide. But what specifically can citizens of the developed world do to achieve this?

Turn the Tide, a U.S.-based nonprofit organization, has an innovative program to help improve the health of the environment. It offers nine simple actions almost anyone can take. None of Turn the Tide's nine actions involve drastic changes, yet each has a positive impact on the environment. For example, every thousand Turn the Tide participants prevent the emission of 4,000,000 pounds of climate-warming carbon dioxide every year. And that's just one benefit. Turn the Tide participants are also saving thousands of trees, millions of gallons of water, and protecting endangered species, and all through nine simple actions. Here are the nine steps:

1. **Eliminate one car trip a week.** The average American drives over 250 miles (402 km.) each week. Replace a weekly 20-mile car trip by telecommuting (working from home), biking, or combining errands and you'll reduce annual emissions of the greenhouse gas carbon dioxide by nearly a thousand pounds.

2. **Replace one beef meal each week.** Meat production is extremely resource-intensive—livestock currently consume 70 percent of America's grain production! Feedlot beef (beef raised in a confined area, not in pastures) is particularly wasteful. Every 1,000 participants who take this action can save over 70,000 pounds (31,752 kg.) of grain, 70,000 pounds of topsoil, and 40 million gallons (152 million l.) of water per year.

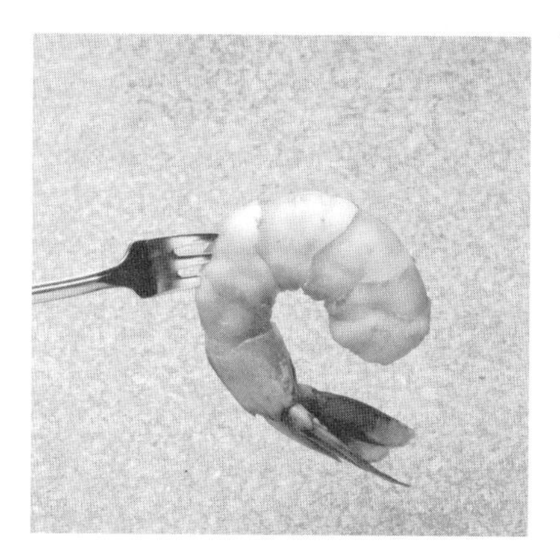
Shrimp

3. **Eat less shrimp.** Shrimp fishing can kill other sea life. Today, nearly 70 percent of the world's fisheries are fully fished or over fished, and about 60 billion pounds (27 billion kg.) of fish, sharks, and seabirds die each year as "bycatch"—animals caught accidentally as a result of wasteful fishing techniques. Every 1,000 participants who stop eating shrimp can save over 12,000 pounds (5,454 kg.) of sea life per year.
4. **Get rid of junk mail** (unwanted mail such as advertising). Nobody likes junk mail. Begin by getting yourself off junk mail lists. Every 1,000 participants who succeed in halving their junk mail save 170 trees, nearly 46,000 pounds (20,865 kg.) of carbon dioxide, and 70,000 gallons (264,978 l.) of water each year.
5. **Replace your light bulbs.** If you replace four standard bulbs with energy-efficient compact fluorescent lights (CFLs), you'll reduce your electricity bills by more than $100 over the lives of those bulbs. More importantly, you'll prevent the emission of 5,000 pounds (2,273 kg.) of carbon dioxide.
6. **Move the thermostat by 3°F.** Heating and cooling represents the biggest part of home energy consumption. Just by turning the thermostat down three degrees in the winter and up three degrees in the summer, you can prevent the emission of nearly 1,100 pounds (449 kg.) of carbon dioxide annually.
7. **Eliminate lawn and garden pesticides.** Americans directly apply 70 million pounds (31.82 million kg.) of pesticides to home lawns and gardens each year and, in so doing, kill birds and other wildlife and pollute precious water resources.

A compact fluorescent light bulb

8. **Use water-saving showerheads and faucets.** Of all natural resources, water is the most essential. But available supply is diminishing rapidly as human populations swell and inefficiently drain precious **aquifers** (water sources). For every 1,000 participants who use water-saving faucets and showerheads, we can save nearly 8 million gallons (30.28 million l.) of water and prevent over 450,000 pounds (204,545 kg.) of carbon dioxide emissions each year.
9. **Inspire two friends.** Here's an easy way for you to triple the positive impact of these nine actions: Convince two friends to join you in your effort.

Source: Turn the Tide website

AFTER READING

A. COMPREHENSION CHECK In small groups, discuss these questions.

1. Why should wealthy countries be particularly responsible for helping to improve the environment?
2. Which steps reduce carbon dioxide emissions?
3. Which steps may lead to cleaner water?

B. VOCABULARY CHECK Look back at the reading to find the words and phrases that match these definitions. Don't use a dictionary.

1. having to do with breathing and/or the lungs (Lines 1–5) respiratory
2. original (Lines 20–25) innovative
3. extreme (Lines 20–25) drastic
4. discharge; giving off (Lines 25–30) emission
5. using a great deal of resources (Lines 30–35) resource-intensive
6. cutting in half (Lines 50–55) halving
7. getting smaller (Lines 75–80) diminishing
8. get bigger (Lines 75–80) swell

Bicycle riders in Chengdu, China

C. TAKING A SURVEY Interview classmates. Find people who agree with at least one of the statements in the chart below. Write their names and explanations.

5\3

Statement	Names	Details
Do you already do all of the nine steps outlined in the reading on pages 273–274? If yes, how long have you been doing them?	Sara	3 years
Do you do *some* of the nine steps in the reading? If yes, which ones?	Nick	Doesn't eat beef
If you don't do any of the nine steps, are you willing to do some of them? If yes, which ones?		
If you don't do any of the nine steps, what other things do you do to help the environment?		

D. EXTENSION The suggestions in the reading were written for people living in the United States. In small groups, discuss some things people in other countries could do to help the environment.

BEFORE READING

A. THINKING AHEAD In small groups, discuss these questions.

1. You read a little about pesticides in Part 1. Have you ever been exposed to pesticides? Explain your answer.
2. Do pesticides affect human health? If so, how?
3. Is it possible to avoid pesticides?

B. VOCABULARY PREPARATION In the sentences below, highlight all vocabulary that is new to you. Then in small groups, compare your highlighted words. Decide which of these words you can guess, which ones aren't very important (so you don't need to look them up), and which ones you should look up.

1. Though pesticide applicators speak of "nontarget organisms," pesticides do not discriminate between targeted and nontargeted living things.
2. The car had been fumigated with the pesticide Phostoxin, and the local coroner found evidence of internal bleeding, a typical sign of pesticide poisoning.
3. In 1987, NEJM [*New England Journal of Medicine*] reported the deaths of three patients from respiratory failure, the result of organophosphate pesticides affecting nerve connections.
4. In the home, pesticides are used in treated fabrics for apparel, diapers, or bedding; in bathroom and kitchen disinfectants such as common household bleach; in insect repellents applied directly to human skin; in pet flea collars and in swimming pool additives.
5. Green, pressure-treated wood, which contains the pesticide copper-chromated arsenate, has made carpenters sick with respiratory illness, coughing, and general ill health, according to a manufacturer's memo obtained by the National Coalition Against the Misuse of Pesticides (NCAMP).
6. No sane person is advocating controlled double-blind cancer tests on human beings, with one group unknowingly exposed to suspected carcinogens and another group—the lucky ones—carefully selected to be controls.
7. Children have a long lifetime of ingesting pesticides ahead of them, and their developing bodies are more susceptible to poisoning.
8. In 1993 a team led by Dr. Mary S. Wolff, of the Mount Sinai School of Medicine, in New York, found a fourfold increase in the relative risk of breast cancer in 58 women with high blood levels of DDE, compared with blood levels in 171 matched control women without cancer, over a six-year period.

READING

The passage you are going to read may seem very long and difficult, but it is just part of one chapter from a book. It is short in comparison to the amount of reading that you will need to do in college. Most students are required to read several hundred pages each week. The reading is also fairly well written and clear compared to some academic reading in college. This chapter will give you a "preview" of a typical assignment. The reading should be done for homework—not in class.

Read the passage without using a dictionary. Highlight main ideas, important details, examples, and vocabulary with different colors. You might also add notes in the margins. Also, highlight the answers to these questions:

- Where do we encounter pesticides?
- What are some of the dangers of pesticides?

Are Pesticides Safe?

WHAT YOU NEED TO KNOW about pesticides is really very simple. They are all designed to kill. "-cide" means "kill," whether the word is *pesticide, insecticide, herbicide, fungicide, termiticide, miticide, rodenticide,* or *bacteriocide*, or any other "*-cide.*" Pesticides are designed to kill unwanted living things, or pests, whether they are insects, weeds, fungi, termites, mites, rodents, or bacteria. All pesticides are dangerous to living things—and that includes human beings. The few, inorganic (noncarbon-containing) pesticides used before World War II were called "economic poisons" because of their economic benefit to farmers. "Economic poisons" became "pesticides," which became, in some circles, "plant protectants." With each change in terminology, the sense of toxicity became more remote.

Insecticide and pesticide

Though pesticide applicators speak of "nontarget organisms," pesticides do not discriminate between targeted and nontargeted living things. "If you go into your back yard with a machine gun and blast back and forth, it is not very choosy about whom it will kill. Pesticides . . . are like that too," says Dr. Janette Sherman, author of *Chemical Exposure and Disease*. While human beings are seldom if ever intentionally targeted for lethal pesticide exposures, pesticides have killed some people (see box on p. 279).

Obviously, pesticides are not something to fool around with. But most of us do not burglarize houses, work for exterminators or lawn-care companies, or hide in boxcars illegally. Where do we encounter pesticides? The answer is "everywhere," or almost everywhere. According to the GAO [Government Accounting Office], "people are exposed to pesticides in the food they eat, the water they drink and swim in, the air they breathe, and in their homes and workplaces. In the home, pesticides are used in treated fabrics for apparel, diapers, or bedding; in bathroom and kitchen disinfectants such as common

Some common household products

household bleach; in insect repellents applied directly to human skin; in pet flea collars and in chemicals added to swimming pools." Their major use is on crops, but pesticides are also used "in homes, backyard gardens, stores, schools, restaurants, office buildings, industrial workplaces, sports facilities, hotels, hospitals, and theaters, on lawns and golf courses, and along highway rights-of-way." As if this were not enough, add to the list churches, synagogues, health clubs; florists, paint, carpeting, deodorant soaps, shampoos, pressure-treated wood; soil, groundwater, and rain and you have an idea of what can expose you to pesticides in twentieth-century America.

Most churches, synagogues, and health clubs hire exterminators for routine spraying, whether needed or not (just ask your church, synagogue, or health club). Pesticides are likely to be on the beautiful plant you bring home from the florist (just ask), in the latex paint you brush on furniture and walls, on the back of wallpaper, and on the brown paper bags you bring home from the supermarket. In 1990, the Environmental Protection Agency [EPA] warned parents against buying "Miraculous Insecticide Chalk," which could cause nausea and flu-like symptoms in children. A 1991 EPA study found pesticide residues in the dust and carpeting of all surveyed houses, making floors potentially hazardous for infants and toddlers. Dust in older houses yielded banned pesticides. Deodorant soaps that kill odor-causing bacteria contain disinfectants and fungicides that *Clinical Toxicology of Commercial Products*

Pesticides Can Kill

- In 1982, U.S. naval lieutenant George Prior, a healthy thirty-year old, died an agonizing death after playing golf on a course that had been repeatedly sprayed with the fungicide Daconil, which was pinpointed as the cause of death. (The capital "D" indicates a trade name.)
- For a man who wanted to take a break after burglarizing an empty house that was being fumigated, crime did not pay. He went back into the house to eat a snack and watch television. Neighbors found him writhing in pain naked on the front lawn of the San Fernando, California, home, having torn off his clothes in an attempt to rid himself of their pesticide contamination. He later died in a local hospital.
- In Texas, four suspected illegal aliens were found dead in a train car half-filled with boxes of tortilla flour. The car had been fumigated with the pesticide Phostoxin, and the local coroner found evidence of internal bleeding, a typical sign of pesticide poisoning.
- In 1987, *NEJM* (*New England Journal of Medicine*) reported the deaths of three patients from respiratory failure, the result of organophosphate pesticides affecting nerve connections.
- Worldwide, anywhere from one million to 25 million people are estimated to suffer from accidental pesticide poisoning each year, with more than 20,000 dying according to the World Health Organization [WHO]. Between 1975 and 1980 in Sri Lanka, 79,961 patients were hospitalized because of pesticide poisonings and 6,083 of them died. In fact, pesticides have become a drug of choice for committing suicide. WHO estimates that each year two million people in undeveloped countries purposely ingest the pesticides so easily available to them. Many more cases of pesticide poisoning worldwide, it is thought, go unrecognized or unreported.

characterizes as moderately or slightly toxic. Certain human (not animal) shampoos contain the fungicide Captan, according to Dr. Marion Moses, a California physician who has treated many migrant farm workers with pesticide-related illnesses and who is now head of San Francisco's Pesticide Education Center. Researchers at Oregon State University discovered pesticides in lanolin-based ointments such as those used for sore nipples by nursing mothers; babies could thus start their pesticide exposures at an early age, though many begin *in utero*, for chemicals can pass through the umbilical cord. You see how they all add up.

Green, pressure-treated wood, which contains the pesticide copper-chromated arsenate, has made carpenters sick with respiratory illness, coughing, and general ill health, according to a manufacturer's memo obtained by the National Coalition Against the Misuse of Pesticides (NCAMP). One carpenter, who had coughed up blood after exposure to sawdust from pressure-treated wood, won a settlement of $667,000 from several companies. Connecticut agricultural scientists in 1989 found ethylene dibromide (EDB), a fumigant banned in 1983, in the soil of a former tobacco farm where it had last been applied in the late 1960s. "The soil is acting as a reservoir," explained Joe Pignatello, one of the scientists, "not only for EDB, but for herbicides, solvents, and PCBs [another banned chemical]."

One kind of reservoir (a place to store drinking water) leads to another: by 1989, eight states had discovered unsafe levels of EDB in their groundwater. And by 1988, according to Lawrie Mott, a Natural Resources Defense Council [NRDC] scientist, 46 pesticides from agricultural runoff had been found in water in 26 states. In North Carolina, for example, groundwater testing had by 1992 found pesticides in eight of 49 randomly selected wells selected for sampling. A 1991 EPA study found that "perhaps" 750 community water supply wells and 60,900 rural domestic water supply wells nationwide are expected to contain pesticides at "levels of health concern." This estimate reflects increasing groundwater contamination, especially in rural states like Iowa. Agricultural runoff—mainly pesticides—now contaminates 55 percent of river miles and 58 percent of lake acres surveyed by the EPA, as reported by Water Quality 2000, a coalition of environmental, business, and governmental groups. In 1993, the GAO put out another of its clearly titled reports: "Drinking Water: Stronger Efforts Needed to Protect Areas Around Public Wells." And rain—heaven's gentle dew—now contains pesticides, in some Midwestern states in concentrations above the EPA's standard for drinking water. Scientists don't know what health effects the contaminated rain may have. (Be sure to carry your umbrella.)

Midwestern farm with well

Pesticides and Your Health

Next to AIDS, cancer is arguably the most feared modern disease. Yet the National Toxicology Program [NTP] by 1990 had identified only 30 agents or processes as definitely causing cancers in human beings. Of these, almost all also cause cancer in animals. Among them is only one pesticide—arsenic and certain of its compounds. However, several hundred other chemicals, including at least 70 of the 400 pesticides used on food crops, cause cancer in animals. Should we wait to find out whether they also cause cancer in humans? Cancer has a long lead time—as long as 40 years. No sane person is advocating controlled double-blind cancer tests on human beings, with one group unknowingly exposed to suspected carcinogens and another group—the lucky ones—carefully selected to be the controls.

Several epidemiological studies (of voluntary though probably unknowing exposure to carcinogens) have shown a possible connection between pesticides and cancer. The National Cancer Institute [NCI] found that Kansas farmers who used the weed killer 2,4-D (a common herbicide) had a higher-than-average risk of contracting malignant cancer of lymph tissues (known as lymphoma), and an Iowa study found that people living in areas with high herbicide use were 60 percent more likely to die of leukemia. A carefully done study reported in the *Journal of Rural Studies* found that "for three of the five categories of cancer [studied], agricultural chemical use was the best predictor of cancer mortality." A 1987 study by the NCI found that children in households where home and garden pesticides were used are up to nine times more likely to develop some form of leukemia than in households where pesticides were not used.

Of 238 Missouri families studied in 1992 for their use of pesticides, 98 percent used pesticides in home or garden at least once a year and 64 percent used them more than five times a year; half of the families used insecticides to control fleas and ticks on pets. A 1993 controlled study of Missouri children showed "statistically significant associations between childhood brain cancer and several types of pesticide use in the home, including no-pest strips and flea and tick collars on pets." According to the NCI, the years 1973 to 1988 saw a "dramatic rise" in brain cancers among children as well as older people.

Children are especially at risk from pesticides. In 1989, the NRDC estimated that "at least 17 percent of the preschool population [three million children out of a total of 17.6 million] are exposed to neurotoxic organophosphate insecticides above safe levels just from eating raw fruit alone." ("Safe" refers to government-set levels based on risk assessments.) Children have a long lifetime of ingesting pesticides ahead of them and their developing bodies are more susceptible to poisoning. Since a fourth of the American public are now contracting cancer by various means, there could be about 4.5 million cancer cases among present preschoolers during their lifetimes. And, estimated Dr. Richard Jackson, chairman of the American Academy of Pediatrics environmental hazards committee, pesticides may cause 5,000 of those cancers.

Actually, the National Academy of Sciences [NAS] has estimated that as many as 20,000 Americans a year will develop cancer because of pesticide residues on produce that they eat. And according to the *Wall Street Journal,* the EPA itself has ranked pesticide residues as the nation's number three cancer risk. Yet for one pesticide alone, alachlor, a pesticide widely used on many crops, the EPA has said that the risk of getting cancer "at current levels in the food or drinking water supply was generally one in a million from such exposure over a 70-year period and added that the dietary risk posed by the substance was reasonable." Reasonable for whom? Is it "reasonable"

Gardener spraying pesticides in vegetable garden

for just one pesticide to cause cancer to one-in-a-million 70-year-olds a few years down the road? Not if you're that one. And what about all the other pesticides? The other routes of exposure? Toxicologist Marvin Legator believes that "the EPA is grossly underestimating the risk to the public" when it sets pesticide tolerances.

Buying produce in a supermarket

Animals get cancer too. Unwittingly, mankind has not been kind to its best friend; dogs whose owners use 2,4-D on their lawns are twice as likely to develop lymphoma as those whose owners don't use it, again according to the NCI. Malignant cancer in dogs is similar to non-Hodgkin's lymphoma in humans, the incidence of which in Americans increased by about 50 percent between 1973 and 1991.

Another cancer whose incidence has increased in the human population is breast cancer, which in the U.S. went up from one in 20 in 1950 to one in nine in the 1990s, up eight percent between 1973 and 1980 among women younger than 50 and up 32 percent among women over 50. The latter are those most exposed to DDT between 1945 and 1972, the years it was in common use. In 1992, a controlled study of 40 women examined at Hartford Hospital, in Hartford Connecticut, by a team led by Dr. Frank Falck, Jr., of the University of Michigan, revealed that the breast tissues of those with breast cancer contained "elevated levels of DDT, DDE, and PCBs, compared with the breast tissues of women with benign breast disease." (DDT is a persistent organochlorine pesticide banned in the U.S. in 1972 for most uses; DDT breaks down in the body to DDE.) In 1993, a team led by Dr. Mary S. Wolff, of the Mount Sinai School of Medicine, in New York, found a fourfold increase in the relative risk of breast cancer in 58 women with high blood levels of DDE, compared with the blood levels in 171 matched control women without cancer, over a six-year period. Said Dr. Wolff, "Given the widespread dissemination of organochlorine insecticides in the environment and the food chain, the implications are far-reaching for public health intervention worldwide." In Israel, after consumer pressure forced the government to ban several pesticides found in dairy products, researchers noted a dramatic drop in breast cancer mortality rates.

In the June 17, 1993, *New Yorker,* Paul Brodeur ended his article "Legacy" with a paragraph on the possible connection between pesticides and breast cancer and the words "Rachel Carson lives." (Carson died of cancer in 1964.) For years, the *New Yorker* has kept a wary eye on twentieth-century technology; in the late 1940s, it devoted almost an entire issue to John Hersey's article on Hiroshima, and in the early 1960s, it published portions of Carson's *Silent Spring,* its title referring to the pesticide-caused deaths of songbirds then occurring across the country. On the publication of this beautifully written and meticulously researched book, Supreme Court Justice William O. Douglas called it "the most important chronicle of this century for the human race."

In January 1988, the *New Yorker* published "The Fumigation Chamber," one of Berton Roueche's always fascinating "Annals of Medicine." This one is the story of a woman doctor in Pennsylvania who gradually developed a series of mysterious symptoms—nausea,

abdominal cramps, diarrhea, heart irregularities, double vision, muscle weakness, chest tightness, twitching in her legs, and a prickling sensation in the soles of her feet. After visiting several specialists without any improvement, she and her doctor husband finally deduced that her symptoms were caused by the routine spraying of organophosphate pesticides in their
215 summer cabin. Later she suffered similar symptoms from insecticide spraying at an indoor tennis court and a flower show. The article ended with the doctor's statement: "I'm just beginning to realize that the world is a very dangerous place. It's something nobody really wants to think about. I mean the thousands and thousands of toxic chemicals that have become so much a part of modern living. I mean the people who use them without really
220 knowing what they can do. I mean the where and how and why they use them. It's frightening. I think I'm pretty much recovered now. I haven't had any trouble for over a year. But you never know. The only thing I'm sure of is that I'm going to have to be very careful for the rest of my life."

Source: *Staying Well in a Toxic World: Understanding Environmental Illness, Multiple Chemical Sensitivities, Chemical Injuries, and Sick Building Syndrome* (Lawson)

AFTER READING

A. COMPREHENSION CHECK Discuss these questions about the reading with a partner. Refer to the information that you highlighted as you read.

1. Where do we encounter pesticides?
2. What are some of the dangers of pesticides?

B. VOCABULARY CHECK Match the words on the left with their definitions on the right. Don't use a dictionary, but look back at the reading if necessary. Write the correct letters on the lines. (**Hint:** Pay attention to the part of speech of the words you are matching.)

f 1. exterminators	a. chemicals that dissolve (melt) other materials
g 2. fumigated	b. deadly
b 3. lethal	c. death
c 4. mortality	d. degree to which something is poisonous
e 5. residues	e. material that remains after most of a product has been used up
a 6. solvents	f. people whose job it is to apply pesticides
d 7. toxicity	g. sprayed with pesticide

C. COLLOCATIONS In small groups, highlight the collocations in the sentences below. Look for noun phrases, adjective phrases, and prepositional phrases.

1. For a man who wanted to take a break after burglarizing an empty house that was being fumigated, crime did not pay.
2. Neighbors found him writhing in pain naked on the front lawn of the San Fernando, California, home, having torn off his clothes in an attempt to rid himself of their pesticide contamination.
3. Obviously, pesticides are not something to fool around with.

Reading Strategy

Organizing Ideas

You have used many graphic organizers in this book. Graphic organizers help you analyze information that you have read. They also serve as study guides. Some of the things graphic organizers can show are main ideas, supporting statements for main ideas, comparisons, and causes and effects.

D. ORGANIZING IDEAS On a separate piece of paper, make your own graphic organizer for the reading (pages 278–283). The information in your graphic organizer can show only one of the relationships in the box above or some other kind of relationship. Look at the graphic organizers in other chapters of this book for ideas. Then in small groups, compare your graphic organizers.

Critical Thinking Strategy

Seeing Both Sides of an Argument

It is often important to be able to see both sides of an argument. Seeing both sides helps you understand a topic more fully. It can also help you better support an argument both in speaking and in writing.

When you read a passage that expresses an opinion, ask yourself what the other side of the argument is and how someone from the other side might disagree with the author.

E. SEEING BOTH SIDES OF AN ARGUMENT In the reading on pages 278–283, the author's position on the use of pesticides is clear. What is the other side of the argument? How might someone on the other side disagree with the author?

It is clear from the reading that pesticides are deadly. However, even though they can be deadly, they might have good uses. In small groups, develop two or three arguments in favor of using pesticides. To help you think, imagine the position of these people:

- a farmer who depends on large, healthy crop production to support his or her family
- a person who owns a fumigation business
- a research scientist who works for a chemical company that makes and sells pesticides

F. MAKING CONNECTIONS In small groups, discuss this question:

- To what extent would Step 7 of "Turn the Tides' Nine Steps" (individual elimination of lawn and garden pesticides) solve some of the problems described in the reading on pages 278–283. Explain your answer.

PART 3 ACADEMIC READING The Effects of E-Waste

BEFORE READING

A child sitting on a pile of recyclable computer waste imported from around the world

A. THINKING AHEAD The research paper that you are going to read is about the health problems caused by the disposal of old or **obsolete** (outdated or old fashioned) computers. In small groups, discuss these questions.

1. What are personal computers made from? In other words, what materials might be used in the manufacturing of computers?
2. What do you know about the materials used in computers? Do you think they are mostly safe, mostly dangerous, or a little of each?
3. What usually happens to personal computers once they are obsolete? Do people throw them away? Do they recycle them? Where are they **discarded** (thrown away) or recycled?
4. Have you ever discarded an old computer? What did you do with it?

B. VOCABULARY PREPARATION In the sentences below, highlight all vocabulary that is new to you. Then decide which of these words you can guess, which ones aren't very important (so you don't need to look them up), and which ones you should look up. Then in small groups, compare your highlighted words.

1. Exposure to discarded computers in the recycling process is extremely hazardous. Women and children, who are especially vulnerable to e-waste contamination, comprise much of the workforce in many of these offshore facilities.

2. What could be dangerous about plastic boxes containing electronic components? Just about everything: personal computers contain lead and other heavy metals, flame retardants, and polyvinyl chlorides (PVCs), all of which have been shown conclusively to affect human health in serious ways.

A recycling center

3. The hazardous substances found in electronics have been linked to human health effects like cancer, birth defects, and hormone disruption.

4. Lead can also cause irreversible neurological damage, especially in children, who are much more vulnerable to lead contamination than adults ("Lead Toxicity," 1992). This is of particular concern in developing nations in Asia, where child workers are exposed to computer waste in recycling centers.

5. The dangers of PDBE exposure in the United States have been noted in a study conducted by Lunder and Sharp (2003), who found that "the average level of bromine-based fire retardants in the breast milk of 20 first-time mothers was 75 times the average found in recent European studies."

6. Dioxin accumulates in the human body and decomposes slowly. It is particularly carcinogenic ("Cancer and the Environment," 2003).

7. Studies have shown that dioxin exposure can also lead to reproductive and developmental problems and increased heart disease and diabetes. Although it has not been shown to cause birth defects in humans, studies in mice have shown that dioxin and similar chemicals can produce congenital defects.

8. This, along with new designs that allow for extended longevity of computers, may someday decrease the human health risks associated with them.

READING

Read through the passage without using a dictionary and highlight main ideas, important details, and important new vocabulary with different colors. Also, highlight the answer to this question:

- What three compounds in computers are dangerous to human health?

E-Waste: The Effects on Human Health of Toxic Substances Found in Personal Computers

Computers educate, entertain, and streamline dull, repetitive tasks. Modern business is unimaginable without them. In law enforcement and healthcare, they've even saved lives. Yet computers, without which most of the industrialized world cannot survive, may be hazardous to our health; moreover, they are becoming an increasing threat to the health of workers in developing nations. The United States alone generates millions of pounds of e-waste (electronic waste) each year. Fifty to 80 percent of this is not recycled domestically; rather, it is sent to recycling facilities in developing nations such as Pakistan, India, and China (Puckett et al., 2002, p. 2). Exposure to discarded computers in the recycling process is extremely hazardous. Women and children, who are especially vulnerable to e-waste contamination, comprise much of the workforce in many of these offshore facilities. What could be dangerous about plastic boxes containing electronic components? Just about everything: personal computers contain lead and other heavy metals, flame retardants, and polyvinyl chlorides (PVCs), all of which have been shown conclusively to affect human health in serious ways.

Computer monitors typically contain up to eight pounds of lead, the harmful effects of which are undisputed. The improper disposal of lead is already an environmental and human health disaster in the United States. According to the Premier Safety Institute (2005):

20 Currently about 40 percent of the heavy metals, including lead, mercury, and cadmium, in landfills come from electronic equipment discards. The health effects of lead are well known; just 1/70th of a teaspoon of mercury can contaminate 20 acres of a lake, making the fish unfit to eat. The hazardous substances found in electronics have been linked to human
25 health effects like cancer, birth defects, and hormone disruption. (¶ 4)

Lead can also cause irreversible neurological damage, especially in children, who are much more vulnerable to lead contamination than adults (Agency for Toxic Substances and Disease Registry [ATSDR], 1992, pp. 7–8). This is of particular concern in developing nations in Asia, where child workers are exposed to computer waste in
30 recycling centers.

Flame retardants such as polybrominated diphenyl ethers (PBDEs) are used in computer screens and casings. Although flame retardants have been added to many household objects to reduce the incidence of fire and as a result, have saved many lives, their use in computers may cause more problems than it prevents. In addition,
35 Birnbaum and Staskal (2004) note that their "use is not evenly spread over the industrialized world. The Americas account for slightly more than 50%, whereas all of Europe accounts for 12%" (¶ 24). The dangers of PDBE exposure in the United States have been noted in a study conducted by Lunder and Sharp (2003), who found that "the average level of bromine-based fire retardants in the breast milk of 20 first-time
40 mothers was 75 times the average found in recent European studies" (p. 5). This study revealed shockingly high levels of these chemicals in breast milk. Several participants had the highest levels ever reported worldwide. "Milk from two study participants contained the highest levels of fire retardants ever reported in the United States" (Lunder & Sharp, 2003, p. 5). PBDEs are considered a threat to humans—especially

45 women and children—because very low levels have been proven to cause learning, memory, and behavior problems in laboratory animals (Lunder & Sharp, 2003, p. 5).

Polyvinyl chloride (PVC), one of the most widely used plastics, was used extensively in the cabling and housing of older-model computers. Some manufacturers have begun using ABS plastic, a less toxic alternative (Silicon Valley Toxics Coalition, n.d., ¶ 36).
50 However, several million older-model computers are discarded and sent from the United States to offshore recycling centers each year. PVC plastic is the main source of dioxin, which is released when PVC plastics are burned, a common practice in third world recycling processes. Therefore, recycling center workers in developing nations tend to be exposed to this highly toxic substance. The U.S. Department of Health and
55 Human Services reports that dioxin builds up in the human body and decomposes slowly. It is particularly carcinogenic (U.S. Department of Health and Human Services, 2003). Studies have shown that dioxin exposure can also lead to reproductive and developmental problems and increased heart disease and diabetes.

Currently, the developed world creates the most e-waste, and the developing world
60 is at the greatest risk from exposure to it. However, as waste from electronics is growing, so are disposal solutions. Industry is increasingly taking responsibility for the collecting, managing, and disposing of their own products when they become obsolete. This, along with new designs that allow for extended longevity of computers, may someday decrease the human health risks associated with them.

References

65 Agency for Toxic Substances and Disease Registry, U.S. Department of Health and Human Services. (1992). *Case studies in environmental medicine: Lead toxicity.* Retrieved March 15, 2005 from http://www.atsdr.cdc.gov/HEC/CSEM/lead/

Birnbaum, L., & Staskal, D. (2004, January). Brominated flame retardants: Cause for concern? [Electronic version]. *Environmental Health Perspectives, 112*, *Number 1*

70 6–12.

Lunder, S., & Sharp, R. (2005). *Mother's milk: Record levels of toxic fire retardants found in American mothers' breast milk*. Retrieved March 15, 2005 from Environmental Working Group http://www.ewg.org

Premier Safety Institute. (2005). *Computers and electronics in healthcare: Informed*

75 *choices for asset management.* Retrieved March 15, 2005 from http://www.premierinc.com/all/safety/resources/computers/

Puckett, J., Byster, L., Westervelt, S., Gutierrez, R., Davis, S., Hussain, A., & Dutta. M. (2002, February 25). Exporting harm: The high-tech trashing of Asia [Electronic version]. The Basel Action Network (BAN) and Silicon Valley Toxics Coalition.

80 Silicon Valley Toxics Coalition. (n.d.). *Just say no to e-waste: Background document on hazards and waste from computers.* Retrieved March 15, 2005 from http://www.svtc.org/cleancc/pubs/sayno.htm#junk.htm

U.S. Department of Health and Human Services. (2003). *Cancer and the environment.* Retrieved March 15, 2005 from

85 http://www.cancer.gov/newscenter/Cancer–and–the–Environment

AFTER READING

A. MAIN IDEAS In small groups, discuss these questions.

- What three compounds in computers are dangerous to human health? In what ways are they dangerous?

B. ANALYSIS: ESSAY FORMAT In small groups, briefly compare the main ideas that you highlighted. Then use what you learned in Chapter 6 about the format of essays to discuss these questions.

1. What is the thesis statement? Where is it placed? What are the three parallel parts?
2. Where is the opener?
3. What are the three topic sentences?
4. Do the topics of the three body paragraphs follow the order of the three topics presented in the thesis statement?
5. Which part of the paper does the conclusion refer back to?

C. CHECKING DETAILS On a separate piece of paper, for *each* of the three body paragraphs, create a clear, logical graphic organizer that depicts main ideas, details, and the relationships between them. When you finish, compare your three organizers with those of other students. Are they similar?

D. IN YOUR OWN WORDS: SUMMARIZING Choose one of the three body paragraphs in the research paper. Fill in the first blank with the topic of the paragraph. Use a noun or noun phrase. Fill in the second blank with the main idea. Complete the sentence.

1. The paragraph is about ______________________________.
2. The writer says that ______________________________

______________________________.

E. MAKING CONNECTIONS The reading in Part 1 lists nine steps that individuals can follow to improve the environment. Is there a tenth step that could help reduce e-waste? Is there something that you, as an individual, can do to help eliminate the dangers associated with the disposing and recycling of used computers? Discuss your ideas in small groups.

F. WORD JOURNAL Which new words from Parts 2 and 3 are important for *you* to remember? Write them in your Word Journal.

G. RESPONSE WRITING Choose one of the following topics and write for 15 minutes. Don't worry about grammar or spelling. Don't stop writing to use a dictionary.

- Some people say that a lot of the information on environmental problems is alarmist (pessimistic) or inaccurate. Agree or disagree.
- Are technological advances (such as personal computers) necessarily dangerous to the environment and human health? Explain your answer.

PART 4 THE MECHANICS OF WRITING

In Part 4, you will learn to reduce adjective clauses to participial phrases, use participial phrases, and use internal citations. You will use this knowledge in Part 5 to write a research paper.

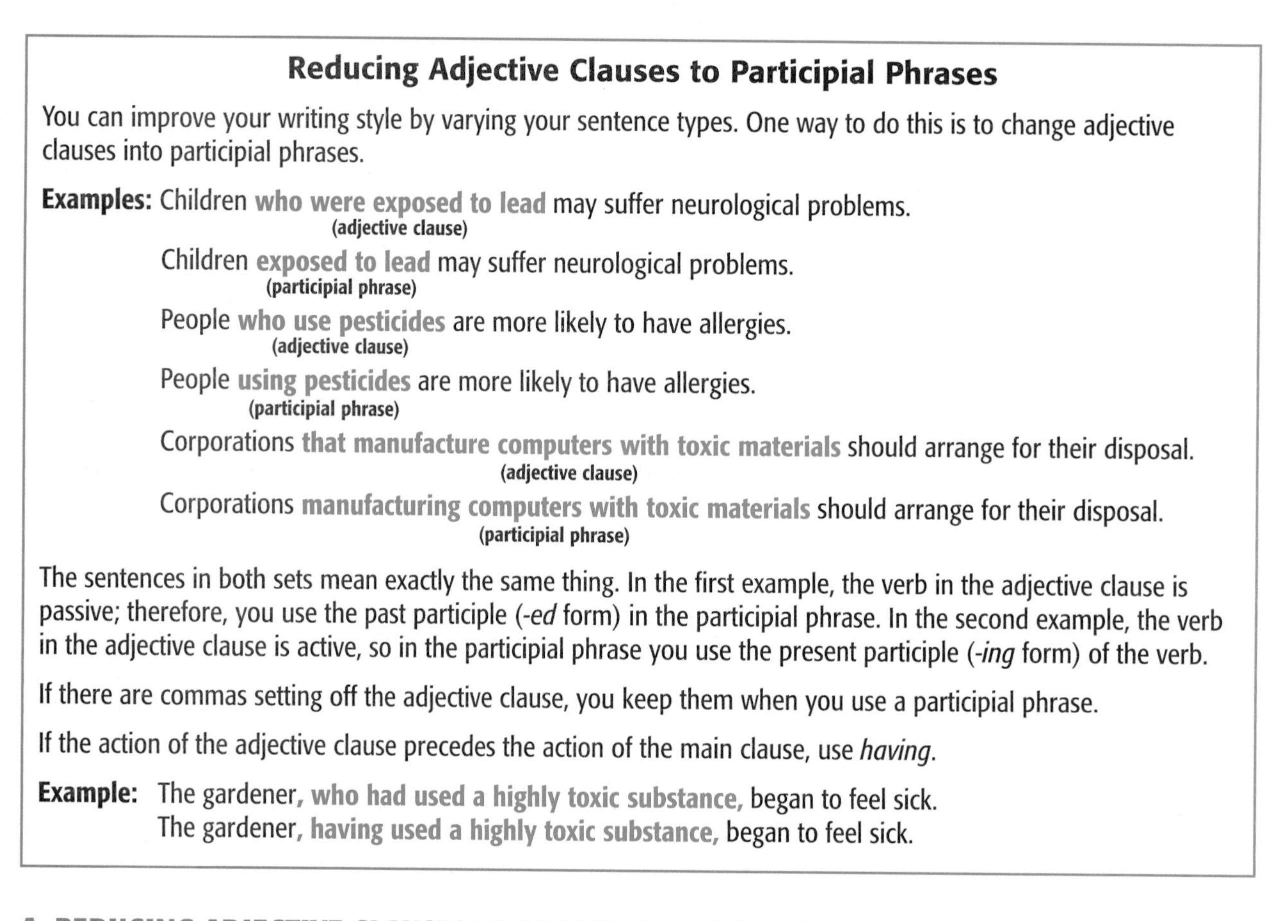

Reducing Adjective Clauses to Participial Phrases

You can improve your writing style by varying your sentence types. One way to do this is to change adjective clauses into participial phrases.

Examples: Children **who were exposed to lead** may suffer neurological problems.
(adjective clause)

Children **exposed to lead** may suffer neurological problems.
(participial phrase)

People **who use pesticides** are more likely to have allergies.
(adjective clause)

People **using pesticides** are more likely to have allergies.
(participial phrase)

Corporations **that manufacture computers with toxic materials** should arrange for their disposal.
(adjective clause)

Corporations **manufacturing computers with toxic materials** should arrange for their disposal.
(participial phrase)

The sentences in both sets mean exactly the same thing. In the first example, the verb in the adjective clause is passive; therefore, you use the past participle (*-ed* form) in the participial phrase. In the second example, the verb in the adjective clause is active, so in the participial phrase you use the present participle (*-ing* form) of the verb.

If there are commas setting off the adjective clause, you keep them when you use a participial phrase.

If the action of the adjective clause precedes the action of the main clause, use *having*.

Example: The gardener, **who had used a highly toxic substance,** began to feel sick.
The gardener, **having used a highly toxic substance,** began to feel sick.

A. REDUCING ADJECTIVE CLAUSES TO PARTICIPIAL PHRASES Rewrite the sentences so that you change the adjective clause into a participial phrase. Follow these steps:

a. Underline the adjective clause in each sentence.
b. Decide if the verb in the adjective clause is active or passive.
c. Rewrite the sentence on the lines, changing the adjective clause into a participial phrase.

1. A woman in India, who had been exposed to dioxin, was diagnosed with heart disease.
A woman in India, having been exposed to dioxin, was diagnosed with heart disease.

2. The discarded computers, which polluted the drinking water, had been sent from the United States.

3. The CEO, who was notified of the dangers of offshore computer recycling, decided to take more responsibility for discarding of his company's product.

____

____

4. Gallons of sewage, which flowed directly into the river last Friday, contaminated New Jersey beaches.

____

____

5. The 50-year-old woman from Utah, who had grown up near a nuclear test site, always wondered if she would someday develop cancer.

____

____

6. According to Lawson, average Americans, who are surrounded by deadly pesticides, are continually risking their health.

____

____

7. The school sent a note home to parents who complained about the use of toxic cleaners in the classrooms.

____

____

8. I knew that the product was dangerous because I read the list of ingredients that appeared on the packaging.

____

____

Using Participial Phrases at the End of a Sentence

You might need to modify a noun (or noun phrase) at the end of a sentence. If so, put the participial phrase after this noun.

Example: Children are at risk from eating **fruit** (noun) **containing dangerous pesticide residues** (participial phrase).

B. SENTENCE COMBINING Change the second sentence of each pair into a present participial phrase (for the active voice) or a past participial phrase (for the passive). Combine them into a complete sentence.

1. This is the woman from Utah. She was diagnosed with heart disease.

____

____

2. The floors of many houses are covered with dust. The dust contains pesticides.

____

____

3. Dust with pesticides makes floors dangerous to babies. Babies crawl across them.

____

____

4. Tim watched the plane. The plane sprayed pesticides on the crops.

____

____

5. Sarah worried about the farm workers. The farm workers are affected by the fumes.

____

____

Using Participial Phrases at the Beginning of a Sentence

A participial phrase at the beginning of a sentence refers to the subject; usually, it indicates either (1) a less important action at the same time as the action in the main clause or (2) the cause of the action in the main clause. (A past participial phrase is used for the passive voice, and a present participial phrase is used for the active voice.) There is a comma between the participial phrase and the subject.

Examples: **Walking along the shore,** we noticed a lot of oil on the sand.
(present participial phrase/active voice)
less important than the action in the main clause ("we noticed . . . ")

Not understanding the danger of pesticides, many farmers continue to use them.
(present participial phrase/active voice)
cause of the action in the main clause (" . . . use . . . ")

Worried about my family's health, I stopped using pesticides in our garden.
(past participial phrase/passive voice)
cause of the action in the main clause (" . . . stopped using . . . ")

If the subject of the sentence is a noun or noun phrase (not a pronoun), the participial phrase may follow it.

Example: Many farmers, **not understanding the danger of pesticides,** continue to use them.

C. ANALYSIS With a partner, study the participial phrase in each of the following sentences. Discuss these questions for each sentence.

- Is it a present or past participial phrase?
- Is this phrase in the active or passive voice?
- Is it less important than the main clause or the cause of the main clause?

1. Angered by an article about offshore computer recycling, the CEO changed his company's policies.
2. The recycling center worker, exposed to dioxin at work, contracted heart disease.
3. Traveling thousands of miles each year on business, Tim always worried about exposure to radiation at high altitudes.
4. Concerned about her family's health, my mother threw away all the toxic household products.
5. The family dog, wearing a highly toxic flea collar, presents an additional danger to babies and small children.

D. SENTENCE COMBINING For each pair of sentences, decide which sentence is either less important than or the cause of the other. Change it into a participial phrase and add it to the other sentence.

1. Pressure-treated wood contains pesticides. Pressure-treated wood can make carpenters sick.

____

____

2. These people live in areas with high herbicide use. These people are 60 percent more likely to die of leukemia.

____

____

3. The CEO called a press conference about recycling practices. The CEO was concerned about how the media would present her company's policies.

____

____

4. I didn't agree with Lawson's ideas. I went to the library to find an article on the other side of the issue.

____

____

____

5. The CEO changed her company's recycling policies. The CEO was angered about an article on offshore recycling.

____

____

Using Internal Citations

You have learned how to refer to sources by paraphrasing, summarizing, and quoting. In a research paper, you do all three, but you also include specific information about your source such as the author's name, publication date, and page number *within* your paper. This information usually appears in or at the end of the sentence or section in which you use your source material. This is called "internal citation." All the information that you need for internal citations should come from the reference list that you create in the research phase of your assignment.

Following are some basic guidelines for APA-style internal citation. Note that there are variations on these rules. You will also find that some APA-style guidelines contradict other guidelines. In addition, many academic departments have their own version of these rules. Therefore, check with your teacher or department for the version of the rules that you should follow.

General Guidelines

The basic citation form for a paraphrase or summary is the author's last name followed by the publication date within parentheses.

Example: **(Smith, 2006)** (author's last name, [comma] year of publication)

The citation form for a quote also requires the page number.

Example: **(Smith, 2006, p. 45)** (author's last name, [comma] year of publication, [comma], page number)

Note that the citation is enclosed in parentheses and that commas separate each element in the citation.

The basic citation form appears at the end of the sentence that contains the paraphrase, summary, or quote and is followed by a period.

Examples: [your paraphrase] **(Smith, 2006).**
["quoted material"] **(Smith, 2006, p. 45).**

Note that there is no period after your material. It appears only after the citation.

Variations

- If there is no author, use a shortened version of the title in place of the author's name. Use quotation marks if the source is an article or a chapter from a book, and italics if the source is a whole book.

Examples: **Reference:** Eliminating pesticides around the home. (2003). *Living Naturally, 100,* 28–31
Citation: **("Eliminating pesticides," 2003)**

Reference: *Controlling pests without chemicals.* (2005). New York, NY: McGraw-Hill
Citation: **(*Controlling Pests*, 2005)**

- If there are two to five authors, list their last names in the same order as they appear in the source, separated by commas if there are more than two. Use an ampersand (&) before the final name.

Examples: **(Jones & Smith, 2006)**
(Jones, Smith, & Turner, 2006)

- If there are six or more authors, list the first author's last name, followed by *et al.* Note the period after *al.*

Example: **(Jones et al., 2006)**

- If you cite the same source more than once, list both names every time if there are only two authors. If there are three, four, or five authors, list only the first name with *et al.* after the first time.

Example **First Citation:** (Jones, Smith, & Turner, 2006)
Subsequent Citations: **(Jones et al., 2006)**

- If the publication has no date, use *n.d.* in place of the year. Note the periods after *n* and *d.*

Example: **(Smith, n.d.)**

- Websites and online publications sometimes do not have page numbers. If you are quoting and the publication has no page number, indicate the paragraph in which the quote appears in place of the page number. Use the paragraph symbol in place of "p.": ¶. (Many word processing programs have this symbol.) Alternatively, you can use the abbreviation *para.* (followed by a period).

Examples: **(Smith, 2006, ¶ 7)**
(Smith, 2006, para. 7)

E. USING INTERNAL CITATIONS With a partner, look through the research paper on pages 287–290. List one example of each of the following internal citation types.

Example: a publication with no date: "Just say no," (n.d.)

1. one author: ____________________
2. two authors: ____________________
3. more than five authors: ____________________
4. a publication with no author: ____________________
5. a direct quote: ____________________

Varying Citation Forms

There are many ways to cite sources within your paper. You should vary your citation formats in order to avoid repetition. You can also vary your formats to emphasze different aspects of your sources. For example, in some cases, you may want to focus on the ideas to which you are referring. In others, you may want to emphasize an author or researcher. In other cases, the date of a publication or study may be important.

Following are some different ways to cite sources in a research paper, using the following source:

Morgan, S. (1995). *Ecology and the environment.* New York: Oxford University Press.

Examples: Population growth leads to habitat loss (Morgan, 1995).

"Habitat loss is one of the most important causes of extinction" (Morgan, 1995, p. 137).

Morgan says that the loss of "habitat . . . is one of the most important causes of extinction" (1995, p. 137).

Morgan (1995) says that the loss of "habitat . . . is one of the most important causes of extinction" (p. 137).

Citing Sources that Cite Sources

If you are citing a source that is in turn citing a source, include the words "as cited in" in your citation and include only the primary source in your reference list.

Example: Your Smith source refers to a study by Wong, so your internal citation reads: **In Wong's study (as cited in Smith, 2006), . . .**

Including Long Quotes

A quote of more than 40 words is called a **block quote**. To include a block quote, introduce it on one line. Start the quoted material on the next line. Indent the entire quote five spaces. Do not use quotation marks. Put a period at the end of the quotation, followed by a parenthetical citation. There is no period after the citation.

Example:

Morgan (1995) makes a convincing case for the role of habitat loss in the process of extinction:

> Habitat loss is one of the most important causes of extinction. As rising populations in many countries lead to the clearing of more land, habitats such as rain forests and grasslands disappear. In East Africa, once renowned for its wildlife, few wild animals survive outside the boundaries of national parks and game reserves. In other parts of the world, coastal ecosystems are cleared for development. Wetland areas such as the Cota Doñana in southern Spain and the Everglades in Florida are drying out as a result of water extraction to support farming and tourism. Bird species are among the worst affected by the loss of wetlands. (p. 137)

Find a block quote in the research paper on pages 287–290. What is the source? On what page number did the quote appear?

F. VARYING CITATION FORMATS Study the three research papers in this book (The Anthropological View of Religion, pp. 23–25, Chapter 1; The Edge of Extinction, pp. 256–259, Chapter 7; and E-Waste: The Effects on Human Health of Toxic Substances Found in Personal Computers, pp. 287–290, Chapter 8). Find as many examples as you can of varying citation formats in the three papers.

G. CITING SOURCES INTERNALLY On a separate piece of paper, use the source material on page 299 to practice summarizing, paraphrasing, quoting, and citing sources internally.

Another cancer whose incidence has increased in the human population is breast cancer, which in the U.S. went up from one in 20 in 1950 to one in nine in the 1990s, up eight percent between 1973 and 1980 among women younger than 50 and up 32 percent among women over 50. The latter are those most exposed to DDT between 1945 and 1972, the years it was in common use. In 1992, a controlled study of 40 women examined at Hartford Hospital, in Hartford Connecticut, by a team led by Dr. Frank Falck, Jr., of the University of Michigan, revealed that the breast tissues of those with breast cancer contained "elevated levels of DDT, DDE, and PCBs, compared with the breast tissues of women with benign breast disease." (DDT is a persistent organochlorine pesticide banned in the U.S. in 1972 for most uses; DDT breaks down in the body to DDE.) In 1993, a team led by Dr. Mary S. Wolff, of the Mount Sinai School of Medicine, in New York, found a fourfold increase in the relative risk of breast cancer in 58 women with high blood levels of DDE, compared with the blood levels in 171 matched control women without cancer, over a six-year period. Said Dr. Wolff, "Given the widespread dissemination of organochlorine insecticides in the environment and the food chain, the implications are far-reaching for public health intervention worldwide." In Israel, after consumer pressure forced the government to ban several pesticides found in dairy products, researchers noted a dramatic drop in breast cancer mortality rates.

Source: Lynn Lawson, *Staying Well in a Toxic World: Understanding Environmental Illness, Multiple Chemical Sensitivities, Chemical Injuries, and Sick Building Syndrome*, 1993, p 112.

PART 5 ACADEMIC WRITING

WRITING ASSIGNMENT

Continue working on the research paper you started in Chapter 7. Your paper will have only five paragraphs and follow the same format that you learned in Chapter 6; the difference is that it will include a reference list and citations. You will need a minimum of five sources on your reference list.

STEP A. DEVELOPING A THESIS STATEMENT AND SUPPORTING IDEAS Once you have chosen a topic and done research on it, you are ready to begin writing your paper. The first step is a general plan of your paper. This consists of your thesis statement and the supporting ideas for it. On a separate piece of paper, write your thesis statement and your three topic sentences, following the guidelines in Chapter 6.

STEP B. FINDING EVIDENCE Now, use the sources you gathered in Chapter 7 to find information that supports each of the topic sentences you wrote in Step A. Do the following:

- On another piece of paper, rewrite your topic sentences with plenty of white space between them.
- For each topic sentence, write in note form relevant facts and details that you will use to develop it. Include any and all citation information in these notes such as authors' last names, publication dates, and page numbers for any direct quotes. (This will save you time later when you are writing the first draft.)
- At this point, you may want to re-evaluate your sources:
  - Do you have enough?
  - Are you using all of them?
- After you complete Step B, you may need to revise your reference list.

Writing Strategy

Planning an Essay by Using a Formal Outline

Before beginning to write, you should organize your ideas in a formal outline like the one you saw in Part 2 of Chapter 7 (pages 253–254). *It is in your outline that you can see problems with organization and fix them before actually writing the essay.* For the supporting ideas, use notes, not complete sentences in the outline, but make sure that every "1" has at least a "2" and that every "a" has at least a "b." Leave your introduction (except for the thesis statement) and conclusion blank at this point. Decide on your introduction and conclusion after you have planned your body paragraphs.

Here is a sample outline for the short research paper on pages 287–290:

I. Introduction

  A. Opener:

  B. Thesis statement: Personal computers contain lead and other heavy metals, flame retardants, and polyvinyl chlorides (PVCs), all of which have been shown conclusively to affect human health in serious ways.

II. Computer monitors typically contain up to eight pounds of lead, the harmful effects of which are undisputed.

  A. Health disaster in the U.S. (Premier Safety Institute)

    1. lead in landfills

    2. cancer, birth defects, and hormone disruption

  B. Neurological damage ("Lead toxicity")

    1. children more vulnerable

    2. child workers in developing nations

III. Flame retardants such as polybrominated diphenyl ethers (PBDEs) are used in computer screens and casings.

  A. Disadvantages outweigh benefits

  B. Use in N. America

    1. Lunder & Sharp study

    2. problems in lab animals (Lunder & Sharp)

IV. Polyvinyl chloride (PVC), one of the most widely used plastics, was used extensively in the cabling and housing of older-model computers.

  A. Older models sent offshore

  B. Dioxin

    1. dioxin released in burning

    2. builds up in body; decomposes slowly

    3. carcinogenic ("Cancer & environment")

    4. other problems

V. Conclusion:

STEP C. ORGANIZING YOUR IDEAS Organize all of your material into a for[...]
300. Use the thesis statement and topic sentences you wrote in Step A and the [...]

Writing Strategy

Writing Introductions

As you saw in Chapter 6 (pages 224–226), an introductory paragraph of an essay begins with an attention-getting device such as a fact, quotation, definition, question, or background information. The device you choose often depends on the topic of your essay. The introductory paragraph also includes your thesis statement, usually at the end. In this chapter, we're going to look closely at the introductory paragraph.

An introductory paragraph contains at least three sentences and leads the reader into the essay. The ideas in these sentences progress from general to specific: you begin with general information (or a question or a fact, quotation, definition, etc.) on your topic that leads to your thesis statement. You can think of an introductory paragraph as an upside down triangle:

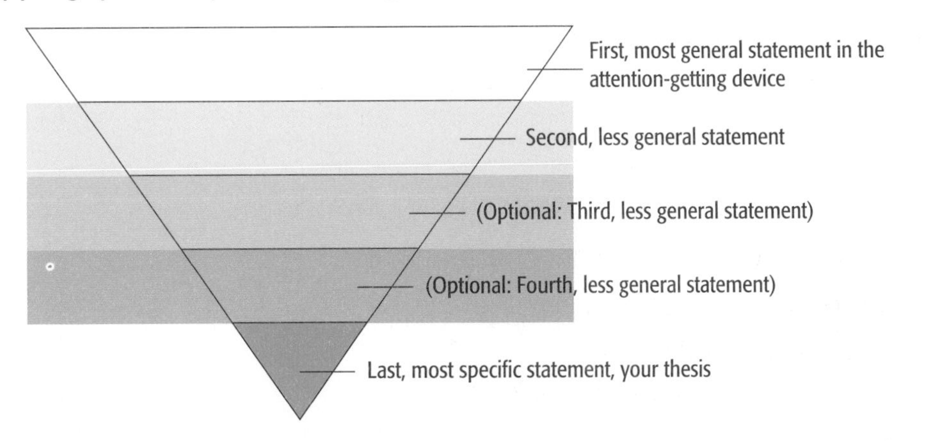

The top of the triangle represents the general information in the introduction, which becomes increasingly specific, and then leads into your thesis.

Writing Conclusions

In Chapter 6 (pages 224–226), you learned that a conclusion restates the main ideas of your essay. A good conclusion gives your reader a feeling of completion and leads the reader away from the essay. In fact, you can think of a conclusion as the opposite of an introduction–in other words, it progresses from specific (a restatement of your thesis) to general ideas on the topic–a right-side-up triangle:

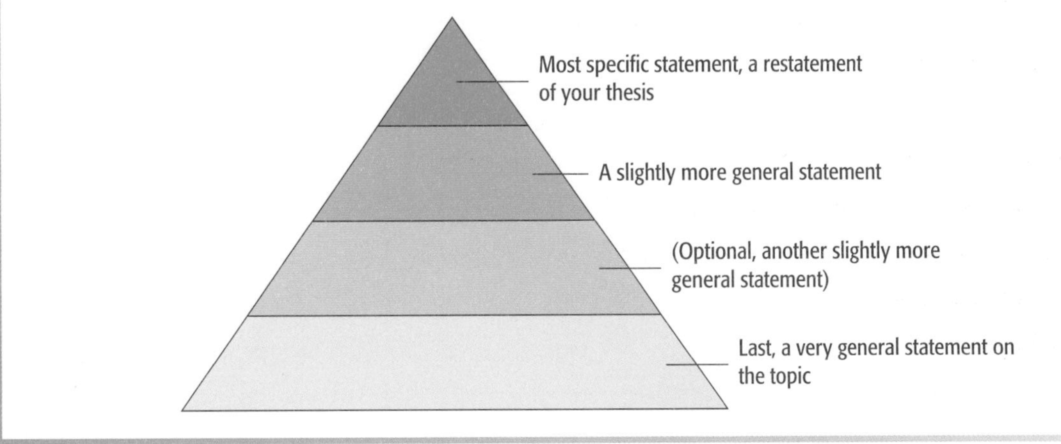

STEP D. WRITING AN INTRODUCTION AND A CONCLUSION Choose an attention-getting device and write an introductory paragraph that progresses from general to specific and concludes with the thesis statement you wrote in Step A. Then write a conclusion following the guidelines on page 301. Exchange your introductory and concluding paragraphs with a classmate and evaluate them: Do they match the triangle models on page 301?

STEP E. WRITING SHORT RESEARCH PAPER Using your outline as a basis, write the first draft of your research paper. Include your citations as your write. Revise your reference list, if necessary.

STEP F. EDITING Read your research paper and answer these questions:

Essay Format

1. Does the thesis statement include a three-part "map" of the body paragraphs?
2. Are the three parts in the thesis statement parallel?
3. Do the body paragraphs follow the order in the thesis statement?
4. Is there strong evidence for each topic sentence?
5. Is the evidence well organized?
6. Does the introduction prepare the reader for the essay?
7. Does it follow the upside-down triangle model?
8. Does the conclusion lead you away from the essay?
9. Does it follow the right-side-up triangle model?
10. Is sentence structure correct (no run-ons, comma splices, or fragments)?

Citation Format

1. Did you do enough library and/or Internet research?
2. Did you use all of your sources?
3. Are all ideas that aren't your own cited?
4. Are all citations in the correct form?
5. Is there enough variation in citations throughout the research paper?
6. Is the reference list in the correct format?

STEP G. REVISING Write your research paper again. This time, try to write with no mistakes.

UNIT 4 VOCABULARY WORKSHOP

Review vocabulary items that you learned in Chapters 7 and 8.

A. ANALYZING WORD CHOICE Find one or more poorly chosen words in each sentence. Cross them out and write better words above them.

1. Ecologists are ~~making a study of~~ studying giant turtles in Malaysia.
2. Avery got malaria when he was living in the tropics.
3. There are some endangered animal species in my country.
4. "Hunters return to the village and tell stories about the day's hunt," she told.
5. Paula got her doctorate in 1996.
6. A lot of animals are killed by poachers.
7. Three things of this problem are important to consider.
8. People internationally got concerned about the endangered aye-aye of Madagascar.
9. The Belize Zoo spends a lot of time on educating children about the importance of rare species in their homeland.
10. Due to global warming, the situation in the Arctic is really bad for polar bears.
11. Many evidences indicate that the number of gorillas in the wild is going down a lot.
12. Jack placed three things on the table.
13. Several recent researches explore the relationship between farmers and wildlife.

B. CHOOSING WORDS WITH THE CORRECT CONNOTATION Read the sentences below. Choose the best word from the box above the sentences and write it on the line. (In a few cases, more than one word is appropriate.)

animal	beast	creature	game	livestock	wildlife

1. The farmer was worried that wolves would kill his ______________________.
2. That criminal is a violent ______________________.
3. There was very little ______________________ left in that part of the forest, so the hunters had to move elsewhere.

environment	neighborhoods	scenery	suburbs	surroundings	terrain	vicinity

4. The ______________________ on Mars is rocky and dry.

5. We traveled through some beautiful ______________________.

6. Is there a lake or river in this ______________________?

be	exist	live	subsist	thrive

7. In winter, the tribe has to ______________________ on potatoes and dried meat.

8. Animals absolutely ______________________ in the safe environment of the Jersey Zoo, and they begin to reproduce.

9. Most scientists believe that the dinosaurs weren't able to ______________________ long after a meteorite struck the Earth.

affluent	fertile	rich	wealthy

10. Their land is ______________________ and their crops are always abundant.

11. The Nile Valley has ______________________ soil deposited there by the annual floods.

12. ______________________ people who are concerned about habitat loss donate millions of dollars to various environmental organizations.

C. MISCELLANEOUS PROBLEMATIC WORDS Discuss the meaning of each pair of words in the box with a partner; check with a dictionary if necessary.

economic/economical	even if/even though	effect/affect
hard/hardly	on the contrary/on the other hand/in contrast	

Now decide if the words in orange have been used correctly or not: Write *OK* on the line if the word is used correctly. Write *X* on the line if the words is used incorrectly. Cross out the incorrectly used words and correct them.

______ **1.** Many South American Indian tribes are working **hardly** to preserve their land.

______ **2.** The **economical** policy of the country is beneficial to developers but not to the environment.

______ **3.** **Even though** this is a natural park, many animals are hunted here by poachers.

______ **4.** "Ecotourists" bring necessary foreign money and concern about the environment into developing countries; **on the contrary**, they also often harm or destroy natural habitat.

_______ **5.** **Even though** we replant millions of trees, it will take hundreds of years before the forest is as thick and diverse as the one that was destroyed.

_______ **6.** I know **hardly** anything about gene banks.

_______ **7.** Indigenous people are not destructive of the environment; **on the other hand**, they protect it.

_______ **8.** There are two main benefits to this electric car: it is **economical** and doesn't pollute the air.

_______ **9.** Human activity has a serious **affect** on the environment.

_______ **10.** **Even if** we begin to replant the forest today, it will take hundreds of years before it is restored.

APPENDIX 1 SUMMARY OF CONJUNCTIONS

There are three groups of conjunctions, each with specific rules for punctuation.

Coordinating Conjunctions

There are exactly seven coordinating conjunctions:

and
but
for (= because)
nor*
or
so (= that's why)
yet (= but)

Use:

1. Join two independent clauses with a comma and a coordinating conjunction.

   Examples: Her family owns a small factory, and she manages it.
   This might look easy, but it's actually rather difficult.

2. If there isn't an independent clause after the coordinating conjunction, don't use a comma before it.

   Examples: Her family owns a small factory and is thinking of expanding.
   This looks easy but is actually rather difficult.

3. In a series of three or more nouns, adjectives, verbs, or phrases, use commas to separate each item; this structure occurs with *and* or *or*.

   Examples: We'll go to Tunisia, Morocco, or Egypt.
   Their business imports fabric, produces clothing, and sells the clothing locally.

**Nor* is used somewhat differently.

1. with different subjects:
    a. Alice won't go to Ghana this year, **nor** will John.
    b. **Neither** Alice **nor** John will go to Ghana this year.

2. with different verbs:
    a. Alice didn't call, **nor** did she write.
    b. Alice **neither** called **nor** wrote.

3. with different objects:
    a. John can't send a fax, **nor** can he send an e-mail.
    b. John can send **neither** a fax **nor** an e-mail.

Subordinating Conjunctions

These are some of the many subordinating conjunctions.

because	when	by the time
although	whenever	as soon as (= immediately after)
as (= because)	before	until
since (= because)	after	as (= while; when)
even though	while (= when)	
while (= although)		if
whereas		unless (= if not)
		in case

Use:

1. If you begin a sentence with a subordinating conjunction, use a comma to separate the dependent and independent clauses.

    Example: **Because** she wanted to do business in Asia, she studied Asian languages and culture.

2. If the subordinating conjunction is in the middle of the sentence, there is usually no comma.

    Example: She studied Asian languages and culture **because** she wanted to do business in Asia.

    Exception: There is often a comma before a subordinating conjunction of contrast.

    Example: The New Kingdom was a period of military success and power in Egypt, **whereas** the Old Kingdom had been a time of defeat and failure.

Adverbial Conjunctions (Conjunctive Adverbs)

These are some of the many adverbial conjunctions.

in addition moreover furthermore also	= and	however nevertheless* even so* (*Use these in a surprising situation.)	= but
therefore consequently thus as a result for this reason	= that's why	in contrast on the other hand	

for example
in other words
that is
i.e.

for instance
e.g.

mostly
for the most part
to some extent (= partly)
to a large extent (= mostly)

first
next
afterwards
finally
then (no comma)

in short
in conclusion

Use:

There are three main ways to use adverbial conjunctions: at the beginning of a sentence, at the beginning of an independent clause, or in the middle of an independent clause. Some conjunctions may appear at the end of a sentence.

Examples: The museum has an extensive collection of religious art. In addition, it houses a fine but small collection of genre paintings.

The exhibit of Egyptian art is extremely rare and valuable; consequently, security will be extraordinarily tight.

Everyone dreams every night. Many people, however, do not remember their dreams in the morning.

Everyone dreams every night. Many people do not remember their dreams in the morning, however.

APPENDIX 2
RESEARCH PAPER IN MLA FORMAT

The Edge of Extinction

Imagine a world without the whale, tiger, panda, or elephant; our planet without the wide-eyed lemur of Madagascar, the gentle manatee of the West Indies, or the beautiful lion tamarin of Brazil; life on Earth without thousands of the fascinating insects, reptiles, amphibians, birds, fish, and mammals that now inhabit it—some in frighteningly small numbers. The famous biologist Edward O. Wilson tells us that "three [species] per hour or 27,000 every year" were becoming extinct by the early 1990s (Morgan 137) and that today, "species are . . . now disappearing . . . a thousand times faster than they are born, due to human activity" ("Speciation" par. 25). Clearly, it is possible for human beings to destroy animal life on a vast scale, for such is the case of most near-extinctions. Now is the time for humans to reverse this trend by focusing on research, breeding programs for endangered species, and safe habitats for animals in the wild, as a number of organizations are attempting to do in different but overlapping ways.

Any action taken to save endangered species must be based on solid research. It is research that informs scientists about the needs, habits, biology, and environment of animals in the wild, and the research, in turn, that educates the public of the need to preserve species. An organization called Earthwatch funds hundreds of research projects throughout the world, mostly by recruiting a corps of volunteers, who "have a critical job" in field projects, such as one looking into "the foraging activities and social behavior" of capuchin monkeys in Venezuela (Perney and Emanoil, par. 21). The marine biologist who began the Earthwatch programs to study and save sea turtles, Tundi Agardy, explains that although the "immediate benefit" of the volunteers "is to help save a generation of endangered turtles . . . the real value is that volunteers themselves become the seed corn of the conservation movement, spreading the word when they return home" (Linden, par. 6).

Human encroachment into what used to be wilderness makes natural habitats increasingly dangerous places for wildlife, necessitating captive breeding programs to save species from extinction. The pioneer of this concept was Gerald Durrell, "the self-described 'champion of the uglies,'" who "founded Jersey Zoological Park in 1958, where he bred endangered species to return to the wild" ("Died," 23). Durrell began by bringing the last few known animals of a species from their endangered habitats to this breeding zoo on the Isle of Jersey, in England. There, in this safe haven where they were protected from environmental pollution, hunters, and human destruction of their habitat, the animals successfully reproduced. The method, still used today and replicated in zoos worldwide, includes providing the animals with "specially landscaped, spacious enclosures which closely resemble their natural homes . . . in the wild" ("Jersey Zoo," par. 3). When the environment is once again safe, the animals are reintroduced to the habitat.

Safe, natural habitats are crucial to species' ultimate survival. "One of the best ways of preserving wildlife is to set aside areas where it can thrive without interference" (Morgan 152). Organizations such as Greenpeace, Nature Conservancy, and Pronatura are doing just that. Among others, the goals of "Greenpeace, an international group that's more than 30 years old, . . . funded mostly by contributions from its 2.5 million members . . . are saving ancient forests, stopping global warming, exposing toxic pollutants, [and] protecting the oceans" (Vann, par. 5). The Nature Conservancy uses money donated by members to buy land and set it aside permanently for nature preserves where no development can take place. The organization admits that it can neither buy all the land nor "protect [it] single-handedly," so its method is to join "together with businesses, governments, partner organizations, indigenous people, and communities" to "preserve our lands and waters for future generations to use and enjoy" ("How We Work," par. 1). While Greenpeace and the Nature Conservancy work internationally, other groups such as the Mexican organization Pronatura work on a national level. In 2005, for example, Mexico launched "the largest conservation project in that nation's history with its plan to protect 370,000 acres of tropical forest on the Yucatan Peninsula," an area that has hundreds of rare species, among them the second largest population of jaguars outside of the Amazon ("Historic Land Save" 1).

The American writer Mark Twain would no doubt approve. As he once pointed out, people should buy land "because they don't make it anymore."

We humans have a history of destruction of the environment, but we needn't repeat the past. By studying animals and their natural habitats, supporting captive breeding programs, and preserving habitats, there is hope that humans may be able to live in harmony with nature.

Works Cited

"Died. Gerald Durrell." Time 13 Feb. 1995: 23.

"Historic Land Save in Mexico." American Forests Winter 2005: 23–28.

"How We Work: Our Methods, Tools, and Techniques." The Nature Conservancy. 2005. The Nature Conservancy. 13 Mar. 2005 <http://nature.org/aboutus/howwework/>.

"Jersey Zoo: A very special place." Durrell Wildlife Conservation Trust. n.d. Durrell Wildlife Conservation Trust. 13 Mar. 2005 <http://www.durrellwildlife.org/index.cfm?a=6>.

Linden, Eugene. "Challenges for Earth Patriots: Stalking Dwarf Hamsters in Siberia." Time 2 Apr. 1990: 70–75.

Morgan, Steven. Ecology and the Environment. New York: Oxford University Press, 1995.

Perney, Linda, and Emanoil, Pamela. "Where the Wild Things Are: 25 Ways to Get Close to Nature this Winter." Audobon Sept.–Oct. 1998: 82–87.

Vann, Kim McCoy. "Report Classifies Woods as Healthy." Tallahassee Democrat 3 Jan. 2005: 5.

Wilson, Edward. "Speciation and biodiversity: Interview with Edward O. Wilson." ActionBioscience.org Ed. Oksana Hlodan. February 2002. American Institute of Biological Sciences. 24 June 2005 <www.actionbioscience.org/biodiversity/wilson.html>.

APPENDIX 3 ACADEMIC WORD LIST

The list on pages 313–316 is Sublist One of the most common words on the Academic World List, compiled by Averil Coxhead. To view the entire list, go to Averil Coxhead's AWL website (http://language.massey.ac.nz/staff/awl/index.shtml).

Each word in italics is the most frequently occurring member of the word family in the academic corpus. For example, *analysis* is the most common form of the word family *analyse*.

The Academic Word List includes both British and American spelling.

analyse
- analysed
- analyser
- analysers
- analyses
- analysing
- *analysis*
- analyst
- analysts
- analytic
- analytical
- analytically
- analyze
- analyzed
- analyzes
- analyzing

approach
- approachable
- approached
- approaches
- approaching
- unapproachable

area
- areas

assess
- assessable
- assessed
- assesses
- assessing
- *assessment*
- assessments
- reassess
- reassessed
- reassessing
- reassessment
- unassessed

assume
- assumed
- assumes
- assuming
- assumption
- assumptions

authority
- authoritative
- authorities

available
- availability
- unavailable

benefit
- beneficial
- beneficiary
- beneficiaries
- benefited
- benefiting
- benefits

concept
- conception
- concepts
- conceptual
- conceptualisation
- conceptualise
- conceptualised
- conceptualises
- conceptualising
- conceptually

consist
- consisted
- consistency
- *consistent*
- consistently
- consisting
- consists
- inconsistencies
- inconsistency
- inconsistent

constitute
- constituencies
- constituency
- constituent
- constituents
- constituted
- constitutes
- constituting
- constitution
- constitutions
- *constitutional*
- constitutionally

Do w/ unit 1

- constitutive
- unconstitutional

context
- contexts
- contextual
- contextualise
- contextualised
- contextualising
- uncontextualised
- contextualize
- contextualized
- contextualizing
- uncontextualized

contract
- contracted
- contracting
- contractor
- contractors
- contracts

create
- created
- creates
- creating
- creation
- creations
- creative
- creatively
- creativity
- creator
- creators
- recreate
- recreated
- recreates
- recreating

data

define
- definable
- defined
- defines
- defining
- *definition*
- definitions
- redefine
- redefined
- redefines
- redefining
- undefined

derive
- derivation
- derivations
- derivative
- derivatives
- *derived*
- derives
- deriving

distribute
- distributed
- distributing
- *distribution*
- distributional
- distributions
- distributive
- distributor
- distributors
- redistribute
- redistributed
- redistributes
- redistributing
- redistribution

economy
- *economic*
- economical
- economically
- economics
- economies
- economist
- economists
- uneconomical

environment
- environmental
- environmentalist
- environmentalists
- environmentally
- environments

establish
- disestablish
- disestablished
- disestablishes
- disestablishing
- disestablishment
- *established*
- establishes
- establishing
- establishment
- establishments

estimate
- estimated
- estimates
- estimating
- estimation
- estimations
- over-estimate
- overestimate
- overestimated
- overestimates
- overestimating
- underestimate
- underestimated
- underestimates
- underestimating

evident
- evidenced
- *evidence*
- evidential
- evidently

export
- exported
- exporter
- exporters
- exporting
- exports

factor
- factored

- factoring
- *factors*

- finance
  - financed
  - finances
  - *financial*
  - financially
  - financier
  - financiers
  - financing
- *formula*
  - formulae
  - formulas
  - formulate
  - formulated
  - formulating
  - formulation
  - formulations
  - reformulate
  - reformulated
  - reformulating
  - reformulation
  - reformulations
- *function*
  - functional
  - functionally
  - functioned
  - functioning
  - functions
- identify
  - identifiable
  - identification
  - *identified*
  - identifies
  - identifying
  - identities
  - identity
  - unidentifiable
- *income*
  - incomes
- *indicate*
  - indicated
  - indicates
  - indicating
  - indication
  - indications
  - indicative
  - indicator
  - indicators
- *individual*
  - individualised
  - individuality
  - individualism
  - individualist
  - individualists
  - individualistic
  - individually
  - individuals
- interpret
  - *interpretation*
  - interpretations
  - interpretative
  - interpreted
  - interpreting
  - interpretive
  - interprets
  - misinterpret
  - misinterpretation
  - misinterpretations
  - misinterpreted
  - misinterpreting
  - misinterprets
  - reinterpret
  - reinterpreted
  - reinterprets
  - reinterpreting
  - reinterpretation
  - reinterpretations
- involve
  - *involved*
  - involvement
  - involves
  - involving
  - uninvolved
- issue
  - issued
  - *issues*
  - issuing
- *labour*
  - labor
  - labored
  - labors
  - laboured
  - labouring
  - labours
- *legal*
  - illegal
  - illegality
  - illegally
  - legality
  - legally
- legislate
  - legislated
  - legislates
  - legislating
  - *legislation*
  - legislative
  - legislator
  - legislators
  - legislature
- *major*
  - majorities
  - majority
- *method*
  - methodical
  - methodological
  - methodologies
  - methodology
  - methods
- *occur*
  - occurred
  - occurrence

- occurrences
- occurring
- occurs
- reoccur
- reoccurred
- reoccurring
- reoccurs

percent
- percentage
- percentages

period
- periodic
- periodical
- periodically
- periodicals
- periods

policy
- policies

principle
- principled
- principles
- unprincipled

proceed
- procedural
- *procedure*
- procedures
- proceeded
- proceeding
- proceedings
- proceeds

process
- processed
- processes
- processing

require
- *required*
- requirement
- requirements
- requires
- requiring

research
- researched
- researcher
- researchers
- researches
- researching

respond
- responded
- respondent
- respondents
- responding
- responds
- *response*
- responses
- responsive
- responsiveness
- unresponsive

role
- roles

section
- sectioned
- sectioning
- sections

sector
- sectors

significant
- insignificant
- insignificantly
- significance
- significantly
- signified
- signifies
- signify
- signifying

similar
- dissimilar
- similarities
- similarity
- similarly

source
- sourced
- sources
- sourcing

specific
- specifically
- specification
- specifications
- specificity
- specifics

structure
- restructure
- restructured
- restructures
- restructuring
- structural
- structurally
- structured
- structures
- structuring
- unstructured

theory
- theoretical
- theoretically
- theories
- theorist
- theorists

vary
- invariable
- invariably
- variability
- variable
- *variables*
- variably
- variance
- variant
- variants
- variation
- variations
- varied
- varies
- varying

VOCABULARY INDEX

UNIT 1
Chapter 1
acquaintances
amulet
anthropomorphic
apply
array
artificial
associated with
based on
bound up
budget cuts
caste system
CEO
chain
charm
chi
cite
clan
closed-book exam
clutter
collocations
combination of
consumption
craze
depict
differ from . . . to
dyeing
examples
fads
feng shui
focus on
foragers
foreign object
gap
graphic organizer
hazardous
head of state
hearth
hierarchy
important detail
infer
inferences
intern
main idea
material (world)
metonym
monotheism
mood
Mount Olympus
named after
notion (about)
nuclear family
open-book exam
polytheistic
prevent
principles
proposal
quest
quotation marks
realm
royalty
spell
stamina
state
supernatural beings
symbol
synthesize
take-home exam
thesis statement
tidbits
totemic ancestor
trance
trivial
turn to
urge
word journal

Chapter 2
adolescence
allies
American Sign Language
analogous
art for art's sake
auctioned
be drawn over
be replaced by
belonging
buzzword (s)
ceremonies of increase
clusters
coincide with
conjunctions
dominance
dominate
ensure
environmental change
exogamy
exploit
fairly recently
fleshy
foresight
from the bottom up
from the top down
give way to
in captivity
in the wild
inflict pain on
initiation rites
instinctive
key point
kinship
leave (home)
macaques
master
microlith
need to
obliterate
omnivorous (diet)
orangutan
outgoing
paint over
paraphrasing
peers
prey
raised in isolation
reenacting
reproductive success
seclusion
superimposed
terrestrial (monkeys)
tribal lore
troop
twigs
withdraw from

Vocabulary Workshop: Unit 1

Academic Word List

adults
aspect
consumption
cooperation
cooperative
cultural
individually
intrinsic
links
nuclear
resources

UNIT 2

Chapter 3

allocation
barriers
beg
bona fide
bribes
brink
burden
capital
capital flight
collateral
compatible with
concept of
crude birth rate
default
destitute
developing countries
eliminate
eradication
evidence
exist on
external debt
extinguish
famine
fluctuations
free enterprise
fronts
frugality
headway
hinder
illiterates
ills
incentive
inflation
invest in
landlocked
launch
life expectancy
macroeconomic polices
national assets
obstacles (to)
on the brink of
plight
population density
predicament
recommendations
rich
shortage of
similar to
stand in the way of
stumbling block
take a toll
take advantage of
tightly knit
trade barriers
vowed
World Bank
zero population growth

Chapter 4

absolute advantage
ad campaign
armament
balance of payments
basis of
be attributed to
bilingual
centers on
comparative advantage
country of origin
crucial
culture
deal with
depend on . . . for
displace
diversifies
dumping
essential raw materials
exotic
exports
free traders
goods
image
imports
impose on
inductive reasoning
infant industries argument
interact
jingle
keep out of
levy
logos
managerial candidates
merchandise
multilingual
object to
opium
place on
potential
print advertisement
protectionists
protective tariff
quantities of
quota
recruit
restricted to
retention
revenue
revenue tariff
sectors
slogan
specialize in
staffing
sweat
take into consideration
tariff
technical support professionals
to the benefit of
turn (something) on and off
undersell
volume
weighed against

Vocabulary Workshop: Unit 2

Academic Word List

attributed
barriers
crucial
displace
fluctuations
imposed
interact
quota
sectors
volume

UNIT 3
Chapter 5
ages and ages hence
ain't never
ain't no
ambiguity
analyze
arrayed
at once
Bach
bewildered
chaos
chilly
civil service
clear-cut
closed form
cold-water flat
comma splice
couplet
course
decent
deferred
definite adverbs
diverged
doesn't make any sense
drop out
essay
face
fair
field
figurative language
fluttered pulses
form
formulas
fragments
free verse
from sole to crown
get off
get through
get to
gin
glittered
grace
gravel
grope
haberdasher
had trodden black
hover
imagery
indefinite adverbs
juxtaposition
layers
matador
metaphors
montage
murmured
mussed up
muttering
nod off
open form
outbreak
paper
patterns
pavement
pleading
put him back
quatrain
rambling
recite
rooming
s'il-vous plait
search
set my feet in glory
similes
speakers
stanzas
surface
symbolism
symbols
take up
talk at once
theme
throne
title
tormented
undergrowth
wanted wear
wood
yet

Chapter 6
as you go on through
blisters
bump into
compassionate
compelled
condensing
deed
descend from
drawing close
ends up
endurance ritual
endure
evoked
evolve (out of)
expanding
fundamental
get aboard
give up
giving yourself to
go out of (his) way
heritage
hero
heroine
impulse
in the nick of time
journey
look about
match
moment of redemption
mythology
nature
only way out of it
original
paid him a visit
profited by
put their foot down
radiantly healthy
recover
redemption
repertoire
resurrection
revolve around
sacrificing (him)self for another
save from
self-preservation
shrewd
skirmish
takes off on
trial
undergo
unsightly
well-fed

Vocabulary Workshop: Unit 3
Academic Word List
apparent
contradictory
focus
formula
initially

instructors
participants
responses

UNIT 4
Chapter 7

abstract
APA
be known for
bibliography
biodiversity
citation
criteria
decline in
dedicated to
documented
encroachment
endangered
entry
extinct
full text
gene pool
greenhouse effect
habitat
indigenous
Infotrac
journals
mammal
microfiche
microfilm
MLA
objective
periodicals index
protection of
references
research paper
respect for
sedentary
soil
style manual
style sheet
subjective
term paper
wilderness

Chapter 8

block quotes
consume
diminishing
discarded
drastic
emission
exterminators
fool around
fumigated
innovative
lethal
mortality
obsolete
residues
resource-intensive
respiratory
rid (him)self of
solvents
swell
take a break
tear off
toxicity

Vocabulary Workshop: Unit 4
Academic Word List

affect
affluent
animal
be
beast
creature
economic
economical
effect
environment
even if
even though
exist
fertile
game
hard
hardly
live
livestock
neighborhoods
on the contrary
on the other hand
in contrast
rich
scenery
subsist
suburbs
surroundings
terrain
thrive
vicinity
wealthy
wildlife

SKILLS INDEX

Academic Focus
Anthropology, 1–84
Cultural Anthropology, 3–43
Physical Anthropology, 45–84
Ecology, 235–302
Endangered Animal Species, 235–270
Human Ecology, 271–302
Economics, 85–158
Developing Nations, 87–120
The Global Economy, 121–158
Literature, 159–232
Human Ecology, 273–305
The Nature of Poetry, 161–192

Academic Skills
Charts, 8, 18, 27, 40, 49, 58, 69, 72, 78, 106, 107, 119, 123, 154, 158, 174, 176, 183, 186, 232, 239, 266, 267, 276
graphic organizers, 7–8, 70, 120 (idea map), 126, 143, 167 (T-chart), 197 (T-chart), 205, 250–251
Critical thinking, SEE Critical Thinking heading
Dictionaries (choosing definitions), 92–93, 131, 163–164, 201–202, 230
Highlighting, 17, 23, 27, 53, 64, 91, 96, 101, 108, 110–111, 125, 127, 135, 145, 164, 168, 242, 255, 277, 278, 284, 286, 287
Outlining, 12, 252–254, 301
Test-taking skills,
avoiding overstatement, 190–191
charts of information, 107
checks (for answers that apply), 58, 61
circling (best choice), 62–63, 99–100, 114, 133–135, 200–201, 208–209,
closed-book exam, 77–78
defining, 11, 21, 51–52, 62–63, 133–135, 163–164, 177, 200–201, 208–209, 216
essay exam, 38
explaining, 18
fill in the blank, 7, 17, 27, 28, 50, 59–60, 71, 82–83, 84, 91, 105, 108, 125, 145, 156–157, 166, 167, 198, 205–206, 231, 232, 249, 275
finding errors, 37, 43, 76, 81, 115, 120, 151, 155, 188, 192, 229, 270, 302
hedging, 190–191
listing, 52, 72
matching, 82, 93, 97, 113, 130, 131, 156, 174, 221, 230, 231, 249, 283, 303–304
multiple choice, 114, 188
overstatement (avoiding), 190–191
sentence completion, 18, 61, 93, 132, 146–147, 150–151, 217, 240, 260, 291
summarizing, 116–117
supporting material in an essay, 228
tables of information, 107
taking a side, 153
underlining, 6, 12

Critical Thinking
Analysis, 42, 81, 152, 191, 226, 259, 291, 295, 302
Application, 28, 132, 144
Categorizing, 249
Cause and effect, 7–8, 118
Comparing, 49
Evaluating sources, 131–132
Inferences, 6, 60, 166, 199, 216
Interpreting, 206
Irony, 240
Making comparisons, 49
Making connections, 28–29, 72, 132, 183, 217, 260, 285, 291
Making inferences, 6, 60, 166, 199, 216
Meaning of poems, 181–183
Outlining, 12, 252–254, 301
Poems (discovering meaning of), 181–183
Seeing both sides of an argument, 284
Summarizing, 18, 61, 93, 132, 144, 183, 217, 240, 260
Synthesizing, 108
Understanding irony, 240
Word journals, 19, 30, 61, 72, 109, 145, 183, 217, 260, 291

Discussion, 19, 28, 30, 50, 123, 126, 144, 199, 285
Chapter introduction discussions, 3, 45, 87, 121, 161, 193, 235, 271
Surveys, 8, 260, 276
Thinking Ahead, 4–5, 9, 20, 46, 51, 62, 88, 94, 98, 122, 127, 133, 162, 167, 176, 194, 199, 207, 236, 241, 255, 272, 277, 285

Expansion/Extension, 97, 276

Group and Partner Work, 3, 4–5, 6, 8, 9, 11, 16, 19, 20, 21, 26, 28, 30, 45, 46, 50, 51, 58, 60, 62–63, 69, 79, 83, 87, 88, 91, 94, 96, 97, 98, 99–100, 101, 105, 106, 107, 108, 112, 121, 122, 123, 125, 126, 127, 130, 132, 133, 142, 144, 153, 154, 161, 162, 165, 166, 167, 170, 175, 176, 177, 181, 182, 186, 194, 194, 197, 198, 199,

200–201, 204, 205, 206, 207, 208–209, 216, 217, 221, 224, 235, 236, 239, 240, 241, 248, 249, 250–251, 252, 253, 255, 259, 260, 262, 263, 270, 271, 272, 275, 276, 277, 283, 284, 285, 286, 291, 295, 297, 302, 304–305

Making Connections, 28–29, 72, 132, 183, 217, 260, 285, 291

READING

Comprehension, 6, 16, 27, 49, 58, 69–70, 91, 96, 106, 125, 130, 142, 165, 197, 204, 239, 248, 260, 275, 283
Details, 126, 205, 250–251, 291
Main idea(s), 25, 216, 248, 259, 291

Literary Content/ Topics
Advertising, 124
Anthropology,
  cultural anthropology, 5–6, 12–16, 23–25
  physical anthropology, 47–48, 53–57, 64–68
Bank for the poor, 95–96
Developing countries, 101–104
Dutch scientist teaches Indians to hunt, 236–239
E-waste, 285–286
Ecology,
  endangered animal species, 236–239, 243–247, 255–259
  human ecology, 273–274, 278–283, 287–290
Economics,
  developing nations, 89–90, 95–96, 101–104
  global economy, 124, 127–129, 135–141
Endangered species, 243–247, 255–259
Environment, 273–274
Feng shui, 5–6
Global marketplace, 127–129
Heroes in literature, 193, 202–204
Humans,
  versus other primates, 53–57
  Stone Age, 64–68
Immigrant travel, 194
International trade, 135–141
Literature,
  heroes in literature, 194–196, 202–204, 209–216
  poetry, 164–165, 168–170, 177–180
Native American rite of passage, 29, 209–216
Orangutans, 47–48
Pesticides, 278–283
Poetry, 164–165, 168–170, 177–180
Poverty, 89–90
Religion, 23–25
Symbolic systems, 12–16
War on poverty, 89–90

Pre-reading Questions/ Activities, 4–5, 9–12, 20–23, 46–47, 51–53, 62–64, 88–89, 94–95, 98–101, 122–124, 127, 133–135, 162–164, 167–168, 176–177, 194, 207–209, 236, 241–243, 255, 272, 277–286, 285–286

Strategies
Analyzing poems, 170–175
Choosing correct dictionary definition, 92–93, 131, 163–164 (parts of speech), 201–202, 230
Collocations, 22–23
Connotation, 304–305
Dealing with too much material, 101
Definitions and examples to check understanding, 143
Euphemisms, 198
Finding themes,
  poems, 175
  stories, 217
Graphic organizers, 7–8
Guessing the meaning of new words,
  choosing correct dictionary definition, 92–93 , 163–164 (parts of speech), 200–201, 230
  context, 10–11, 51–52, 166
  essential vs. nonessential words, 242
  multiple definitions, 92–93, 131
Having questions in mind, 64
Italics, 7, 209 (for foreign words)
Knowing which new words to focus on, 242
Marking a book, 17
Organization of research paper, 26
Organizing ideas, 284
Outlining, 12, 252–254
Passive voice, 248
Poems,
  analyzing, 170–175
  form, 170–175, 181
  meaning, 181–183
  sound, 170–175, 181
  themes, 175
Previewing,
  headings, 52, 63, 135
  pictures and captions, 3, 4, 45, 46, 63, 87, 88, 94, 121, 122, 161, 162, 193, 207, 236, 271, 272
  subtopics, 167
Pronoun references, 60–61, 166
Questions (having them in mind), 64
Quotation marks, 50
Recognizing euphemisms, 198
Summarizing your reading, 144
Tables to find information, 107
Themes of poems, 175
Understanding italics, 7, 209 (for foreign words)
Understanding organization of a research paper, 26
Understanding passive voice, 248
Understanding pronoun references, 60–61, 166
Understanding quotation marks, 50

Using tables to find information, 107
Word journals, 19, 30, 61, 72, 109, 145, 183, 217, 260, 291

Surveys, 8, 260, 276

Thinking Ahead, 4–5, 9, 20, 46, 51, 62, 88, 94, 98, 122, 127, 133, 162, 167, 176, 194, 199, 207, 236, 241, 255, 271, 277, 285

Vocabulary
Academic words, 84, 157, 232, Appendix 3 (313–316)
Affixes, 83
Checks/review, 7, 17, 28, 50, 59–60, 71, 91, 97, 105, 125, 130, 142,166, 198, 216, 249, 275
Collocations, 22–23, 82–83, 205–206 (with prepositions), 231, 249, 284
Phrases, 59
  verb phrases with prepositions, 71
  with prepositions, 27, 108, 145, 156–157, 205–206
Preparation activities, 21, 51–52, 62–63, 99–100, 133–135, 177, 200, 208–209, 242, 255, 277, 286
Stems, 83
Topics,
  advertising, 125
  bank for the poor, 97
  developing nations, 91, 97, 99–100, 105
  feng shui, 7
  e-waste, 286
  endangered species, 243, 249, 255
  environment, 275
  global marketplace, 130
  heroes in literature, 193, 200–201, 208–209, 216
  humans
    versus other primates, 51–52, 59
    Stone Age, 62–63, 71
  immigrant travel, 194
  international trade, 133–135
  literature, 198
  Native American rite of passage, 208–209, 216
  orangutans, 50
  pesticides, 277, 283
  poetry, 163–164, 166, 177
  poverty, 91, 97
  religion, 21, 28
  symbolic systems, 17
Workshops,
  Anthropology (Unit 1), 82–84
  Ecology (Unit 4), 303–306
  Economics (Unit 2), 156–158
  Literature (Unit 3), 230–232

WRITING
Response Writing
Art, 72
Developing nations, 109
Economics, 109
Endangered species, 260
Environmental problems, 291
Feng shui, 30
Heroes, 217
Humans, 72
International trade, 145
Luck, 30
Microlending, 109
Poetry, 183
Religion / rituals, 30
Symbolism, 20
Zoos, 260

Strategies
Brainstorming, 78–79
Choosing a topic, 39, 78, 118, 153, 189, 223, 264–265
Essay writing,
  choosing a topic, 223
  editing, 229
  gathering ideas, 223–224
  organization, 224–226, 228
  rewriting, 229
  supporting material, 228
  thesis statement, 227
  topic sentences, 227–228
  writing the essay, 229
Gathering supporting material/evidence, 39, 110–111, 119, 154, 189, 223–224
Organizing information, 41, 81, 120, 155, 189, 224–226, 229
  idea mapping, 120, 189
  outlining, 301
Paragraph writing,
  choosing a topic, 39, 78, 118, 153, 189
  editing your paragraph, 43, 81, 120, 155, 192
  gathering supporting material/evidence, 39, 110–111, 119, 154, 189
  organizing information, 41, 81, 120, 155, 189
  planning the paragraph, 189 (idea mapping)
  rewriting the paragraph, 43, 81, 120, 155, 192
  types,
    analysis, 191
    argument (cause and effect), 118, 120 (idea mapping), 152 (inductive reasoning)
    cause and effect, 118, 120 (idea mapping)
    comparison, 80–81
    definition, 40–41
  writing the paragraph, 43, 81, 120, 155, 192
Paraphrasing, 79–80
Research paper,
  choosing a topic, 264–265
  developing a thesis statement, 300
  editing a reference list, 270
  editing a research paper, 302
  finding evidence, 299
  reading sources in detail, 268
  revising a research paper, 303
  writing conclusions, 301–302

writing introductions, 301–302
writing reference lists, 268–270
writing research papers, 264, 302
Synthesizing, 39
Writing and editing a reference list, 268–270
Writing conclusions, 301–302
Writing essays, 223–229
Writing introductions, 301–302
Writing supporting material in an essay, 228
Writing the theme (of a poem), 189
Writing the thesis statement, 227
Writing topic sentences in an essay, 227–229

Word Journals, SEE Word Journals (under Reading Strategies)

Writing Skills (Mechanics of Writing)
Avoiding sexism, 206
Brackets, 261
Citing sources, 42, 111–112, 132, 296–299, Appendix 2: MLA formatting (309–312)
Condensing (using synonyms), 221
Ellipses, 261
Evaluating online sources, 265–266
Expanding (using synonyms), 221
Finding supporting information, 110–111
Grammar,
adjective clauses, 31–32, 37
reduction of (to participial phrases), 292–293, 295–296
with prepositions, 32–33, 37
adverbial conjunctions, 35–36, 37, 73–74, 76, 149–151, Appendix 1 (306–308)
as . . . as, 186
comma splices, 187–188
conditionals,
present unreal, 146–147, 151
with *without,* 147–148, 151
conjunctions,
adverbial, 35–36, 37, 73–74, 76, 149–151, Appendix 1 (306–308)
coordinating, 33–34, 37, 149–151, Appendix 1 (306–308)
subordinating, 74–76, 149–151, Appendix 1 (306–308)
coordinating conjunctions, 33–34, 37, 149–151, Appendix 1 (306–308)
fragments, 36–37, 187–188
modals, 184–185 (possibility/probability)
must, 219–220
ought to, 219–220
participial phrases,
beginning of sentence, 294, 295–296
end of sentence, 293–294, 295–296
reduced from adjective clauses, 292–293, 295–296
passive voice, 248
possibility/probability, 184–185
present unreal conditionals, 146–147, 151
relative clauses, SEE adjective clauses
run-on sentences, 187–188
sentences,
comma splices, 187–188
fragments, 36–37, 187–188
run-ons, 187–188
should, 219–220
similes, 186
subordinating conjunctions, 74–76, 149–151, Appendix 1 (306–308)
transitional expressions,
adverbial conjunctions, 149–151
cause and effect, 149–151
coordinating conjunctions, 149–151
followed by phrases, 149–151
subordinating conjunctions, 149–151
without (in conditionals), 147–148, 151
Hedging, 190–191
Library research, 266–267
Making a strong argument, 219–220
Organizing information, 18
Outlining, 301
Parallelism, 218–219
Paraphrasing, 79–80, 112, 222–223
Phrases for symbols, 185
Providing evidence, 155
Punctuation,
brackets, 261
ellipses, 261
Quotations, 112–115, 132, 261
Source material, 110, 261–263
Strong argument, 219–220
Summarizing, 18, 61, 93, 132, 144, 183, 217, 240, 260
Supporting information, 110–111
Synonyms, 112, 220–221
Using source material, 110

Writing Topics
Anthropology, 39–43, 78–81, 265, 300–303
Ecology, 265, 300–303
Economics, 265, 300–303
Free trade, 153–155
Heroes, 223–229
Humans (versus nonhumans), 78–81
Poem, 188–192
Poverty, 118–120
Rite of passage, 223–229

CREDITS

Text Credits

p. 5 Adapted from "San Francisco Legislator Pushes Feng Shui Building Codes" by John Gaeddert from *The Skeptical Inquirer*, May-June 2004, Vol. 28, issue 3. Used by permission of The Skeptical Inquirer, www.csicop.org. p. 29 "Alone on a Hilltop". Reprinted with the permission of Pocket Books, a division of Simon & Schuster Adult Publishing Group from *Lame Deer Seeker of Visions* by John (Fire) Lame Deer and Richard Erdoes. Copyright © 1972 by John Fire Lame Deer and Richard Erdoes; copyright renewed © 1994 by Pocket Books. p. 48 Adapted from "The Orangutans" as appeared on Tourismindonesia.com, and Tiergarten Schonbrunner, accessed 10/18/04. www.zoovienna. p. 89 From "Bono" by Bobby Shriver, *Time*, April 26, 2004, Volume 163, issue 17. p. 124 "You Say Potato" by Ilana DeBare. *San Francisco Chronicle* by Ilana DeBare. Copyright © 1997 by San Francisco Chronicle. Reproduced with permission of San Francisco Chronicle in the format Textbook via Copyright Clearance Center. p. 128 "Microsoft's Call Center Business in India Gets an American Accent" by Brier Dudley, *Seattle Times*, August 16, 2004. Copyright © 2004 Seattle Times Company. Used with permission. p. 165 "Poetry Lessons" by Ivars Peterson. *Science News* by Ivars Peterson. Copyright © 1990 by SCI Service Inc. Reproduced with permission of SCI Service Inc. in the format Textbook via Copyright Clearance Center. Reproduced with permission from Science News the weekly newsmagazine of science, copyright 1990 Science Service. p. 172 "Marrying" by Charles Harper Webb. Reprinted from *Stand Up Poetry* edited by Charles H. Webb, 2002 by permission of the University of Iowa Press. p. 173 "Going to Norway" by Jack Anderson. p. 179 "Deferred" by Langston Hughes from *The Collected Poems of Langston Hughes* by Langston Hughes, copyright © 1994 by The Estate of Langston Hughes. Used by permission of Alfred A. Knopf, a division of Random House, Inc. p. 179 "The History Teacher" From *Questions About Angels* by Billy Collins, © 1991. Reprinted by permission of the University of Pittsburgh Press. p. 181 "The Road Not Taken" by Robert Frost from *The Poetry of Robert Frost* edited by Edward Connery Lathem. p. 197 "My Name is Aram" by William Saroyan. Reproduced by permission of The Trustees of Leland Stanford Junior University. p. 205 From *The Power of Myth* by Joseph Campbell & Bill Moyers, copyright © 1988 by Apostrophe S Productions, Inc. and Bill Moyers and Alfred Van der March Editions, Inc. for itself and the estate of Joseph Campbell. Used by permission of Doubleday, a division of Random House, Inc. p. 212 "Ta-Na-E-Ka" by Mary Whitebird. From *Scholastic Voice*, December 13, 1973. Copyright © 1973 by Scholastic Inc. Reprinted by permission of Scholastic Inc. p. 244 From "The Human Factor" by Sally Morgan, *Ecology and the Environment*, 1995, pp. 136–143. p. 280 Excerpt adapted from "Which Pesticides Are Safe?" by Lynn Lawson, from *Staying Well in a Toxic World: Understanding Environmental Illness, Multiple Chemical Sensitivities, Chemical Injuries, and Sick Building Syndrome* by Joan Carolyn Prouty Lawson, 1993. Reprinted by permission of Lynn Lawson.

Photo Credits

Cover (top right): © Nicholas Nick/National Georgraphic Image Collection; (middle left): © Amos Morgan/Getty Images; (bottom right): © Tim Hall/Getty Images. **Unit 1.** P. 1: © Archivo Iconografico, S.A./CORBIS; p. 3: © Tim Hall/Getty Images; p. 4 (top left & bottom left): © Ryan McVay/Getty Images; p. 4 (right): © David N. Averbach; p. 9: © Ryan McVay/Getty Images; p. 11: © Royalty-Free/CORBIS; p. 13: © Robert Harding World Imagery/Getty Images; p. 15 (left): © Ian Waldie/Getty Images; p. 15 (right): © Superstock, Inc./Superstock; p. 16 (left): Courtesy Newberry Library; p. 16 (right): © Peter Thompson/Getty Images; p. 20 (left): © Photodisc/Getty Images; p. 20 (middle): © Siede Preis/Getty Images; p. 20 (right): The McGraw-Hill Companies Inc./Ken Cavanagh Photographer; p. 34: © PhotoLink/Getty Images; p. 45: © Nicholas Nick/National Georgraphic Image Collection; p. 46 (top left): © Digital Vision/ PunchStock; p. 46 (top right): © Alan and Sandy Carey/Getty Images; p. 46 (bottom left): © Brand X Pictures/Punchstock; p. 46 (bottom right): © Martin Harvey/CORBIS; p. 48: Photos by Jutta Kirchner; p. 53: © Nicholas Nick/National Georgraphic Image Collection; p. 54 (top right): © Tom & Pat Leeson/Photo Researchers; p. 54 (bottom left): © Karl Ammann/CORBIS; p. 55: © James Balog/Getty Images; p. 56 (left): © Royalty-Free/CORBIS; p. 56 (right): © Connie Bransilver/Photo Researchers; p. 65: © Douglas Mazonowicz/Bruce Coleman; p. 67 (top): © Dr. Parvinder Sethi; p. 67 (bottom): © Reunion des Musees Nationauz/ Art Resource, NY; p. 68: © Gary Irving/Getty Images. **Unit 2.** P. 85: © Stockbyte/PictureQuest; p. 87: © Dag Sundberg/Getty Images; p. 88 (left): © Stephane Cardinale/People Avenue/CORBIS; p. 88 (right): © David N. Averbach; p. 90 © Adrian Brooks; p. 94 (top left): © Karen Kasmauski/CORBIS; p. 94 (bottom left), p. 95: © Rafiqur Rahman/Reuters/CORBIS; p. 98: Dana Fradon © 1998 from The Cartoon Bank; p. 109: © Digital Vision/PunchStock; p. 115: © D. Normark/ PhotoLink/

Getty Images; p. 121: © BananaStock/PictureQuest; p. 122 (all):): © David N. Averbach; 124: © Linda S. O'Roke; p. 128: © Howard Huang/Getty Images; p. 129: © Ami Vitale; p. 133: AP/Wide World Photos; p. 136: © Sean Sprague/Stock Boston; p. 141: © Joseph Nettis/Stock Boston. **Unit 3.** P. 159: © Stockbyte/PictureQuest; p. 161: © Hulton Archive/Getty Images; p. 162 (left): © Dynamic Graphics/PictureQuest; p. 162 (right): © Ryan McVay/Getty Images; p. 170: © Royalty-Free/CORBIS; p. 172: © Bettmann/CORBIS; p. 173: The Granger Collection/New York; p. 180: © Raymond Gehman/Getty Images; p. 195: © Warner Bros./DC Comics/The Kobal Collection; p. 196: AP/Wide World Photos; p. 201 (both): © Lucasfilm/20th Century Fox/The Kobal Collection; p. 209 (top left): © Patrick Ward/CORBIS; p. 209 (middle right): © Comstock/PictureQuest; p. 209 (bottom left): © Lisa Larsen/Time & Life Pictures/Getty Images; p. 212: © John Eastcott/Yva Momatuik/Stock Boston; p. 215: © Jim Reed/Photo Researchers. **Unit 4.** P. 235: © Andrea Pistolesi/Getty Images; p. 237: © Digital Vision/ PunchStock; p. 238 & 240: Juan Pratginestos/Worldwide Fund for Nature; p. 243: © Chon Day , Yankee Magazine, July 1992; p. 245: © Rod Berriedale-Johnson/Panos Pictures; p. 246 (left): © Digital Vision/Getty Images; p. 246 (right): © Martin Harvey; Gallo Images/CORBIS; p. 247: © Digital Vision/PunchStock; p. 248: © Brand X Pictures/ PunchStock; p. 249: © Thinkstock Images/PictureQuest; p. 273: © J-P NOVA/Stock Image/PictureQuest; p. 274 (top left): © C. Sherburne/ PhotoLink/Getty Images; p. 274 (top right): © PhotoLink/ Getty Images; p. 274 (bottom left): © Paul Grebliunas/ Getty Images; p. 247 (bottom right): © Alberto Moreno/ Reuters/CORBIS; p. 275: © Bill Aron/PhotoEdit; p. 276 (top): © Ernie Friedlander/Cole Group/Getty Images; p. 276 (bottom): The McGraw-Hill Companies, Inc./Roger Loewenberg, photographer; p. 277: © David C. Johnson; p. 280, 281: © Linda S. O'Roke; p. 282: © Carl & Ann Purcell/ CORBIS; p. 283: © Image Source/PictureQuest; p. 284: © Digital Vision/Getty Images; p. 287, 288: Courtesy of SVTC and the Basel Action Network.

We apologize for any apparent infringement of copyright and if notified, the publisher will be pleased to rectify any errors or omissions at the earliest opportunity.

NOTES

NOTES

NOTES

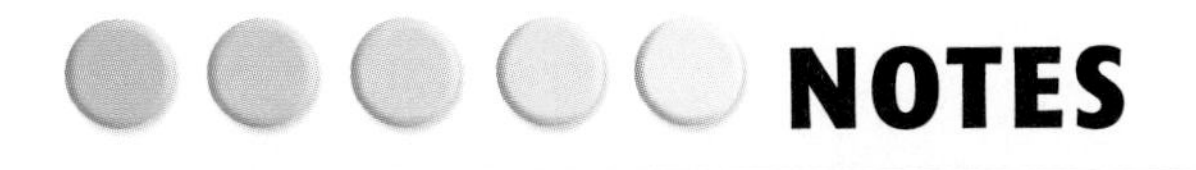

NOTES

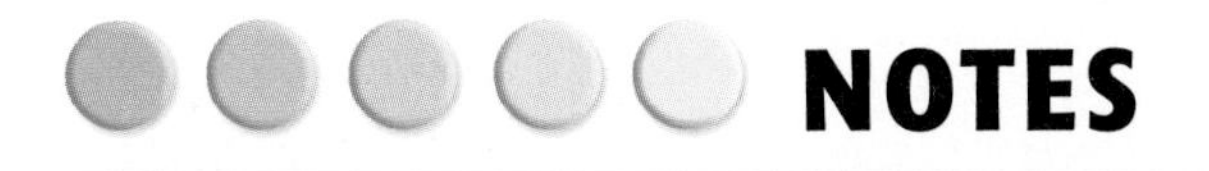

NOTES